A precarious equilibrium

Manchester University Press

Key Studies in Diplomacy

Series Editors: J. Simon Rofe and Giles Scott-Smith

Emeritus Editor: Lorna Lloyd

The volumes in this series seek to advance the study and understanding of diplomacy in its many forms. Diplomacy remains a vital component of global affairs, and it influences and is influenced by its environment and the context in which it is conducted. It is an activity of great relevance for International Studies, International History, and of course Diplomatic Studies. The series covers historical, conceptual, and practical studies of diplomacy.

Previously published by Bloomsbury:

21st Century Diplomacy: A Practitioner's Guide by Kishan S. Rana
A Cornerstone of Modern Diplomacy: Britain and the Negotiation of the 1961 Vienna Convention on Diplomatic Relations by Kai Bruns
David Bruce and Diplomatic Practice: An American Ambassador in London, 1961–9 by John W. Young
Embassies in Armed Conflict by G.R. Berridge

Published by Manchester University Press:

Reasserting America in the 1970s edited by Hallvard Notaker, Giles Scott-Smith and David J. Snyder
Human rights and humanitarian diplomacy: Negotiating for human rights protection and humanitarian access by Kelly-Kate Pease
The diplomacy of decolonisation: America, Britain and the United Nations during the Congo crisis 1960–64 by Alanna O'Malley
Sport and diplomacy: Games within games edited by J. Simon Rofe
The TransAtlantic reconsidered edited by Charlotte A. Lerg, Susanne Lachenicht and Michael Kimmage
Academic ambassadors, Pacific allies: Australia, America and the Fulbright Program by Alice Garner and Diane Kirkby

A precarious equilibrium

Human rights and détente in Jimmy Carter's Soviet policy

Umberto Tulli

Manchester University Press

The right of Umberto Tulli to be identified as the author of this work has been asserted
by him in accordance with the Copyright, Designs and Patents Act 1988.

Published by Manchester University Press
Oxford Road, Manchester M13 9PL
www.manchesteruniversitypress.co.uk

British Library Cataloguing-in-Publication Data
A catalogue record for this book is available from the British Library

ISBN 978 1 5261 4602 1 hardback
ISBN 978 1 5261 6077 5 paperback

First published 2020

The publisher has no responsibility for the persistence or accuracy of URLs for any external or
third-party internet websites referred to in this book, and does not guarantee that any content on
such websites is, or will remain, accurate or appropriate.

Typeset by Newgen Publishing UK

Contents

Author's note   vi

List of abbreviations   vii

Introduction   1

1   Setting the stage for a human rights policy   10

2   Human rights and the 1976 presidential election   48

3   Firmness abroad, consensus at home, 1977–1978   82

4   Coping with critics: the choice in favour of quiet diplomacy, 1978   122

5   Critics' triumph: quiet diplomacy, SALT II and the invasion of
    Afghanistan, 1979–1980   152

    Conclusion   190

Select bibliography   199

Index   206

Author's note

This book is a revised and updated version of the Italian *Tra diritti umani e distensione. L'Amministrazione Carter e il dissenso in Urss* (FrancoAngeli, 2013). While the structure and the main ideas of the book remain fundamentally the same, sections have been rewritten, new archival research has been conducted and new books on Carter's human rights policy, the CSCE process and the role of the United States during the 1970s have been consulted. No book is written in complete isolation and this one owes numerous debts to many scholars, colleagues and friends. Suggestions and support have always been abundant. I am extremely grateful to Sara Lorenzini and Mario Del Pero. Sara gave a fundamental encouragement to complete the book as well as generous advice. Mario has followed this research with an extraordinary intellectual acumen. I have been discussing these themes with many other scholars. Shortening as much as possible what otherwise would be an endless list, I would like to thank Federico Romero, Antonio Varsori, Piero Craveri, Silvio Pons, Fred Logevall, Jeremi Suri, Tatiana Yankelevich, Barbara Keys, Arne O. Westad, Piers Ludlow, Ilaria Zamburlini, Alessandra Bitumi, Dario Fazzi, Matteo Risari, Sabrina Paolucci, Lucrezia Cominelli, Flavia Tudini and Simone A. Bellezza. Finally, I would like to thank J. Simon Rofe, Giles Scott-Smith and Jonathan de Peyer for the opportunity to publish with Manchester University Press and Helen Flitton of Newgen Publishing UK.

Abbreviations

AAP	Andrei Amalrik Papers, Houghton Library, Harvard University, Cambridge, MA
ABM	Anti-ballistic missile
ACDA	Arms Control and Disarmament Agency
ADSA	Andrei D. Sakharov Archives, Houghton Library, Harvard University, Cambridge, MA
AFL-CIO	American Federation of Labor and Congress of Industrial Organizations
AI	Amnesty International
AIPAC	American Israel Public Affairs Committee
ALCM	Air-launched cruise missile
CF	Country Files
CHRDR	Center for Human Rights Documentation and Research, Columbia University, New York
CJH	Center for Jewish History, New York
CL	Office of Congressional Liaison
CPD	Committee on the Present Danger
CSCE	Conference on Security and Cooperation in Europe
DPMP	Daniel Patrick Moynihan Papers, Library of Congress, Washington, DC
EEA	Enzo Enriques Agnoletti Papers, Historical Archives of the European Union, Florence
FCO	Records of the Foreign and Commonwealth Office, The National Archives, Kew
GDR	German Democratic Republic (East Germany)
GFPL	Gerald R. Ford Presidential Library, Ann Arbor, MI
HAEU	Historical Archives of the European Union, Florence
HMJP	Henry M. Jackson Papers, University of Washington, Seattle, WA
HRC	Human Rights Collection, Andrei D. Sakharov Archives, Houghton Library, Harvard University, Cambridge, MA
HRW	Human Rights Watch
HU	Human Rights

ICBM	Intercontinental ballistic missile
IOC	International Olympic Committee Archives, Lausanne, Switzerland
JCPL	Jimmy Carter Presidential Library, Atlanta, GA
LOC	Library of Congress, Washington, DC
MBFR	Mutual and Balanced Force Reductions
MFN	Most Favored Nation
MIRV	Multiple Independently Targetable Re-entry Vehicle
NA	National Archives, Kew, London
NARA	National Archives and Records Administration, College Park, MD and Washington, DC
NATO	North Atlantic Treaty Organization
NCSJ	National Conference for Soviet Jewry
NGO	Non-Governmental Organization
NSA	National Security Advisor
NSC	National Security Council
OAU	Organization of African Unity
PE0	Records of the European Parliament before Direct Elections, Historical Archives of the European Union, Florence
PREM	Prime Minister's Office
PRM	Presidential Review Memorandum
RFE	Radio Free Europe
RG	Record Group
SALT	Strategic Arms Limitation Talks
SF	Subject Files
SLBM	Submarine-launched ballistic missile
SS	Office of Staff Secretary
USIA	United States Information Agency
WCP	Warren Christopher Papers, National Archives and Records Administration, College Park, MD and Washington, DC
WHCF	White House Central Files
ZBM	Zbigniew Brzezinski Donated Materials, Jimmy Carter Presidential Library, Atlanta, GA

Introduction

In January 1981, just days before Jimmy Carter left the White House, many of the president's officials were well satisfied with the campaign promoting human rights and its accomplishments. According to Lincoln Bloomfield, who dealt with the issue at the National Security Council (NSC), Carter's human rights policy "represented the clearest change from policies pursued by the previous two administrations. It produced some of the most notable moral and political successes" and was a "definite plus for the United States in its international position". Nevertheless, he admitted, the policy had also "generated the sharpest criticism" and was "the one least likely to be followed" by the incoming Reagan administration.[1]

As Bloomfield anticipated, the new president seemed inclined to abandon Carter's commitment to defending human rights. Repeatedly, in his electoral campaign, Reagan had thundered against Carter's flawed approach to human rights. To him, the policy had failed to address Soviet abuses and to confront Soviet power and growing influence. Moreover, his words about the need to rebuild American foreign policy on strong anti-communist foundations had raised doubts both in Congress and among activists about his administration's commitment to the promotion of human rights abroad. Joshua Rubenstein – at the time an Amnesty International representative and a leading expert on Soviet dissent – claimed that activists feared "the Reagan administration will not have a positive emphasis on human rights and in some parts of the world his election has been taken as a green light, an encouragement for repressive forces".[2]

These fears were confirmed within days when President Reagan proposed Ernest Lefever as the new undersecretary for human rights. Lefever, a long-time researcher at the Brookings Institution and the founder of the conservative Ethics and Public Policy Center, had been an outspoken critic of Carter's human rights efforts. In 1978, he had published an essay titled "The Trivialization of Human Rights" in which he attacked the "futility and irresponsibility of human rights standards" seen as such because they added up to "confusing guideline[s] for responsible statecraft".[3] The following year, during a Congressional hearing, he had argued that "we cannot export human rights ... in dealing with Third World countries ... their foreign policy behavior should be the determining factor, not their domestic practices".[4] Lefever's appointment was firmly rejected by the Senate; indeed, the Republican majority within the Senate Foreign Relations Committee went so far as to vote with the Democrats to reject him by thirteen votes to four. A full four months passed before the Reagan administration named its second choice, thirty-three-year-old Elliott Abrams, who had earlier served as an aide to conservative Senators Henry Jackson (D – Washington) and Daniel Patrick Moynihan (D – New York). Abrams became crucial for the definition of what he called a "conservative human rights policy". With an explicit anti-Soviet twist, he welded human rights to the promotion of democracy abroad. As such, the new American stance on international human rights bore little resemblance to Carter's "absolute commitment to human rights", a policy that led the United States to criticize its international allies as much as its rivals.[5]

These controversies are telling. The Lefever fiasco and Abrams' determination to pursue a human rights agenda were deeply rooted in the popularity of human rights both in Congress and in the American public at large. By the early 1980s, only a tiny minority considered human rights as marginal to American foreign policy. This was probably Carter's most important legacy. Although he was not the initiator of the human rights policy, he played a crucial role in making human rights a central concern for American diplomacy. Yet to say that Carter's human rights-based policy, its forms and its outcomes enjoyed popularity in Congress would be misleading. In the four years he spent in office, Carter had failed both to persuade the American public that he had a clear grasp on the US's role in the world, and to build a lasting domestic consensus on foreign policy. Many blamed Carter's emphasis on the promotion of human rights for many of the difficulties the United States was facing at the time.

A first strand of criticism, at the time extremely popular, came from those who began to call themselves neoconservatives. They saw Carter's human rights campaign as a failure, an expression of morality without power that did not pay enough attention to the Soviet Union, and that trained the focus against America's authoritarian allies. Another line of criticism, embraced by many liberals, pointed to a sense of delusion and frustration at the accomplishments of Carter's campaign. Despite some significant and important outcomes, many claimed the human rights policy did not meet expectations and the White House had been too selective in its implementation.[6] Further criticism came from those who had advocated for better relations with the Soviet Union. Members of the business community, supporters of arms control and the demilitarization of American foreign policy, as well as many academicians holding realist assumptions about the international system, blamed Carter's campaign for worsening bipolar relations.[7]

Indeed, there were many contradictions and shortcomings in Carter's human rights campaign. How could the White House integrate the promotion of human rights into other foreign policy concerns? How could it develop a policy that was supposed to be at once universal and based on case-by-case action? How could it alleviate the suffering of victims of human rights violations? How could an ideological assault on the foundations of Soviet power be reconciled with Carter's commitment to develop détente and reach a new SALT agreement with Moscow? How could the administration follow a global human rights agenda without jeopardizing other concerns for

American foreign policy? And finally – something that probably troubles scholars more than policy-makers – did the human rights campaign aim to move American foreign policy beyond the Cold War horizon or to renew ideological confrontation with the Soviet Union?

Many scholars – historians and political scientists alike – have tried to answer these questions, offering disparate interpretations of Carter's human rights-based foreign policy. Since the mid-1990s, a growing body of scholarship has argued that Carter tried to move American foreign policy beyond the Cold War and the bipolar horizon.[8]

In part, the president himself contributed to this idea. Carter's rhetoric, especially in the early months after assuming office, sought to tone down the Cold War and demonstrate that it was possible to cooperate with the Soviets to address new global challenges. Even some of his early opponents, neoconservative intellectuals like Jeane Kirkpatrick and Joshua Muravchik, or president Ronald Reagan, were instrumental in enhancing the alleged irrelevance of bipolar relations to Carter's foreign policy, attacking his diplomacy for allowing the Soviets to increase their power and influence.

In part, scholarly appreciation of Carter's international action as an early attempt to develop a post-Cold War foreign policy benefited and still benefits from an ongoing reappraisal of the 1970s as a crucial decade of transformation for the international system and for the United States. Several different processes had interacted to produce radical changes that no longer fitted into traditional Cold War categories: the emergence of global interdependence; the erosion of the bipolar balance of power and the rise of new actors in international relations; the affirmation of new political cleavages along with the rise of new global challenges. It was the moment in which a new and interdependent global order began to emerge.[9] To many historians, Carter's human rights policy was a major part of his attempt to manage an interdependent, post-Cold War international system. Daniel J. Sargent, for example, has suggested that Carter tried to develop a new foreign policy imbued with a mix of technocracy (Carter himself was an engineer) and moral beliefs, in which the management of global interdependence was matched by a new attention to human rights. Heavily influenced by the works of the Trilateral Commission, Carter developed a "world order politics" to replace the more traditional "balance of power politics".[10] Other scholars, for example David Schmitz, Vanessa Walker and Itai Nartzizenfield Sneh, saw the formulation of Carter's human rights as an explicit attempt to move American foreign policy beyond bipolar paradigms and perspectives and to develop a post-Cold War foreign policy. The subtitle of Sneh's book is eloquent enough: through the human rights campaign, *The Future Almost Arrived*.[11] In so doing, Sneh and many others imply that Carter's failure to move beyond the Cold War was manifest in his conversion to Cold War politics soon after the Soviets invaded Afghanistan in December 1979.[12]

Departing from most of these interpretations, this book is based on three main ideas.

First, it aims at placing Carter's foreign policy and his human rights initiative in the Cold War context. The Cold War was the central reality of Carter's foreign policy; the president himself "was a Cold Warrior from day one" who never abandoned anti-communism, as Nancy Mitchell wrote. From his first days in office, for example, Carter sought to elaborate a new SALT proposal to limit the arms race and check Soviet rearmament. He did not overlook the deployment of Soviet SS-20 missiles, which began in 1976 and ended in 1979, and the need to elaborate a NATO response. He proposed that NATO Allies increase their defence spending. He also followed with anxiety the growing Soviet (and Cuban) military intervention in the Horn of Africa. Even strategic and military decisions that, to many, represented Carter's conversion to containment after the Soviets invaded Afghanistan began well before the invasion. Moreover, the White House was keen on completing normalization with China, an action to which the White House attached great geopolitical meaning. Similarly, Carter's proclaimed global and total commitment to human rights was calibrated to the Soviet Union and its violations of human rights. Even domestic politics did not allow Carter to overlook bipolar relations. Controversy over Soviet and Cuban adventurism in Africa, the Committee on the Present Danger, the political storm over Paul Warnke's double appointment to the head of both the United States Arms Control and Disarmament Agency and the SALT negotiations team, and protests over the presence of a Soviet Brigade in Cuba – all these were reminders that many Americans still believed the Cold War to be an appalling reality.[13]

While the book does not deny that Carter's human rights campaign had global extension and impact, it suggests that the Soviet Union was a specific target of both direct and indirect actions. By wielding the human rights "sword", the Carter administration renewed the United States' ideological competition with the Soviet Union. It followed a consistent approach to human rights violations in the world, denouncing allies' abuses and distancing the United States from many of them, but it specifically targeted the Soviet Union. Engaging the Soviets on human rights was an important weapon in Carter's strategy, one that allowed the United States to create new tensions and fuel political ferment within the Soviet Union, tarnish communism's image and global appeal and renew the global perception of America as a beacon of fundamental freedoms and rights.

Second, the book points out that détente and human rights intertwined and overlapped in unexpected, ambiguous and contradictory ways in the 1970s. Benefiting from growing contact between the blocs, dissidents in the Soviet Union and communist Europe found an international sounding box for their demands, strengthening Western interest in the state of human rights beyond the Iron Curtain. The bipolar dialogue and growing global interdependence thus favoured greater attention to human rights. This was an unexpected and paradoxical result of détente, a policy that was conceived as conservative in nature and, often, in opposition to the promotion of human rights. This forms the second element of the relationship between human rights and détente and shows the tension and apparent irreconcilability between them. Moscow perceived every action in favour of dissidents as an intolerable interference in Soviet domestic affairs and part of an ideological offensive aimed at delegitimizing the Soviet State, and therefore denounced it as irreconcilable with bipolar dialogue. Still more importantly, genuine indignation at the repression of political dissent became a weapon in the hands of critics and opponents of détente within the United States. Led by Senator Henry M. Jackson (D – Washington), the heterogeneous coalition that opposed Richard Nixon and Henry Kissinger's détente continuously denounced bipolar dialogue as a "one-way street" in which there was no room for human rights. They made the same argument to the Carter administration, casting a prolonged shadow over any attempt to develop a dialogue with the Soviet Union. This tension formed the backdrop against which Carter developed his Soviet policy. From his first days in office Carter had tried to develop a human rights policy that was complementary and functional to détente. The simultaneous promotion of human rights and détente was based on the idea that the Soviets needed to understand that the repression of dissent was detrimental to détente and the attempt to conclude a new SALT Treaty for the control of nuclear weapons. In other words, by linking foreign policy to American domestic politics, and détente to human rights, Carter was seeking to legitimate détente within the United States once again, silencing or at least containing charges from those who repeatedly affirmed it to be a form of appeasement of Soviet totalitarianism. For this reason, the book argues that Carter's Soviet policy in its entirety was conceived as a double process of negotiations geared to making the Soviets accept the reduction of internal repression so as to strengthen détente and the prospects for the ratification of the SALT II agreements in the United States. In doing so, the book also offers a fresh interpretation of Jimmy Carter's détente. Benefiting from Zbigniew Brzezinski's intellectual contribution, the president elaborated a conception of détente as a dynamic process that could stabilize bipolar relations in order to allow the United States to compete politically and ideologically.

The political balance between détente and human rights soon revealed itself to be unable to simultaneously satisfy both the Soviets and the American public. This is the basis of the third major idea of this book: the origins, changes, results and failures of Carter's human rights campaign can be explained in large part by analysing the political debate within the United States and Congress's criticism of the White House's foreign policy. Trying to appease domestic critics of détente, the Carter administration overlooked the negative impact of its human rights campaign on bipolar relations.

For this reason, the book adopts an "intermestic approach" to the study of Carter's foreign policy. A traditional diplomatic history approach, one that focuses on government-to-government relations, fails to assess the complexity and the main constraints the White House faced when developing its human rights campaign, as well as the debates Carter's foreign policy elicited within the United States and within Congress. By assuming an intermestic approach, the book aims to uncover how domestic politics shaped Washington's foreign policy, its promotion of human rights and its attempt to develop bipolar détente. It also aims to understand how the evolution of international politics, and the deterioration of bipolar détente, affected the American domestic debate over Carter's foreign policy.[14] The legislative branch, in particular, came to play a crucial role. On the one hand, it contributed to the emergence of human rights in American foreign policy and, in the post-Vietnam, post-Watergate climate, it was determined to keep its role in foreign policy discussions. On the other, the Carter administration itself immediately identified Congressional support as fundamental for its foreign policy, as well as Senate ratification of the SALT II Treaty as the crucial obstacle for policy vis-à-vis the Soviet Union. Through this perspective, the main limits and shortcomings of Carter's foreign policy emerge: the inability to create a lasting consensus for his foreign policy, the failure to guide American attention to human rights and the failure to confer a new sense of legitimacy to détente.

The main ideas explored in the book are thus the implication of Carter's new universalism on human rights for the Cold War, the manifold and contradictory ties between human rights and détente and Carter's domestic failure.

In the first two chapters, I describe the rise of human rights in American foreign policy and the rationale for Carter's emphasis on human rights during the 1976 presidential elections. Specifically, the first chapter focuses on the emergence of human rights in international politics and American foreign policy. Human rights became what historian Samuel Moyn has defined as a global and non-political "last utopia", and many activists genuinely believed that their advocacy transcended politics on behalf of a new moral lingua franca to rebuild international relations.[15] But the actions of these defenders of human rights were filtered by politicians who did not transcend their own ideologies or interests. Therefore, the first chapter focuses on Congress and its attempts to introduce human rights into American foreign policy. It argues that the Congressional human rights surge was based on the experience of the Vietnam War and the rejection of Kissinger's alleged amoral foreign policy. Human rights became common ground for both liberals and "neo-internationalists", who asked the American government to rediscover its traditional values and define a foreign policy for growing global interdependence, and for conservatives and neoconservatives, who wanted to abandon détente with the USSR and relaunch a traditional policy of containment.

The second chapter focuses on the role of human rights and Soviet dissidents in the 1976 presidential campaign. It highlights three major changes: the creation of the Congressional Committee on the Conference on Security and Cooperation in Europe (CSCE) (known as the Helsinki Commission); the influence of Zbigniew Brzezinski's reflections on Carter's campaign; and the electoral relevance that Soviet violations of human rights assumed in 1976. As a latecomer to the language of human rights, Carter's adoption of their promotion as a platform for his foreign policy was intended both to bring together the different components of the Democratic Party, divided over foreign policy at the time, and as a new consensual principle for American international action.

The third chapter focuses on 1977 and Carter's open diplomacy addressing Soviet violations of human rights. While prioritizing human rights, the administration constantly recalled the importance of détente and arms control. Although several historians consider this the major contradiction in the administration's foreign policy, the chapter argues that Carter truly believed he could preserve détente while, at the same time, promoting human rights in the USSR. His strategy was based on a reconceptualization of Kissinger's linkage, which was supposed to play a pivotal role in the domestic debate, helping Carter to develop a political dialogue with those conservative and neoconservative Cold Warriors who were dissatisfied with détente. In this view, American diplomatic efforts aimed both at making the Soviets willing to accept human rights criticisms and at creating new legitimation for SALT II within the United States.

The fourth chapter analyses the decision to shift the human rights policy towards the Soviet Union from open to quiet diplomacy. This change occurred in mid-1978 after the closing of the CSCE Belgrade conference. While many historians have argued that after 1978 human rights no longer figured prominently in Carter's agenda, this chapter highlights how the United States and the Soviet Union continued to discuss human rights in private talks. To explain the choice for quiet diplomacy, the chapter stresses two points. First, as seen from Washington, the Soviets were making some positive moves to openness, especially regarding the free emigration of Soviet Jews or CSCE humanitarian provisions. Reducing public criticism was conceived as a tool to reward the Soviets for their cooperative attitude. Second, within the United States, a number of liberal critics began to point out how Carter's firm stance on Soviet violations of human rights was detrimental to détente and arms control negotiations, while others denounced the selectiveness of a supposedly universal campaign. The Carter administration decided to move discussions of Soviet violations of human rights from open to quiet diplomacy, in order to address such growing criticism and Soviet protests. Yet this shift occurred at a moment when, because of Soviet actions in Africa and the conclusion of trials of a number of well-known dissidents such as Yuri Orlov and Natan Sharansky, American scepticism towards détente and Soviet intentions was at its peak.

The fifth chapter discusses how conservative and neoconservative critics of Carter's foreign policy lashed out at the president's quiet diplomacy, denouncing it as a betrayal of his firm commitment to human rights and Soviet dissidents. To them, as Jeane Kirkpatrick wrote in a well-known *Commentary* article in late 1979, the human rights campaign was targeting allied countries and ignoring the Soviet Union. By exploiting détente and its misconceived human rights campaign – critics argued – the Carter administration had allowed the Soviets to strengthen their military capabilities, to expand their global influence and to continue their violations of human rights. The Soviet invasion of Afghanistan seemed to confirm this criticism. Soon after the invasion, the administration decided to interrupt détente with the Soviets while continuing to focus on Soviet violations of human rights. Yet the meaning of the campaign was now different. Human rights had lost their dynamic linkage with détente: no attempt to advance human rights in the Soviet Union was possible; and ideological coverage to create domestic support in favour of détente was no longer required. The human rights campaign was now just another tool to score propaganda points against the Soviets.

Notes

1 L. Bloomfield, "The Carter Human Rights Policy. A Provisional Appraisal", 16 January 1981, JCPL, ZBM, Box 34, Folder "NSA Accomplishment – Human Rights".
2 Associated Press, "Soviet Dissident Calls Reagan Human Rights Policy Dangerous", 10 February 1981.
3 E.W. Lefever, "The Trivialization of Human Rights", *Policy Review* 3 (Winter 1978), pp. 13–34.
4 House Committee on Foreign Affairs, *Human Rights and U.S. Foreign Policy*, Hearings Before the Subcommittee on International Organizations, 96th Congress, 1st Session (Washington, DC: US Government Printing Office, 1979), pp. 230–231.

5 M. Freudenheim and B. Slavin, "White Hats Have a Practical Use", *New York Times*, 8 November 1981; R. Sinding Søndergaard, "'A Positive Track of Human Rights Policy': Elliott Abrams, the Human Rights Bureau, and the Conceptualization of Democracy Promotion, 1981–1984", in R. Pee and W.M. Schmidli (eds), *The Reagan Administration, the Cold War, and the Transition to Democracy Promotion* (Basingstoke: Palgrave Macmillan, 2018), pp. 31–53.

6 J. Muravchik, *The Uncertain Crusade: Jimmy Carter and the Dilemmas of Human Rights Policy* (Washington, DC: American Enterprise Institute for Public Policy Research, 1988), pp. 8–9.

7 G.F. Kennan, *The Cloud of Danger: Current Realities of American Foreign Policy* (Boston: Little, Brown & Company, 1978); C. Marcy (ed.), *Common Sense in U.S.–Soviet Relations* (Washington, DC: American Committee on East–West Relations; New York: Norton, 1978).

8 John Dumbrell was among the first to propose such interpretation. See J. Dumbrell, *The Carter Presidency: A Re-Evaluation* (Manchester and New York: Manchester University Press, 1993). See also J.A. Rosati, "Continuity and Change in the Foreign Policy Beliefs of Political Leaders: Addressing the Controversy over the Carter Administration", *Political Psychology* 9:3 (September 1988), pp. 471–505; J.A. Rosati, "The Rise and Fall of America's First Post-Cold War Foreign Policy", in H.D. Rosenbaum and A. Ugrinsky (eds), *Jimmy Carter: Foreign Policy and Post-Presidential Years* (Westport, CT: Greenwood Press, 1994), pp. 35–52; D. Skidmore, *Reversing Course: Carter's Foreign Policy, Domestic Politics, and the Failure of Reform* (Nashville, TN: Vanderbilt University Press, 1996).

9 C. Maier, "Consigning the Twentieth Century to History: Alternative Narratives for the Modern Era", *American Historical Review* 105:3 (2000), pp. 807–831; N. Ferguson, C. Maier, E. Manela and D.J. Sargent (eds), *The Shock of the Global: The 1970s in Perspective* (Cambridge, MA: Harvard University Press, 2010). The concept of interdependence was first discussed in R. Keohane and J. Nye, *Power and Interdependence: World Politics in Transition* (Boston: Little, Brown & Company, 1977).

10 D.J. Sargent, *A Superpower Transformed: The Remaking of American Foreign Relations in the 1970s* (Oxford and New York: Oxford University Press, 2015), pp. 233.

11 D.F. Schmitz and V. Walker, "Jimmy Carter and the Foreign Policy of Human Rights: The Development of a Post-Cold War Foreign Policy", *Diplomatic History* 28:1 (January 2004), pp. 113–143; D.F. Schmitz, *The United States and Right-Wing Dictatorships* (Cambridge and New York: Cambridge University Press, 2006); I.N. Sneh, *The Future Almost Arrived: How Jimmy Carter Failed to Change U.S. Foreign Policy* (New York: Peter Lang, 2008).

12 The first to offer such a perspective was W. Lafeber, "From Confusion to Cold War: The Memoirs of the Carter Administration", *Diplomatic History* 8:4 (1984), pp. 1–12.

13 N. Mitchell, *Jimmy Carter in Africa: Race and the Cold War* (Palo Alto, CA: Stanford University Press and Woodrow Wilson Center Press, 2016), quotation at p. 8; N. Mitchell, "The Cold War and Jimmy Carter", in O.A. Westad and M.P. Leffler (eds), *The Cambridge History of the Cold War*, vol. 3: *Endings* (Cambridge and New York: Cambridge University Press, 2010), pp. 66–88; A.H. Cahn, *Killing Détente: The Right Attacks the CIA* (University Park: Pennsylvania University Press, 1998); B.J. Auten, *Carter's Conversion: The Hardening of American Defense Policy* (Columbia: University of Missouri Press, 2008).

14 F. Logevall, "Domestic Politics", in F. Castigliola and M.J. Hogan (eds), *Explaining the History of American Foreign Relations* (3rd edn) (Cambridge and New York: Cambridge University Press, 2016), pp. 151–167; C. Craig and F. Logevall, *America's Cold War: The Politics of Insecurity* (Cambridge, MA: Harvard University Press, 2010); W.M. Schmidli, *The Fate of Freedom Elsewhere: Human Rights and U.S. Cold War Policy toward Argentina* (Ithaca, NY and London: Cornell University Press, 2013).

15 S. Moyn, *The Last Utopia: Human Rights in History* (Cambridge, MA: Harvard University Press, 2010).

1

Setting the stage for a human rights policy

During the 1970s, human rights gained unexpected and sudden prominence in international politics. Discussions of human rights were everywhere, providing a vocabulary to oppressed religious groups, national minorities and political dissidents, as well as workers' or women's groups. However different these claims were, they all converged on making human rights the central concern of the decade. As popular as the concept was, it was also a contested one.

For many activists around the world, human rights offered a tool to transcend political divisions on behalf of a universal idea and what historian Samuel Moyn labelled an apolitical "last utopia" to transform international relations.[1] To governments and movements from the "global South", human rights language meant above all self-determination and the rejection of neo-colonial practices.[2] Socialist countries offered their own version of human rights, one that was based on their egalitarian ideology and on the need to respond to international criticism of their abuses of individual freedom.[3] Western European governments' discourse on human rights was based on their post-1945 experiences and on their ambitious political will to prove that the European Economic Community was a global "civilian power". In a broad definition of human rights, Western Europeans began referring to political freedoms, social and economic rights, the right to development and a vague notion of "third generation rights".[4]

Nowhere was the debate on human rights more intense than in the United States. The reasons for the emergence of human rights within the United States were multiple and diverse. Many activists were galvanized by broader changes occurring both at the national and at the international level since the 1960s, such as decolonization, the achievements of the civil rights movement, as well as President Johnson's "war on poverty". Involvement with the many movements from the "long 1960s" provided activists with experiences, sensitivity to rights violations and a jargon for advocating a rights-based political proposal.[5] Grassroots activism, however, had to struggle to make its way through the legislative and the political process. In this sense, historians Samuel Moyn and Barbara Keys are probably right in pointing out a political discontinuity between the civil rights movement's experience of the 1960s and the human rights surge of the 1970s. The Vietnam War and its legacies provided this discontinuity. The war was not an "incubator" of human rights ideas. Nevertheless, it produced three major changes that contributed to the prominence of human rights in American foreign policy during the 1970s.[6] First, to many Americans, the Vietnam War proved the moral bankruptcy and imperialist bias of their country's foreign policy.[7] The war opened the Pandora's box of American Cold War alliances with authoritarian regimes and of the USA's responsibility in human rights violations around the world. To many Americans, the war generated "a deep sense of shame and embarrassment, feelings of guilt that cried for expiation". Prioritizing the promotion of human rights abroad could favour such an expiation.[8] Second, the war accelerated the collapse of Cold War liberalism, that consensual doctrine that had sustained America's Cold War policies both at home and abroad for about twenty years. New principles for American foreign policy had to be found. Human rights could offer a new consensual doctrine, one that fitted well with the American tradition; one that could bring morality, legalism and idealism all together in inspiring Washington's action abroad.[9] Finally, the war fuelled the political and institutional ambitions of a resurgent Congress that found in the promotion of human rights an arena to affirm its role and to challenge the White House handling of foreign affairs.[10]

However, for those members of Congress who elevated human rights to a high priority, the issue intertwined with their own beliefs and ideological preferences. Accordingly, as popular as the concept of human rights was in Congress, it was also divisive and ambiguous. Attention to human rights soon proved to be double-edged and contradictory, with two opposing understandings of the concept's political meaning for American foreign policy.

From neglect to denial: the United States and human rights, 1948–1972

It is tempting to read the history of American foreign policy as driven by the promotion of rights, democracy and freedom. Yet, human rights entered American foreign policy as a marginal aside during the Second World War in planning for the post-war order. In preparing for America's entry into the war, President Franklin D. Roosevelt announced his "four essential freedoms" to rebuild the international system: "the freedom of speech and expression", the freedom to "worship God", the "freedom from want" and, finally, "freedom from fear".[11]

Roosevelt's manifesto was a list of both the essential rights Nazi fascism had violated and the basic principles to rebuild and remodel the international community. It defined a new conception of liberty, which combined into a single category civil and political rights, economic and social rights and people's right to self-determination.[12] The "Four Freedoms" speech was also a human rights manifesto that asserted a substantial equation between freedom and human rights. In concluding his address, Roosevelt remarked that "freedom means the supremacy of human rights everywhere" and that "our support goes to those who struggle to gain those rights or to keep them".[13]

Roosevelt's speech fuelled a variety of debates among many organizations, such as the International League for Human Rights, the National Association for the Advancement of Colored People and the American Jewish Committee. It inspired dozens of books, pamphlets and articles, as well as a series of four paintings by illustrator Norman Rockwell. It became a sort of ideological blueprint for what historian Mark Philip Bradley identified as the "human rights moment of the '40s" and for the definition of many human rights treaties, declarations and covenants, such as the United Nations Universal Declaration of Human Rights (1948), the Nuremberg Principles (1946), the American Declaration of the Rights and Duties of Man (1948), the Convention on the Prevention and Punishment of Genocide (1948), the Fourth Geneva Convention on the Protection of Civilian Persons in Time of War (1949) and the European Convention on Human Rights (1950).[14]

The United Nations Declaration on Human Rights was the capstone of this panoply of international documents. Yet, it also revealed the limits of the human rights discourse of the 1940s. Many of these had already emerged during early negotiations of the new international system. The final communiqué of the 1944 Dumbarton Oaks Conference for the creation of the United Nations, for example, mentioned human rights only in a brief paragraph, fuelling international protests. Within the United States, for example, Jacob Blaustein and Joseph Proskauer, both members of the American Jewish Committee, started a petition for the adoption of an International Charter for Human Rights. Similarly, Frederick Nolde, executive secretary of the Joint Committee on Religious Liberty, prepared three memoranda for Secretary of State Edward Stettinius urging the creation of an international mechanism to implement Roosevelt's "Four Freedoms".[15] Abroad, on the eve of the 1945 San Francisco conference where the United Nations was officially established, some international allies of the United States urged the introduction of an international system for the protection of human rights. To address their demands, Stettinius responded that the idea was not feasible at that moment and that the only viable solution was to wait for the establishment of a specific committee that would write an international covenant on human rights.[16]

This committee was announced to the world on 26 June 1946, when the UN Economic and Social Council inaugurated its Commission on Human Rights, whose main task was to draw up what would later become the Universal Declaration of Human Rights. Originally, the Commission was supposed to define a binding text. However, its mandate was immediately curtailed. Contrary to original plans, members of the Commission would not be independent experts, but rather political representatives of states. Its members further contributed to the reduction of their mandate when they decided to disavow the right of the individual to petition the Commission. Denunciations of human rights abuses would be channelled through states and governments. Moreover, the UN debate over the adoption of a binding covenant to protect human rights that incorporated socio-economic rights encountered firm opposition from American conservative politicians and intellectuals as well as professional organizations and lobbies, such as the American Medical Association. Domestic opposition intertwined with the Cold War and growing international confrontation.

The fundamental document became a far-reaching declaration that was supposed to be integrated by other more specific treaties. However, the American delegation at the Commission on Human Rights was instructed to keep socio-economic rights out of the covenant while appearing non-hostile on these rights. A non-cooperative attitude would have created a geopolitical disadvantage for the United States because many states supported a strong commitment on socio-economic rights. Thus, the American diplomatic strategy became one of defining an international covenant that "mirrored the principles and rights" protected by the US Constitution and proposing further covenants or "other measures concerning economic, social, and cultural rights".[17] In February 1952 the General Assembly authorized the two-covenant solution. The International Covenant on Civil and Political Rights and the International Covenant on Economic, Social and Cultural Rights supplemented the Universal Declaration of Human Rights, but both were adopted only in 1966.

The ideological reconceptualization of human rights produced by the Cold War had relevant consequences. Within the United States, many began perceiving social and economic rights, one of Roosevelt's "Four Freedoms", as ancillary to individual freedoms. It was a clearly self-serving understanding, with a patently anti-Soviet and anti-communist bias. Nevertheless, it was also deeply rooted in the historical evolution of human rights – civil and political rights came first, then economic and social rights – and in their own nature: unlike individual freedoms, economic and social rights required state intervention that could not be universally ensured soon after the war. On their side, the Soviets overturned such concepts to point out that material equality was a prerequisite for assuring fundamental freedoms and that economic and social rights were modern and intrinsically superior rights. The confrontation between civil and political rights and economic and social rights became a continuous leit-motiv in mutual accusations between the United States and the Soviet Union. The UN Commission on Human Rights became a battlefield for ideological confrontation between East and West.[18]

The new meaning the United States attributed to human rights became clear with the "Truman Doctrine" (1947). In one of its best-known paragraphs, Truman's address to a joint session of Congress pointed out what he saw as the striking opposition between two "alternative ways of life". The Western one was "based upon the will of the majority, and is distinguished by free institutions, representative government, free elections, guarantees of individual liberty, freedom of speech and religion, and freedom from political oppression". The Soviet way of life was based "upon the will of a minority forcibly imposed upon the majority. It relies upon terror and oppression, a controlled press and radio, fixed elections, and the suppression of personal freedoms."[19] Truman's Manichean vision of world affairs drew a clear and total opposition between two systems of values – democracy versus totalitarianism, freedom versus oppression – and, incidentally, gave an anti-communist twist to the American definition of human rights.[20] Within weeks of expounding this doctrine, Truman clarified that Americans were "a people who not only cherish freedom and defend it, if need be, with our lives, but we also recognize the right of other men and other nations to share it. While the struggle for the rights of man goes forward in

other parts of the world, the free people of America cannot look on with easy detach-
ment, with indifference to the outcome."[21]

Anti-communism, rather than human rights, would drive America's foreign policy.
Accordingly, Washington began to show a high degree of tolerance for human rights
violations occurring in allied countries. In 1950, back from Latin America, diplomat
George Kennan wrote:

> We cannot be too dogmatic about the methods by which local communists
> can be dealt with. These vary greatly, depending upon the vigor and efficacy of
> local concepts and traditions of self-government. ... [W]here the concepts and
> traditions of popular government are too weak to absorb successfully the intensity
> of the communist attack, then we must concede that harsh governmental measures
> of repression may be the only answer; that these measures may have to proceed
> from regimes whose origins and methods would not stand the test of American
> concepts of democratic procedure; and that such regimes and such methods may
> be preferable alternatives, and indeed the only alternatives to further communist
> successes.[22]

At home, anti-communism produced a dramatic tightening. It was embodied by
Senator Joseph McCarthy's crusade against communist infiltration in American cul-
ture, politics and society. A Republican from Wisconsin, McCarthy claimed that the
US State Department was "thoroughly infested with communists" in February 1950.
It was a groundless allegation, yet it epitomized the political climate of the time, when
an anti-communist hysteria favoured stricter political control and produced a clear
paradox: anti-communism, the essential basis for protecting freedom during America's
Cold War, became the fundamental argument for supporting right-wing dictatorships
and to limiting some of the rights of American citizens.[23]

McCarthy's campaign was matched by Senator John W. Bricker's (R – Ohio) crusade against international human rights treaties. In January 1953, he introduced a proposal to amend the Constitution so that Congress, not the executive branch, would
wield authority over the ratification of international treaties. Bricker was supported by
a heterogeneous coalition: Cold Warriors, McCarthy sympathizers, conservatives who
feared a resumption of New Deal policies through international covenants, isolationists
and segregationists who feared that international treaties could impose measures for
real racial equality. Even the US Chamber of Commerce, the National Association of
Manufacturers, the Daughters of the American Revolution, the Veterans of Foreign
Wars and the American Bar Association (ABA) sided with Bricker because, as ABA
president Frank Holman clarified, international human rights treaties were a threat to
the American constitutional system and an attempt to "promote State socialism, if not
communism".[24] Bricker's campaign targeted the 1948 Convention on the Prevention
and Punishment of the Crime of Genocide, under discussion in the Senate at the
time. It came to be associated with a project that threatened American sovereignty
and that surreptitiously aimed at building "a wall of socialistic and communist containment" around the United States, as Bricker himself claimed.[25] Between 1953 and

1954, President Eisenhower took a strong position against Bricker, contributing to halt his campaign.[26] Nevertheless, Bricker's shadow was so prolonged that the United States would join neither the Convention against the Crime of Genocide nor any other human rights treaty for several years.[27]

Human rights did not disappear completely during the 1950s. In Western Europe, a vast coalition of conservatives, Christian Democrats and anti-communists succeeded in creating a regional human rights regime, epitomized by the signing of the European Convention on Human Rights and, later, by the creation of the European Court of Human Rights. The Convention delineated human rights along Cold War divisions, promoting the idea of a substantial equivalence between Nazi fascism and communism. Denouncing human rights abuses in communist countries contributed to distinguish democratic Europe from "the other" Europe. The West German journal *Die Menschenrechte* ("Human Rights"), for example, hosted a regular column "that drew parallels between Nazi and communist crimes, juxtaposing stories of victims of Nazism with stories of victims of communism".[28]

Some attention to human rights survived in the United States, too. The issue was initially confined to groups and organizations such as the National Association for the Advancement of Colored People, Freedom House, the International League for the Rights of Man, the World Council of Churches and the World Jewish Congress. However, these associations could not boast a vast membership nor capillary organization and their discussion of human rights remained confined to diplomatic circles and legal scholars. Human rights barely entered political debates.[29] By the late 1950s, however, efforts to promote racial equality and emancipation took centre stage in American society. Later on, there were also new movements on university campuses over freedom of speech and association, as well as for women's rights. Progressively, Americans rediscovered the human rights lexicon. Yet, despite global transformations elicited by decolonization and early transnational contacts – many black advocacy groups, for example, linked their struggle to the global battle against racial discrimination – these rights movements were an inward-looking phenomenon. Mobilization focused on domestic issues, although in some circumstances human rights violations across the world engendered deep concerns for many American activists.[30]

Meanwhile, the United States entered the Vietnam quagmire. By the mid-1960s, both Republicans and Democrats were disappointed at their country's inability to win the war within a short time. By 1966, disappointment had turned into embarrassment. That year, Senator Mike Mansfield (D – Montana) began urging US troop reduction in Europe, while Senate Foreign Relations Committee Chairman William Fulbright (D – Arkansas) started Congressional hearings on the American war in Vietnam. Pointing the finger at the mantra of the credibility of the American commitment to contain communism, Fulbright denounced what he defined as "the arrogance of American power", a tendency that led to equating "power with virtue and major responsibilities with a universal mission".[31] Over the following months, the anti-war stance gained momentum. Many debated the legal basis for the American intervention and concluded that the war was illegal. Others began to question the war's moral foundation and, more generally, that of American Cold War foreign policy. Both were considered flawed because, as scholar Trevor McCrisken has written, "the United States was using its immense power in ways inconsistent with the principles, the values and the ethical standards of the American people".[32]

The Vietnam War accelerated the multifaceted crisis of containment and eroded the domestic consensus that had sustained America's Cold War policy for twenty years. To political scientist and future National Security Advisor Zbigniew Brzezinski, the war was "the Waterloo of the WASP elite" and of its foreign policy consensus.[33] It was time to identify new directions for American foreign policy and to elaborate a new consensual doctrine to sustain American engagement with the world.

At one of the extremes of this debate, many conservatives criticized the Democratic establishment for its inability to win a war in a remote Third World country and, by extension, they lashed out at the supposedly self-defeating moderation of containment. They urged a more muscular foreign policy that should not leave the initiative to the Soviets, as they believed containment had done since its beginnings. At the opposite extreme, the "New Left" found in the Vietnam War both a natural consequence of Cold War logic and a demonstration of the imperial hubris of American foreign policy. With revolutionary rhetoric, the "New Left" proposed a heterogeneous panoply of initiatives that encompassed the rejection of any form of militarism, called for nuclear disarmament and espoused a vague notion of Third Worldism. Between these two extremes, different solutions were proposed. To the now-discredited Cold Warriors, the solution to the crisis of containment passed through the reaffirmation of containment itself and of its fundamental pillars: a new moral, political and military American leadership to confront Soviet communism. To the contrary, much of the Democratic establishment embraced what became the buzzword of the decade: interdependence. To them, the Cold War and its unambiguous categories had become too rigid to usefully understand an increasingly pluralistic world in which new international actors, ranging from transnational movements to international institutions, were playing an important role, and new international problems were emerging. To cope with these global transformations, they argued, the United States should work for negotiated and collective solutions and re-evaluate the positive role of international regimes and organizations.[34]

A more conservative proposal for the future direction of American foreign policy was elaborated by Republican President Richard Nixon, who entered office in 1969, and his National Security Advisor, Henry Kissinger. Nixon and Kissinger did not deny that an increasingly pluralistic world was developing. "The post-war order of international relations – the configuration of power that emerged from the Second World War – is gone", they wrote to Congress in 1971. "With it are gone the conditions which have determined the assumptions and practice of United States foreign policy since 1945." To them, a new multipolar international system was progressively emerging, one in which the economic growth of Western Europe and Japan, the rise of a Chinese alternative within the communist world and Soviet nuclear parity with the United States were fostering the relative decline of American power.[35]

However grandiose their slogans on multipolarism were, their understanding of international affairs remained defined by Cold War categories. Any international event was analysed through traditional Cold War bipolar prisms and appreciated for its impact on the Cold War. This analytical dimension slipped quasi-automatically into a prescriptive one. Bipolarism was a political perspective to (re)impose onto international relations. International stabilization and order would become their buzzwords.[36]

The pillar of their foreign policy was a realist approach to a comprehensive détente with the Soviet Union. Far from representing the end of the Cold War, détente was an attempt to rationalize, stabilize and renew bipolar confrontation, recognizing that it was possible to introduce some areas of dialogue and cooperation with the Soviets, within a framework that remained substantially competitive. For this reason, détente was based on an attempt to de-emphasize the ideological warfare that went together with America's Cold War, while promoting a form of "containment by other means", suitable for an age of strategic, economic and political limits, as the 1970s were perceived. Through negotiations with the Soviets, détente aimed to strengthen American security and to promote its interests. The dialogue with the Soviets was meant, among other things, to stabilize the Cold War division into blocs, to impose a new discipline within the Western alliance at a moment when many Western allies were protesting American hegemony, to elaborate an exit strategy from the Vietnamese quagmire, to reduce the financial burden of containment and to prevent the spread of Soviet-inspired communism to new areas of the world.[37]

Beginning in 1972, the United States and the Soviet Union signed a variety of documents and treaties, encompassing a broad range of topics and issues, such as scientific and technological cooperation, space exploration, a twelve-point declaration on "Basic Principles of Mutual Relations between the United States and the Soviet Union", a commitment to reducing conventional forces and the summoning of a multilateral conference on security and cooperation in Europe. The very essence of negotiations, and indeed the very essence of détente, was nuclear weapons. During President Nixon's historic visit to Moscow, he and Brezhnev signed the Interim Agreement on the Limitation of Strategic Arms (SALT) that froze the number of nuclear weapons each country could have. Under the terms of the agreement, the United States could maintain 1,054 intercontinental ballistic missiles (ICBMs) and 656 submarine-launched ballistic missiles (SLBMs), while the Soviets could keep 1,618 ICBMs and 950 SLBMs. This quantitative advantage for the Soviet Union was balanced by an American qualitative advantage, for the United States had developed multiple independently targetable re-entry vehicle (MIRV) technology that allowed missiles to carry multiple warheads. They also signed an Anti-Ballistic Missile (ABM) Treaty, which allowed each party to develop two ABM sites, thereby institutionalizing deterrence.[38]

Détente aimed also to rebuild the domestic consensus over foreign policy. To do that, Nixon and Kissinger proposed a "centrist national security agenda", which combined security imperatives with the need to contain "massive military retrenchment (left) and massive military escalation (right)".[39] Prior to becoming a policymaker, Kissinger the professor wrote: "the acid test of a policy ... is its ability to obtain domestic support".[40] To do that, Kissinger the policy-maker developed a political discourse that presented détente as a new policy that would ensure international stability, a reduction of American burdens and a new structure of peace, as he pompously claimed. Selling détente to the American public became a pivotal mission for the White House, a mission that was achieved almost immediately. Nixon and Kissinger succeeded in portraying détente as a dramatic reduction in both the risk of a nuclear war and Cold War tensions with the Soviet Union.

Kissinger's diplomacy was welcomed by those Democrats who favoured more stable contact with the Soviets, the SALT Treaty, the 1972 US–Soviet trade treaty and growing scientific and economic contacts. To them, these achievements represented a deep break with the discredited policy of containment, and could eventually permit both a demilitarization of American foreign policy and a shift of resources in favour of domestic priorities. Equally successful was the diplomatic opening to China. Although it was conceived as a strictly bipolar initiative to push the Soviets towards a more cooperative attitude for the American disengagement from Vietnam and for détente in general, Nixon's visit to Beijing envisaged better trade relations with the potentially almost limitless Chinese market. And, of course, most Americans openly supported Kissinger's peace negotiations with Vietnam, which led to the signing of the 1973 Paris Peace Accords.[41]

Although many members of Congress were in favour of détente, they nevertheless grew sceptical of Kissinger's realism. His strong emphasis on stability and control soon triggered accusations of amorality or even immorality for the explicit abandonment of traditional notions of American exceptionalism and its national mission. Kissinger's secretive and centralized style, and the progressive marginalization of both Congress and allies further fuelled criticism, as did the lack of any major commitment to the promotion of democracy and human rights.

To Kissinger and Nixon, human rights represented a multifaceted challenge to their foreign policy. Despite the frequent claims that the administration supported a "quiet diplomacy" approach to human rights violations, Kissinger constantly thundered against making human rights an issue in American foreign policy and dismissed them as irrelevant, "quixotic" or even dangerous.[42] To Kissinger, proposals for a human rights-based foreign policy were a quintessential expression of that Wilsonian idealism which encouraged the United States to "espouse great causes, such as making the world safe for democracy, or human rights", and which Kissinger wanted to eradicate from American foreign policy. Human rights were an expression of a dangerous and deceptive morality: "the nettle we have to grasp is if this [attention on human rights] goes on another two years, we are going to see a precipitant slide of the American position in the world that is totally unprecedented. That is what we are going to see. And all the other stuff is sentimental nonsense."[43] On the contrary, Kissinger claimed that his aim was to promote the real national interest that "should be narrowly constructed to exclude moral commitments or causes that do not promise a clear, direct, predictable payoff in increased security or prosperity for the nation".[44]

To Kissinger and Nixon, human rights were both outside legitimate foreign policy concerns and in opposition to two fundamental assumptions of realist thought about international politics: respect for national sovereignty and the principle of non-interference in domestic affairs. As Nixon affirmed, it was dangerous "to make the domestic politics of countries around the world a direct objective of American foreign policy", because

> the protection of basic human rights is a very sensitive aspect of jurisdiction of … governments …. If the infringement of human rights is not so offensive that we cannot live with it, we will seek to work out what we can with the country involved in order to increase our influence. If the infringement was so offensive that we cannot live with it, we will avoid dealing with the offending country.[45]

Not only did human rights constitute a challenge to Nixon and Kissinger's cultural premises, but they also introduced several problems in American relations with other countries. They were a twofold threat to bipolar détente, since they represented an unacceptable interference in Soviet domestic affairs and also revived the ideological fervour that in the past had led the United States to perceive the Soviet Union as a total, illegitimate and absolute enemy. In a telephone conversation on the eve of the 1972 Moscow meeting, for example, Kissinger invited Nixon to avoid "lecturing [the Soviets] about freedom of speech".[46]

Similarly, Kissinger and Nixon resisted considering human rights in American relations with Third World countries. If the aim of their foreign policy was to bring order and stability to the international system, the United States should avoid all those actions that, like the promotion of human rights, could have destabilizing effects that might eventually permit the Soviets to increase their influence in the world. Instead, in order to achieve international stability and to reduce the costs of hegemony, the United States had to reinforce its economic, political and military relations with many authoritarian regimes.

It was in the context of these analyses that Congress openly challenged Kissinger's approach to international affairs and introduced human rights into State Department priorities. From Kissinger's perspective, Congressional actions represented an isolationist assault on American power that was based on the assumption that the United States was "too depraved to participate in international politics".[47] On this point, a limitation of Kissinger's analysis was evident. Far from advocating an isolationist intent – the "spearhead of retreat", in one contemporary's words – Congressional actions on human rights were rooted in a growing international movement and in the circulation of ideas that from Europe to Latin America, from the Soviet bloc to the United States, were succeeding in putting human rights under the spotlight.[48]

Liberals' vision for a human rights policy in an interdependent world

Discontent with Kissinger's diplomacy increased over the months, leading Congress to propose alternative visions for world affairs and to position human rights at the centre of American foreign policy. One of these was deeply rooted both in the United States'

exceptionalist self-perception and in growing global interdependence. Another aimed
at renewing containment. On this point, there is a broad consensus among historians,
who point out that since 1973, Congress had been able to inscribe human rights legislation into American foreign policy.[49] Yet, before Congress could articulate and impose
such proposals, the American government found itself in opposition to the global
rediscovery of human rights.

The origins of the human rights surge of the 1970s were multiple and complex. They
intertwined international, transnational and national contexts, as well as long-term
processes and sudden accelerations. However, they all converged on criticism of the
American government and Kissinger's foreign policy.

One of these transformations was decolonization. Although decolonization did not
represent a human rights phenomenon, it nevertheless contributed to an international
debate on the very nature and meaning of human rights.[50] By the late 1960s, many
would agree with the Colombian Ambassador to the UN, Clara Ponce De Leon, who
realized that "an awakening of the world conscience" was developing; an "awakening
of peoples to a clear right – that of strengthening the foundations of justice, a society
based on equality, the obligations of States to promote conditions that will permit
every person the full enjoyment of his rights".[51] It was largely a consequence of the
growth in UN membership of new states born of former colonial territories. They
found in the United Nations an important forum for their anti-colonial struggles and
for the advancement of a new conception of human rights, one that magnified the right
to self-determination and that was at odds with Western ideals of individual rights,
repudiating them as a form of Western neo-colonialism. As a moral aside of popular
liberation from external domination, human rights were meant to be collective and
national rights to protect recently independent countries from former imperial
rulers. This anti-Western mood soon translated into characterization of the Universal
Declaration as an instrument of neo-colonialism and into attacks on its universality in
the name of cultural integrity, self-determination of peoples or national sovereignty.[52]
Under this new impulse, the UN Commission on Human Rights changed its nature.
For twenty years, it had been the locus of Cold War debates over human rights. By the
late 1960s, when its member states grew from twenty-one to thirty-two, it became an
arena for North–South confrontation, with developing countries having the power to
impose their agenda on the Commission. A similar development took place in the
General Assembly, where Third World countries' numerical superiority was indisputable. The adoption of the Convention on the Elimination of All Forms of Racial
Discrimination in 1965 inaugurated an era in which Third World countries set the UN
agenda. By 1974, more than 10 per cent of all General Assembly resolutions attacked
apartheid and other forms of racial segregation. In the very same year, the General
Assembly adopted both the Declaration on the New International Economic Order
and the Charter of Economic Rights and Duties of States.[53] The right to development –
Senegalese jurist Keba M'Baye argued in 1972 – should be viewed as a fundamental
human right.[54]

As controversial as this approach to human rights was, it found resounding
approval in Western Europe, where the human rights surge intertwined with several

transformations. First, a new wave of anti-Americanism entered European politics during the 1970s, triggered by the Vietnam War, alleged American responsibilities in the 1973 Chilean coup and, more broadly, the role the United States was supposed to have had in the authoritarian involution of many Latin American countries. This was, for example, the official conclusion of the Second Russell Tribunal that investigated the social, cultural and economic foundations of violations occurring in Chile, Brazil and other Latin American countries. After conducting a series of hearings with émigrés, human rights activists and prominent scholars, the tribunal was unequivocal in condemning the United States for violations of human rights occurring in the Americas. Not only was Washington supporting Latin American regimes, thus sharing political responsibility for their human rights abuses, but the tribunal also concluded that US corporations' economic interests in those countries were a fundamental motivation for those violations.[55] Moreover, pressures exerted on national governments and European Community (EC) institutions by nongovernmental organizations (NGOs), trade unions and some political parties should not be overlooked. In Great Britain, for example, a movement of solidarity with Chile spread over the country. In Italy and France, leftist parties constantly denounced the brutality of the Chilean dictatorship. Moreover, the rise of human rights in the 1970s intertwined with the emergence of a new specific identity discourse for the EC that was aiming at affirming European distinctiveness vis-à-vis the United States on the world stage: despite its own difficulties, the EC was willing to offer the world a political model that was eventually different from the American one.[56] Human rights could offer a symbolic area to prove the difference between the EC and Nixon and Kissinger's America. EC institutions started to issue declarations condemning the brutal repression of Pinochet's regime and to discuss some symbolic gestures, including holding meetings between leaders of the Chilean opposition and EC representatives, or moving EC diplomatic representation from Santiago to Caracas. The EC even decided to revise its development aid policy towards Chile, channelling its programmes through NGOs and churches.[57]

These global transformations contributed to putting the expression "human rights" under the spotlight and to projecting a clear perception of transformation in the international system, something that was confirmed by heated academic debates on interdependence. Used in connection with other more popular expressions such as "global village", "transnational society" or "world community", interdependence was the new buzzword to describe the growing interconnections in the world, as well as the emergence of many new problems and challenges.[58] Interdependence and its related concepts were so popular that in 1977 the historian Thomas H. Etzold underlined the many meanings the concept was assuming. Etzold wrote, "A first meaning is the common reliance on the biosphere. A second is the dependence of all governments and people on the nuclear powers to refrain from world-shattering, all-out war. A third meaning is the trend toward tightening relations between foreign and domestic affairs." In the most important of all the meanings in use – he admitted – "interdependence is the global web of transactions".[59] According to Representative Dante Fascell (D – Florida), growing interdependence among nations in areas such as energy and food production, along with technological advances in communications and transportation, had "created an enormous increase in transnational ties among nations". As part of this process, "structures within a society, whether cultural, business, education, professional, or scientific" had to some extent become involved in international relationships. "These nongovernmental groups and individuals", Fascell wrote, "now play an important role in world affairs ... [and] are demanding a say in the traditional agreements, exchanges, and relationships among world government leaders."[60]

Fascell's words pointed to the blossoming of NGOs, transnational networks and foundations, which magnified the growing prominence human rights had for the interdependent world.[61] The American branch of Amnesty International offers the best example to understand NGOs' new prominence. Established in 1961 in London by lawyer Peter Benenson, Amnesty International quickly became an international movement, establishing chapters in a number of different countries. In 1965, the American branch inaugurated its offices. After going through financial instability, charges of political bias and moments of difficulty, Amnesty International became the leading group of the human rights lobby of the 1970s. Its thematic mobilization and the creation of specific adoption groups that lobbied on behalf of single victims equally distributed among Western, communist and less-developed countries boosted Amnesty International's credibility as "a non-political, non-sectorial, international movement to guarantee the free exchange of ideas and the free practice of religion", as Benenson claimed.[62] Within the United States, its membership skyrocketed between 1968 and 1976, with roughly 8,000 new members per year; its annual budget jumped to $1 million and new offices were opened across the country. The American branch became a model and a source of inspiration for other human rights groups. By the end of the decade, more than a hundred human rights NGOs were operating in the DC area. It was "an amorphous yet multifaceted aggregate" of organizations advocating a specific legislation to enhance human rights abroad. NGOs began to publish newsletters, reports and detailed bulletins, and to collaborate with members of the US government and Congress. As William Korey underlined, the "offices of some 40 to 50 Congressmen were responsive to Amnesty's concern and the organization had close links particularly with a key subcommittee on international organisations of the House Foreign Affairs Committee".[63] They provided "a vital input" to political discussions and initiatives through the wide circulation of fast, credible and precise information on human rights abuses abroad.[64]

NGO pressures found in a specific group of members of Congress a receptive audience. They defined themselves as "new internationalists". They formed a non-structured and informal group, made up almost exclusively of Democrats, whose ambition was to define a new international role for the United States, free from the Cold War's rigid dichotomies and more responsive to global challenges. To them, Senator Harold Hughes (D – Iowa) claimed, "a new internationalism" based "on the demilitarization" of foreign policy and "an increased emphasis on cultural and economic factors" was emerging. It was up to the empowered Congress to "develop a moral foreign policy".[65] Human rights offered the best area to advance new internationalists' claims and proposals because – international lawyer Richard Falk argued – they could become the driving force in the realization of a new global community where the "traditional notions of territorial sovereignty" were undermined.[66] Their proposals encompassed all aspects of American foreign policy, and, although they were often vague, they embodied the widespread belief that it was time to move beyond bipolarism. The new internationalists' proposals were far from Kissinger's realism, secrecy, ruthlessness, his obsession with the Soviet Union and his lack of any humanitarian evaluation. To them, not only had Kissinger abandoned traditional American values, but he was also following a morally repugnant path, as his closeness to authoritarian dictators in Latin America indicated. Human rights came to symbolize the new universal language that provided a means both to transcend the division of the world into two blocs and to move beyond Kissinger's perceived amoral realism.[67]

The first clash between new internationalists and the White House arrived in 1971, when an amendment urging the White House to deny any economic assistance to non-democratic Brazil was introduced. During the Congressional debate, Ted Kennedy (D – Massachusetts) explained that Congress should prevent the White House from using federal funds to aid authoritarian regimes.[68] While the amendment was defeated, Ted Kennedy pointed out the path Congress should follow to give human rights a prominent position in American foreign policy:

> Despite our strong tradition of democracy, the United States continues to support regimes in Latin America that deny basic human rights. We stand silent while political prisoners are tortured in Brazil ... I point this out ... because Brazil is ruled by a government that we fully support with money. ... The Council of Europe has condemned the Greek military dictatorship for political oppression and the torture of political prisoners. The Organization of American States can do no less. ... Much of the $673 million in military aid granted in the past nine years has gone to those governments that displayed their contempt for democratic principles.[69]

A more determined effort arrived when James Abourezk (D – South Dakota) introduced an amendment to Section 32 of the 1973 Foreign Assistance Act that called on the president to deny any economic or military assistance to any country with political prisoners.[70] Much to Abourezk's chagrin, a watered-down, non-binding version of the amendment would finally be approved. Nevertheless, he explained to an Italian supporter of his initiative that he made some "real accomplishments in this effort". First, he had demonstrated, "to foreign governments that Congress is deeply concerned with the abuse" and violations of human rights. Second, "we built a foundation of support ... that will be vital in future sessions" and, finally, "we formed a national coalition of Congressmen, religious leaders, national press and concerned citizens which will convincingly prove to all foreign governments that this issue is not dead".[71]

The Abourezk amendment harbingered a major Congressional action in favour of human rights. By late 1973, Donald Fraser (D – Minnesota) started a series of hearings to investigate the place of human rights in American foreign policy. Noting the "rampant violations of human rights" and the need for a more effective strategy from both the United States and the world community, Fraser held fifteen hearings with officials from the executive branch, international legal scholars and experts and representatives from human rights and humanitarian NGOs. With the exception of executive branch officials, who looked like the accused rather than witnesses, they all agreed on three major points. First, the growing interdependence between the United States and the rest of the world had made the American public more responsive to human rights violations. Second, the United States ought to reinforce cooperation with NGOs and transnational networks. Third, the US government ought to be more active in the promotion of human rights and fundamental freedoms abroad. Fraser's hearings proposed to rediscover the (perceived) traditional values of American foreign policy in order to face the challenges of interdependence and move beyond the Cold War. As Fraser himself admitted:

> Because we have been so preoccupied with the context of ideologies that formed the framework of the Cold War that we have not replaced that way of measuring events, judging nations and looking to international relationships with some new framework. It is my impression that one useful framework would be an increased emphasis on the observance of human rights by various societies around the world, which has the value, in pragmatic terms, of putting to societies, both the left and right, a rather standard set of ideas in terms of how they treat their own people.[72]

Nor was the Nixon administration immune from Fraser's criticism: "our Government ... does not believe that human rights should be a significant factor in determining our bilateral relations with other States. Human rights issues are not raised with other States ... for fear of jeopardising our friendly relations."[73]

After more than 1,000 pages of transcription, the Fraser Committee's conclusions were published in the 1974 report *Human Rights in the World Community: A Call for U.S. Leadership*. Already in the preamble, which reported that "the human rights factor is not accorded the high priority it deserves in our country's foreign policy", and that human rights violations were "not limited to any particular ideological persuasion" because "governments of the right, centre and left have been responsible for violating the fundamental rights of men and women", Fraser listed twenty-nine recommendations to give human rights greater priority. Among these, the report invited the State Department to:

> 1. Treat human rights factors as a regular part of U.S. foreign policy decision-making ...; 2. discourage governments which are committing serious violations of human rights ...; 3. respond to human rights practices of nations in an objective manner without regard to whether the government is considered friendly, neutral, or unfriendly ...; 4. upgrade the consideration given to human rights in determining Soviet–American relations.[74]

The report called on the State Department to create a specific office for human rights or to appoint an officer for human rights in each bureau of the department, and on Congress to play an active role through the extension of the Civil Rights Commission's competencies or, alternatively, through the creation of a new agency devoted to the promotion of human rights abroad. Finally, it suggested certain political initiatives, such as the adoption of the human rights treaties not yet ratified by the United States, or linking military and economic aid to the promotion of human rights.[75]

The report was poorly received by the White House. In June 1974, Kissinger's staff held a meeting to discuss Congressional activism on human rights and Fraser's hearings. It was a problem with a "substantive meaning" that foreshadowed "language in the aid bill prohibiting us from providing any military aid to Chile almost completely because of human rights. If that happens, we can look at it in Korea, it will impact on our maintaining troops in Korea. And you can go down the line to about fifteen places." To make matters worse, the meeting proved the widespread awareness that the administration was not prepared to face the Congressional challenge on human rights, especially because the State Department lacked adequate staff to handle such an issue, as it had only "two guys now, one in L[egal] and one in I[nternational] O[rganizations] designated as the Human Rights guys".[76] To confirm the lack of preparation in Kissinger's staff, the following day Robert Ingersoll had to admit to the House Committee on Foreign Affairs that the State Department had not yet adopted any effective measure to introduce human rights considerations into foreign development and military aid programmes.[77]

By October, Winston Lord, director of the Policy Planning Staff, provided Kissinger with the conclusions of an early study on the origins, meaning and possible consequences of Congressional activism on human rights. To Lord, the human rights surge was favoured by four developments:

> 1. Recent events in four countries ... 2. The debate on the Jackson amendment ... 3. The charge that the US Government is insensitive to human rights issues in its overall conduct of foreign policy surely hinders development of a domestic 'consensus' on some aspects of foreign policy because it has tended to alienate significant elements in Congress, the media, the universities and the natural foreign affairs constituency. American publications are giving increasing attention to repressive measures by regimes with which the United States is identified and are editorializing against our policies toward them 4. In Congress, these developments have led to support for a stronger US official posture on human rights. Dissatisfaction with the Government's present policies on human rights issues abroad has been a factor in the increase of legislative restrictions on aid programs for countries with authoritarian regimes and has provided additional arguments for opposing foreign aid programs generally.[78]

Many feared that Congress could interrupt aid to Chile and South Korea. To prevent such an outcome and, more broadly, "to strengthen a domestic consensus in support of US foreign policy, to promote détente and to improve our ability to deal effectively with troublesome issues that obstruct our national objectives abroad", Lord suggested some "selective changes" through sporadic public remarks and quiet diplomacy actions.[79]

While the State Department was struggling with how to cope with Congressional actions, the *New York Times* reported that Kissinger had reprimanded the American ambassador in Chile for having discussed human rights with the military junta.[80] Although minor, the incident seemed to confirm the idea that Kissinger had no interest in human rights violations occurring abroad, thus providing a new boost to Congressional initiatives. Indeed, Congress introduced a number of proposals to modify the 1974 Foreign Assistance Act. One focused on Chile: while the White House proposed $60 million in aid to the country, Congress authorized only a $25 million package. Another amendment, sponsored by Fraser, modified Section 502 of the Foreign Assistance Act by proposing that:

> The President shall substantially reduce or terminate security assistance to any government which engages in a consistent pattern of gross violations of internationally recognized human rights, including torture or cruel, inhuman or degrading treatment or punishment; prolonged detention without charges; or other flagrant denials of the rights to life, liberty and the security of the person.[81]

While it did not contain any binding language, Fraser's amendment introduced three other human rights provisions: it invited the US government to assure a peaceful transition in favour of national self-determination in former Portuguese colonies in Africa; it proposed appointing a State Department Coordinator for human rights and humanitarian affairs; and it urged the State Department to present an annual report on the state of human rights in countries receiving American foreign aid.[82]

Much to Fraser's chagrin, the first report prepared by the State Department, which was presented on 14 November 1975, was "a bland, unsigned summary report", which listed several human rights violations occurring "within both those countries receiving U.S. security assistance and those that do not" and suggested that "quiet but forceful diplomacy" was the best way to improve human rights abroad.[83] The report triggered a number of negative reactions. Fraser criticized it as a "defense of the State Department's apparent intention not to comply with the law", while Alan Cranston (D – California) said the report "amount[ed] to a cover-up of information that American taxpayers and legislators are entitled to".[84] Above all, the dismissive attitude Kissinger's State Department had shown with its first report offered a new opportunity for firmer action on human rights. Foreshadowing this, in September 1975, Democrat Tom Harkin (Iowa) introduced a binding amendment to the International Development and Food Assistance Act. It prohibited any form of economic assistance to:

> Any country which engages in a consistent pattern of gross violations of internationally recognized human rights, including torture or cruel, inhuman, or degrading treatment or punishment, prolonged detention without charges, or other flagrant denial of the right to life, liberty, and the security of person unless such assistance will directly benefit the needy people in such country.[85]

A second proposal was the Humphrey–Cranston amendment. It made previous provisions binding, especially those relating to Section 502B of the Foreign Assistance

Act, which called on the president of the United States to cut any economic assistance programme wherever he found "a consistent pattern of gross violations of internationally recognized human rights".[86]

Cold Warriors' appropriation of Soviet dissent: the Jackson–Vanik amendment and the campaign against the CSCE

The Soviet Union was not immune from human rights criticism. Growing contacts between East and West favoured awareness among activists on both sides of the Iron Curtain. To many dissidents within the Soviet bloc, the new language of human rights offered a renewal of the revolutionary past and a fulfilment of communist promises of social rights.[87] To others, there was no possible mediation between human rights and the Soviet system: Soviet political control was in opposition to human rights.

Relations between Soviet communism and human rights were ambiguous and ran deep into the origins of the Soviet Union. Similarly, political dissent was also far from being a new phenomenon. Its origins were multiple, and its genealogy depended on various sources and experiences, as did the forms it assumed over the years. It encompassed writers' search for truth and justice, human rights and democratic groups, seekers of greater religious freedom, free emigration advocates and left-wing critics of the Soviet system, who argued that Soviet leaders had betrayed the revolution. One source dated back to Khrushchev's years, when the thaw fuelled expectations of more intellectual freedom. Khrushchev's almost immediate reversal turned expectations into protests.[88] The fate of authors Yuli Daniel and Andrei Sinyavsky, who were arrested for anti-Soviet propaganda in 1965, elicited Soviet citizens' protests and early Western attention towards the plight of dissidents. To curtail them, Soviet authorities began arresting other dissidents. Yuri Galanskov, Aleksandr Ginzburg, Alexey Dobrovolsky and Vera Lahkova were among those arrested for their personal involvement both in demonstrations and in *samizdat* publication of materials related to Daniel and Sinyavsky. The "trial of the four", as the Western press named it, led to the dissidents being sentenced to labour camps and thrust Soviet repression into public awareness in the West.[89]

Another major source of what came to be known as Soviet dissent was the plight of Soviet Jews. After fifty years of Soviet assimilationism, most Soviet Jews did not represent a problem for Soviet authorities. They were the "Jews of silence", as Nobel laureate Elie Wiesel wrote, who had no interest in affirming their identity in the public sphere, although they were aware of their origins.[90] During the 1960s, however, agitation for Jewish rights spread among Soviet Jews. This was largely an outcome of certain international events. First, the Israeli government contributed to highlight the plight of Jewish refuseniks, as Soviet Jews who were denied the right of emigration began to be known. It established Nativ in 1952, an organization whose aim was supporting *aliyah* (immigration) to Israel. In 1955 Nativ launched operation Bar, aimed at Soviet Jews. Nativ was designed to function covertly, making contacts, fostering Jewish education and aiding immigration to Israel, as well as orchestrating international campaigns in support of Soviet Jews. In its campaign, it went as far as establishing contact with leading Americans, such as Supreme Court Judges William Douglas and Arthur J. Goldberg, and Senators Abraham Ribicoff (D – Connecticut), Jacob Javits (R – New York) and Henry M. Jackson (D – Washington).[91] Second, the Eisenhower and, later, the Johnson administrations touched upon the repression of Soviet Jews in international fora. Nevertheless, Soviet authorities' firm rejection of American pressures prevented any decisive action.[92] Most notably, the Six-Day War in 1967 provided Soviet Jews with new momentum for the affirmation of their identity. As Alexander Sirotin has suggested, it "really helped to revive hope after the long-time of fear and terror".[93] Pride in Israel's victory pushed thousands of Jews to openly challenge Soviet power: those Elie Wiesel referred to as the "Jews of Silence" were now speaking against their repression and demanding the right to emigrate to Israel.[94]

As the Six-Day War was a catalyst for the affirmation of Jewish identity within the USSR, it also stirred up Soviet authorities' anti-Jewish and anti-Zionist policies. Anti-Zionist articles were published in the most important newspapers. The first edition of *Ostorozhono: Sionizm* (Caution: Zionism) made is appearance in 1969 and the following year a new edition was distributed. Soviet authorities even distributed abroad an English version to denounce globally "the ideology, a ramified system of organisations and the practical politics of the wealthy Jewish bourgeoisie which has closely allied itself with monopoly circles in the USA and other imperialist countries".[95] Soviet anti-Zionism was rooted in the traditional animosity towards Jews deep in the Russian people, but the Soviets embarked on the anti-Zionist campaign only after 1967.[96] Scholar William Korey claims that the campaign had also the "pragmatic, political purpose" of finding a scapegoat for Soviet Arab allies' military defeat. Moreover, it was also an element of Soviet policy towards the Middle East and Arab countries. Building on a denunciation of Zionist imperialism, the Soviet Union could strengthen its political ties with them.[97]

The plight of Soviet Jews elicited global attention and mobilization. American citizens were particularly receptive. On a general level, it was part of a much longer history of American concerns for religious freedom, as well as an irresistible propaganda vehicle during the Cold War, one that allowed the comparison of the Soviet Union with Nazi Germany. There was also genuine solidarity between Soviet Jews and American Jews, who elicited attention to the plight of their coreligionists in the Soviet Union. Moreover, during the 1960s a revival of Judaism and Jewish cultural identity, which until that moment had undergone erasure due to high rates of secularization, took place in the United States. Culturally and politically, the traditional positions of Jewish organizations in Western countries were defined by two images: "Diaspora" and "Holocaust". Fighting for Soviet Jews' right to emigrate meant avoiding a new Holocaust and, at the same time, ensuring a reunification of the Diaspora communities. The Israeli Nativ played also a significant role. Beyond contacts with some selected politicians, it also contributed to the establishment of the American Conference on Soviet Jewry, which summoned the first World Conference on Soviet Jews in 1965.[98]

Mobilization, however, was not limited to Soviet Jews. By the late 1960s, other developments contributed to the rise of international attention to human rights abuses in the Soviet bloc.

In Czechoslovakia, the development of "socialism with a human face" – as the attempt to develop a programme of hitherto unexperienced economic and political liberalization was known – and the Soviet-led military suppression of it showed the world the contradiction between the socialist system and freedom. Although the Prague Spring, as Western media called socialism with a human face, was not framed in the language of human rights, it helped cement the idea that the Soviet Union could not accept freedoms and rights. In January 1969, Czechoslovak student Jan Palach set fire to himself in Prague to protest censorship and the suppression of free speech. Palach's self-sacrifice was a tragic inspiration to other self-immolations among Czechoslovakians that outraged the world, galvanized Czechoslovakian dissidents and favoured the rise of rights-based discussions to oppose Soviet brutality.[99]

Within the Soviet Union, scientist Andrei Sakharov published *Peace, Coexistence and Intellectual Freedom* in 1968. Calling for a new foundation for socialism in order to incorporate human rights and to develop a truly peaceful coexistence, Sakharov's pamphlet set off an alarm for Soviet authorities.[100] One reason for concern was Sakharov's prestige. As KGB chief Yuri Andropov explained to the Politburo, the pamphlet's author was "a full member of the Academy of Sciences of the USSR … three times hero of Socialist Labor; recipient of State and Lenin Prizes; deputy director of research at All-Union Research Institute of Experimental Physics".[101] Another was its impact. The *New York Times* published in July 1968 Sakharov's appeal for total intellectual freedom and bipolar cooperation in order to overcome the dangers of nuclear war, famine, cults of personality and bureaucracy.[102] Two months later, Senator Dodd (D – Connecticut) asked the staff of the Library of Congress to update a 1966 report on *Intellectual Ferment in the Soviet Union*. Significantly, the new report's title was *Intellectual Ferment and Political Dissent in the Soviet Union* because, as the introduction explained, the phenomenon "had already achieved epidemic proportions" and represented a major challenge to the Soviet system.[103]

The very same year, the *samizdat Chronicle of Current Events* made its first appearance. It reported documented violations of human rights by the Soviet government and it soon became the main voice of human rights activists across the Soviet Union. In 1970, Andrei Sakharov, Valery Chalidze and Andrei Tverdokhlebov founded the Committee on Human Rights in the Soviet Union. Its detailed information and its founders' prestige earned the group international attention. For his activities in this committee, Valery Chalidze was stripped of his citizenship while he was lecturing in the United States. Once there, he founded an English-language version of the *Chronicle of Current Events* and further spread information on Soviet dissidents among Western observers. Andrei Sakharov remained in the USSR under the authorities' close scrutiny. By 1973, the KGB noted that Sakharov "persistently appeals to the West not to embark on the course of rapprochement with the USSR without extracting from Soviet leadership concessions of an ideological and political nature". Yet, the KGB recognized that preventing Sakharov from casting the Soviet Union in a negative light would have been detrimental to Soviet interests and prestige: punitive measures would "lead to vigorous anti-Soviet outcries in the West, and may be met with less than full understanding by some fraternal parties".[104]

Within the United States, the plight of political dissidents and of Soviet Jews prompted deeply emotional reactions and human rights organization were determined not to remain silent. Their campaigns were framed in the language of universal human rights and they often recalled international declarations and covenants. To many activists, the plight of Soviet Jews was no different from that of victims of human rights abuses elsewhere. Yet, others appropriated the issue of human rights in the Soviet Union to fight against Kissinger's détente. Among the former, the most influential and important figure was Senator Henry "Scoop" Jackson (D – Washington).

Jackson was an outspoken opponent of détente. Far from Kissinger's détente and new internationalists' vision of cooperation in an interdependent world, his views were a quintessential expression of Cold War liberalism. To him, a new emphasis on containment and on its ideological and material underpinnings was the solution to reaffirm American primacy. Refusing any logic based on the acceptance of interdependence, he believed that American security and peace could be achieved by reaffirming a position of preponderance of power, rather than by accepting strategic parity, and by a firm commitment to spreading democratic values in the world. For this reason, he proposed maintaining a strong presence of American conventional forces in Europe, fully developing the antiballistic missile system (ABM) and, above all, ensuring the superiority of the American nuclear arsenal. The 1972 SALT agreement became the first target of his anti-détente campaign. Jackson constantly claimed that the treaty would favour Soviet rearmament and, consequently, American vulnerability. He succeeded in introducing an amendment to the ratification law of the SALT agreement to ensure parity in the number of nuclear weapons in all future SALT negotiations.[105]

Jackson's security concerns were matched by an ideological rejection of détente as a whole, which he labelled a new and immoral form of appeasement with Soviet totalitarianism. According to Jackson, the lack of morality in détente was particularly clear in the repression of political dissent. Not only was it a demonstration of the totalitarian nature of Soviet power, but, he argued, Western countries were also legitimizing the repression of political dissent through détente.[106]

Jackson succeeded in connecting growing dissent in the Soviet Union, a genuine interest in the promotion of human rights abroad and his fight against détente. By mid-1971, Jackson's staff started to collect information on Soviet violations of human rights and refuseniks, becoming a sort of hub among dissidents, NGOs and a growing (although still minority) group of anti-détente politicians. Jackson's emphasis on human rights was not only a consequence of his anti-détente stance. According to some biographers and scholars, his personal experiences and his education contributed to his sensitivity to human rights issues. His mother was active in defending Jews in their Washington community, while the initial difficulties his father experienced after he emigrated from Norway came to represent a perpetual reminder.[107] Sarah Snyder argued that a tour of the Soviet Union in the mid-1950s cemented his ideas about the oppressive and totalitarian nature of Soviet power.[108] In a similar vein, his former aide Charles Horner suggested that Jackson's commitment to human rights in the Soviet Union resulted from his reading of Robert Conquest's description of Stalinism in *The Great Terror*.[109] Moreover, Jackson's approach to human rights was also tied to his political career. He heartily endorsed civil rights, social welfare, Roosevelt's domestic policies and his failed "Second Bill of Rights", as well as the adoption of the 1948 Universal Declaration of Human Rights.[110]

Jewish emigration from the Soviet Union became Jackson's best chance to raise the issue of human rights and morality in East–West détente. In July 1971, with his colleague William Brock (R – Tennessee), Jackson tabled a resolution that urged the president to demand the Soviets cease discrimination and assure the right to free emigration. In February 1972, he introduced a proposal for the creation of a biannual $250 million programme to support Soviet Jews' resettlement in Israel.[111]

More importantly, he introduced an amendment to the 1972 trade agreement between the United States and the Soviet Union. It urged making the granting of most favoured nation status (MFN) to all non-market economies contingent on those countries allowing their citizens to emigrate freely. The opportunity for such an initiative was offered by the Soviets themselves when, in August 1972, they introduced an emigration tax based on level of education. The tax fell particularly hard on Soviet Jews, who generally had higher levels of education. It varied between 5,000 and 30,000 roubles – up to seven years' salary for a highly qualified engineer – and, consequently, it virtually closed off any possible path to emigration. Soviet officials justified the introduction of the tax as a self-protection tool for the Soviet Union and as a reimbursement for decades of free education provided to those men who were taking Soviet "scientific knowledge" to capitalist countries.[112] The decision was also an opening to Arab countries. As the Middle Eastern conflict intensified, many Arab countries were increasingly questioning Moscow's emigration policy, which they claimed favoured new Jewish settlements in the area.[113]

The Soviet tax led to several protests within the United States and in Western Europe. Six thousand academics signed an appeal against it, while the National Conference on Soviet Jewry (NCSJ), an umbrella organization established in 1971, condemned Soviet action and organized a day of national solidarity with Soviet Jews, with public rallies and demonstrations in all major American cities. In New York, the solidarity day brought together approximately 100,000 people who urged Nixon to "speak out" in defence of Soviet Jews.[114]

Jackson benefited from this protest and linked it to his political campaign against bipolar détente. On 4 October 1972, he introduced an amendment to the US–Soviet Trade Bill, linking the concession of the MFN to free emigration.[115] In February 1973, Wilbur Mills (D – Arkansas) and Charles Vanik (D – Ohio) introduced the same amendment on the House floor. In a press release, they declared they had a vast majority in both Houses (289 and 78 cosponsors). Over the following months, Jackson's stance became stronger, and the Soviets first reduced the tax and later abolished it.[116] Jackson's campaign gained further momentum in September 1973, when Sakharov wrote an appeal to the American Congress to express his support for the Jackson–Vanik amendment:

> [T]he world is … entering on a new course of detente and it is therefore essential that the proper direction be followed [from] the outset. This is a fundamental issue, extending far beyond the question of emigration. Those who believe that the Jackson Amendment is likely to undermine anyone's personal or governmental prestige are wrong. Its provisions are minimal and not demeaning. … The abandonment of a policy of principle would be a betrayal of the thousands of Jews and non-Jews who want to emigrate, of the hundreds in camps and mental hospitals, of the victims of the Berlin Wall.[117]

Within days, eighty-four Jews from Moscow and Vilnius sent a similar plea to Congress, urging the legislature to continue the struggle for the promotion of human rights in the USSR.[118]

The more Jackson's campaign strengthened, the fiercer opposition to his initiative became. The Soviets protested at unacceptable American interference in their domestic affairs. To Moscow, international discussions of its human rights record was an ideological assault inconsistent with bipolar détente. Within the United States, Kissinger repeated that only quiet diplomacy could alleviate the plight of Soviet Jews. Privately, however, Kissinger lamented with President Nixon that "the emigration of Jews from the Soviet Union is not an objective of American foreign policy. And if they put Jews into gas chambers in the Soviet Union, it is not an American concern. Maybe a humanitarian concern."[119] Even the American business community took a firm position against the Jackson–Vanik amendment. As part of the economic détente between East and West, General Electric, PepsiCo and Occidental Petroleum had signed important contracts with the Soviets and regarded the Jackson–Vanik amendment as a potential threat to reaching the Soviet market. In July 1974, they established the American Committee on US–Soviet Relations, whose aim was to strengthen economic ties between East and West and to prevent Congress from adopting the Jackson–Vanik legislation.

Despite these efforts, the House approved the Trade Bill with the Jackson–Vanik amendment by an overwhelming majority. It was a clear demonstration, Jackson triumphantly claimed, that the American people urged a "détente with a human face".[120] A triangular negotiation among Kissinger, Jackson and the Kremlin was now unavoidable. In October, they reached an agreement on the emigration of 60,000 Soviet Jews in return for a waiver of the amendment, to be negotiated each year.[121] By the end of the year, TASS announced that the Soviet Union would renounce the trade agreement. American interference in Soviet domestic affairs had pushed Moscow to renounce the economic and trade benefits that the White House had conceived as a major tool to strengthen détente.[122] To Jackson, this was a major victory: his amendment succeeded both in concretely weakening détente and in proving that Kissinger's bipolar dialogue was conceived in opposition to the promotion of human rights.

The debate on Soviet dissidents and détente did not end with Soviet renunciation of the trade agreement. Benefiting from the growing contact between Western and Eastern societies promoted by détente, the plight of Soviet dissidents remained under the international spotlight. Despite Soviet crackdowns, dissidents intensified their actions. New groups were formed, such as the Soviet section of Amnesty International, created by Yuri Orlov in 1974 over the opposition of the International Secretariat.[123]

Around the same time, Soviet authorities ordered the expulsion of Aleksandr Solzhenitsyn for the publication of *The Gulag Archipelago*. First published in France, the book was immediately translated into many languages and became an international bestseller that – a reviewer commented – was a detailed account "of the other great Holocaust of our century – the imprisonment, brutalization and very often murder of tens of millions of innocent Soviet citizens by their own Government, mostly during Stalin's rule from 1929 to 1953".[124] Solzhenitsyn's expulsion – the *Washington Post* commented – was the demonstration that "the Soviet system was still the same".[125] The White House was soon concerned with Solzhenitsyn and the need to contain the echo of his expulsion. Secretary of State Kissinger, for example, urged Voice of America to minimize the impact of Solzhenitsyn and not to air an exclusive interview the international radio broadcaster had recorded just weeks before.[126]

Solzhenitsyn became one of the strongest symbols of Cold Warriors' human rights crusade. Jackson pounced on the White House's reluctance to condemn the expulsion. "[I]t [was] clear that the administration has narrowed its conception of détente to exclude issues of human rights", Jackson commented to the *Seattle Post*.[127] On another occasion he added:

> At a time when men and women throughout the free world – ordinary citizens, government officials, and even heads of State – have voiced their revulsion at the mistreatment and brutal expulsion of this great and brave man, I cannot allow the silence of the President to be understood as representing the sentiments of the American people; it does not. ... It is false and misleading to suggest that the pursuit of peace requires official indifference to the fate of those brave men and women who are struggling to resist tyranny.[128]

Many intellectuals as well as politicians joined Jackson's campaign, such as socialist Michael Harrington, liberal James McGregor Burns, neoconservative Irving Kristol and George Meany, president of the American Federation of Labor and Congress of Industrial Organizations (AFL-CIO). Jesse Helms and other Republicans asked the president to grant honorary American citizenship to Solzhenitsyn.[129] When the dissident finally arrived in the United States, a major political crisis erupted for the new president, Gerald Ford.

Gerald Ford had replaced Nixon, who resigned over the Watergate scandal in August 1974. With a reputation for honesty and an in-depth knowledge of legislative and political dynamics – he had led the Republican minority in the House from 1965 to 1973 – Ford promised what the presidency needed in 1974: probity and good skills to overcome the tensions between the executive and the legislative branches. Yet, he had no foreign policy experience and lacked Nixon's instinct for foreign affairs. For this reason, he relied heavily on Kissinger's input. Following Kissinger's advice, Ford announced he would not attend an AFL-CIO-sponsored dinner in Solzhenitsyn's honour. Within days, he also refused to meet the dissident when he visited the White House on 4 July. A political crisis erupted when a White House spokesperson explained, first, that the president had a "heavy schedule of commitments" and, later, that he "did not like meetings that are symbolic and empty of substance".[130] Jackson and many others lashed out at the president, who was then forced to invite Solzhenitsyn to the White House. Solzhenitsyn refused because, as he explained, "nobody needs symbolic meetings".[131] All major newspapers criticized Ford. *Washington Post* columnist George F. Will commented: "Obviously Mr. Ford decided that meeting with Solzhenitsyn would be inconsistent with détente. Obviously, Solzhenitsyn is correct: Détente as practiced by the United States prevents even gestures of support for the cause of human rights in the Soviet Union."[132] In the same newspaper, cartoonist Herb Block portrayed Kissinger and Ford hiding in a hole as Solzhenitsyn went by. In another cartoon, President Ford was hiding under the desk in the Oval Office while Solzhenitsyn waited outside the White House, and Kissinger was whispering: "It's all right to come out now. If you had met him, Brezhnev might have disapproved."[133] Jackson accused the president of "cowering in fear of the Soviet reaction".[134] Former Governor of California Ronald Reagan wrote that "some of President Ford's … advisers are so nervous about bruising the sensibilities of the Soviets that they have persuaded him not to meet the man who is considered by many to be the world's … most profound spokesman for human freedom and morality".[135]

The "Solzhenitsyn affair", as the incident came to be known, set the stage for another major controversy when, within days, President Ford announced his participation in the closing session of the CSCE to sign its Final Act. Conceived by the Soviets as early as 1954 to legitimate their domination over Eastern Europe, the proposal to summon a European conference for continental security was rejected by Western countries until the late 1960s. Negotiations opened in Helsinki only in 1972, involving thirty-five countries. It was soon clear that participants had different priorities. To the Soviets, the conference should have brought the formal recognition of post-war boundaries, which implied Western recognition of their domination over half of Europe.[136] To Kissinger, the CSCE was a marginal process. His interest was so limited that he confessed to his staff: "They can write it in Swahili for all I care."[137] Despite this dismissive attitude, the United States participated in negotiations because, as Kissinger later explained, "We didn't want to break with our allies or confront the Soviets on it."[138] Not only were CSCE negotiations consistent with Kissinger's linkage strategy to obtain Soviet cooperation in other areas, but they could also have helped the United States reaffirm its leadership in transatlantic relations at a moment in which tensions on both sides of the Atlantic were multiplying. After all, Kissinger explained, American allies considered the "European security negotiations as their equivalent to SALT – as the vehicle by which Western European governments can engage visibly in negotiations with the East on issues relating to their security".[139]

Indeed, CSCE talks were particularly relevant for EC member states that took centre stage in negotiations and succeeded in setting the agenda of the meeting. One of their basic aims would soon be identified in overcoming the division of Europe. In this sense, contrary to Kissinger's definition of détente as a conservative policy, Western European countries considered détente as a dynamic process whose aims were to promote and reinforce economic, cultural and human contacts and exchanges between the two Europes, to make frontiers more permeable and, eventually, to overcome the Cold War in Europe. As French President Georges Pompidou explained to German Chancellor Willy Brandt: "we could dissolve the blocs, a little bit … and bring together all nations, east and west".[140]

The CSCE Final Act reflected these differences. Structured around four different parts (officially renamed baskets) and introduced by a ten-point preamble, the document listed the fundamental principles governing security and cooperation in Europe. As such, it was not immune from contradictions. Principle VI of the Preamble affirmed that all participating states would refrain from any intervention in the internal affairs of any other participating state; Principle VII introduced respect for human rights and fundamental freedom, as well as "the right of the individual to know and act upon his rights and duties". Differences emerged also among the baskets. The first affirmed a general commitment to non-intervention in internal affairs, the respect of sovereignty and national boundaries, and renunciation of the use of force among the convening parties. The second basket introduced some measures to foster economic, scientific and technological cooperation, while the third introduced measures for cultural contact, the dissemination of information, contact between peoples and solutions for humanitarian problems. A final section called upon the participating states to hold a follow-up conference to review progress and shortcomings in the implementation of the Final Act.[141]

Soviet resistance to Principle VII and other references to human rights were easily overcome. First, the CSCE envisaged increased economic contact and exchanges. Second, the political outcome of the conference was the culmination of one of Moscow's longstanding political aims: the recognition of its superpower status. Above all, as Gromyko commented, the treaty left the Soviets "masters in [their] own house", thanks to its provisions about non-interference and the respect of national sovereignty. "If you clear away the rubbish", he maintained on another occasion, "[the CSCE] boils down to three items: borders; respect for sovereignty and non-interference; military détente."[142]

A similar perception soon developed within the United States. To critics of Kissinger's détente, the Final Act became a new target of their campaign because, as the *New York Times* noted, "Nothing signed at Helsinki will in any way save courageous free thinkers in the Soviet empire from the prospect of incarceration."[143] Pointing to the contradiction between Moscow's commitments at Helsinki and the Soviet authorities' refusal to allow Sakharov to fly to Oslo to be awarded the Nobel Prize, Jackson recalled that "there are times in international diplomacy when the president of the United States ought to stay home". Helsinki was one of those occasions because the Helsinki Final Act was "yet another example of the sort of one-sided agreement that has become the hallmark of the Nixon-Ford administration".[144] Foreshadowing his upcoming candidacy against Ford for the Republican nomination, Ronald Reagan said that Ford's trip to Helsinki had placed "our stamp of approval on Russia's enslavement of the captive nations" and forthrightly declared "I am against it and I think all Americans should be against it."[145] Major newspapers ran negative op-eds against this "new Munich" and, even worse, this "super Yalta". *Newsweek* writer Alfred Friendly, for example, wrote that "in practice Basket III proves relatively empty".[146] Public attitudes focused on the "betrayal of Soviet dissenters" and on the "inviolability of the borders" theme.[147] Some ethnic lobbies denounced the Helsinki Agreements as a "miserable and un-American treaty" that legitimized Soviet domination over half of Europe.[148] Solzhenitsyn blamed Ford for sacrificing Eastern Europe on the altar of East–West détente.[149] From Helsinki, Ford did his best to uphold the correctness of his choice to sign the agreements and to confirm his commitment to their respect and promotion: "It is important", he declared during the signing ceremony, "that you recognize the deep devotion of the American people and their government to human rights and fundamental freedom."[150]

Conclusion

Historian Thomas Borstelmann has recently reminded us that the United States in the 1970s "is not separate from the larger narrative" of global history.[151] The rise of human rights in American policy during that decade is no exception. It was part of a broader trend in which widespread activism and transformations of the international system questioned the political landscape of a world still dominated by Cold War divisions. Citizens began to form networks across national boundaries to promote new ideas and programmes. In Washington and New York, as well as in Rome, Paris, Buenos Aires and Moscow, human rights advocates began to call for their governments to respect and promote human rights. "In these actions, human rights became", historian Samuel Moyn wrote, "a sort of international *lingua franca* for diverse voices."[152]

Although part of a global surge, the American attention to human rights had some very specific characteristics. The "shock of the global" of the 1970s intersected with, and gained momentum from, the "American shocks" of the 1970s. The political reaffirmation of human rights concerns was a reply to the crisis of American internationalism, to the Vietnam War, to the Watergate scandal, to the Church Committee's revelations about CIA assassination plots, to the American role in the Chilean coup and to America's support of many authoritarian regimes. Abroad, these choices triggered a wave of protests against the United States' role in the world. Intellectuals, journalists and many politicians in Western Europe and Latin America denounced the United States' turn against international freedom and basic human rights. Rediscovering human rights and aligning the United States with the international and transnational movement for the promotion of human rights would have contributed to a reformulation of the American image abroad. At home, a human rights-based foreign policy would provide the expiation that, according to Barbara Keys, American society was searching for after the sense of guilt, shame and embarrassment left by the Vietnam War.[153] But human rights would also provide principles to displace the now-discredited Cold War liberalism: the emergence of human rights was a reply to the crisis of American internationalism.

Widespread American attention towards human rights was above all an unintended consequence of Nixon, Ford and Kissinger's foreign policy and of their inability to create a domestic consensus on détente. Grassroots organizations, human rights lobbyists in Washington and sympathetic members of Congress consciously embodied a countermovement that was highly critical of Kissinger's realist foreign policy, where no room was left for the promotion of human rights. Congress succeeded in introducing human rights legislation into American foreign policy. As the Friends Committee on National Legislation wrote in 1976 in its newsletter:

> Human rights has changed from a rather tedious subject of low visibility to one of the most relevant issues on Capitol Hill. Over strenuous administration objections, Congress has written human rights provisions into foreign military and economic aid bills. It has cut off military aid to Chile and Uruguay. Congressional hearings have been held on human rights violations in some eighteen countries. And the State Department, prodded by Congress, has created a Coordinator for human rights and humanitarian affairs.[154]

However, the human rights interest turned out to be ambiguous, contradictory, "two-headed" and dependent upon two ideological definitions of the American role in the world. On the one hand, the advancement of human rights permitted new internationalists such as Donald Fraser to define a new foreign policy to face future challenges, transcend the Cold War and respond to the growing interdependence between states. It was a vague position, which criticized Kissinger's realist assumptions and style, his secrecy, his unscrupulousness and his amorality, but that accepted bipolar détente because, from this perspective, it reduced bipolar rivalry, facilitating the demilitarization of American foreign policy and, eventually, the definition of a policy to lead growing global interdependence. Conversely, Jackson and those who were starting to call themselves "neoconservatives" firmly opposed both Kissinger's realism and the globalist agenda embraced by new internationalists. They rejected the idea that interdependence could reduce and limit American moral, political and military capabilities and resources. To them, by wielding the human rights ideological weapon it was possible to fight both Soviet totalitarianism and Kissinger's détente, which they claimed was a new form of appeasement.

These two approaches reinforced each other. Kissinger himself admitted that "conservatives who hated communists and liberals who hated Nixon came together in a rare convergence, like an eclipse of the sun".[155] He made this even clearer in his *Diplomacy*, where he described how:

> In the absence of a morally persuasive presidency, many of those reared on the traditional approach to American foreign policy joined forces in opposing Nixon's new approach. Liberals did so because they considered the new emphasis on national interest amoral, conservatives because they were more committed to the ideological competition with Moscow than to the geopolitical one.[156]

Convergence between liberals and conservatives had two immediate outcomes. First, it contributed to the definition of human rights as a central tenet of American foreign policy. Favouring a consensual foundation for a human rights-based foreign policy would be a major challenge for the next administration. Second, it contributed to the delegitimization of Kissinger's approach to détente. Indeed, after the mid-1970s, détente was a weakened process. However, its weaknesses did not lead to its end. On the contrary, it initiated an attempt to redefine it in order to take into consideration proposals concerning the protection of human rights.

Notes

1 S. Moyn, *The Last Utopia: Human Rights in History* (Cambridge, MA: Harvard University Press, 2010).

2 For a recent review of the links and contradictions between decolonization and the rise of human rights during the 1970s see J. Eckel, "Human Rights and Decolonization: New Perspectives and Open Questions", *Humanity: An International Journal of Human Rights, Humanitarianism, and Development* 1:1 (2010), pp. 111–135.

3 K. Chernenko, *Human Rights in Soviet Society* (New York: International Publishers, 1981) [originally published as *SSSR – KPSS, stsialisticheskoe obshchestvo, prava cheloveka* (Moscow: Novosti Press)]. A similar point was made by the East German government in its publication *Freedom, Democracy, and Human Rights. For Whom and for What? The GDR Presents Its View* (Berlin: Panorama DDR, 1976).

4 K. Vasak, "Human Rights: A Thirty-Year Struggle: the Sustained Efforts to give Force of law to the Universal Declaration of Human Rights", *UNESCO Courier* 30:11 (1977), pp. 38–35.

5 S.B. Snyder, *From Selma to Moscow: How American Activists Transformed U.S. Foreign Policy* (New York: Columbia University Press, 2018), pp. 3–15; T.F. Jackson, *From Civil Rights to Human Rights: Martin Luther King, Jr., and the Struggle for Economic Justice* (Philadelphia: University of Pennsylvania Press, 2007), pp. 223–227.

6 Moyn, *The Last Utopia*, p. 159; B. Keys, *Reclaiming American Virtue: The Human Rights Revolution of the 1970s* (Cambridge, MA: Harvard University Press, 2014); J. Renouard, *Human Rights in American Foreign Policy: From the 1960s to the Soviet Collapse* (Philadelphia: University of Pennsylvania Press, 2016), p. 11.

7 J. Suri, *Power and Protest: Global Revolution and the Rise of Détente* (Cambridge, MA and London: Harvard University Press, 2003), p. 131.

8 Keys, *Reclaiming American Virtue*, p. 9.

9 M. Del Pero, *The Eccentric Realist: Henry Kissinger and the Shaping of American Foreign Policy* (Ithaca, NY: Cornell University Press, 2010); R.A. Melanson, *American Foreign Policy since the Vietnam War: The Search for Consensus from Nixon to Clinton* (Armonk, NY and London: M.E. Sharpe, 2000); T.B. McCrisken, *American Exceptionalism and the Legacy of the Vietnam War: US Foreign Policy since 1974* (Basingstoke and New York: Palgrave Macmillan, 2003).

10 R.D. Johnson, *Congress and the Cold War* (New York and Cambridge: Cambridge University Press, 2006).

11 "FDR's Four Freedom Speech", in M. Beschloss (ed.), *Our Documents: 100 Milestone Documents from the National Archives* (New York: Oxford University Press, 2003), p. 170.

12 R. Normand and S. Zaidi, *Human Rights at the UN: The Political History of Universal Justice* (Bloomington: Indiana University Press, 2008), pp. 88–89; E. Borgwardt, *A New Deal for the World: America's Vision for Human Rights* (Cambridge, MA: Harvard University Press, 2005).

13 Beschloss, *Our Documents*, p. 171.

14 M.P. Bradley, *The World Reimagined: Americans and Human Rights in the Twentieth Century* (New York: Cambridge University Press, 2016), pp. 13–69.

15 R. Traer, *Faith in Human Rights: Support in Religious Tradition for a Global Struggle* (Washington, DC: Georgetown University Press, 1991), pp. 173–174; K. Sikkink, *Mixed Signals: U.S. Human Rights Policy and Latin America* (Ithaca, NY and London: Cornell University Press, 2004), pp. 30–34.

16 Normand and Zaidi, *Human Rights at the UN*, p. 132; M.R. Ishay; *The History of Human Rights: From Ancient Times to the Globalization Era* (Berkeley and Los Angeles: University of California Press, 2008), pp. 211–225.

17 Department of State Instruction to the United States Delegation to the Fifth Regular Session of the General Assembly, 5 September 1950, in US Department of State, *Foreign Relations of the United States, 1950*, vol. 2: *The United Nations; The Western Hemisphere* (Washington, DC: US Government Printing Office, 1950): https://history.state.gov/historicaldocuments/frus1950v02/d300 (accessed October 2011). See also C.N.J. Roberts, *The Contentious History of the International Bill of Human Rights* (Cambridge and New York: Cambridge University Press, 2015), pp. 190–223.

18 "The Balance between Civil and Political Rights and Economic and Social Rights: Origins of the Human Rights Declaration and Covenants and Subsequent Developments", NA, FCO 28/3652; J.F. Matlock, Jr, "US Policy on Human Rights in Relations with the USSR", in D. Liang-Fenton (ed.), *Implementing US Human Rights Policy* (Washington, DC: United States Institute for Peace, 2004), pp. 245–263.

19 J. Suri, *American Foreign Relations since 1898: A Documentary Reader* (Hoboken, NJ: Wiley-Blackwell, 2010), pp. 90–92.

20 M.P. Leffler, *For the Soul of Mankind: The United States, the Soviet Union and the Cold War* (New York: Hill and Wang, 2008), pp. 62–64; C. Craig and F. Logevall, *America's Cold War: The Politics of Insecurity* (Cambridge, MA: Harvard University Press, 2010), pp. 66–90; F. Romero, *Storia della Guerra fredda. L'ultimo conflitto per l'Europa* (Turin: Einaudi, 2009), pp. 18–72.

21 H.S. Truman, "Address at the Jefferson Day Dinner", 5 April 1947, in J. Woolley and G. Peters, "The American Presidency Project": www.presidency.ucsb.edu/ws/index.php?pid=12859 (accessed June 2010).

22 G. Kennan, "Report on Latin America", in US Department of State, *Foreign Relations of the US 1950*, vol. 2, p. 607; R.R. Trask, "George F. Kennan's Report on Latin America (1950)", *Diplomatic History* 2:3 (1978), pp. 307–312.

23 Craig and Logevall, *America's Cold War*, pp. 122–127.

24 M. Mazower, "The Strange Triumph of Human Rights, 1933–1950", *Historical Journal* 47:2 (2004), pp. 379–398; L. Henkin, "U.S. Ratification of Human Rights Conventions: The Ghost of Senator Bricker?", *American Journal of International Law* 89:2 (April 1995), pp. 341–350; P. Grant, "The Bricker Amendment Controversy", *Presidential Studies Quarterly* 15:3 (1985), pp. 572–582; P. Weiss Fagen, "The United States and International Human Rights, 1946–1977, *Universal Human Rights* 2:3 (1980), pp. 19–33.

25 A. Kirkup and T. Evans, "The Myth of Western Opposition to Economic, Social and Cultural Rights? A Reply to Whelan and Donnelly", *Human Rights Quarterly* 3:1 (2009), pp. 221–238.

26 President Eisenhower to W. Knowland, 25 January 1954, in *The Papers of Dwight D. Eisenhower*, vol. 15: www.eisenhowermemorial.org/presidential-papers/first-term/documents/684.cfm (accessed June 2010).

27 Henkin, "U.S. Ratification of Human Rights Conventions".

28 P. Betts, "Socialism, Social Rights, and Human Rights: The Case of East Germany", *Humanity: An International Journal of Human Rights, Humanitarianism, and Development* 3:3 (Winter 2012), pp. 407–442; T. Buchanan, "Human Rights, the Memory of War and the Making of a 'European' Identity, 1945–75", in M. Conway and K.K. Patel (eds), *Europeanization in the Twentieth Century: Historical Approaches* (Basingstoke: Palgrave Macmillan, 2010), pp. 151–171; M.R. Madsen, "From Cold War Instrument to Supreme European Court: The European Court of Human Rights at the Crossroads of International and National Law and Politics", *Law & Social Inquiry* 32:1 (2007), pp. 137–159; S. Moyn, *Christian Human Rights* (Philadelphia: University of Pennsylvania Press, 2015), p. 159; M. Duranti, *The Conservative Human Rights Revolution: European Identity, Transnational Politics, and the Origins of the European Convention* (Oxford: Oxford University Press, 2017).

29 W. Korey, *NGOs and the Universal Declaration of Human Rights: A Curious Grapevine* (New York: St. Martin's Press, 2001).

30 Keys, *Reclaiming American Virtue*. See also Roberts, *The Contentious History of the International Bill of Human Rights*, pp. 190–223; M.L. Dudziak, *Cold War Civil Rights: Race and the Image of American Democracy* (Princeton, NJ and Oxford: Princeton University Press, 2000) pp. 12 and 79–114. Sara B. Snyder has recently offered a different interpretation that emphasizes the role of transnational activism during the 1960s. See Snyder, *From Selma to Moscow*.

31 J.W. Fulbright, *The Arrogance of Power* (New York: Random House, 1966), p. 3.

32 McCrisken, *American Exceptionalism and the Legacy of Vietnam*, p. 26; J. Suri, *Power and Protest: Global Revolution and the Rise of Detente* (Cambridge, MA: Harvard University Press, 2003).

33 S. Serfaty, "Brzezinski: Play It Again, Zbig", *Foreign Policy* 32 (Fall 1978), pp. 3–21.

34 Del Pero, *Eccentric Realist*, pp. 39–42; J. Ehrman, *The Rise of Neoconservatism: Intellectuals and Foreign Affairs* (New Haven, CT and London: Yale University Press, 1995), pp. 33–62.

35 R. Nixon, "Second Annual Report to the Congress on United States Foreign Policy", 25 February 1971, in *Public Papers of the Presidents of the United States: Richard Nixon, Containing the Public Messages, Speeches and Statements of the President, 1971* (Washington, DC: US Government Printing Office, 1972), pp. 231–232.

36 Del Pero, *Eccentric Realist*, pp. 43–75; J.M. Hanhimäki, *The Flawed Architect: Henry Kissinger and American Foreign Policy* (Oxford and New York: Oxford University Press, 2004); R. Dallek. *Nixon and Kissinger: Partners in Power* (New York: HarperCollins, 2007). See also, F. Logevall and A. Preston (eds), *Nixon in the World: American Foreign Relations, 1969–1977* (Oxford and New York: Oxford University Press, 2008).

37 On the nature of détente, see A. Stephanson, "Fourteen Notes on the Very Concept of the Cold War", H-Net Diplomatic History List (H-Diplo), 24 June 1996: www.h-net.org/~diplo/essays/PDF/stephanson-14notes.pdf (accessed October 2011). On its conservative nature and its aims: J.L. Gaddis, *Strategies of Containment: A Critical*

Appraisal of Postwar American National Security Policy (Oxford and New York: Oxford University Press, 1982).

38 R.L. Garthoff, *Détente and Confrontation: American-Soviet Relations from Nixon to Reagan* (Washington, DC: The Brookings Institution, 1994), pp. 146–223.

39 J.E. Zelizer, "Détente and Domestic Politics", *Diplomatic History* 33:4 (September 2009), pp. 633–652.

40 H.A. Kissinger, *A World Restored: The Politics of Conservatism in a Revolutionary Age* (New York: Grosset & Dunlap, 1964), p. 326.

41 P. Williams, "Détente and US Domestic Politics", *International Affairs* 61:3 (July 1985), pp. 431–447; Dan Caldwell, "The Legitimization of the Nixon-Kissinger Grand Design and Grand Strategy", *Diplomatic History* 33:4 (September 2009), pp. 633–652.

42 H.A. Kissinger in *Department of State Bulletin* 69:1792 (29 October 1973), pp. 527–552.

43 Minutes of the Secretary's Staff Meeting", Washington, 22 October 1974, in *Foreign Relations of the United States, 1969–1976*, vol. E-3: *Documents on Global Issues, 1973–1976*: http://history.state.gov/historicaldocuments/frus1969–76ve03/d244 (accessed October 2011).

44 G.F. Will, *New York Times*, 23 December 1973.

45 House Committee on Foreign Affairs, Subcommittee on International Organizations and Movements, *International Protection of Human Rights: The Work of International Organizations and the Role of U.S. Foreign Policy*. Hearings 93rd Congress, 1st Session (Washington, DC: US Government Printing Office, 1974). See also C. Apodaca, *Understanding US Human Rights Policy: A Paradoxical Legacy* (New York: Routledge, 2006), p. 31.

46 Quoted in R.D. Schulzinger, "Détente in the Nixon–Ford Years, 1969–1976", in M.P. Leffler and O.A. Westad (eds), *The Cambridge History of the Cold War*, vol. 2: *Crises and Détente* (Cambridge: Cambridge University Press, 2010), p. 380.

47 J. Suri, *Henry Kissinger and the American Century* (Cambridge, MA: Harvard University Press, 2007), pp. 244–245.

48 See H. Brandon, *The Retreat of American Power* (New York: Doubleday, 1973), pp. 140–153; W. Bundy, *A Tangled Web: The Making of Foreign Policy in the Nixon Presidency* (New York: Hill & Wang, 1998), pp. 383–399.

49 Among the most recent, see, M.C. Morgan, "The Seventies and the Rebirth of Human Rights", in N. Ferguson, C. Maier, E. Manela and D.J. Sargent (eds), *The Shock of the Global: The 1970s in Perspective* (Cambridge, MA: Harvard University Press, 2010), pp. 237–250; B. Keys, "Congress, Kissinger, and the Origins of Human Rights Diplomacy", *Diplomatic History* 34:5 (2010), pp. 823–851; J. Renouard, *Human Rights in American Foreign Policy: From the 1960s to the Soviet Collapse* (Philadelphia: University of Pennsylvania Press, 2016); D.J. Sargent, *A Superpower Transformed: The Remaking of American Foreign Relations in the 1970s* (Oxford and New York: Oxford University Press, 2015).

50 R. Burke, *Decolonization and the Evolution of International Human Rights* (Philadelphia: University of Pennsylvania Press, 2010); A. Eckert, "African Nationalists and Human Rights, 1940s-1970s", in S.-L. Hoffmann (ed.), *Human Rights in the Twentieth Century* (Cambridge: Cambridge University Press, 2010), pp. 283–300.

51 C. Ponce de Leon quoted in M. Flores, *Storia dei diritti umani* (Bologna: Il Mulino, 2008), p. 239.

52 Moyn, *The Last Utopia*, pp. 93–128.

53 R.J. Vincent, "The Response of Europe and the Third World to United States Human Rights Diplomacy", in D.D. Newsom (ed.), *The Diplomacy of Human Rights* (Lanham, MD: University Press of America, 1986), pp. 31–42; G. Sluga, "The Transformation of International Institutions: Global Shocks as Cultural Shock", in Ferguson, Maier, Manela and Sargent, *The Shock of the Global*, pp. 223–236; R. Burke, "From Individual Rights to National Development: The First UN International Conference on Human Rights, Tehran, 1968", *Journal of World History* 19:3 (September 2008), pp. 275–296.

54 K. M'Baye, "Le droit au développement comme un droit de l'homme", *Revue des droits de l'homme* 5:2–3 (1972), pp. 503–534.

55 See, for example, "Il Tribunal Russell II", HAEU, EEA 201.

56 A.É. Gfeller, *Building a European Identity: France, the United States, and the Oil Shock, 1973–74* (New York: Berghahn Books, 2012); A. Bitumi, *Un ponte sull'Atlantico. Il "Programma di visitatori" e la diplomazia pubblica della Comunità europea negli anni Settanta* (Bologna: Il Mulino, 2014).

57 L. Ferrari, *Sometimes Speaking with a Single Voice: The European Community as an International Actor, 1969–1979* (Brussels: Peter Lang, 2016), p. 179.

58 Sargent, *A Superpower Transformed*, pp. 166–175.

59 T.H. Etzold, "Interdependence 1976?", *Diplomatic History* 1:1 (1977), pp. 35–45.

60 D.B. Fascell, "The Helsinki Accords: A Case Study", *Annals of the American Academy of Political and Social Science* 442:1 (1979), pp. 69–76.

61 D. Weissbrodt, "The Contribution of International Nongovernmental Organizations to the Protection of Human Rights", in T. Meron (ed.), *Human Rights in International Law: Legal and Policy Issue* (Oxford: Oxford University Press, 1984), pp. 403–438; and Korey, *NGOs and the Universal Declaration*.

62 P. Benenson, *Persecution 1961* (London: Penguin Books, 1961), pp. 161–162; T. Buchanan, "The Truth Will Set You Free: The Making of Amnesty International", *Journal of Contemporary History* 37:4 (October 2002), pp. 575–597.

63 Korey, *NGOs and the Universal Declaration*, p. 168; K. Cmiel, "The Emergence of Human Rights Policy in the United States", *Journal of American History*, 86:3 (1999), pp. 1231–1250, and K. Cmiel, "The Recent History of Human Rights", *American Historical Review* 109:1 (February 2004), pp. 117–135.

64 D. Ottaway, "The Growing Lobby for Human Rights", *Washington Post*, 17 December 1976.

65 H. Hughes, *Congressional Record*, 92nd Congress, 1st Session, 19 May 1971, pp. 15953.

66 R. Falk, *Legal Order in a Violent World* (Princeton, NJ: Princeton University Press, 1968), p. 75.

67 Johnson, *Congress and the Cold War*, pp. 190–241; Sargent, *A Superpower Transformed*, pp. 165–196.

68 *Congressional Record*, 92nd Congress, 1st Session, 16 September 1971, pp. 32156–32157.

69 Sikkink, *Mixed Signals*, p. 58.

70 J. Abourezk, "Amendment to the Foreign Assistance Act", *Congressional Record*, 93rd Congress, 2nd Session, 21 June 1974, pp. S1–S4.

71 J. Abourezk to E.E. Agnoletti, 30 November 1973, HAEU, EEA 209.

72 See, for example, T. Kennedy, T.J. Frarer and R. Falk, in House Committee on Foreign Affairs, Subcommittee on International Organizations and Movements, *International Protection of Human Rights*. Fraser's words are at p. 434.

73 Ibid., p. 219.

74 House Committee on Foreign Affairs, Subcommittee on International Organizations and Movements, *Human Rights in the World Community: A Call for U.S. Leadership* (Washington, DC: US Government Printing Office, 1974), p. 3.

75 Ibid., pp. 11–15 and 19–30.

76 "Minutes of the Acting Secretary's Functional Staff Meeting", Washington, DC, June 12,1974, in *Foreign Relations of the United States, 1969–1976*, vol. E-3: http://history. state.gov/historicaldocuments/frus1969–76ve03/d236 (accessed October 2011).

77 "Letter from the Assistant Secretary for East Asian and Pacific Affairs (Ingersoll) to the Chairman of the House Foreign Affairs Committee (Morgan)", Washington, June 27, 1974, in *Foreign Relations of the United States, 1969–1976*, vol. E-3: http://history.state. gov/historicaldocuments/frus1969–76ve03/d237 (accessed October 2011).

78 "Summary of Paper on Policies on Human Rights and Authoritarian Regimes", Washington, October 24, 1974, in *Foreign Relations of the United States, 1969–1976*, vol. E-3: https://history.state.gov/historicaldocuments/frus1969–76ve03/d243 (accessed October 2011).

79 Ibid.

80 S.M. Hersh, "Kissinger Said to Rebuke U.S. Ambassador to Chile", *New York Times*, 27 September 1974.

81 "Legislation Enacted on Human Rights", LOC, DPMP, Box 1603, Folder 4.

82 Committee on International Relations, *Congress and Foreign Policy, 1975* (Washington, DC: US Government Printing Office, 1976).

83 Department of State, *Report to Congress on the Human Rights Situation in Countries Receiving U.S. Security Assistance* (Washington, DC: Government Printing Office, 15 November 1975); "Legislation Enacted on Human Rights", LOC, DPMP, Box 1603, Folder 4; Keys, *Reclaiming American Virtue*, pp. 133–137.

84 B. Gwertzman, "U.S. Blocks Human Rights Data, on Nations Getting Arms", *New York Times*, 19 November 1975.

85 T. Harkin, *Congressional Record*, 94th Congress, 1st Session, 10 September 1975, p. 8607–8612; M. McGrory, "Freshman Presses a Point", *Washington Star*, 29 September 1975.

86 "Legislation Enacted on Human Rights", LOC, DPMP, Box 1603, Folder 4. C. Apodaca, *Understanding US Human Rights Policy*, p. 39; W.M. Schmidli, *The Fate of Freedom Elsewhere: Human Rights and U.S. Cold War Policy toward Argentina* (Ithaca, NY and London: Cornell University Press, 2013), pp. 73–74.

87 B. Nathans, "The Disenchantment of Socialism: Soviet Dissidents, Human Rights and the New Global Morality", in Jan Eckel and S. Moyn (eds), *The Breakthrough: Human Rights in the 1970s* (Philadelphia: University of Pennsylvania Press, 2013), pp. 33–47; M.P. Bradley, "Human Rights and Communism", in J. Fürst, S. Pons and Mark Selden (eds), *The Cambridge History of Communism*, vol. 3: *Endgames? Late Communism in Global Perspective, 1968 to the Present* (Cambridge: Cambridge University Press, 2017), pp. 151–202.

88 P. Reddaway, *Uncensored Russia: Protest and Dissent in the Soviet Union* (New York: American Heritage Press, 1972); R.L. Tökés, *Dissent in the USSR: Politics, Ideology, and People* (Baltimore, MD: Johns Hopkins University Press, 1974); L. Alexeyeva, *Soviet Dissent: Contemporary Movement for National Religious and Human Rights* (Middletown, CT: Wesleyan University Press, 1985); V. Zubok, *Zhivago's Children: The Last Russian Intelligentsia* (Cambridge, MA and London: The Belknap Press of Harvard University Press, 2009).

89 P. Litvinov and P. Reddaway, *The Trial of the Four: A Collection of Materials on the Case of Galanskov, Ginzburg, Dobrovolsky and Lashkova, 1967–68* (New York: Viking Press, 1972); Zubok, *Zhivago's Children*, pp. 254–265; C. Vaissié, "La COMES (1958–1969), une association d'écrivains dans la guerre froide", in J.-F. Sirinelli and G.H. Soutou (eds), *Culture et Guerre Froide* (Paris: Presses de l'Université Paris-Sorbonne, 2008), p. 298.

90 H.L. Feingold, *"Silent No More": Saving the Jews of Russia. The American Jewish Effort, 1967–1989* (Syracuse, NY: Syracuse University Press, 2006); G. Perkovich, "Soviet Jewry and American Foreign Policy", *World Policy Journal* 5:3 (Summer, 1988), pp. 435–467.

91 W. Orbach, *The American Movement to Aid Soviet Jews* (Amherst: University of Massachusetts Press, 1979), p. 19; P. Peretz, *Let My People Go: The Transnational Politics of Soviet Jewish Emigration during the Cold War* (Piscataway, NJ: Transaction Publishers, 2015), pp. 57–62.

92 W.R. Tayler to the Secretary, "Representations to the Soviets Government on Behalf of Soviet Jews", 23 July 1964, NARA, RG 59, Entry 5563, Box 3, Folder 1.

93 A. Orlek, *The Soviet Jewish Americans* (Westport, CT: Greenwood Press, 1999), pp. 49–50.

94 Ibid.

95 Y. Ivanov, *Caution Zionism! Essays on the Ideology, Organisation and Practice of Zionism* (Moscow: Progress Publishers, 1970), p. 6 [originally published as *Ostorozhno: Sionizm! Ochercki po ideologii, organizatzi, i praktike sionzima* (Moscow: Izdatelstvo politicheskoy literatury, 1969)].

96 J. Frankel, *The Soviet Regime and Anti-Zionism: An Analysis* (Jerusalem: Hebrew University of Jerusalem, 1984), pp. 21–59; J. Frankel, "The Anti-Zionist Press Campaign in the Soviet Union, 1969–1971: An Internal Dialogue?", *Soviet Jewish Affairs* 2:1 (May 1972), pp. 3–26; T. Freedman (ed.), *Anti-Semitism in the Soviet Union: Its Roots and Consequences* (New York: Freedom Library Press of the Anti-Defamation League, 1984).

97 W. Korey, *Russian Anti-Semitism, Pamyat, and the Demonology of Zionism* (Jerusalem: Hebrew University of Jerusalem, 1995), p. 14.

98 Perkovich, "Soviet Jewry and American Foreign Policy"; A. Preston, *Sword of the Spirit, Shield of Faith: Religion in American War and Diplomacy* (New York and Toronto: Alfred A. Knopf, 2012), pp. 559–572.

99 *Chronicle of Current Events* 6 (1969); A.J. Stoneman, "Socialism with a Human Face: The Leadership and Legacy of the Prague Spring", *History Teacher* 49:1 (November 2015), pp. 103–125.

100 A.D. Sakharov, "Razmyslenija o progresse, mirnom sosuscestvovanii i intellektual'noj svobode", ADSA, HRC, Box 4, Folder 1.

101 Y. Andropov to Central Committee, 22 May 1968, "The Appearance of Progress, Coexistence, and Intellectual Freedom", in J. Rubenstein and A. Gribanov (eds), *The KGB File of Andrei Sakharov* (New Haven, CT and London: Yale University Press, 2005), pp. 86–88.

102 T. Shabad, "A Russian Physicist's Plan: US–Soviet Collaboration", *New York Times*, 22 July 1968.

103 Legislative Reference Service of the Library of Congress, *Aspects of Intellectual Ferment in the Soviet Union* (Washington, DC: US Government Printing Office, 1966); Legislative

Reference Service of the Library of Congress, *Aspects of Intellectual Ferment and Dissent in the Soviet Union* (Washington, Dc: US Government Printing Office, 1968).

104 Document 64: Chebrikov and Rudenko to Kosygin, "Proposals on how to deal with Sakharov and Solzhenitsyn", 28 September 1973, in Rubenstein and Gribanov, *The KGB File of Andrei Sakharov*, pp. 160–166.

105 H.M. Jackson, "The Moscow Arms Agreements", 1 June 1972, HMJP, Accession no. 3560-06/9/97.

106 Del Pero, *Eccentric Realist*, pp. 110–143.

107 R.G. Kaufman, *Henry M. Jackson: A Life in Politics* (Seattle and London: University of Washington Press, 2000); Preston, *Sword of the Spirit*, p. 567.

108 Snyder, *From Selma to Moscow*, p. 37.

109 C. Horner, "Human Rights and the Jackson Amendment", in D. Fosdick (ed.), *Staying the Course: Henry M. Jackson and National Security* (Seattle: University of Washington Press, 1987), pp. 109–128.

110 J. Bloodworth, "Senator Henry Jackson, the Solzhenitsyn Affair, and American Liberalism", *Pacific Northern Quarterly* 97 (Spring 2006), pp. 69–77.

111 Senator Muskie to the President, 7 January 1972; H.M. Jackson, "Senator Jackson Introduces Two-Year Program of Aid to Resettle Soviet Jews in Israel", 3 February 1972; both in HMJP, Accession no. 3560-06/43/16.

112 TASS Interview with Vice-Minister Shulimin, 6 January 1973, HMJP, Accession no. 3560-05/315/27.

113 Peretz, *Let My People Go*, pp. 200–201.

114 Orbach, *The American Movement*, p. 90.

115 H.M. Jackson to Members of the Senate, 27 September 1972, HMJP, Accession no. 3560-05/4/12.

116 H.M. Jackson, "Freedom of Emigration and East–West Trade", 18 April 1973, HMJP, Accession no. 3560-06/17/9A.

117 A.D. Sakharov to Congress, 14 September 1974, HMJP, Accession no. 3560-06/37/18.

118 "Appeal to U.S. Congress by Jews from Moscow and Vilnius", 19 September 1973, HMJP, Accession no. 3560-06/40/9.

119 Quoted in " 'It Wouldn't Be U.S. Concern if U.S.S.R Sent Jews to Gas Chambers', Kissinger Told Nixon": www.haaretz.com/it-wouldn-t-be-u-s-concern-if-u-s-s-r-sent-jews-to-gas-chambers-kissinger-told-nixon-1.330106 (accessed October 2015).

120 H.M. Jackson, "House Passage of the Jackson-Mills-Vanik Amendment to the Trade Reform Act", 11 December 1973, HMJP, Accession no. 3560-06/40/9.

121 H.A. Kissinger to H.M. Jackson, 18 October 1974, HMJP, Accession no. 3560-029/1/1.

122 H.M. Jackson, "On Secretary Kissinger's Announcement of January 14", 26 January 1975, HMJP, Accession no. 3560-06/11/55. In his memoirs, Dobrynin blamed Jackson's decision to make the details of the agreement public for the failure of the trade agreement. A. Dobrynin, *In Confidence: Moscow's Ambassador to America's Six Cold War Presidents* (Seattle: University of Washington Press, 1995), pp. 335–336.

123 The creation of AI's USSR branch initiated a debate between the international Secretariat and the American section. The former was in opposition, fearing that a Soviet section could be detrimental to détente and its capability to negotiate with Soviet authorities. The latter argued for a major commitment on communist countries in order to contain the idea that Amnesty was a liberal organization,

focused only on human rights violations occurring in Latin America. A. Blaine to I. Morris, 31 January 1974, CHRDR, A.I. USA Archives, RG I, Series I.1., Box 1, Folder "Meetings 1974"; and Memorandum to the Directors of AI USA and "Then to Be Circulated as Appropriate for Comments and Support by Other National Section", 17 December 1974, CHRDR, AI USA Papers, National Office Records, RG I, Series I.2, Box 1, Folder "Executive Committee Meetings, Nov.–Dec. 1974". See also, Keys, *Reclaiming American Virtue*, pp. 90–97 and 184–195.

124 S. Cohen, "The Gulag Archipelago", *New York Times*, 16 June 1974.
125 R. Kaiser, "Arrest Shows Soviet System Still the Same", *Washington Post*, 13 February 1974.
126 Keogh to Kissinger, 4 March 1974; Kissinger to Keogh, NARA, RG 59, Entry 5552, B.5, Folder "USIA–Voice of America (1953–1978)".
127 "Jackson Ired at Silence on Solzhenitsyn", *Seattle Post – Intelligencer*, 16 February 1974.
128 H.M. Jackson, "Solzhenitsyn and Détente", 15 February 1974, HMJP, Accession no. 3560-05/260/82.
129 "News Release of the Committee for Intellectual Freedom", HMJP, Accession no. 3560-06/38/1; Del Pero, *Eccentric Realist*, pp. 143–144.
130 H.M. Jackson, "Speech by Solzhenitsyn by Invitation of the AFL-CIO", Washington, DC, 30 June 1974, HMJP, Accession no. 3560-06/37/31; J. Keogh, "Memorandum for Henry Kissinger", 4 March 1974; H.A. Kissinger to J. Keogh, undated, NARA, RG 59, Entry 5552, Department of State, Bureau of European Affairs, Office of Soviet Union Affairs, Box 5, Folder "USIA–Voice of America (1953–1978)".
131 Hanhimäki, *Flawed Architect*, pp. 433–435.
132 G.F. Will, "Solzhenitsyn and the President", *Washington Post*, 11 July 1975.
133 H. Block, *Washington Post*, 8 July 1975 and 18 July 1975.
134 Henry Jackson, Press Release, 17 July 1975, HMJP, Accession no. 3560-006/11/112.
135 "The Ronald Reagan Column", 18 July 1975, R.T. Hartman Papers, Box 175, GFPL.
136 The best reconstruction of CSCE negotiations and impact, as well as of Soviet rationale, is S.B. Snyder, *Human Rights Activism and the End of the Cold War* (New York and Cambridge: Cambridge University Press, 2012), esp. pp. 15–37.
137 J.M. Hanhimäki, "They Can Write It in Swahili: Kissinger, the Soviets and the Helsinki Accords", *Journal of Transatlantic Studies* 1:1 (Spring 2003), pp. 37–58. A different interpretation is in J. Suri, "Détente and Human Rights: American and West European Perspectives on International Change", *Cold War History* 8:4 (November 2008), pp. 527–545.
138 Memorandum, Cabinet Meeting, 8 August 1975: http://cdn.geraldrfordfoundation. org/memcons/1553206.pdf (accessed November 2012).
139 Memorandum from Secretary of State Rogers to the President, "United States and Allied Approaches to the Current Issues of European Security", 31 October 1969, in *Foreign Relations of the United States, 1969–1976*, vol. 39: *European Security*: http://history.state.gov/historicaldocuments/frus1969–76v39/d10 (accessed November 2015).
140 G.-H. Soutou, "The Linkage between European Integration and Détente", in N.P. Ludlow (ed.), *European Integration and the Cold War: Ostpolitik-Westpolitik, 1965–1973* (New York: Routledge, 2007), pp. 11–35; F. Romero and S. Pons, "Europe between the Superpowers, 1968–1981", in A. Varsori and G. Migani (eds), *Europe in*

the International Arena during the 1970s (Brussels and New York: Peter Lang, 2011), pp. 85–97; A. Romano, *From Détente in Europe to European Détente: How the West Shaped the Helsinki CSCE* (Brussels: Peter Lang, 2009); Romero, *Storia della Guerra fredda*, p. 245.

141 CSCE Final Act: www.osce.org/documents/mcs/1975/08/4044_it.pdf (accessed June 2010).

142 Gromyko in Dobrynin, *In Confidence*, p. 346. For further discussions of the Soviet rationale, see Snyder, *Human Rights Activism*, pp. 31–36. According to Snyder, it is also possible that Kissinger made the Soviets believe that the United States would not discuss respect of Basket III.

143 "Brezhnev at Helsinki", *New York Times*, 1 August 1975.

144 H.M. Jackson, "General Release on the Helsinki Summit", 22 July 1975, HMJP, Accession no. 3560-06/11/115; and "Statement on Soviet Rejection of Sakharov Visa", 12 November 1975, HMJP, Accession no. 3560-06/17/18.

145 G. Ford, *A Time to Heal: The Autobiography of Gerald R. Ford* (New York: Harper and Row, 1979), p. 300.

146 "European Security and Real Détente", *New York Times*, 21 July 1975; "Jerry, Don't Go!", *Wall Street Journal*, 23 July 1975; "Solzhenitsyn Says Ford Joins in Eastern Europe's Betrayal", *New York Times*, 22 July 1975; Alfred Friendly, Jr, "Cold War to Cold Peace", *Newsweek*, 21 July 1975.

147 Hon. Millicent Fenwick, "Monitoring the Helsinki Accord", *Congressional Record*, 94th Congress, 2nd Session, p. 7737; "Memorandum of Conversation", 11–12 August 1975, NARA II, RG 59, Accession A1, 5552, Box 1, Folder Leg 7: CODEL Albert.

148 The Presidents of the Polish American Committee, the Ukrainian Congress of America, the Slovak League of America, the Hungarian Organization of Churches, the Albanian Liberation Fund, the Lithuanian Organization Center, the Croatian Organization of Michigan, the Latvian Association of Michigan, the Estonian War Veterans and the Byelorussian Association of Michigan to President Ford, 23 July 1975, GFPL, White House Central Files, Box 13, Folder "CSCE, 8/9/74–7/31/75"; Abraham J. Bayer, Memorandum to Files, "Telegrams to Ford Prior His Departure for European Security Conference", 24 July 1975, NCSJ Papers, Box 63, Folder 1.

149 H.M. Jackson, "Congress Welcomes Solzhenitsyn", HMJP, Accession no. 3560-06/11/110.

150 G. Ford, "Address in Helsinki Before the Conference on Security and Cooperation in Europe", 1 August 1975, in US Department of State Bulletin, *The Conference on Security and Cooperation in Europe*.

151 T. Borstelmann, *The 1970s: A New Global History from Civil Rights to Economic Inequality* (Princeton, NJ and Oxford: Princeton University Press, 2012), p. 175.

152 Moyn, *The Last Utopia*, p. 144.

153 Keys, *Reclaiming American Virtue*.

154 Friends Committee on National Legislation, *Newsletter*, December 1976.

155 H.A. Kissinger, in Walter Isaacson, *Kissinger: A Biography* (New York and London: Simon & Schuster, 1992), p. 607.

156 H.A. Kissinger, *Diplomacy* (New York: Simon & Schuster, 1994), pp. 742–743.

2

Human rights and the 1976 presidential election

In his memoirs, Jimmy Carter has underlined how his personal attention to human rights had a long history that preceded his announcement to run for the Democratic nomination on 12 December 1974. Similarly, many historians have pointed out that his commitment to human rights was rooted in his strong moral and religious beliefs, as well as in the experience of the civil rights movement. The human rights campaign, Carter's speechwriter Hendrik Hertzberg wrote, was "pure Jimmy".[1] However, human rights became a specific theme that qualified Carter's platform for American foreign policy only in 1976. Therefore, it seems more appropriate to trace back his strong commitment to some specific issues that entered the American political debate between 1975 and 1976. This chapter will discuss, first, the early and unintended consequences of the CSCE Final Act and what scholars have labelled the "Helsinki effect". The blossoming of groups to monitor compliance with the Helsinki Accords in Eastern Europe and in the Soviet Union was matched by the creation of a specific Congressional Commission that contributed to changing the American perception of the Final Act and its humanitarian provisions. The chapter will then highlight how the commitment to promoting human rights offered an opportunity to unify the Democratic Party, which was split over foreign policy issues. Finally, it will narrow its focus on Carter's advisers for foreign policy during the electoral campaign, Cyrus R. Vance and Zbigniew Brzezinski. Brzezinski, in particular, played a significant role in shaping Carter's campaign. Reflecting his voluminous academic writings, Brzezinski proposed to ideologically challenge the Soviet Union while renewing bipolar détente. Human rights, which had never been at the core of Brzezinski's analyses, could serve this ambitious aim.

Détente in crisis: from Angola to creation of the "Helsinki Commission"

When Gerald Ford entered the White House in August 1974, after he had served in the House of Representatives for twenty-five years, he had no experience in foreign affairs. Yet, global transformation became a major problem for his administration. As president, he was forced to confront new dilemmas and to find creative solutions. The collapse of the Bretton Woods financial system in 1971, skyrocketing inflation and rising unemployment, the need for a new energy policy in the aftermath of the 1973 oil shock and the challenge posed by the "Global South" converged in transforming the relationship between the United States and the world and in eroding the pre-eminence of American–Soviet relations.[2] However, relying heavily on Kissinger's judgements and advice, Ford immediately reaffirmed the American central commitment to détente and international stability. He was keen to sign the Vladivostok agreement in November 1974 that introduced numerical parity between the missiles that the United States and the Soviet Union could hold. Similarly, he did not hesitate to sign the Helsinki Final Act in 1975, despite growing protest among American ethnic lobbies, human rights activists and many members of Congress.

Two other issues confirmed the prominence of bipolar relations for American policymakers and tested the limits of bipolar détente. First, the Angolan civil war demonstrated the inability of détente to restrain superpowers' global rivalry and, in the end, to build lasting peace. Second, human rights did not disappear in the aftermath of the Jackson–Vanik controversy, the Solzhenitsyn affair or the signing of the CSCE. On the contrary, Congress succeeded in creating a commission to monitor compliance with CSCE norms, thus welding human rights to bipolar relations.

The Angolan civil war was the last great crisis of decolonization and, specifically, a consequence of the collapse of the Portuguese regime in 1974. Kissinger initially paid little attention to the Portuguese colony of Angola. He was more concerned with the prospect of a communist government in Portugal and its implications for NATO and the Mediterranean.[3] In early 1975, the new regime in Lisbon agreed to recognize Angolan independence by the end of that year. The announcement precipitated the crisis among different factions, most of whom had established relationships with external powers, with the CIA, the communist camp and Cuba supporting opposite armed groups. Cuba became one of the most influential players in the civil war. Yet, it was not until April 1975 that the White House began to see the conflict as a proxy war in which – Kissinger claimed – the Soviets were trying to "tilt the political balance of Africa".[4]

Kissinger and Ford were now determined to prevent a communist takeover in Angola. Aware that the public would not support overt American intervention, they provided new covert support to the anti-Marxist forces. During the fall of 1975, American media reported on the US operation. Congress grew alarmed. In 1975, no issue dominated the headlines and Congressional debates more than reports of CIA abuses. To many, the agency had trespassed its original mandate by engaging in domestic espionage activities, assassination plots and coups to overthrow foreign governments. Kissinger described Congress as "violently opposed to intervention abroad, especially in the developing world, ever suspicious of the CIA, deeply hostile to covert operations, and distrustful of the veracity of the executive branch".[5] Outraged by CIA covert operations and with Vietnam in mind, in December 1975 Congress prohibited the use of funds in Angola, without a specific Congressional authorization.[6]

This bitter defeat for Ford proved the limits of bipolar détente. Détente did not prevent global competition between the United States and the Soviet Union but, for the first time during the Cold War, the United States had to stand aside as communist influence was expanding. Kissinger found the defeat even more difficult to accept because, over the previous months, Congressional conservatives had been criticizing Ford's weakness vis-à-vis the Soviet Union, but now, when the administration was firmly confronting the Soviets, these same conservatives undermined the White House's attempt to resist communism. This was a further problem. By 1975, the barrier that détente architects had envisaged between domestic issues and foreign policy was eroding and the White House found itself in a contradiction. On one hand, Congress was preventing the White House from resisting Soviet and Cuban adventurism in Africa. On the other, it was increasingly questioning the validity of bipolar détente. To critics, Angola was a further demonstration that the dialogue with the Soviets was immoral, dangerous and detrimental to American interests.[7]

Over the same months, Congress undertook another major initiative for bipolar affairs, namely the creation of a specific Commission to monitor signatory states' compliance with CSCE norms. Once again, the White House was opposed to Congressional actions, thus strengthening the idea that Kissinger and the architects of détente had envisioned the bipolar dialogue in opposition to human rights and American values.

There was a clear paradox in the Helsinki Final Act and to some extent in US–Soviet détente: what began as a conservative policy that aimed to consolidate the division of Europe became a transformative process whose unintended consequences were to legitimize dissidents' activities in the communist bloc and foster contact between them and Western societies.[8]

Soon after the signing of the Final Act, the Soviet press celebrated Brezhnev's perceived diplomatic success. Newspapers such as *Pravda* and *Izvestia* published the entire text of the Final Act, including those provisions concerning human rights.[9] Over the following months, the Final Act became a consistent source of inspiration for Soviet dissidents, as well as an international legitimation and a transnational resounding box. Their condition – Soviet Ambassador Anatoly Dobrynin argued in his memoirs – "certainly did not change overnight, but they were definitely encouraged by this historic document" that led to the creation of a transnational network of activists committed to forcing communist countries to respect CSCE human rights provisions.[10]

Soviet scientist and dissident Andrei Sakharov was among the first to understand the revolutionary importance of the Final Act. In late 1975, the KGB noted that Sakharov "continually expressed the idea that the CSCE created opportunities for exerting pressures on Soviet authorities" and that he had explained to a British journalist that "the task of the West is to use the tools it has at hand to assist the Soviet Union in fulfilling its obligations".[11] Sakharov, who was awarded the Nobel Peace prize in 1975, became "public enemy number 1" and, in the eyes of the Soviet state, had to be stopped.[12] Following Sakharov's activism, many other dissidents formed groups to monitor their governments' compliance with CSCE norms. First in Moscow, where Yuri Orlov, Elena Bonner, Natan Sharansky and others inaugurated the Public Group to Promote Fulfilment of the Helsinki Accords in the USSR and, later, in Ukraine,

Georgia, Lithuania, Armenia, Poland, Czechoslovakia and Hungary, Helsinki monitoring groups mushroomed. They all demanded that communist authorities embrace openness, enforce human rights and respect legality and CSCE humanitarian provisions. Ferment constantly increased and forced KGB chief Yuri Andropov to focus on techniques to neutralize dissidents. In March 1976, he offered numerous details on KGB activities: "In carrying out the operative-investigative projects in 1975, the KGB uncovered and prevented criminal activity of 53 hostile nationalistic and antisocial groups … As of January 1, 1976, the State security organs have issued warrants for the arrest of 964 individuals."[13] Despite these measures, the Soviet security services were unable to contain dissidents' activities. Clandestine publications such as *samizdat* and *tamizdat* were no longer confined to Moscow and St Petersburg, and were reaching small, peripheral cities. Refuseniks, prisoners of conscience, political dissidents and religious and ethnic minorities in the Soviet Union were now under the spotlight of international organizations and NGOs. In other words, dissent in the Soviet Union was on the rise.[14]

Dissidents' activities and authorities' actions to cope with them strengthened Western attention to human rights within the Soviet bloc. By late 1975, groups for the implementation of the Final Act were established in Norway and Great Britain and public demonstrations took place in Paris, Bonn, Rome and other Western cities. The same year, some Soviet émigrés in Denmark and other Western human rights activists convened the International Sakharov Hearings. This non-governmental tribunal succeeded in investigating human rights abuses occurring in the Soviet Union and in drawing attention to the CSCE Final Act. Similar initiatives fuelled political debates on the meaning of human rights in East–West relations and on the ambiguous relationship between communism and human rights. In France, for example, the issue of human rights in East–West relations contributed to a transformation of the liberal left and to a redefinition of an anti-totalitarian milieu, which found in human rights a crucial watershed. Similarly, Italian social democrats wielded the human rights weapon to challenge the Italian Communist Party, which, at the time, was assuming a moderate stance in both domestic and international affairs. The Italian Socialist Party led the offensive against human rights violations occurring in communist Europe and became an authoritative interlocutor of many dissidents.[15]

In the United States, the growing attention to political dissent in communist Europe was best represented by a Congressional initiative to create a specific Commission to Monitor States' Compliance with the Final Act.[16] The idea first emerged one week after the signing of the Helsinki Final Act, when a Congressional delegation led by Carl Albert (D – Oklahoma) flew to Moscow to discuss détente and its problems. During the first meeting, Representative John Brademas (D – Indiana) tried to explain to the Soviets some of the implications of the Helsinki Agreements and why Americans were sceptical about their true meaning:

> If you want serious, permanent détente you must adhere to Helsinki: détente can die in 1976, if there is not Soviet willingness … to adhere in fact, in reality, in action to Basket III commitments. Otherwise, this will be a major partisan issue

in the 1976 presidential campaign. I speak as a strong partisan of détente, but to become permanent it requires adherence to the Helsinki commitments and more openness on military and economic arrangements.[17]

The Soviets rebuked this without ambiguity: the Final Act had to be understood "in full, in toto, in its full complexity".[18] Over the following days, Soviet and American delegations tackled the different meanings they attributed to the role of human rights in détente and to the Helsinki process. Representatives Millicent Fenwick (R – New Jersey) and Sidney Yates (D – Illinois) even named the names of many refuseniks, as Soviets citizens who were denied authorization to emigrate were known in the West. Thanks to a *New York Times* Moscow correspondent, Christopher Wren, Fenwick succeeded in meeting Yuri Orlov and Vladimir Turchin, founders of the Soviet section of Amnesty International.

Back in the United States, Fenwick introduced House Resolution 9466, which called for the creation of the Congressional Commission on Security and Cooperation in Europe.[19] Composed of six Senators, six Representatives and three officials from the executive branch, the "Helsinki Commission", as it was immediately called, was supposed to undertake two main tasks: monitoring states' actions to comply with the Final Act and encouraging governmental and private actions and programmes for the promotion of the Helsinki Agreements.[20]

Within days, Clifford Case (R – New Jersey) introduced the same proposal in the Senate. In doing so, he explained that it was up to Congress to take such a bold initiative on human rights, given the White House's dismissive approach to the issue.[21] While the text of the resolution discussed the entire Final Act without privileging one basket to the detriment of the others, the Congressional debate focused almost exclusively on human rights, humanitarian issues and even free emigration, something that was not openly addressed by the Final Act. This overlap between the Helsinki Agreements and the Jackson–Vanik amendment demonstrated that American attention to human rights in the Soviet Union was as broad as it was vague. Moreover, like the Jackson–Vanik amendment, the creation of the "Helsinki Commission" triggered a harsh debate between Congress and the White House, as well as between the United States and the Soviet Union.

In January, the administration expressed its opposition to the Fenwick–Case proposal, a measure that was "neither useful nor desirable".[22] Writing to John Sparkman, chairman of the Senate Foreign Relations Committee, Robert J. McCloskey, Assistant Secretary for Congressional Relations, listed the administration's objections. From the executive branch's perspective, the Commission was a superfluous body that duplicated the functions of the State Department. The administration, McCloskey added, had "taken all the necessary steps for monitoring the implementation and compliance with CSCE by the other signatory states". Finally, even its "extraordinary composition would not seem to provide an appropriate or effective means for coordinating or guiding our efforts".[23]

This firm stance was also rooted in Soviet reactions to the Congressional initiative. Not only did the Soviets launch a new wave of repression and arrests of dissidents, but they also started a campaign denouncing what they considered to be continuous American interference in their domestic affairs and the hypocritical American approach to the Helsinki process. After all, the Soviets protested, Washington was maintaining an unreasonable restriction on travel to the United States for members of communist parties who were as a result constantly denied visas, thus violating the Helsinki Accords. They also claimed that the Americans had not published the text of the Final Act, something that was denounced as a violation of the right of the individual to know and act upon his rights.[24] Finally, the Soviets put under the spotlight human rights violations occurring within the United States. Increasingly, they denounced racial inequality and discrimination against African Americans and Native Americans, Washington's support for authoritarian regimes in Latin America and the lack of any satisfactory mechanism to ensure social and economic rights.[25]

The indignant Soviet response prompted a growing polarization within the United States. On the one side, the administration took a more critical position vis-à-vis the Fenwick–Case proposal. On the other side, supporters of the initiative claimed that Soviet actions made it even more necessary. Fenwick reiterated that the commission was the only tool to ensure respect for the Helsinki Accords and to be aware of "what is happening to the Ukrainians, the Baltic peoples, the Jews and the Anabaptists of Russia; to the Poles, Hungarians, Czechs, and Bulgarians; and in Romania, to the Germans, Hungarians, Baptists, Catholics, and Jews". Its creation would have provided the Final Act with real meaning because "non-binding international agreements … are significant only to the extent that they actually succeed in changing the behavior of the countries concerned".[26]

The Senate Foreign Relations Committee unanimously approved the Fenwick–Case proposal in April. In doing so, it introduced an amendment calling on the president to present Congress with a six-month report on all member states' respect for the CSCE Final Act. Over the following months, Congress started its hearings. Several witnesses pointed out that the commission was the only tool to ensure that the Helsinki Agreement was respected. Senator James Buckley (R – New York), for example, demanded "some assurance that the Helsinki Accords will be observed by all signatories", in order to avoid the possibility that CSCE could "become, as détente has become, a one-way street". Joshua Eilberg (D – Pennsylvania) stressed that "there should be no doubt that unless there is a constant public monitoring of how the various signatories to the Helsinki declaration live up to the promises of the section on human rights that section will be ignored by the Soviet Union and, quite probably, other East European countries".[27]

Ethnic lobbies and captive nations' organizations abandoned their initial critical stance towards the proposal and openly supported it. The Polish-American Congress, the Joint Baltic American Committee and the Union of Councils for Soviet Jews agreed to consider the Monitoring Commission as a tool to press the Soviet and East European governments to comply with the Helsinki rules.[28] The NCSJ coordinated a campaign in favour of the Commission. According to its president, Jerry Goodman, this "should not be so designed as to preclude the possibility that the Soviet Union will at some point disregard the provision completely". It was necessary to act "intelligently … not embarrass the Russians so much that they can scrap it completely".[29] Above all, the NCSJ started to see the document as a substitute to promote freer emigration from the USSR. Through the articles concerning the reunification of families, it would have been possible to reverse the negative trend in Soviet exit visas, which decreased from 20,628 in 1974 to 13,221 in 1975.[30] And in March 1976, even Senator Jackson openly endorsed it.[31]

Soviet authorities provided an unintended and definitive boost for the creation of the Commission, when they issued a warning to Yuri Orlov. TASS officially reported that:

> Seeking to gain popularity among opponents of relaxation of international tensions as well as among the enemies of the USSR, Orlov, among others, began to hammer together a group of dissidents, calling it pretentiously and provocatively an organization of control over Soviet implementation of the Final Act of the Conference on Security and Cooperation in Europe. It is difficult to classify Orlov's actions as anything but an attempt to cast doubts in the eyes of the world community about the sincerity of the Soviet efforts aimed at uncompromising realization of the undertaken international responsibilities.[32]

If the communiqué aimed to stop Orlov's activities and to prevent further Western actions in support of dissidents, it completely failed. On 17 May 1976, five days after the group's formation, Congress approved the creation of the Helsinki Commission.[33] During the vote, Representative Dante Fascell (D – Florida), who became the first Chairman of the Commission, told the floor that Congress should play a more vigorous role in the promotion of human rights, and then went on to confess:

> When I first learned of Mrs. Fenwick's proposal I was skeptical about the wisdom of setting up yet another government entity for such a specific purpose … I am now convinced that such an entity would not only be useful but could play a vital role in the promotion of human rights and in making certain that détente will be a two-way street and will mean substantive progress on fundamental humanitarian issues.[34]

Once the proposal was approved, an intense debate developed within the administration on how to cope with this Congressional initiative. The State Department proposed to overlook the apparent problems of the bill (a duplication of its tasks; its "hybrid" composition; the submission of a six-month report) and "permit the bill to become law without presidential signature".[35] Staff member Jim Cannon suggested the president should not veto the bill because such an action "would be perceived by the American Jewish community and others as an effort to hamper the work of the Commission"; in fact, "a number of Jewish community leaders have called to urge [presidential] approval".[36] Similarly, believing that "presidential disapproval of the legislation at this time might be construed by the public, albeit incorrectly, as evidence of a callous Administration attitude toward the question of human rights", the Department of

Commerce proposed an official ceremony for the signature.[37] A compromise solution prevailed: on 3 June 1976, President Ford signed the bill in the presence of Case, Fenwick and her legislative aide Bill Canis.[38]

The confrontation between the White House and Congress did not end with the adoption of the law. Over the following months, the administration tried to obstruct the Commission's actions by postponing the appointment of executive branch officials. Officially, the State Department was concerned about their role in the Commission. Off the record, Kissinger confessed to his staff the political implications of such a body:

> Kissinger: The President signed the bill only because I had not been told what was happening. I would have fought it to the death. It never would have passed if I had known more about it. … I put DOD up to send their General Counsel. What would the Congressional members of the Commission think if DOD sent a substantive man from ISA and I don't send Hartman? I don't want the Executive branch to be helpful.
>
> Hartman: The bill has been signed. We are now in a position of having to comply whether we like it or not.
>
> Kissinger: While I am the Secretary of State there will be no questioning of the Secretary by State Department personnel in public, not if they want to keep their jobs. I will not have the Executive branch participants used to encourage disputes between its various branches. It will not be Monroe Leigh's job to bring forth information for the committee. That function is to be performed by the witnesses. I am worried about Senator Jackson setting up a similar Commission on SALT compliance with three generals. If that happens the department will lose control completely. We might as well put Jackson in the Pentagon.[39]

In July, the administration proposed to restrict the tasks and powers of representatives from the executive branch by denying them the right to vote in the Commission or the chance to question witnesses during Congressional hearings. Although Senator Case was close to the concerns of the White House, Fascell and the other members did not accept such a proposal.[40] The deadlock was broken in late September, after four months of public and private pressure from the commissioners and "ethnic lobbies", and a month before the presidential elections. On the one hand, Fascell accepted the White House suggestion to appoint officials from the executive branch as "observers", instead of "full members". On the other, he publicly lashed out at the White House for its tardiness and repeated that he had solicited the appointment of the members.[41] Fascell's pressures intersected with those of the electoral campaign. According to scholar William Korey, Carter's running-mate Walter Mondale leaked the news he would touch upon this during his television debate with Bob Dole, Republican vice-presidential candidate.[42] On 7 October, Ford appointed Mansfield Sprague from the Department of Commerce, Monroe Leigh for the State Department and Henry E. Bergold from Defense to the Commission. In doing so, the president clarified that they would serve as observers and that the State Department, not the Commission, had "primary responsibility within the United States government for ensuring compliance with the Helsinki Accord".[43]

Relations between the administration and the Helsinki Commission remained strained until Ford's electoral defeat. According to some press leaks, Kissinger tried to obstruct the commissioners' first mission in Europe to develop contacts within monitoring groups and European parliaments. Claiming that the three officials from the administration were mere observers, the Secretary of State prevented their participation.[44] In addition, when *Washington Post* conservative columnists Rowland Evans and Robert Novak reported that Soviet and other Eastern European embassies had refused to issue a visa to the commissioners, a new controversy erupted. They blamed Kissinger for the decision because "the State Department [did] not lift a finger to get visas. What's more Commission members and administration officials told us the State Department privately concurred in the Soviet obstruction." Accordingly, the article concluded, "Dr. Kissinger and Soviet Ambassador Anatoliy Dobrynin were in the same boat on this."[45] Recently declassified documents, however, offer a partly different picture. Understanding the Helsinki Commission's growing influence over the political debate, Kissinger urged American embassies in Eastern Europe to protest at the denial of visas to commissioners. Nevertheless, it was a late action, which was implemented only after Jimmy Carter's electoral victory. Equally revealing, Kissinger justified it because "an atmosphere" had developed in the United States, "which tends to obscure what progress has been made", thus emphasizing more the American domestic debate rather than compliance with CSCE provisions.[46]

The clash between the Commission and Kissinger contributed to reinforce the idea that the administration was deliberately ignoring Soviet dissidents and that human rights and Kissinger's détente were in opposition. More broadly, the debate over its creation showed an early evolution in the American appreciation of the CSCE Final Act. When it was signed, the Final Act was denounced as Brezhnev's ultimate triumph and as an American betrayal of dissidents. By the end of 1976, the Final Act was perceived as a tool for the promotion of human rights in Eastern Europe and in the Soviet Union.

This change is best exemplified by the evolution of Democratic candidate Jimmy Carter's declarations regarding the Helsinki Final Act during the electoral campaign. At first, the Democratic candidate had embraced critics' buzzwords against the CSCE. He had defined the Final Act as "an agreement that, in effect, ratified the take-over of Eastern Europe by the Soviet Union". Helsinki, Carter continued, had been a mistake and there was "no reason for us to participate in the Helsinki conference" that had provided the Soviets with "a tremendous diplomatic victory".[47] In early October 1976, Dante Fascell wrote to Carter to explain that the incumbent administration had the opportunity to promote human rights in the Soviet Union through the Helsinki Accords and his Commission.[48] Fascell's letter arrived when Carter was developing a new understanding of the Helsinki Accords.

Human rights and détente during the primary elections

While Congress was pressing the White House on its tardiness with the appointments to the Helsinki Commission, American newspapers raised a new controversy over

Kissinger's détente. In March 1976, *Washington Post* columnists Novak and Evans reported that Kissinger's aide Helmut Sonnenfeldt had explained to American diplomats that the purpose of American foreign policy should have been to favour stable relations between the Soviet Union and its satellites because "Eastern Europe [was] within their scope and area of natural interest. It is doubly tragic that in this area of vital interest and crucial importance it has not been possible for the Soviet Union to establish roots of interest that go beyond sheer power."[49] To Evans and Novak, Sonnenfeldt's words had a clear meaning: the United States should favour "a permanent Union" between the Soviet Union and Eastern Europe and the "stabilization of the Soviet empire".[50] A major controversy began within the United States, forcing the White House to take an unquestionable position against the alleged Sonnenfledt doctrine. Even Kissinger was forced to address a letter to Senator James Buckley (R – New York) to explain that there was no Sonnenfeldt doctrine, and that the president's policy towards Eastern Europe was opposed to the idea of spheres of influence.[51]

The controversy blew up on the eve of Republican primary vote in North Carolina, during which former California Governor Ronald Reagan succeeded in defeating President Ford. Other victories soon arrived for Reagan. His ascendancy within the Republican Party was made possible by a conservative upsurge in American society that drew from different sources. It was in part a reaction against the social ferment of the long 1960s – a reaction that brought new vitriolic crusades against materialism, abortion and gay rights. In part, the troubled economy, with rising unemployment and skyrocketing inflation, weakened Ford's moderate agenda and played a major role in the conservative upsurge of the mid-1970s.[52] Foreign policy and the perception of American weakness vis-à-vis the Soviet Union should not be overlooked. Reagan found in détente Ford's soft underbelly. He did not hesitate to strike him there. In announcing his candidacy, Reagan clearly stated that his decision to run for the nomination was mostly based on Kissinger's flawed policy vis-à-vis the Soviet Union. The perceived decline in American security and military strength became a major issue in his campaign. Détente and the SALT agreement had relegated the United States to "Number Two in military power in a world where it is dangerous – if not fatal – to be second best".[53] Reagan's persistent attacks on détente forced Ford to reassess his foreign policy, so much that he banished the use of the word "détente". Reagan derided such a decision: "The slogan has a nice ring to it but neither Mr. Ford nor his new Secretary of Defense will say that our strength is superior to all others."[54] Following victory in North Carolina, Reagan reiterated his opposition to the Final Act and détente and honoured Solzhenitsyn as "a true moral hero snubbed by Ford and Kissinger".[55]

By the end of the primaries, Ford succeeded in securing the Republican nomination, but the race was so close that he was forced to accept Reagan's plank for foreign policy. *Morality in Foreign Policy*, as the section was named, distanced the Republican Party from Kissinger's experience:

> The principles by which we act to achieve peace and to protect the interests of the United States must merit the restored confidence of our people. We recognize and commend that great beacon of human courage and morality, Alexander

Solzhenitsyn, for his compelling message that we must face the world with no illusions about the nature of tyranny. Ours will be a foreign policy that keeps this ever in mind. Ours will be a foreign policy which recognizes that in international negotiations we must make no undue concessions; that in pursuing *detente* we must not grant unilateral favors with only the hope of getting future favors in return. Agreements that are negotiated, such as the one signed in Helsinki, must not take from those who do not have freedom the hope of one day gaining it. Finally, we are firmly committed to a foreign policy in which secret agreements, hidden from our people, will have no part.[56]

In the rest of the plank, human rights popped up to criticize different specific targets, such as China or South Korea. Yet, it was far from being a call for the promotion of human rights in the world, for the platform completely ignored human rights violations in Latin America and many other international allies of the United States.[57] Nevertheless, Ford was "furious" and felt humiliated by a section in which the Republican Party disavowed his foreign policy, which was now perceived as guilty of having sold out American moral, political and military superiority to promote a new appeasement.[58]

While human rights proved a highly divisive issue among Republicans, Democrats found in a strong commitment to human rights a guarantee of unity for their own party, which at the time appeared fractured on foreign policy issues. Nevertheless, it took time for Democrats to place human rights at the centre of their platform. During the race for nomination, the only Democrat who prioritized human rights was Senator Henry Jackson. A Cold War liberal who supported civil rights at home and a strong anti-communist commitment abroad, Jackson believed that the protection of internationally recognized human rights should be a major element of American foreign policy and a fundamental weapon to renew the Cold War. Other Democrat contenders seemed not to care about the place of human rights in American foreign policy. Liberal candidate Morris Udall, who had a long record of support for the civil rights legislation, did not embrace human rights during the race. He believed the United States should avoid meddling in other countries' domestic affairs and that détente with the Soviet Union should be reinforced, even though it implied leaving human rights backstage. Frank Church had a similar stance. Instead of a global agenda to transform the world through the promotion of human rights, he advocated restraints and moderation as the best way to renew American foreign policy.[59] Nor did human rights qualify Jimmy Carter's race during the primaries. On the contrary, he had not hidden his doubts on the Jackson–Vanik legislation. Calling the amendment "ill-advised", he blamed it for the worsening in bipolar détente and proposed revising it. To him, "Russia is a proud nation like we are, and if Russian communist leaders had passed a resolution saying that they were not going to do this or that if we didn't do something domestically, we would have reacted adversely to it. That's exactly what's happened."[60]

With no expertise in foreign affairs, Carter resisted making foreign policy a central issue during his race for the Democratic nomination. He followed Jackson in advocating a more reciprocal détente, in criticizing Ford and Kissinger for their secretive and amoral foreign policy and in promising better relations with European allies. The distinctive mark of his race was being an outsider in Washington politics, at a moment in which Americans' distaste for and aversion to professional policy-makers was profound and overwhelming. He was an almost unknown candidate who, in announcing his decision to run for the presidency, had to introduce himself to journalists who ignored him. "My name is Jimmy Carter and I am running for President of the United States" became a winning slogan and made an appearance on campaign materials for the Democratic Party.[61]

Being an outsider was important to Carter's race for the White House, as were his profound morality and strong religious beliefs. Since his early days as a local politician in Plains, Georgia, Carter had been a moderate supporter of the civil rights movement. He witnessed the contradictions of an unequal society at first hand and, by the early 1960s, he was advocating a desegregationist stance. He was elected to Georgia State Senate in 1963 with a moderate integrationist programme but, when he ran for governor in 1966, he lost the election to segregationist Lester Maddox. In 1970, Carter ran for governor again, this time disavowing his pro-integrationist stance. This angered some of his supporters but got him elected. As governor, Carter changed his tone completely. He declared at his inauguration that "the time for racial discrimination is over" and then worked to increase the number of African Americans serving in the state government. *Time* magazine put him on its cover as a representative of a "New South" that embraced integration and civil rights.[62]

A born-again Christian, he promised a moral rebirth to American politics. Leaning on theologians Reinhold Niebuhr and Paul Tillich, Carter frequently claimed that Christians should participate in politics without compromising their beliefs. Yet, while relentless pessimism and historical realism about the limitations of human existence seem to dominate Niebuhr's writings, Jimmy Carter was confident that individuals, institutions and states could advance ideals, promote peace and alleviate suffering: "the … duty of politics", Carter used to repeat, "is to establish justice in a sinful world". Through this religious language, he promised to bring America to new redemption.[63]

Carter was the perfect candidate. He was an outsider who promised to restore American policy to its lost morality after the bankruptcy of the Vietnam War, the Watergate scandal and Kissinger's unscrupulous realism. His deep religiosity appealed to the rising New Right, and neoconservatives could favour his proposed fiscal policies.[64] Above all, as Bert Lance, one of Carter's earliest supporters and campaigners, later recalled, "Jimmy was a formidable campaigner. He was a moderate to the moderates, a conservative to the conservatives, and a liberal to the liberals. He was all things to all voters."[65] Carter was a conservative who did not hide his moral aversion to abortion, but he was also a liberal who upheld women's and minorities' rights, and he showed specific attention to problems relating to education and the environment. His combination of modernity and conservatism, as well as his ability to maintain a balance between religious devoutness and respect for the separation of church and state, helped to appeal to both religious and secular voters.[66]

As his campaign gained strength, Carter began talking about foreign affairs. His proposals were vague enough to appeal to as many voters as possible. He promised more attention to the new challenges of interdependence, disarmament and international trade; better relations with allies; a new policy for less-developed countries; and the strengthening of bipolar détente. Above all, taking on the growing mistrust towards the establishment, he promised an injection of morality into foreign policy. Human rights fitted into these moral and religious convictions, but Carter embraced them only in spring 1976, when the race for the Democratic nomination was almost over.

Carter's conversion to human rights was probably due to the adoption of a strong human rights commitment by the Democratic platform drafting committee. During an April meeting of the committee, differences over foreign policy immediately emerged among Democrats. While Jeane Kirkpatrick, Daniel Patrick Moynihan and Ben Wattemberg, representing the more conservative wing of the party, proposed a firmer stance on Soviet communism, Sam Brown and Bella Abzug, on behalf of the liberal wing, supported a programme based on a positive evaluation of interdependence, antimilitarism and détente. The only area of agreement concerned the need to introduce an explicit commitment to human rights. According to Moynihan's report, Sam Brown presented a resolution demanding that all American foreign aid be cut off to regimes violating human rights. Moynihan objected that such a formula would favour the Soviets to the detriment of American and allies' interests. He then proposed, "Why not oppose any form of aid? 'We'll be against the dictators you don't like the most ... if you'll be against the dictators we don't like the most.' The result was the strongest platform commitment to human rights in our history."[67] Not only was this formula a compromise between two opposite factions, but it was also the only possible glue binding a Democratic Party that was neatly divided over foreign policy issues. Accordingly, through a strong commitment to the promotion of human rights, the presidential candidate Carter could meet both liberals' expectations for a radical reform of American foreign policy and conservatives' expectations for a firmer stance on the Soviet Union. As Elizabeth Drew wrote in the *New Yorker*, "surveys by Patrick Caddell, Carter's campaign pollster, had shown that human rights was an issue that united liberals and conservatives – a very strong issue around the table."[68]

In July, the New York Democratic Convention approved the electoral platform. The document started with a condemnation of Kissinger's style inspired by "a balance-of-power diplomacy suited better to the last century than to this one". Above all, it accused Nixon, Ford and Kissinger of jeopardizing American security and repudiating American traditional commitments to democracy and freedoms.[69] As such, it was not radically different from what Republicans were writing in their platform. Like their Republican counterparts, Democrats wanted to continue bipolar détente, despite its flaws and shortcomings. For this reason, they were advocating a "strong American military deterrent, hard bargaining for our own interest, recognition of continuing competition and the refusal to oversell the immediate benefits of such a policy to the American public". Détente would not erase competition but its continuation was the only option "for human survival".[70]

Like the Republican platform, Democrats pledged a commitment to human rights:

> We will reaffirm the fundamental American commitment to human rights across the globe. America must work for a release of political prisoners ... in all countries. America must take a firm stand to support and implement existing U.S. law to bring about liberalization of emigration policy in countries which limit or prohibit free emigration. America must be resolute in its support of the right of workers to organize and of trade unions to act freely and independently, and in its support of freedom of the press. America must continue to stand as a bulwark in support of human liberty in all countries. A return to the politics of principle requires a reaffirmation of human freedom throughout the world.[71]

To many, this section reflected the influence of Jackson and his supporters over the definition of the Democratic proposal for foreign policy. Indeed, the focus on free emigration and other civil and political freedoms was inspired by those human rights controversies in which Jackson played a major role.[72] Nevertheless, this firm stance was balanced by a commitment to arms reduction and by a long section that, under the title "The Challenge of Interdependence", introduced some new issues for American foreign policy, inspired by the new internationalists' reflections.

Bringing all its foreign policy parts together, the platform was more ambitious, and more ambiguous, than the Republican one. It tried to address two major problems: the need to differentiate Democrats' plans from Kissinger's realpolitik, which was increasingly perceived as indicative of the moral decay of the United States, and the need to keep cohesion within the Democratic Party, split between those who wanted to find a new foundation for American foreign policy and those who continued to look at international relations from a bipolar perspective.

Carter's first mission was to develop a synthesis between them. He tried to offer such a synthesis in his acceptance speech. He appropriated human rights as a quintessential expression of the American past and, obviously, of the Democratic Party. The American Revolution, he claimed, had established "a pioneer [state] in shaping more decent and just relations among people and among societies". Two centuries later, the legacy of the revolution for American politicians was "a sustained architectural effort to shape an international framework of peace within which our own ideals gradually can become a global reality".[73] Carter's ideals were those of the one who

> inspired and restored this nation in its darkest hours, Franklin D. Roosevelt ....
> A fighting democrat who showed us that a common man could be an uncommon leader – Harry S. Truman .... A brave young President who called the young at heart, regardless of age, to seek "a New Frontier" of national greatness – John F. Kennedy .... A great-hearted Texan who took office in a tragic hour and who went on to do more than any other President in this century to advance the cause of human rights – Lyndon Johnson.[74]

When a journalist from *Playboy* asked Carter to clarify why he had praised Johnson as a champion of human rights, Carter replied that the Vietnam War had destroyed President Johnson's "whole life". He then added that "there hasn't been another President in our history – with the possible exception of Abraham Lincoln – who did so much to advance the cause of human rights".[75]

To Carter, the promotion of human rights abroad was an extension of American traditional values. With a parallel between his early political experiences in Georgia during the 1960s and the situation of the United States in the mid-1970s, Carter pointed out that the roots of his dedication to human rights were in his "personal knowledge of the devastating effect of racial segregation in my region of the country".[76] A strong commitment to human rights was a purifying and restorative principle for the moral crisis the United States was facing, much as President Johnson's civil rights reforms had contributed to absolve America from its racist sins.[77]

Moreover, Carter's determination to introduce the promotion of human rights in American foreign policy resulted also from numerous appeals that his staff received from NGOs and human rights activists. Within days of the Democratic Convention, for example, Amnesty International addressed the first of many memoranda to the Democratic candidate urging him to raise the issue of human rights during the elect-oral campaign.[78] In September 1976, Andrei Sakharov and ninety Soviet Jews appealed to both presidential candidates not to abandon the promotion of human rights abroad.[79] Above all, Carter's electoral committee received a number of pleas urging him to clarify his stance vis-à-vis the Jackson–Vanik amendment and free emigra-tion from the Soviet Union. In July, he reiterated his doubts on that legislation. In an interview with the *New York Times*, he described the Jackson–Vanik amendment as a mistake: "here was an instance where I think the Soviet Union would have been much more amenable to quiet but firm diplomatic negotiations than highly publicized pressure placed on the Soviet Union by an act of Congress".[80] To leaders of the NCSJ, the vast campaign in support of the Jackson–Vanik amendment had been the only leverage to favour freer emigration from the USSR, and Carter's words contrasted with his proclaimed commitment to promote human rights.[81] Protests were so strong that Richard Holbrooke and Stu Eizenstat, both members of the Carter campaign committee, urged Carter to speak publicly about Soviet dissidents, to reply to Sakharov's appeal and, above all, to modify his stance on the Jackson–Vanik amendment.[82]

Carter followed this advice. He assured Senator Jackson that he shared his "deep concern over the protection of human rights and freedom of emigration in the Soviet Union and throughout the world" and that the Jackson–Vanik amendment would be "effectively implemented by a Carter–Mondale administration".[83] Speaking to B'nai B'rith, he made a pledge to discuss "the fate of men like Bukovsky and Slepak" in all negotiations with the Soviets. He also added that "if any nation, whatever its political system, deprives its people of basic human rights, that fact will help shape our people's attitude towards that nation's government. … Despite our deep desire for successful negotiation on strategic arms and nuclear proliferation, we cannot pass over in silence the deprivation of human rights in the Soviet Union."[84] Finally, he also touched upon free emigration in two telegrams he sent to Stuart A. Wurtman and Irene Manekovsky,

President and Vice-President of the Union of Councils for Soviet Jews. If elected, Carter assured the former, he would work "strongly and honorably to represent the interest of Soviet Jewry during direct negotiations with the Soviet Union".[85] To the latter he pledged to do

> everything I possibly could as President to encourage the Soviet Union to liber-
> alize its emigration policies for Jewish citizens who want to move. In my private
> discussions, in all negotiations including those concerning trade, and in other
> relationships, one of the prominent considerations and advantages I would hope
> to secure for our own country would be the release and freedom of Soviet Jews.
> I should not hesitate to use trade pressures to effectuate that purpose.[86]

In being able to unify the Democratic Party behind the human rights banner, Carter could criticize Ford from both right and left, asking for a major commitment to a mor-ally based policy. Echoing Jackson and Reagan, Carter criticized Kissinger's approach to international relations and promised a more reciprocal détente. At the same time, he adopted liberals' criticism of Kissinger's obsession with balance of power, his neglect of North–South relations and his support for allied authoritarian regimes.

In Brzezinski's shadow

Economic problems and moral issues dominated the presidential race between Gerald Ford and Jimmy Carter. Yet, foreign policy was at the centre of the concluding month of the electoral campaign.

On foreign policy issues, candidate Carter counterbalanced his inexperience with the advice he received from Zbigniew Brzezinski. Following Brzezinski's suggestions, Carter made Kissinger's legacy a centrepiece of his electoral campaign and a major target of his attacks. He promised to continue détente with the Soviets, while departing from the most controversial features of Kissinger's approach and introducing new com-petitive elements. Instead of secret diplomacy, back channels and a lack of any moral grounding, he committed himself to open diplomacy, morality and human rights. Centralization would be replaced by an open foreign policy in which both Congress and allies would be consulted. Rather than the bipolar obsession Kissinger had shown with his foreign policy, Carter promised to address new global challenges.

Carter first met Brzezinski in 1973 during a session of the Trilateral Commission, a private organization of around 200 prominent figures seeking to foster closer cooper-ation among North America, Western Europe and Japan. The ultimate goal of the commission was to agree upon "workable trilateral policies designed not only to enhance closer trilateral cooperation but also to progress towards a more just commu-nity" and to face the challenges of global interdependence.[87] Carter was invited to join the Trilateral Commission because he was considered "a bright upcoming Democrat" who had succeeded in relaunching Georgia's economy by prioritizing international trade.[88] He avidly participated in all meetings and summits sponsored by the Trilateral Commission, studying its reports and forging some personal connections. Carter would later describe this experience as "profoundly important". Not only did it introduce him to the foreign policy establishment (as president, Carter would appoint many trilateralists to diplomatic positions), but it was also important for the intellectual contribution the Trilateral forum gave to Carter: "those Trilateral Commission meetings for me were like classes in foreign policy", he confessed.[89] Brzezinski became a sort of mentor to the young Governor of Georgia. He lectured him on international affairs, on the evolution of bipolar relations, on the rise of global challenges and the nature of international relations in the era of interdependence and on the need to reverse the course of American diplomacy. Brzezinski's ideas shaped Carter's thoughts, ambitions and style. As Walter Isaacson wrote, when Kissinger first heard Carter's earliest proposals on foreign policy, he was impressed by "hearing Brzezinski's snide words slung at him each day, not with a slightly embittered Polish accent but a smiling Georgia accent".[90]

By late 1975, Brzezinski had risen to become Carter's top adviser on foreign policy matters. In December, the candidate urged Brzezinski to draw up a memorandum on some viable solutions to relaunch American international actions. By the end of the month, Brzezinski presented a scheme with some general principles:

> (1) as the first priority to create a stable inner core for world affairs, based on closer collaboration among the advanced democracies (open-ended trilateralism);
> (2) secondly, to shape on the above basis more stable North–South relations …;
> (3) thirdly, to promote détente with the Soviet Union and to court China. Détente, of course, is desirable but it ought to be more reciprocal. Moreover, since the element of rivalry remains a reality, it cannot be the basis for coping with global problems.[91]

This document was fundamental to Carter. Not only did it provide him with an initial blueprint for the electoral campaign but, over the following months, Brzezinski also worked with Richard Gardner and Henry Owen to turn it into a forty-five-page memorandum that would inspire the future president's early foreign policy actions. Above all, the three points of the memorandum described some of Brzezinski's intellectual developments, fluctuating between an invitation to surpass the bipolar horizon and his inability to get free of Cold War paradigms.

The son of a Polish diplomat, Brzezinski was a public intellectual whose ascendancy was deeply rooted in the transformation of American Cold War academia during the 1960s.[92] From the privileged position of a Columbia University professor of Soviet affairs and international relations, Brzezinski did not hesitate to chasten many administrations for their shortcomings and to commend others' foresight and correctness. In doing so, he showed both a certain tendency to combine his academic reflection with his role as a public intellectual and a penchant "to move with the intellectual fashions of the day".[93] Indeed, his books and articles are quite heterogeneous, touching on studies on the totalitarian nature of the Soviet Union or the impact of what he labelled the "technetronic age" on the international community. Nevertheless, there are some core beliefs in his intellectual position that inspired Carter's campaign and, later, foreign policy: his deep hostility towards Soviet communism; the possibility of developing a dialogue with Central and Eastern Europe; and the idea that the United States should develop a more dynamic foreign policy to engage and challenge the Soviet Union in order to foster its decline.

Although Brzezinski's first book discussed the Soviet Union as a totalitarian state whose political model prevented any possible political transformation, Brzezinski tried throughout the 1960s to move beyond the totalitarian model to study the Soviet Union and to define new prescriptions for American foreign policy.[94] First, he invited the United States to embrace a policy of "peaceful engagement" of Eastern Europe, in order to encourage political evolution and differentiation within the bloc. This was hardly conventional, for Brzezinski was arguing for an expansion of economic and trade links with communist Europe at a moment in which fierce anti-communists within the United States were rejecting any hypothesis of dialogue with the Soviet bloc.[95] Second, questioning the usefulness of the totalitarian model to describe the USSR, he argued for an evolutionary interpretation of Soviet rule, one which passed through different phases. However, as historian David Engerman notes, Brzezinski's analyses from the early 1960s were actually arguing for a transformation "within, not a departure from, totalitarianism".[96] Third, focusing on modernization processes that were transforming Soviet society, Brzezinski discussed the possible convergence between capitalism and communism, as well as global modernization processes. Yet, unlike his colleagues, he excluded the possibility of a complete convergence between the United States and the Soviet Union, given their different ideologies and historical evolutions.[97]

Moreover, with the publication of *The Soviet Bloc: Unity and Conflict* in 1960, Brzezinski began considering the communist camp as "neither homogeneous, monolithic, nor unchanging. Underneath the external façade of unity a continuing process of change is taking place."[98] A number of transformations could point to a possible conflict within the bloc, Brzezinski argued, and consequently to its possible decline: institutional, ideological and national differences between people's democracies and the Soviet Union; polycentrism in Eastern Europe; and the challenge represented by Chinese neo-orthodoxy: "The Soviet bloc is thus changing into a far more complex communist camp."

Brzezinski further discussed these ideas in a forum sponsored by the journal *Problems of Communism* and, later, in a new book: *Dilemmas of Change in Soviet Politics*. He described the Soviet Union as a modern and industrialized system. However, contrary to the Western experience, this would not lead to a democratization or a liberalization of the Soviet political system. Instead, should an evolution take place, this would lead the Soviet Union towards degradation. To face this challenge, Soviet leaders should work for a redistribution of power in favour of talented technocratic leaders, thus reducing the importance of ideology. However, Brzezinski concluded that this would not be possible. Instead, he predicted a "sterile bureaucratic phase" and a stagnation that in the long run would trigger the degeneration of the Soviet state.[99]

This analysis implied a clear prescription for American policymakers. The United States should not be a passive spectator to these transformations; on the contrary, it should develop a more dynamic foreign policy in order to favour Soviet decline and differentiation within the Soviet bloc. Washington should undertake two major actions: it should develop a "positive engagement" with Eastern Europe and a policy of détente with the Soviet Union. This policy should:

(1) aim at stimulating further diversity in the communist bloc;
(2) thus increasing the likelihood that the East European states can achieve a greater measure of political independence from Soviet domination;
(3) thereby ultimately leading to the creation of a neutral belt of states which, like the Finnish, would enjoy genuine popular freedom of choice in internal policy while not being hostile to the Soviet Union and not belonging to Western military alliances.[100]

Studies on positive engagement earned Brzezinski an appointment to the State Department's policy planning staff as an expert on European affairs. His contribution was clear when, on 7 October 1966, President Johnson announced that the United States would try to develop the peaceful involvement of Eastern Europe or, as the president himself said, "to build bridges across the gulf which has divided us from Eastern Europe".[101]

In early 1968, Brzezinski left the State Department to go back to his role as a public intellectual. To Brzezinski, Soviet tanks rolling in the streets of Prague in 1968 confirmed his analyses of the failure of ideology to ensure the bloc's cohesion. It also introduced a further challenge to Soviet rule that, eventually, became a new point of his analysis of Soviet decline: nationalism. On the eve of the invasion, Brzezinski had criticized many Western Sovietologists' inclination to "minimize what I fear may be potentially a very explosive issue in the Soviet polity ... we still live in the age of nationalism ... it is going to be exceedingly difficult for the Soviet Union to avoid having some of its many nationalities go through a phase of assertive nationalism".[102]

After Richard Nixon's victory in November 1968, Brzezinski became an outspoken critic of Kissinger's foreign policy. In condemning his colleague, Brzezinski moved between two consistent patterns: the growing economic interdependence and the ideological competition between East and West. Economic interdependence or, as Brzezinski called it, the "technetronic age", was the focus of a 1970 book, *Between Two Ages*. The world, Brzezinski predicted, was entering a new era, marked by the end of European reconstruction and the beginning of a post-industrial age. New problems and challenges were emerging with the technetronic society: "a society", Brzezinski wrote, "that is shaped culturally, psychologically, socially, and economically by the impact of technology and electronics – particularly in the area of computers and communications".[103] In this new international system, the Cold War would remain the central concern of American foreign policy. "In the foreseeable future", Brzezinski continued, the Soviet Union "will remain too strong externally not to be a global rival to the United States." Still, the technetronic age would have transformed competition by favouring some innovative trends within the Soviet system.[104] To Brzezinski, the uncertainties brought by the 1970s could be particularly difficult for the Soviet Union given its growing bureaucratization, ideological weakness and the emergence of nationalistic tensions. The rise of the technetronic age, Brzezinski claimed, would push the Soviet Union towards a constant and unavoidable, although slow, decline. In this process, the United States could exploit bipolar détente to relaunch an ideological confrontation with the Soviets.

This variety of suggestions, and the contradiction between interdependence and Brzezinski's failure to escape Cold War divisions, entered Carter's electoral campaign. In late 1975, Brzezinski invited Carter to "take the Kissinger foreign policy head-on. … Kissinger's foreign policy ought to be attacked directly, and his personal role in shaping it and giving it its somewhat dubious moral-political outlook ought to be the major focus."[105] A few months later, he drew up a detailed memorandum on the shortcomings of Kissinger's foreign policy. According to Brzezinski, Kissinger's "secretive personal diplomacy of the 19th century" proved to be "relatively short-sighted and unsuccessful" because it marginalized allies, "virtually ignore[d] the importance of international economics" and misled "Congress and the country". Despite its shortcomings, détente "should be continued and extended", Brzezinski wrote, but the "main challenge … will be to come to grips with the full implications of the interdependence of effective decision-making in such areas as inflation, energy, trade, food, population and environment". The Democratic candidate should recall that the United States had to pursue the two basic national interests, namely "national security and promoting the democratic principles for which the US (ought to) stand".[106]

Carter followed Brzezinski's instructions. From Chicago, he promised a new partnership among the United States, Western Europe and Japan and major cooperation with Congress because "in every foreign venture that has failed – whether it was Vietnam, Cambodia, Chile, Pakistan, Angola or in the excesses of the CIA – our Government forged ahead without consulting the American people, and did things that were contrary to our basic character".[107] In another speech, he thundered against Kissinger's penchant to act as a "Lone Ranger" committed to a "one-man policy of international adventure".[108]

Drawing from the Democratic platform and from Brzezinski's suggestions, Carter pledged to cooperate with the Soviets and other Eastern countries but, at the same time, he admitted that the United States and the Soviet Union would continue to compete. Brzezinski's influence on Carter's ideas about détente became increasingly evident as the Democratic candidate began referring to "more reciprocal" and "dynamic" détente. Indeed, Brzezinski had repeatedly criticized Kissinger's détente as "a conservative balance of power arrangement, devoid of any moral content" that failed to incorporate a political and ideological competition.[109] Many of Brzezinski's criticisms of Kissinger echoed those of Jackson and other hardliners, but Brzezinski ultimately drew a different conclusion. Rather than abandoning détente, as some irreconcilable critics were claiming, the United States should continue to pursue it, but it had to become "more comprehensive and more reciprocal".[110]

The opportunity to develop new links with Eastern and Central Europe in the same way the Soviets had done with Western Europe was a further reason to continue détente. Far from both the traditional "benign neglect" the United States had demonstrated towards Eastern Europe and the "Sonnenfeldt doctrine", Brzezinski proposed taking advantage of "the differences and even the conflicts between the communist States". Differentiation within the communist world required "a differentiated American policy". This could be achieved through the Helsinki Agreement, which gave the United States the opportunity to reject "the notion that Eastern Europe is an exclusive Soviet sphere of influence" and to "reaffirm the commitment to East European independence".[111] Following this idea, Carter pledged to develop stronger ties with Eastern Europe within the framework of a more reciprocal détente.[112] In the same vein, Brzezinski urged Carter:

> Do not attack the Agreement as a whole. The so-called "Basket III" gives us the right – for the first time – to insist on respect for human rights without this constituting interference in the internal affairs of communist states. Accordingly, this is a considerable asset for us, and you should hammer away at the proposition that the Republicans have been indifferent to this opportunity. The Helsinki Agreement also provides for the permanence of existing borders in Europe, and this happens to be in our interest. Insecurity about borders tended to drive the East Europeans (notably the Czech and Poles) into Soviet hands. Thus, it is not in your interest to suggest that it would have been better if we had not accepted the existing borders.[113]

This was a unilateralist and maximalist approach to the Helsinki process. It pointed out many potential advantages for the United States but failed to discuss the reasons why the Soviet Union should accept this kind of détente. Nevertheless, it was a synthesis of Brzezinski's thoughts. As original as it was vague, it seemed to call for a rollback of Soviet communism through the promotion of interdependence and links with Eastern Europe. At the same time, it was a perfect electoral strategy that allowed Carter to show the difference between his reciprocal, active and human rights-based version of détente and Republicans' amoral and one-sided bipolar dialogue. Contrary to Kissinger's static and conservative version of détente, Brzezinski and Carter were now proposing to further promote differentiation within the Eastern bloc. Similarly, far from the rejection of ideological competition that was at the core of Kissinger's détente, Carter's proposals for the bipolar dialogue exalted ideological competition or rather, as Brzezinski wrote in November 1976, they aimed at forging a détente that should "reduce direct tensions, while competing effectively on the political and ideological planes".[114]

Carter followed this strategy during the October television debate, the second of three, with Ford. As Sarah Snyder has argued, Ford's staff devoted considerable time to preparing him for questions and charges on the Helsinki Agreement. Ford, however, addressed this issue badly during the debate, ending up denying Soviet hegemony over Eastern Europe: "There is no Soviet domination of Eastern Europe, and there never will be under the Ford administration." To make things worse, when *New York Times* journalist Max Frankel offered Ford the opportunity to clarify his statement with a follow-up question, Ford reiterated: "I don't believe, Mr. Frankel, that the Yugoslavians consider themselves dominated by the Soviet Union. I don't believe the Rumanians consider themselves dominated by the Soviet Union. I don't believe that the Poles believe themselves dominated by the Soviet Union."[115] Carter took the opportunity to attack the Republican candidate: "I would like to see Mr. Ford convince the Polish-Americans and the Czech-Americans and Hungarian-Americans in this country that those countries don't live under the domination and supervision of the Soviet Union behind the Iron Curtain."[116]

This quick exchange conditioned the closing of the presidential campaign. At a general level, the tone of the debate and its follow-up showed how bipolar relations were still on the top of Carter's agenda. As journalist Elizabeth Drew lamented, the electoral campaign was dominated by the Cold War and proved both candidates' inability to cope with the new reality of interdependence: "They have talked about obsolete formulations", she wrote, "[t]he talk about a bipolar world is the ragged end of an old argument."[117] Moreover, while foreign policy had taken a backseat to economic issues up to that point, Ford's gaffe became a major issue. Over the following days, the *Los Angeles Times* described Ford's words as "either a momentary lapse of reason or evidence of a profound misunderstanding of one of the most important world security problems". Similarly, the *New York Times* pointed out that Ford's declarations had boosted Carter's popularity among ethnic lobbies and human rights advocates in Illinois and Ohio, where the Democrat was closing the gap with Ford.[118] Carter was able to exploit Ford's faux pas. Following the debate, he declared himself to be "shocked by the insensitivity and lack of knowledge which Mr. Ford displayed in his remarks about Eastern Europe".[119]

Strengthening Carter's image as a leader with sound moral principles and standards – historian Barbara Keys has recently argued – human rights "satisfied the public emotional craving to move beyond the moral taint of the [Vietnam] War".[120] Still, far from enjoying an overwhelming victory, Carter won in a very tight race, with 51.05 percent of the popular vote to Ford's 48.95. If the place of human rights had been a contested one up to this point, the vote did not untie the knots of the role they would assume.

Assembling a team for foreign policy

After the November victory, Carter wasted no time in collecting advice on priorities and strategies for American foreign policy. From his position as Carter's most influential adviser, Zbigniew Brzezinski submitted a memorandum – prepared with Richard Gardner and Henry Owen – to the president-elect in early November. It listed and explained the priorities the administration had to cope with in the first six months. The United States, they wrote, "had no choice but to be engaged in a protracted architectural process to reform and reshape the existing international system". It was not a call for "an assertive American leadership, but for more subtle inspiration and cooperation on a much wider front" that included "the entire international community. .... [T]hat community, in addition to the traditional problems of war and peace, now confronts global problems never before faced by mankind."[121] Four issues were identified "as the most urgent of all: the need to put the East–West relationship on a more stable basis;

the need to set in motion a process pointing towards a comprehensive Middle Eastern settlement; the need to initiate comprehensive and constructive North–South negotiations; the need to contain the arms race and to rationalize our defense posture". The memorandum argued that the United States should also seek cooperation with the Soviet Union and other communist countries. In other words, the United States should seek to "widen the scope of détente to include ... more constructive and cooperative Soviet involvement in coping with global problems". The reduction of direct tensions would have moved confrontation to the "political and ideological" levels.[122]

Although the memorandum called for going beyond "the Atlanticist/East–West Cold War framework of the years 1945–1976" and hoped for a renewed dialogue with the Soviet Union, it nevertheless identified Moscow as the major threat to American interests. For this reason, the United States should avoid going back to containment and seek a new SALT agreement, as well as:

> a) Commencement of political talks regarding the definition of common rules of restraint regarding regional conflicts and regarding reciprocal military abstention from areas not yet subject to U.S./Soviet military competition. b) Exploration of ways of developing greater cooperation regarding such global problems as food and nuclear proliferation. c) Informal understandings regarding the implementation of the human rights provisions of the Helsinki accords. d) These proposals might be accompanied by quiet suggestions to the USSR that it take specific steps to ease the plight of Soviet Jewry, you would ask Congress to repeal the Jackson–Vanik Amendment and grant most favored nation treatment to the Soviet Union.[123]

Therefore, the memorandum pushed for the United States to harness the Soviet Union to the international system, strengthening contacts, exchanges and, in the end, détente. It articulated a concept of détente that was broad and, at the same time, narrow. Expressing the desire to define an intricate web of contacts between East and West, Brzezinski was calling for a far-reaching form of détente. Yet, the aim of Brzezinski's détente was not overcoming competition between the Soviet Union and the United States. Rather, reducing the risk of an overt conflict, détente should be conceived as a tool to launch a new ideological competition. As in all the other memoranda Brzezinski prepared during the electoral campaign, he ambiguously moved across interdependence and the Cold War, détente and ideological confrontation. However, regardless of whatever compass the new administration were to follow, the memorandum highlighted that building "broad popular and Congressional support" was paramount. This would require "public enunciation of your overall concept and direction; adoption of specific actions on pressing issues; seizing the initiative in several policy areas in order to foreshadow and advance your overall strategy".[124]

Brzezinski was hardly alone in contributing to the definition of Carter's foreign policy. Since late 1975, Cyrus R. Vance had joined Carter's advisers for foreign affairs and began contributing to his race for the White House. Many historians have pointed out the differences, even the rivalry, between Brzezinski and Vance.[125] Once in office,

Carter appointed the former as National Security Advisor and the latter as Secretary of State. Tensions between the two plagued the Carter administration's attempt to develop a consistent foreign policy and caused many troubles to the president. To focus on the conflict between Brzezinski and Vance, however, is to risk overstating their differences at the expense of their areas of agreement and similarities. Indeed, their ascendancy within the foreign policy establishment, their experience within the Trilateral Commission and much of their advice to the Democrat candidate were similar.

A graduate of Yale Law School and a lawyer in New York, Vance had forged good connections to the Democratic foreign policy establishment during the early 1960s. President Kennedy appointed him as general counsel to the State Department and, later, Secretary of the Army. President Johnson designated him as Deputy Secretary of Defense. Vance proved to be an able negotiator who led several delicate diplomatic missions in Panama after the 1964 anti-American riots, in the Dominican Republic in 1965, in Vietnam in 1966 and in Cyprus in 1968. The lessons Vance had learned from his legal career, political and diplomatic assignments from Presidents Kennedy and Johnson and membership of the Trilateral Commission gave him a technocratic grasp of world affairs and the opportunity to elaborate a worldview that celebrated global interdependence, international cooperation and economic issues over traditional Cold War schemes.[126]

At the heart of Vance's worldview was his firm belief that "our national interests encompassed more than U.S.–Soviet relations", and that many "developments did not fit neatly into an East–West context".[127] To him, it was time to free America's foreign policy from Cold War schemes and obsessions. Embracing analyses on global interdependence and growing complexity in world affairs, Vance claimed that new challenges such as economic and financial problems, regional conflicts or nuclear proliferation were equally important. Similarly, since his encounter with the Vietnam War in 1968, he had reached the conclusion that crises in the developing world had a local nature, independent of bipolar relations and that one of the most serious flaws in America's containment was to bring back local conflicts and tensions to the Cold War.[128]

Vance elaborated these ideas in a memorandum he prepared for Carter in late October 1976, just days before the presidential elections. Sharing many of Brzezinski's concerns and priorities, he defined three major points for any eventual Carter foreign policy. His first point had more to do with process and legitimacy than with the content of foreign policy. Capturing the need for a new legitimacy for foreign policy and growing tension between the executive and the legislative branches, Vance emphasized that Congress needed to be "an active partner in developing foreign policy objectives". To meet this goal, he proposed that the administration keep Congress constantly informed and work with it over major initiatives for foreign affairs.[129]

The second element of Vance's foreign policy strategy focused on the importance of global changes. Vance asserted that a failure to address problems associated with "human rights, economic development, energy, population growth, environmental damage, food, nuclear proliferation, and arms transfers", would not only exacerbate current suffering in Third World countries, but also possibly lead to "uncontrollable conflicts that could draw the nuclear powers into potentially disastrous military action". Vance emphasized the value of gaining an in-depth understanding of these issues, on a country-by-country basis, without necessarily fitting these issues into East–West policy.[130]

Finally, Vance supported a renewed détente with the Soviet Union. According to him, Carter had to explain to Americans that "the scope and prospects for cooperation were modest" and that bipolar relations would continue to be a mix of cooperation and confrontation. He hoped the new administration would be able to value cooperation more than confrontation. To him, arms control was the most important issue in US–Soviet relations and the most likely area to produce results. He rejected the idea that arms agreements would necessarily have a positive effect on the broader US–Soviet relationship, and more generally any explicit linkage between arms control and other bipolar issues. The most important rationale for an arms agreement was on its own terms: "The best argument for SALT is a tough-minded description of what it could do for the United States and Western security, as opposed to unrealistic and unsustainable claims about a new era in U.S.–Soviet relations."[131] Accordingly, he exhorted the incoming president to immediately work on a SALT II Treaty and, eventually, to define "a possible agenda for SALT III". Vance proposed a comprehensive summit in the autumn of that year that should go beyond the SALT problem and, recognizing the importance of human rights in bipolar relations, he specified:

> Should an early attack be made on the most-favored-nation problem – which is of great importance to the Soviets – and on the elimination of the Jackson Amendment? I believe the trade question need not be addressed at an early date. It is wise to use this item for a bargaining lever and to keep the cat on their back for a while.[132]

Vance and Brzezinski touched upon the same points and issues in their memoranda. Yet, there were major differences in their worldview and suggestions to the incoming president.

First, Brzezinski and Vance differed in their interpretation of the place of the Soviet Union for American foreign policy in the era of interdependence. Vance tended to see global interdependence and North–South relations as replacing East–West relations. For this reason, he proposed to focus on a country-by-country approach and to separate bipolar relations from local crisis. Brzezinski, by contrast, tended to merge them and to assess the impact of growing interdependence on East–West relations.

Second, they differed on their definition of détente. To Vance, détente meant almost exclusively arms control. All bipolar initiatives should be subordinate to the signing of a new arms control treaty. No issue should be allowed to prevent the United States and the Soviet Union from signing a new SALT agreement. However, Brzezinski never abandoned his anti-Soviet attitude. To him, détente should stabilize bipolar relations and reduce the risk of a direct confrontation between superpowers, in order to relaunch the ideological competition between the United States and the Soviet Union.

Human rights – never at the core of Brzezinski's analyses or Vance's memorandum – were a further area of difference between Carter's two top advisers on foreign affairs. Both recognized the importance of human rights in American foreign policy as a tool to build a cooperative relationship with Congress and to strengthen domestic support for the new administration's foreign policy. Yet, to Brzezinski, human rights should become a wedge for ideological competition with the Soviet Union and an essential component in bipolar relations. For his part, Vance argued for a pragmatic and limited human rights policy. He cautioned against the risks of a radical human rights approach. In December 1976 he had reiterated his unwillingness "to meddle in the affairs of other nations" and his determination to reach a new arms control agreement with the Soviet Union.[133] Assuming that it could be detrimental to the administration's will to reach a new SALT Treaty with the Soviets, he invited the incoming administration to minimize the impact of human rights in bipolar relations.

This latent tension between Vance and Brzezinski emerged soon after Carter entered office. The intersection between human rights and détente would soon become an area of major disagreement between the two.

Conclusion

Carter was a latecomer to the human rights surge of the 1970s. A commitment to the promotion of human rights reflected both his deep moral and religious beliefs and the sudden prominence human rights had acquired in the American political debate. Through a major commitment to human rights, Carter could break with Kissinger's realist legacy and the moral bankruptcy of the Vietnam War, and renew America's image in the world. Furthermore, centring the Democratic proposal for foreign affairs on human rights was also a reply to the 1976 electoral imperatives: maintaining the cohesion of the Democratic Party at a moment in which, on foreign policy issues, it was divided; differentiating his proposal from Ford and Kissinger's; and maximizing the broad and vague attention to human rights that was growing in American society. A third element that contributed to the emphasis on human rights was Brzezinski's intellectual analysis of international relations. In the memoranda he prepared for candidate Carter, as well as in his articles and books, Brzezinski had briefly discussed human rights. However, the issue fitted perfectly within his vast intellectual reflection both in terms of his ideas about détente, which in his view should become more reciprocal, aggressive, with a strong ideological dimension, and in terms of his globalist drive that hoped for closer cooperation among industrial democracies and with the Soviet Union.

Finally, the proposal for a human rights-based foreign policy and for human rights in East–West relations was also based on the creation of the Congressional "Helsinki Commission". On the eve of President Carter's inaugural address, Chairman Fascell sent Vance a note inviting him to reiterate in his meetings with the Soviets "that we are serious about the implementation of the Helsinki Accords, especially those provisions dealing with basic human rights". For this reason, he had enclosed a draft version of President Carter's inaugural address that prioritized human rights:

> There can no higher priority than a renewed effort to end the madness of the arms race. The negotiations on SALT II and MBFR will have the urgent attention of this administration. The success of these endeavors will require patience – skill – caution – determination – and faith. In that regard, all sides must try to act in ways which will increase trust and faith in one another's words and commitments.
>
> The promises made in Helsinki must be kept – especially those that promise to recognize basic human rights and to provide for greater movement of people, information and ideas among nations. Our nation, our people and this administration are – as Americans always have been – irrevocably committed to basic human rights, individual freedom and guaranteed justice – not only for ourselves – but for all people everywhere. We shall therefore place great importance to the Helsinki follow-up conference in Belgrade later this year.
>
> Progress in the area of international human rights is no less important to world security than progress in SALT II or MBFR. Good faith efforts toward each of these goals are absolutely and inextricably linked to each other in the quest for peace.[134]

Carter's proposals during the electoral campaign left many unanswered questions. He did not clarify how the new administration would integrate the promotion of human rights abroad with other priorities and concerns for American policy. Nor was his position vis-à-vis the Soviet Union clearer. Good will and the commitment to develop a new détente would not suffice alone to ensure Soviet cooperation on global issues. Similarly, Carter never specified how he could succeed in promoting a more reciprocal détente that accepted ideological competition, as Brzezinski had indicated.

Notes

1 J. Carter, *Keeping Faith: Memoirs of a President* (New York: Bantam Books, 1982); J. Muravchik, *The Uncertain Crusade: Jimmy Carter and the Dilemmas of Human Rights Policy* (Washington, DC: American Enterprise Institute for Public Policy Research, 1986); R. Balmer, *Redeemer: The Life of Jimmy Carter* (New York: Basic Books, 2014).

2 On Gerald Ford's foreign policy, see D.J. Sargent, *A Superpower Transformed: The Remaking of American Foreign Relations in the 1970s* (Oxford and New York: Oxford University Press, 2015), pp. 175–197 and 214–220.

3 D. Binder, "Kissinger Weights Effect of a Communist Portugal", *New York Times*, 18 April 1975; M. Del Pero, " 'Which Chile, Allende?' Henry Kissinger and the Portuguese Revolution", *Cold War History* 11:4 (2011), pp. 625–657; M. Del Pero, "A European Solution for a European Crisis. The International Implications of Portugal's Revolution", *Journal of European Integration History* 15:1 (2009), pp. 15–34.

4 O.A. Westad, *The Global Cold War: Third World Interventions and the Making of Our Times* (New York: Cambridge University Press, 2005), pp. 207–249; P. Gleijeses, *Conflicting Missions: Havana, Washington, and Africa, 1959–1976* (Chapel Hill and London: University of North Carolina Press, 2002). The Kissinger quotation is in Sargent, *A Superpower Transformed*, p. 221.

5 H.A. Kissinger, *Years of Renewal* (New York: Simon & Schuster, 1999, pp. 823–835, 826. See also A.H. Cahn, *Killing Détente: The Right Attacks the CIA* (University Park: Pennsylvania University Press, 1998), pp. 53–57.

6 R.D. Johnson, "The Unintended Consequences of Congressional Reform: The Clark and Tunney Amendments and US Policy toward Angola." *Diplomatic History* 27:2 (2003), pp. 215–243.

7 G. Ford, *A Time to Heal: The Autobiography of Gerald R. Ford* (New York: Harper and Row, 1979), p. 346.

8 J.M. Hanhimäki, "Conservative Goals, Revolutionary Outcomes: The Paradox of Détente", *Cold War History* 8:4 (2008); S.B. Snyder, *Human Rights Activism and the End of the Cold War* (New York and Cambridge: Cambridge University Press, 2012); Sargent, *A Superpower Transformed*, pp. 209–220.

9 *Current Digest of Soviet Press*, 27 August 1975, pp. 14–15.

10 A. Dobrynin, *In Confidence: Moscow's Ambassador to America's Six Cold War Presidents* (Seattle: University of Washington Press, 1995), p. 346.

11 Document 108: Andropov to the Central Committee, "Appeals to Western Communist Parties and the Need for Continuing Internal Repression", 29 December 1975, in J. Rubenstein and A. Gribanov (eds), *The KGB File of Andrei Sakharov* (New Haven, CT and London: Yale University Press, 2005), pp. 223–224.

12 Document 101, Andropov to the Central Committee, "Sakharov Receives the Nobel Prize for Peace", 10 October 1975, in Rubenstein and Gribanov, *The KGB File of Andrei Sakharov*, pp. 190–191.

13 Andropov to the Central Committee, No. 545, "On the Results of Search for Authors of Anti-Soviet Anonymous Documents in 1975", 13 March 1976: www.gwu.edu/~nsarchiv/NSAEBB/NSAEBB191/KGB%2003-13-1976.pdf (accessed June 2015).

14 Document 101, Andropov to the Central Committee, "Sakharov Receives the Nobel Prize for Peace".

15 "Toward the International Sakharov Hearings in Rome", undated, ADSA, HRC, Box 11, Folder 1. M. Corti, *Le testimonianze del Tribunale Sacharov sulla violazione dei diritti dell'uomo nell'Unione Sovietica* (Milan: La Casa di Matriona, 1976); A.W. Blaser, "How to Advance Human Rights without Really Trying: An Analysis of Nongovernmental Tribunals", *Human Rights Quarterly* 14:3 (1992), pp. 339–370; D.C. Thomas, *The Helsinki Effect: International Norms, Human Rights, and the Demise of Communism* (Princeton, NJ: Princeton University Press, 2001); M.S. Christofferson, *French Intellectuals Against the Left: The Antitotalitarian Movement of the 1970s* (New York and Oxford: Berghahn Books, 2004), pp. 88–228; C. Ripa di Meana and G. Mecucci, *L'Ordine di Mosca. Fermate la Biennale del dissenso* (Rome: Liberal Edizioni, 2007); V. Lomellini, *L'appuntamento mancato. La sinistra italiana e il dissenso nei regimi comunisti, 1968–1989* (Florence and Milan: Le Monnier-Mondadori 2010).

16 W. Korey, *The Promises We Keep: Human Rights, the Helsinki Process and American Foreign Policy* (New York: Institute for East–West Studies, 1993); Snyder, *Human Rights Activism*, pp. 38–51.

17 Memorandum of Conversation, "Working Sessions between Delegation of the U.S. House of Representatives and Members of the USSR Supreme Soviet", 11–12 August 1975, NARA, RG 59, Lot Files 73D368, Box 1, Folder Leg 7: CODEL Albert. Members of the American delegation were Carl Albert, R. Michel, M. Price, C. Zablocki, E. Boland, P. Landrum, J. Brademas, D. Latta, J. Quillen, P. Burton, W. Green, S. Yates, Tim L. Carter, T. Foley, T. Bevill, B. Archer, G. Danielson and M. Fenwick.

18 Ibid.

19 A. Schapiro, *Millicent Fenwick: Her Way* (New Brunswick, NJ: Rutgers University Press, 2003), pp. 168–170.

20 Snyder, *Human Rights Activism*, pp. 38–50; C.P. Peterson, *Globalizing Human Rights: Private Citizens, the Soviet Union, and the West* (Abingdon and New York: Routledge, 2012), pp. 18–28.

21 Korey, *Promises We Keep*, p. 24.

22 B. Scowcroft to J. Collins, "HR 10193 (Establishment of a Commission on Security and Cooperation in Europe)", GFPL, NSA – NSC Europe, Canada and Ocean Affairs Staff, Folder CSCE 1975(6) WH, Box 44.

23 R.J. McCloskey to J. Sparkman, 19 January 1976, in Senate Committee on Foreign Relations, *Establishing a Commission on Security and Cooperation in Europe*, Report No. 94-756 (Washington, DC: US Government Printing Office, 23 April 1976).

24 Mr Clift to B. Scowcroft, "Soviet Propaganda on U.S. Violations of the CSCE Final Act", 2 December 1975, GFPL, NSA – NSC Europe, Canada and Ocean Affairs Staff, Folder CSCE 1975(7) WH, Box 44; and G. Arbatov, "Reciprocity After Helsinki", *New York Times*, 8 October 1975.

25 Clift to Scowcroft, "Soviet Propaganda on U.S. Violations of the CSCE Final Act". See also C. Andrew and O. Gordievsky, *Instructions from the Centre: Top Secret Files on KGB Foreign Operations, 1975–1985* (London: Hodder and Stoughton, 1991), pp. 91–92; Peterson, *Globalizing Human Rights*, pp. 42–43.

26 M. Fenwick, "Monitoring the Helsinki Accords", *Congressional Record*, 94th Congress, 2nd Session, 23 March 1976, p. 7737.

27 Subcommittee on International Political and Military Affairs of the Committee on International Relations of the House of Representatives, *Hearings on H.R.9466 (S.2679) and Related Bills to Establish a Commission on Security and Cooperation in Europe* (Washington, DC: US Government Printing Office, 1976), pp. 15–16 and 24.

28 Ibid., pp. 43–51.

29 J. Goodman to S.H. Lowell, 22 October 1975, CJH, NCSJ Papers, Box 6, Folder "Jerry Goodman 1975".

30 See J. Goodman, in *Hearings on H.R.9466 (S.2679)*, pp. 29–41.

31 H.M. Jackson's General Release, "Jackson Urges Action on Helsinki Accords", 26 March 1976, HMJP, Accession no. 3560-06/12/26.

32 P. Goldberg, *The Final Act: The Dramatic, Revealing Story of the Moscow Helsinki Watch Group* (New York: Morrow, 1988), pp. 53–54.

33 R. Drinan, in *Congressional Record*, 94th Congress, 2nd Session, 17 May 1976, p. 14052; Fenwick, "Monitoring the Helsinki Accord", p. 14190.

34 D. Fascell, in *Congressional Record*, 94th Congress, 2nd Session, 17 May 1976, p. 14052.

35 Memorandum for the President, "Enrolled Bill S.2679 – Commission on Security and Cooperation in Europe – Sen. Case (R – New Jersey)", 28 May 1976, GFPL, White House Record Office, Box 46, Folder "6.3.76 – S.2679".

36 J. Cannon to President Ford, "H.R. 15813 – To Amend the Act Establishing the CSCE", GFPL, White House Record Office, Box 65.

37 Memorandum for the President, "Enrolled Bill S.2679 – Commission on Security and Cooperation in Europe – Sen. Case (R – New Jersey)", 28 May 1976, GFPL, White House Record Office, Box 46, Folder "6.3.76 – S.2679".

38 Statement by S.H. Lowell on Signing the Fenwick–Case Bill, 3 June 1976, CJH, NCSJ Papers, Box 73, Folder 1.

39 Memorandum of Conversation, H. Kissinger, A. Hartman et al., 26 July 1976, GFPL, NSA –NSC Europe, Canada and Ocean Affairs Staff, Box 44, Folder CSCE 1976(1) NSC, Box 44.

40 Memorandum from A. Hartman and M. Leigh to the Secretary, "CSCE Commission – Executive Branch Participation", 30 July 1976, GFPL, Bobbie Greene Kilberg Papers, Box 4, Folder "Helsinki Agreement – Commission on Security and Cooperation in Europe".

41 D. Fascell, Press Release, NARA, RG 519, Box 8, Folder 4.

42 Korey, *Promises We Keep*.

43 President Ford to D. Fascell, 7 October 1976, GFPL, NSA – NSC Europe, Canada and Ocean Affairs Staff, Box 44, Folder CSCE 1976(4) NSC; and S. Oliver to D. Fascell, "Eagleburger Meeting", 6 October 1976, NARA, RG 519, Box 48, Folder "State Department Correspondence 1976–1977".

44 "3 on Helsinki Panel Curbed by Kissinger", *New York Times*, 2 November 1976; "Kissinger Curbs Administration Officials on Trip", *Christian Science Monitor*, 19 November 1976; M.W. Browne, "Curbed U.S. Tour of Western Europe Ending", *New York Times*, 22 November 1976.

45 R. Evans and R. Novak, "An Unholy Partnership", *Washington Post*, 10 November 1976.

46 Outgoing Telegram State 277519, 11 November 1976, GFPL, NSA – NSC Europe, Canada and Ocean Affairs Staff, Folder CSCE 1976(8) WH, Box 45; A. Hartman to D. Fascell, 1 December 1976, NARA, RG 519, Box 48, Folder "State Department Correspondence 1976–1977"; Fascell to Oliver, "Eagleburger Meeting", 6 October 1976, NARA, RG 519.

47 "Carter Quotes on Eastern Europe", GFPL, Michael Raoul-Duval Papers, Box 25, Folder "Carter on Foreign Policy (1)"; R. Trautman, "Second Debate Tonight", *Daily News*, 6 October 1976".

48 D. Fascell to J. Carter, 2 October 1976, NARA, RG 519, Box 48, Folder "Fascell Correspondence".

49 R. Novak and R. Evans, "A Soviet–East Europe Organic Union", *Washington Post*, 22 March 1976.

50 Ibid.

51 Buckley to Ford, 23 March 1976; Scowcroft to Cheney, 27 March 1976; Janka to Scowcroft, 30 March 1976, GFPL, Marsh Files, Box 84, NSC March 4–31, 1976; "Proposed Reply Regarding Sonnenfeldt Doctrine", 20 April 1976, GFPL, WHCF, Box 5, Folder CO1-4.

52 Y. Mieczkowski, *Gerald Ford and the Challenges of the 1970s* (Lexington: University Press of Kentucky, 2005), pp. 304–310; S. Wilentz, *The Age of Reagan: A History, 1974–2008* (New York: HarperCollins, 2008), pp. 26–47.

53 S.F. Hayward, *The Age of Reagan: The Fall of the Old Liberal Order, 1964–1980* (New York: Three Rivers Press, 2001), p. 465.

54 "Reagan's TV Address", 31 March 1976, GFPL, WHCF, Box 6, Folder "04/17/76 (3)"; "Reagan – Issues, Foreign Affairs", GFPL, Ron Nessen Papers, Box 3, Folder "Ronald Reagan (2)"; "Reagan, in National TV Talks, Attacks Ford Foreign Policy", *Washington Post*, 1 April 1976.

55 Quoted in Cahn, *Killing Détente*, p. 47.

56 The document is available online: www.presidency.ucsb.edu/ws/index.php?pid=25843 (accessed June 2014).

57 B. Keys, *Reclaiming American Virtue: The Human Rights Revolution of the 1970s* (Cambridge, MA: Harvard University Press, 2014), p. 225.

58 Ford, *Time to Heal*, p. 398.

59 Keys, *Reclaiming American Virtue*, pp. 227–228.

60 Committee on House Administration, *The Presidential Campaign, 1976*, vol. 1, part 1: *Jimmy Carter* (Washington, DC: US Government Printing Office, 1978), pp. 83–84.

61 R.A. Rutland, *The Democrats: From Jefferson to Clinton* (Columbia and London: University of Missouri Press, 1995), p. 228.

62 E.S. Godbold, Jr, *Jimmy and Rosalynn Carter: The Georgia Years, 1924–1974* (Oxford and New York: Oxford University Press, 2010), pp. 156–190, quotation at p. 170.

63 H. Shapiro, "A Conversation with Jimmy Carter", *New York Times*, 19 June 1977; W. Standing, *Presidential Faith and Foreign Policy: Jimmy Carter the Disciple and Ronald Reagan the Alchemist* (Basingstoke: Palgrave Macmillan, 2014); J. Waltz, "Jimmy Carter and the Politics of Faith", in Mark J. Rozell and G. Whitney (eds), *Religion and the American Presidency* (New York: Palgrave Macmillan, 2007), pp. 171–188.

64 S. Kaufman, *Plans Unraveled: The Foreign Policy of the Carter Administration* (DeKalb: Northern Illinois University Press, 2008), pp. 6–17.

65 B. Lance, *The Truth of the Matter: My Life In and Out of Politics* (New York: Summit Books, 1991), p. 30.

66 Carter, *Keeping Faith*, pp. 73–74. A similar point is in D.E. Rosenbaum, "Carter's Position on Issues Designed for Wide Appeal", *New York Times*, 11 June 1976.

67 D.P. Moynihan, "The Politics of Human Rights", *Commentary* 64:2 (1977)

68 E. Drew, "Reporter at Large: Human Rights", *New Yorker*, 18 July 1977.

69 "Democratic Party Platform", 12–15 July 1976: www.presidency.ucsb.edu/ws/index.php?pid=29606 (accessed July 2015).

70 Ibid.

71 Ibid.

72 S. Rosenfeld, "Secretary of State Scoop Jackson?", *New York Times*, 18 June 1976.

73 J. Carter, "Acceptance Speech", 15 July 1976: www.jimmycarterlibrary.gov/assets/documents/speeches/acceptance_speech.pdf (accessed July 2015).

74 Ibid.

75 "*Playboy* Gets Answers: Carter Talks of Faith, Writers, Deserters, Sex, Death, and Victimless Crimes in Interview", *Spokane Daily Chronicle*, 25 September 1976.

76 J. Carter, *Our Endangered Values: America's Moral Crisis* (New York: Simon & Schuster, 2005), p. 8.

77 M.E. Stuckey, *Jimmy Carter, Human Rights, and the National Agenda* (College Station: Texas A&M University Press, 2008), p. 128.

78 W. Turnbull (AI USA) for Governor Carter, JCPL, 1976 Presidential Campaign, Box 36, Folder 1.

79 "Draft of a Speech", JCPL, Lipshutz Personal Files, Box FG 51, Folder "Presidential Campaign (May 1976)".

80 "Excerpts from the Interview with Carter on His Concepts in Foreign Policy", *New York Times*, 7 July 1976.

81 NCSJ to Carter, 13 July 1976, JCPL, 1976 Presidential Campaign, Box 312, Folder 4.

82 R. Holbrooke to S.E. Eizenstat, 14 October 1976, JCPL, 1976 Presidential Campaign – Stu Eizenstat, Box 23, Folder "Jewish Affairs, 10/76".

83 W. Orbach, *The American Movement to Aid Soviet Jews* (Amherst: University of Massachusetts Press, 1979), pp. 152–153.

84 *Presidential Campaign 1976*, vol. 1, part 2, pp. 711–712.

85 J. Carter to S.A. Wurtman, 16 September 1976, CJH, NCSJ Papers, Box 55, Folder "Presidential Campaign 1976 – Democratic Party".

86 J. Carter to I. Manekovsky, 14 September 1976, CJH, NCSJ Papers, Box 55, Folder "Presidential Campaign 1976 – Democratic Party".

87 Quoted in Sargent, *A Superpower Transformed*, p. 171; S. Gill, *American Hegemony and the Trilateral Commission* (Cambridge: Cambridge University Press, 1990), pp. 130–142.

88 Z. Brzezinski, *Power and Principle: Memoirs of the National Security Adviser, 1977–1981* (New York: Farrar, Straus and Giroux, 1983), p. 5; Z. Brzezinski, Interview, 18 February 1982, Jimmy Carter Presidential Oral History Project, Miller Center of Public Affairs, University of Virginia: http://webstorage3.mcpa.virginia.edu/poh/transcripts/ohp_1982_0218_brzezinski.pdf (accessed July 2015).

89 R. Scheer, "Jimmy, We Hardly Know Y'All", *Playboy*, November 1976, p. 192; D. Brinkley, "The Rising Stock of Jimmy Carter: The Hands-On Legacy of Our Thirty-Ninth President", *Diplomatic History* 20:4 (Fall 1996), p. 516; H. Jordan, *Crisis: The Last Year of the Carter Presidency* (London: Michael Joseph, 1982), p. 45; H. Sklar (ed.), *Trilateralism: The Trilateral Commission and Elite Planning for World Management* (Boston: South End Press, 1980), pp. 91–92.

90 R. Scheer, "In Search of Brzezinski", *Washington Post*, 6 February 1977; W. Isaacson, *Kissinger: A Biography* (New York and London: Simon & Schuster, 1992), p. 700.

91 Brzezinski, *Power and Principle*, p. 7.

92 J. Vaïsse, "Zbig, Henry, and the New Foreign Policy Elite", in Charles Gati (ed.), *Zbig: The Strategy and Statecraft of Zbigniew Brzezinski* (Baltimore, MD: Johns Hopkins University Press, 2013).

93 "Zbigniew Brzezinski: Special Assistant to the President for National Security Affairs", NA, PREM 16/1911. See also, S. Serfaty, "Brzezinski: Play It Again, Zbig", *Foreign Policy* 32 (Fall 1978), pp. 6–7.

94 Z. Brzezinski, "U.S. Foreign Policy in East Central Europe. A Study in Contradiction", *Journal of International Affairs* 11:1 (1957), pp. 60–71; C.J. Friedrich and Z. Brzezinski, *Totalitarian Dictatorship and Autocracy* (Cambridge, MA: Harvard University Press, 1956); A. Gleason, *Totalitarianism: The Inner History of Cold War* (Oxford and London: Oxford University Press, 1995), pp. 125–126; D. Engerman, *Know Your Enemy: The Rise and Fall of America's Soviet Experts* (New York: Oxford University Press, 2009), pp. 207–210.

95 P.G. Vaughan, "Zbigniew Brzezinski: The Political and Academic Life of a Cold War Visionary" (PhD dissertation, West Virginia University, 2003), pp. 43–49.

96 Z. Brzezinski, "The Nature of the Soviet System", *Slavic Review* 20:3 (October 1961), pp. 351–368; D.C. Engerman, "The Fall of Totalitarianism and the Rise of Zbigniew Brzezinski", in Gati, *Zbig*, pp. 27–40, here p. 35.

97 Z. Brzezinski and S. Huntington, *Political Power: USA/USSR* (New York: Penguin Books, 1971) (1st edn 1965).

98 Z. Brzezinski, *The Soviet Bloc: Unity and Conflict* (Cambridge, MA: Harvard University Press, 1960), p. xvii.

99 Z. Brzezinski, "The Soviet Political System: Transformation or Degeneration?", *Problems of Communism* 15:1 (January 1966), pp. 1–15; Z. Brzezinski (ed.), *Dilemmas of Change in Soviet Politics* (New York: Columbia University Press, 1969).

100 Z. Brzezinski and W.E. Griffith, "Peaceful Engagement in Eastern Europe", *Foreign Affairs* 39 (July 1961), pp. 642–653; Z. Brzezinski, *Alternative to Partition: For a Broader Conception of America's Role in Europe* (New York: McGraw-Hill, 1965).

101 "Columbia's Brzezinski Joins State Department", *New York Times*, 12 May 1966; *Department of State Bulletin* 50:1303, 15 June 1964, p. 923. See also, P. Vaughan, "Beyond Benign Neglect: Zbigniew Brzezinski and the Polish Crisis of 1980", *Polish Review* 64:1 (1999), pp. 3–28. The quotation is from T.A. Schwartz, *Lyndon Johnson and Europe: In the Shadow of Vietnam* (Cambridge, MA: Harvard University Press, 2003), p. 19.

102 Z. Brzezinski, "Reflections on the Soviet System", *Problems of Communism* 17:3 (May–June 1968), p. 47.

103 Z. Brzezinski, *America in the Technetronic Age* (New York: School of International Affairs, Columbia University, 1967), p. 9.

104 Ibid.

105 Quoted in Vaughan, "Zbigniew Brzezinski", pp. 232–233.

106 "The Inadequacy of Kissinger Foreign Policy: The Agenda for Foreign Policy in the Decade Ahead", JCPL, 1976 – Presidential Campaign, Box 17, Folder 1.

107 "Carter, Outlining Foreign Policy Views, Urges Wider Discussion", *New York Times*, 16 March 1976.

108 J.T. Wooten, "Carter Pledges an Open Foreign Policy", *New York Times*, 24 June 1976.

109 Z. Brzezinski to S. Hertzberg, 7 November 1973, JCPL, ZBM, Box 1, Folder: "Correspondence File: 11/1/73–11/30/73".

110 Z. Brzezinski to D. Spiegel, 20 January 1976, JCPL, ZBM, Box 6, Folder: "Z. Brzezinski Chron File, 1/1/76–4/30/76"; Brzezinski, *Power and Principle*, pp. 146–150.

111 Z. Brzezinski, "Draft of a Speech", 14 September 1976, JCPL, ZBM, Box 19, Folder "USSR–US Relations 7.76–9.76". See, also, Z. Brzezinski, "Observations on East–West Relations: Détente in the '70s", *New Republic*, 3 January1970, p. 18.

112 *Presidential Campaign 1976*, vol. 1, part 1, pp. 116–117. See also, E. Drew, *American Journal: The Events of 1976* (New York: Random House, 1977), p. 91.

113 Z. Brzezinski to Carter and Vance, "Points to Bear in Mind on East West Relations", 6 October 1976, Cyrus R. and Grace Sloane Vance Papers, Yale University, Libraries and Manuscripts, Box 8, Folder 7.

114 Z. Brzezinski, R. Gardner and H. Owen, "Foreign Policy Priorities. November 3, 1976–May 1, 1977", 3 November 1976, JCPL, Plains Files, Box 41, Folder 7 "Transition. Foreign Policy Priorities".

115 "Transcript of Foreign Affairs Debate between Ford and Carter", *New York Times*, 7 October 1976; "Carter Blasts Ford Insensitivity on Eastern Europe", 7 October 1976, JCPL, 1976 – Presidential Campaign, Box 16, Folder 2; L.P. Ribuffo, "Is Poland a Soviet Satellite? Gerald Ford, the Sonnenfeldt Doctrine and the Election of 1976", *Diplomatic History* 14:3 (Summer 1990), pp. 385–403; S.B. Snyder, "Through the Looking Glass: The Helsinki Final Act and the 1976 Election for President", *Diplomacy and Statecraft* 21:1 (2010), pp. 87–106.

116 "Transcript of Foreign Affairs Debate between Ford and Carter", *New York Times*, 7 October 1976.

117 Drew, *American Journal*, p. 465.

118 D. Sullivan, "The Debates as Theater", *Los Angeles Times*, 8 October 1976; K. Reich, "Carter, Ford Do Battle Over Eastern Europe", *Los Angeles Times*, 8 October 1976; D.S. Broder, "Now the Burden is on Ford", *Washington Post*, 10 October 1976; "Oops!", *New York Times* 10 October 1976; R.W. Apple, Jr, "The President Slipped in Front of Just the Wrong Audience", *New York Times*, 10 October 1976.

119 "Carter Blasts Ford Insensitivity on Eastern Europe", 7 October 1976, JCPL, 1976 – Presidential Campaign, Box 16, Folder 2; Snyder, "Looking Glass".

120 Keys, *Reclaiming American Virtue*, p. 240.

121 Brzezinski, Gardner and Owen, "Foreign Policy Priorities".

122 Ibid.

123 Ibid.

124 Ibid.

125 G. Smith, *Morality, Reason and Power: American Diplomacy in the Carter Years* (New York: Hill and Wang, 1986); J. Dumbrell, *The Carter Presidency: A Re-Evaluation* (Manchester and New York: Manchester University Press, 1993); Kaufman, *Plans Unraveled*.

126 M.J. Laucella, "A Cognitive-Psychodynamic Perspective to Understanding Secretary of State Cyrus Vance's Worldview", *Presidential Studies Quarterly* 34:2 (June 2004), pp. 227–271; Mary DuBois Sexton, "The Wages of Principle and Power: Cyrus R. Vance and the Making of Foreign Policy in the Carter Administration" (PhD dissertation, Georgetown University, 2009).

127 C. Vance, *Hard Choices: Critical Years in America's Foreign Policy* (New York: Simon & Schuster, 1983), p. 27.

128 Ibid. See also, Kaufman, *Plans Unraveled*, pp. 17–19.

129 C. Vance, "A Suggested Carter Administration Agenda", 24 October 1976, Cyrus R. Vance and Grace Sloane Vance Papers, Box 8, Folder 4.

130 Ibid.

131 Vance, *Hard Choices*, p. 136.

132 C. Vance, "A Suggested Carter Administration Agenda". See also C. Vance, "Overview of Foreign Policy Issues and Positions", in Vance, *Hard Choices*, pp. 441–462.

133 C. Vance, Draft for Inaugural Address, JCPL, SS, 1976 Campaign Transition File, Box 2, Folder "Inaugural Speech Drafts – Notes and Suggestions".

134 The letter is in Goldberg, *The Final Act*, pp. 486–487.

3

Firmness abroad, consensus at home, 1977–1978

Jimmy Carter entered office in January 1977 without a detailed strategy for foreign affairs. He had to navigate among different priorities and pressures. Domestically, Congress and human rights activists wasted no time in reminding the White House that the president had promised a total commitment to human rights. Conversely, Secretary of State Cyrus Vance cautioned against the risks of a too radical human rights approach, urged decentring the Soviet Union from America's top priorities and pushed for a rapid conclusion of arms control negotiations. For his part, National Security Advisor Zbigniew Brzezinski was determined to use human rights as an ideological weapon to challenge the Soviet Union and, eventually, to favour differentiation within the communist bloc. Furthermore, as the president himself discovered, the human rights policy had to overcome resistance from diplomats and State Department personnel. Moreover, it was unclear how the administration could integrate human rights into American foreign policy, balancing the pledge for an absolute commitment with other concerns for American diplomacy.

While the executive branch was scrabbling over the meanings of the human rights campaign, President Carter moved swiftly to give human rights high priority in America's foreign policy. He transformed the State Department's Desk for Human Rights into an effective Bureau, increasing its budget, power and personnel. He elevated the coordinator for human rights to the status of undersecretary. He appointed Warren Christopher to lead the newly established Interagency Group on Human Rights and Foreign Assistance, whose goal was to coordinate US departments and agencies in the implementation of the human rights policy. Based on human rights considerations, the administration cut aid to Argentina, Uruguay, Ethiopia, Nicaragua, Uganda, Cambodia, Laos, Mozambique and Guatemala and approved economic sanctions against Pinochet's Chile. Carter then appointed African American pastor and civil rights activist Andrew Young as American ambassador to the United Nations. By the end of the year, the president had signed the two covenants on human rights that the United Nations had approved in 1966, as well as the American Convention on Human Rights and the Convention on the Elimination of All Forms of Racism. In submitting these documents to the Senate for ratification, he also urged the ratification of the Convention on the Prevention and Punishment of Genocide, which had been languishing in the Senate since the early 1950s. Human rights took centre stage in bipolar relations as well. While the president was determined to strengthen détente, he repeatedly chastened the Soviets for their human rights abuses.[1]

To many scholars, these early initiatives contributed to moving American international action away from Cold War priorities, laying the foundation for a post-Cold War policy.[2] To others, they were a major demonstration of Carter's naïve approach to foreign affairs. In bipolar relations, in particular, Carter's will to promote human rights while preserving détente has been considered at least contradictory.[3] This chapter argues that Carter conceived human rights and détente as interdependent and mutually reinforcing. Conscious that the American public's attitude towards détente represented a major obstacle for the bipolar dialogue, the White House hoped to build a domestic consensus on détente, through a firm stance on Soviet violations of human rights. At the same time, through the continuation of détente, it tried both to ideologically challenge the Soviet Union and to promote human rights there.

The United States on the offensive

Over the first months in office, human rights were at the core of President Carter's declarations and major decisions. Yet, the administration had not set a clear agenda for the promotion of human rights abroad. Early problems encompassed the definition of the specific rights the United States would protect, how human rights could fit into foreign policy and integrate other relevant concerns, what were the basic aims, the tools and the limits of the human rights policy. Indeed, American interventions on human rights were frequent and bombastic, but unsystematic and apparently lacking a clear planning.[4]

Secretary of State Cyrus Vance tried to bring some order into the human rights policy. In an April address at the University of Georgia's Law School, he proposed a minimalist and pragmatic approach to human rights in international relations. Speaking as a lawyer rather than a politician, he provided a threefold definition of human rights, in which the right to the inviolability of the person would take precedence over civil and political freedoms and social and economic rights. He then called for a pragmatic, case-by-case approach, listing sixteen questions the United States should ask before taking any action, and advising that any concrete initiative for the defence of human rights should consider "the limits of our power and our wisdom".[5]

The following month, however, President Carter used a different tone to describe his human rights commitment. In a major address at Notre Dame University, Carter chose inspiring words and defined human rights "a fundamental tenet" of American foreign policy. With a Wilsonian subtext, he called for a moral rebirth of American foreign policy and for a renewal of America's image as a beacon of democracy, freedom and human rights. By proclaiming that the United States was "now free of that inordinate

fear of communism", Carter seemed to accept those invitations to move American foreign policy beyond the Cold War that had been the focus of new internationalists since
the early 1970s and to lay the groundwork for a new foreign policy. In reality, in iden-
tifying human rights as the ideological cornerstone of American action in the world,
Carter was not renouncing bipolar antagonism. On the contrary, he was calling for a
new strategy to cope with the Soviet Union on the ideological level.[6]

Carter was conscious that containment had pushed the United States to adopt "the
flawed and erroneous principles and tactics of our adversaries, sometimes abandoning
our own values for theirs" and that the Vietnam War had proved the "intellectual and
moral poverty" of this approach. Yet, he was also confident in American capabilities to
recover from past mistakes. Echoing theologian Ronald Niebuhr, he admitted that the
"world was imperfect" and "will always be imperfect", but, departing from Niebuhr's
pessimistic worldview, the president reaffirmed his confidence in "our own political
system". What Carter was criticizing was not the American determination to confront
Soviet communism, but the forms containment had assumed over the years, especially in developing countries: "We've fought fire with fire, never thinking that fire is
better quenched with water", Carter declared. Adapting bipolar antagonism to both
the legacies of the Vietnam War and an age of growing global interdependence, he
was calling for new ways to cope with old threats. A consistent approach to human
rights – one that distanced the United States from traditional authoritarian allies; that
did not deny that American record on human rights was far from being totally sat-
isfying; and that openly addressed Soviet violations of human rights – would make
America's commitment to democracy more consistent and effective.[7]

Indeed, while the White House never spared criticism of the poor Soviet record
on human rights, it was also committed to following a global approach to human
rights violations in the world. Latin America, in particular, had become a laboratory
for Carter's new diplomacy. The Carter administration was conscious that American
military aid and financial support to authoritarian right-wing regimes was inconsistent
with America's commitment to democracy and that it had fuelled anti-Americanism
well beyond the region. Moreover, thanks to Amnesty International and other NGOs,
as well as Latin American émigrés in the United States, abuses and violence occurring
in Chile, Argentina, Brazil and other countries were widely known in the United
States and could not be ignored.[8] By cutting economic and military assistance to these
regimes, the president could develop a more consistent approach to human rights,
present the human rights campaign as a universal and global policy and renew the
American image abroad.

If the new universalism of human rights was the first pole of Carter's Soviet policy,
détente and arms control represented the second. To prevent ideological confrontation
becoming a military clash, it was fundamental to preserve the bipolar dialogue and
reach a new arms control agreement. Indeed, securing peaceful coexistence and easing
nuclear tensions with the Soviet Union was another major theme of Carter's Notre
Dame Speech. With a conciliatory tone, Carter recalled that there was no alternative
to détente and urged the Soviets to "halt the strategic arms race. This race is not only
dangerous, it is morally deplorable." In one of the drafts the president had prepared,

there was a firmer commitment to a reciprocal détente; one that should balance arms control and human rights and should not jeopardize American security.[9] However, the final version omitted these lines. The reason for such a change – one might speculate – was the need to contain Soviet irritation with human rights criticism.

Carter's bipolar policy constantly oscillated between these two poles, intertwining cooperative attitudes with firmness on human rights. At first, the United States assumed a firm stance vis-à-vis the Soviets. In November 1976, as president-elect, Carter wrote a letter to refusenik Vladimir Slepak and, in December, incoming Secretary of State Cyrus Vance met Andrei Amalrik, who had been exiled from the USSR earlier in the year. Once in office, the administration worked closely with the newly established "Helsinki Commission" to intensify American warnings regarding Soviet compliance with CSCE humanitarian provisions. The State Department officially intervened on behalf of Andrei Sakharov.[10] The president even addressed a letter to the prominent Soviet scientist. He pledged his "commitment to promote respect for human rights and … seek the release of prisoners of conscience".[11] In early February, during the first official meeting with Soviet ambassador Anatoly Dobrynin, Carter and Secretary of State Vance explained that their aim was not to "embarrass the Soviet Union" over human rights issues and handed the ambassador a list of fifteen refuseniks whose plight was particularly important for the American public. They also protested at the expulsion of George Krimsky, an American journalist charged of being a spy, and urged Soviet authorities to free several gaoled dissidents.[12] Within days, the administration officially protested at the arrest of Yuri Orlov, Aleksandr Ginzburg and other members of the Moscow-based Helsinki Group. The following month the White House condemned Soviet authorities for the arrest of the members of the Ukrainian Helsinki Group and other dissidents such as Natan Sharansky. On 1 March, Cyrus Vance and Vice President Walter Mondale met Vladimir Bukovsky at the White House. The exiled dissident denounced a new Soviet crackdown on human rights activists and invited the administration not to give up on human rights. President Carter joined them and reassured Bukovsky that the American commitment to human rights was "permanent".[13]

White House actions were not limited to declarations and symbolic gestures. In early March, Congress approved Carter's proposal to increase the budget of Radio Free Europe and Radio Liberty. Before the vote, the president explained that "our most crucial audiences for international broadcasting are in the Soviet Union and Eastern Europe."[14] Meanwhile, National Security Advisor Zbigniew Brzezinski urged the CIA to focus on political dissidents in the Soviet Union and to define an adequate policy on their behalf. Despite the absence of detailed information, CIA analyses suggested that "President Carter's statements … give evidence of a new policy that is designed to cause trouble for the USSR."[15] Based on this conclusion, Brzezinski authorized some initiatives to support Soviet dissidents. Available sources seem to confirm that the American action resulted in an ambitious propaganda effort within Soviet boundaries based on the diffusion of forbidden literary and political works, the distribution of *samizdat*, *tamizdat* and anti-Soviet pamphlets, open support to transnational networks of activists focusing on Soviet violations of human rights and CSCE humanitarian provisions.[16]

Carter's firmness on human rights abuses outraged the Soviets. As seen from Moscow, American and Western critiques on human rights represented an ideological assault on the very foundations of the Soviet system and an unacceptable interference in its domestic affairs. The attack on human rights – the Soviets repeatedly claimed – was inconsistent with, and in opposition to, détente.

Major Soviet newspapers published a variety of articles denouncing American hypocrisies and interferences as well as the fact that the American jargon of human rights served only to cover the imperialist intentions of its capitalist promoters. An anonymous commentator lashed out at American "furor" as a way to make world public opinion look away from the many successes of socialism.[17] In another article, Georgy Arbatov argued that Carter's human rights campaign was a hypocritical assault:

> If we established close ties with the American Indians who fought at Wounded Knee, with whom we sympathize deeply, wouldn't this be regarded as interference in your domestic affairs? ... It is difficult for us to take the United States as a teacher who has a moral right to give us lessons all the time and teach us how to behave in our internal affairs. We know a bit more about the United States, about the many violations of civil rights, the situation of black Americans and so on. And for us, the United States is a country which for years has supported some of the most terroristic and dictatorial regimes, in South Korea, now Chile, and many others.[18]

In early February, Ambassador Dobrynin was instructed to protest at American interference and the hypocritical stance of the president, who ignored the fact that the Soviet system "proclaimed and provided in reality the right for work, education, social security, free medical assistance, and retirement to all Soviet citizens." Dobrynin was also supposed to list the many human rights violations occurring in the United States: "multi-million unemployment, deprivation of rights of ethnic minorities, race discrimination, unequal rights for women, the violation of citizens' rights by [State] organs, the persecution of people with progressive opinions", as well as the "systematic support by the USA of dictatorial, anti-populist regimes in some countries". Finally, he was instructed to provocatively ask his American counterpart how the United States would respond if the Soviets started a well-orchestrated campaign against those violations.[19]

To many historians, Carter's actions on human rights and the indignant Soviet response were a demonstration of Carter's inconsistent and naïve approach to international affairs. Yet, by adopting a different perspective, one that privileges the link between domestic and foreign policies, these contentious issues seem to indicate that the Carter administration was aware that the promotion of human rights in the Soviet Union and in Eastern Europe had to overcome three major obstacles.

First, the White House had to contain Soviet irritation with human rights criticism. According to the White House, the Soviets had many interests in the continuation of détente, ranging from Soviet international status and Soviet leaders' personal prestige to material benefits resulting from arms control and, possibly, from better trade relations. To the White House, this variety of interests should have convinced the Soviets to loosen repression or, at least, to tolerate American critique on human rights.[20] After all, the Soviets had rebutted American criticism but they were still committed to continue détente and to reach a new arms agreement. Moreover, the fact that the human rights policy was not anti-Soviet propaganda, but a universal initiative, could help limit negative Soviet attitudes.[21] The second obstacle concerned the leverages the United States had in order to promote human rights in the Soviet bloc. Only the continuation and the strengthening of détente could allow the United States to promote human rights in the USSR. For this reason, while criticizing the Soviets for their poor record on human rights, Carter had also sent reassuring messages to the Soviets. In August 1976, months before his election, he had urged former diplomat Averell Harriman to explain to Brezhnev and Gromyko that his priorities were détente, a reduction of nuclear weapons and strengthening economic ties with the Soviet Union. For this reason, Harriman reported to the Soviets that Carter intended "in no way to interfere in internal affairs of the Soviet Union but he is for supporting all the provisions of the Helsinki Agreement", and he was in favour of a major initiative to repeal the Jackson–Vanik amendment.[22] A similar conciliatory attitude was at the core of the first letter Carter wrote to Brezhnev. The American president underlined that his basic objectives were to reach a new SALT agreement and to work with the Soviets in order to prevent conflict around the world. He reaffirmed his will to improve trade relations between the two countries but also that the United States "cannot be indifferent to the fate of freedom and individual human rights".[23]

Here, the administration had to face the third major obstacle, namely the need to find a new domestic legitimacy for détente. To many conservative and neoconservative opponents, détente had become a one-way street that had allowed the Soviets to increase their power, had created new threats for American national security and had forced the United States to avoid any discussion of human rights with the Soviets.[24] Indeed, by early 1977, many Americans believed that something went wrong with bipolar détente. While most still supported attempts to develop a dialogue with the Soviet Union, a larger majority was determined to reaffirm American primacy vis-à-vis the USSR.[25]

Carter's strategy for dealing with the Soviet Union needed to address these problems. Apparently, the central point was an explicit rejection of Kissinger's linkage. The president had never hidden his personal hostility towards Kissinger's strategy of binding together different negotiations. Not only did he consider such a practice immoral, but he also believed that it was detrimental to American interest in reaching a new SALT agreement:

> I think we come out better in dealing with the Soviet Union if I am consistently and completely dedicated to the enhancement of human rights, not only as it deals with the Soviet Union but all other countries. I think this can legitimately be severed from our inclination to work with the Soviet Union, for instance, in reducing dependence upon atomic weapons and also in seeking mutual and balanced force reductions in Europe. I don't want the two to be tied together. I think the

previous administration, under Secretary Kissinger, thought that there ought to be this linkage; that if you mentioned human rights or if you failed to invite Mr. Solzhenitsyn to the White House that you might endanger the progress of the SALT talks.[26]

In reality, Carter was not abandoning the linkage. Rather, he was proposing a re-elaboration of it, linking together the American domestic debate and foreign policy. Whereas the main architects of détente, Richard Nixon and Henry Kissinger, had erected a barrier between domestic politics and diplomacy, Carter was welding Soviet respect for human rights to détente, and the chance to conclude a new SALT Treaty to American domestic politics. The promotion of human rights in the Soviet Union was both an objective of Carter's Soviet policy and an instrument to legit-imate détente within the United States. By safeguarding détente, the administra-tion could concretely advance human rights in the Soviet bloc and, possibly, launch an ideological challenge to Soviet hegemony. At the same time, by attacking the Soviets on human rights violations, Carter could negotiate with domestic critics of détente. Embracing conservative claims in favour of a "détente with a human face", Carter hoped to obtain their support for a new SALT agreement. As *New York Times* journalist Anthony Lewis commented in an early assessment of Carter's bipolar policy: "The Soviets forced an early and awkward test of the Carter policy when they expelled an American correspondent, threatened Andrei Sakharov and arrested other dissidents. If the president had not responded clearly, he would … [have looked] weak, and he would have hurt his chances of selling any future arms control agreement to the Senate."[27] Even more clearly, White House Press Secretary Jody Powell wrote to the president in February:

It seems to me that the Soviets should understand your feeling that it is necessary to build domestic political support for initiatives in arms control and for détente in general. One of the reasons Ford–Kissinger failed in this effort and had to back away from détente was because the American people would not support a policy which seemed to abandon our position in support of human rights. … Surely the Soviets are sophisticated enough to understand that the domestic political flexi-bility we need to make progress in other areas is enhanced by your position on human rights.[28]

Powell's memorandum continued with an invitation to explain this problem to Dobrynin "on an informal basis", something that Carter had already done.[29] Indeed, during the February meeting with the ambassador, Carter explained "it would be helpful if the Soviet Union would respond on human rights issues. … [T]his would help in dealing with Congress."[30]

To the White House, human rights and détente became the two sides of the same coin; as parts of a strategy that entailed a double negotiation. Negotiating with the Soviets, the administration was trying to use détente in order to promote human rights in the Soviet Union. Within the United States, building a new consensus on détente through human rights was paramount to Carter. Accordingly, well before the administration could set a clear strategy for human rights, it had identified American society support as one of its most fundamental aims.

Building a domestic consensus over foreign policy and détente

Within days of Carter's election, anti-détente arguments were relaunched in the American political debate. On 11 November 1976, Paul Nitze and Eugene Rostow summoned a press conference to announce the creation of the Committee on the Present Danger (CPD). Officially a bipartisan organization, the CPD was filled with Jackson's Democrats and opponents of détente. The CPD repeatedly pointed out that "the Soviet drive for world dominance based upon an unparalleled military buildup" represented a major threat for the United States.[31] Should the Soviet Union reach a condition of strategic superiority – Nitze had explained in *Foreign Affairs* just a few weeks before this announcement – it "would adjust its policies and actions in ways that would undermine the present détente situation, … resurrect the danger of nuclear confrontation or, alternatively, increase the prospect of Soviet expansion through other means of pressure".[32] Therefore, to Nitze and other CPD members, it was necessary to close this "window of vulnerability" through a programme to strengthen American nuclear arsenals, differentiate American weapons and, eventually, reach a new SALT agreement with stricter limits for Soviet weapons and better tools to verify Soviet compliance.

The White House seemed inclined to accept some of these suggestions and to develop a dialogue with the CPD and proponents of a firmer stance towards the Soviets. In March, Carter confirmed the European allies' commitment to a 3 per cent increase in defence spending and promised to develop new weapons, such as the B1 bomber, the neutron bomb and the Trident submarine.[33] Above all, in early February, Carter urged hawkish Senator Henry Jackson to prepare a memorandum with his suggestions for a new SALT agreement. Lecturing the president with the memorandum, Jackson intertwined his staunch anticommunism with strategic considerations. He reminded the president that "not all negotiable agreements are in our interest; that some agreements may be worse than none" and "that an unsound agreement now could make it difficult or impossible to obtain a sound one later". Jackson's proposal was based on a radical reduction in intercontinental missiles, with no limit for theatre forces, bombers and ALBMs (Air Launched Ballistic Missiles). In addition, Jackson specified that the new treaty should redefine heavy missiles "such that the Soviet SS-19 is not considered light". Jackson also urged the president to include a ban on the Soviet "Backfire" bomber in the new treaty. Finally, the new agreement needed better capabilities to verify compliance and the means to redress the results of a violation. Carter found the memorandum "excellent and of great help".[34]

The initial dialogue on strategic issues did not prevent the CPD and Jackson from opposing the administration's decision to appoint Paul Warnke as both Director of the United States Arms Control and Disarmament Agency (ACDA) and head of the SALT negotiations team.[35] Since 1975, Warnke had been advocating a unilateral reduction in nuclear weapons based on the assumption that the Soviets had no ambition to reach a condition of nuclear superiority. Although the White House eventually succeeded in Warnke's double appointment, this was just a partial success: a large majority (70:29) of Senators supported Warnke's appointment to the ACDA while only fifty-eight Senators voted in favour of him leading the SALT negotiating team, far below the necessary threshold for the ratification of the potential SALT II Treaty.[36]

If Carter wanted to win Senate ratification of the SALT II Treaty, once it had been negotiated, he had to convince critics and opponents of détente that the agreement was in America's interest and that détente itself was not a form of appeasement with Soviet totalitarianism, as they had been claiming since the early 1970s. Building on their campaign to push human rights in East–West relations, Carter could prove détente did not imply a renunciation of American values. On the contrary, it could become a more aggressive policy – one that could engage the Soviets on human rights and fundamental freedoms.

From the start, Carter's human rights policy had been also a public relations programme that was supposed to rebuild a consensus for foreign policy in general and for détente specifically. One area of agreement among Carter's foreign policy advisers was the need to develop a cooperative attitude with Congress. During the electoral campaign, both Vance and Brzezinski suggested that a morally based foreign policy with the promotion of human rights as its central pillar could help with Congress and the American public.

Carter's human rights campaign found broad support within the United States. The American Council of Captive Nations, the NCSJ, many local chapters of Amnesty International and the president of the American Bar Association, Jerome Shestak, were among the first to commend Carter's firm stance on human rights. The Executive Committee of the World Slovak Congress approved a resolution guaranteeing the organization's support to what was labelled the "Carter doctrine on human rights". Similarly, the Ukrainian Congress Committee of America organized a demonstration in support of Carter's campaign.[37] Soviet-born cellist Mstislav Rostropovich lauded the "noble, brilliant and courageous" defence of human rights. Months later, Carter would invite him to give a televized concert from the White House in tribute to freedom.[38] Polls reported high approval ratings among American citizens. According to public interest opinion research in July 1977, 59 per cent of Democrats and 49 per cent of Republicans supported the new course Carter had given to American foreign policy, even if human rights would be detrimental to a new arms control treaty.[39] Congressional reactions were similar. Both liberals and conservatives in Congress commended the renewed emphasis on human rights. Liberals appreciated both the attempt to revive détente on moral grounds and Carter's consistent approach to human rights, which did not spare criticism of America's authoritarian allies, such as Argentina, Brazil or South Korea. For example, in February 1977, Don J. Pease (D – Ohio) sent a message to the president announcing he would introduce a resolution to praise his approach to human rights. Similarly, Senator Howard Metzembaum (D – Ohio) invited Carter to continue with his strong defence of human rights in the world.[40] On 2 March, Frank Church admitted he was "delighted that the new administration" had clarified that "we are not only prepared to speak out in favor of human rights wherever it is appropriate, but that ... we are also ready to cut back on American aid programmes, particularly military aid programmes, that heretofore have gone to non-communist governments of totalitarian character, where the jails are filled with political prisoners". The following day Benjamin Rosenthal (D – New York) lauded Carter's decision to address Soviet violations of human rights within the framework provided by détente.[41]

For their part, conservatives commended Carter's firmness in asking the Soviets to adhere to the Helsinki Agreement. In late January, both houses approved by a large majority (90 votes in favour in the Senate, 400 in the House) a resolution that, with "the full endorsement of the administration", urged the Soviet Union to comply with the "Helsinki declaration, including their pledge to facilitate freer movement of people". Significantly, Republicans Edward Brooke, Clifford Case, Pete Domenici, Mark Hatfield, Jacob Javits, Paul D. Laxalt and conservative Democrats Jackson and Moynihan were among the cosponsors of the resolution.[42] Jackson and Moynihan were among the first to commend Carter's declaration and to underline that Congressional action on human rights was "parallel to the initiatives undertaken by President Carter. ... [I]n speaking on behalf of fundamental human rights, the president of the United States has the clear and unambiguous support of the Senate and the House and the people of the United States."[43] Even Republican Jack Kemp celebrated Carter's "courage and conviction as an example to us all to speak out for the principles on which our country was founded", and he remarked that only with the Soviets' realization that "we will not forsake our stand in the name of détente, SALT, or the Olympic Games, can we make an honest attempt to reach a long-term understanding with them".[44]

The Helsinki Commission contributed to strengthening Carter's stance on human rights. Presenting the second Congressional hearings on the Final Act, chairman Dante Fascell pointed out that both his commission and the White House were working to renew and sustain détente. To him, talking about Soviet violations of human rights was not detrimental to détente; "on the contrary, we seek only to further a process of understanding between two very different and long-opposed systems".[45] Similarly, in February 1977, sixty-three Representatives addressed a letter to the president to congratulate him on his stance on human rights.[46] The following month, fifty-seven Senators joined the chorus of those who officially supported Carter's campaign.[47]

The apparent cohesion of the American public and Congress on human rights hid the dual-headed interest on human rights that had contributed to the erosion of Kissinger's détente. While everyone agreed on the importance of human rights to American foreign policy; its political role and meaning was a contested one. Ultraconservative "Senator Jesse Helms's endorsement of your standing on human rights" – a liberal member of the North Carolina Legislative Assembly wrote to the president – "should be reason enough for you to assess your position."[48] Since the last months of the electoral campaign, Carter's challenge had been how to turn this dual-headed attention into a single unifying principle. Early Congressional approvals were just a partial achievement. Conservatives and neoconservatives were determined to challenge the Soviet Union and fight détente; liberals and neo-internationalists continued to advocate a global human rights campaign, in order to free American foreign policy from its bipolar obsession.

Soviet reactions and the failure of the Moscow summit

Soviet reaction to Carter's human rights offensive was not limited to protest. On the contrary, it was a multifaceted and multilevel response. Apparently contradictory, it intertwined a counterpropaganda offensive and a new crackdown on dissidents but also some pragmatic concessions.

Early Soviet reactions to Carter's election were not totally negative. The Kremlin openly welcomed Carter's remarks on détente and arms control. Nevertheless, the Soviets had good reason to be worried once Carter took office.[49] First, although the Soviets believed that Carter and Secretary of State Vance were truly committed to strengthening détente, they also feared the president could fall under the influence of National Security Advisor Zbigniew Brzezinski, who was perceived as an uncompromising Cold Warrior. His Polish origins and his academic experience foreshadowed a firmer approach to bipolar affairs.[50] A second problem was the new regionalist approach within the State Department, namely the attempt to cope with global challenges by considering them in their local, indeed regional, framework rather than viewing them through the traditional bipolar lens. This new approach to international affairs was mostly a result of Vance's appointment as Secretary of State. As he had announced to Carter during the transition period, as Secretary of State he would prevent bipolar affairs to dominate American foreign policy, trying to deal with them according to their own specificities. While this approach could have contributed to reducing bipolar tensions, it wounded Soviet pride, which found in the very nature of détente the recognition it craved from the United States, signalling its equal status.[51]

Nevertheless, it was Carter's firm stance on human rights that fuelled tensions between Moscow and Washington. As Ambassador Dobrynin recalled in his memoirs: "inside the Kremlin" the reaction was a mix of "indignation, irritation, and concern".[52] To the Soviets, Carter's actions were not only in opposition to the very nature of détente, but they were also fuelling unrest and leading a transnational movement that was highlighting Soviet violations of human rights. As the CIA documented, unrest in the Soviet bloc was constantly growing, increasing "chronic Soviet fears of a spillover into the Soviet Union itself". Indeed, new groups were established and, confirming Soviet fears, they openly submitted petitions, letters and appeals to the White House urging Carter not to step back from his human rights commitment. "The US human rights offensive", CIA analysts pointed out, "heartened Soviet dissidents, and temporarily emboldened them to make more vigorous protests and to channel their appeals directly to the US Administration."[53]

Beyond diplomatic protests, the Kremlin's attempt to cope with Carter's campaign was based on the suppression of dissent. Soviet authorities conducted new arrests and intimidations in early 1977 to curb dissidents' activities. A new crackdown was supposed to show "the ruling circles of Western countries … the ineffectiveness of their policy of sabotage and pressure towards the Soviet Union. We should emphasize that in keeping with the policy of détente, we will decisively stop any attempts at interference in our internal affairs and denigration of the socialist achievements."[54] Communist Party officials from the USSR, Czechoslovakia, Poland, the German Democratic Republic, Hungary, Romania, Cuba and Mongolia reiterated this commitment during a March meeting in Sofia that called for ideological cooperation for a "decisive battle" against the human rights campaign started by "imperialist circles".[55]

In addition to arrests, the Soviets used an increased propaganda effort to undermine dissidents' credibility. In January, for example, *Pravda* published an article denouncing the dissidents as just "a little heap of renegades … they exist only because they are supported, paid and praised by the West". On other occasions, Soviet authorities referred to them as "enemies of the state" or "traitors", while Vladimir Bukovsky, who had been received at the White House, was "only a small step from … terrorism".[56] Activists for free emigration were frequently labelled "social parasites", traitors and "agents of Zionism". Anti-Zionistic campaigns were not new in the USSR but now they became more frequent and vitriolic. Soviet television even broadcast a documentary film, *Buyers of Souls*, which denounced them as agents of an anti-Soviet conspiracy orchestrated by Western countries. According to viewers, the sixty-five-minute documentary openly incited anti-Semitism. While the film revealed the names and addresses of Jewish activists, the commentary repeated that "these people are all soldiers of Zionism within the Soviet Union, and it is here that they carry out their subversive activities".[57] In early March, S.L. Lipavski denounced the alleged connection between the CIA and refuseniks. In an open letter published by *Izvestia*, he confessed to being in collusion with the Americans. Together with Vladimir Slepak and Natan Sharansky, he stated, he had been ordered to fuel protest and to persuade Jewish families in the Soviet Union to emigrate in order to destroy the foundation of the Soviet State.[58]

Nevertheless, by late February, many in the Politburo noted that Soviet actions were not preventing Carter from other interventions in Soviet domestic affairs. Accordingly, Gromyko, Ustinov and Andropov stated that Carter was trying an "unacceptable and futile" attempt to "impose on us his own approach to the basis of Soviet–American relations even before we set about negotiating".[59] For this reason, they urged Brezhnev to write to the American president and reiterate Soviet indignation. The letter, signed on 25 February, blamed the United States and its approach to "the so-called human rights" for the worsening in bipolar relations. Contemptuously, Brezhnev clarified once again that:

We have no intention to enforce our customs on your country or other countries, but we will not allow interference in our internal affairs, no matter what kind of pseudo-humane pretense is used for the purpose. And how should we treat such a situation, when the President of the USA sends a letter to General Secretary of the CC CPSU and at the same time starts a correspondence with a renegade, who proclaimed himself to be an enemy of the Soviet State and who stands against, normal, good relations between the USSR and the USA? We should not like our patience to be tested while dealing with any matters of foreign policy, including the questions of Soviet–American relations. The Soviet Union must not be dealt with like that.[60]

Brezhnev's firmness was echoed by Arbatov, who met with the American ambassador, Malcolm Toon. After repeating the traditional litany of accusations, Arbatov openly threatened the collapse of the forthcoming Moscow summit between Gromyko and Vance to discuss arms control.[61]

As Vance headed to Moscow in late March 1977, he found himself in a highly charged atmosphere. To make things worse, Carter had anticipated the content of the American "deep-cuts proposal" just days before Vance's departure. Not only was such an openness a radical departure from the confidentiality that surrounded previous SALT talks, but the content of the proposal was hardly acceptable to the Soviets since it was calling for a radical reduction of land-based missiles that constituted the bulk of Moscow's strategic forces.[62] Once in Moscow, Vance further bemused the Soviets by presenting two different proposals: beyond the "deep-cuts proposal, the United States elaborated also a Vladivostok-style proposal that foreshadowed a 10 percent reduction in weapons".[63]

The Soviets rejected both proposals, without "even a hint of a counterproposal".[64] Human rights criticism fuelled Soviet irritation, but it could hardly explain the Soviet rebuff. The American proposal itself contained a number of problems. First, by arriving in Moscow with two conflicting schemes, Vance showed an ambiguous and dismissive stance on arms control. Second, both Carter's early remarks and Vance's negotiations confirmed that the Americans were considering the "deep-cuts proposal" as the real basis for negotiations, thus departing from the 1974 Vladivostok Agreements. On the contrary, to Brezhnev, "Vladivostok had become politically sacrosanct" and any new arms control treaty should be based on it.[65] Moreover, the administration was acting on the assumption that the Soviets would accept any arms control plan and that the major obstacle for a new SALT agreement, if not the only real obstacle, was Senate ratification. By advancing a proposal inspired by Jackson's priorities, the Carter administration was trying to build a further bridge to anti-détente forces within the United States, instead of laying the ground for serious negotiations with Moscow.[66]

The Soviets' strategy to cope with human rights criticism also considered some degree of yielding to international pressures in order to address American concerns. While Soviet leaders acknowledged that their record was still incomplete, they were working for improvements. After all, in late 1977 the Soviets adopted a new Constitution that included a series of civil and political rights – such as freedom of speech, of assembly, of religious belief and worship – as well as social and economic rights. Brezhnev himself dwelt on the democratic features of the Soviet system, "a democracy that covers the political, social, and economic spheres, … social justice and social equality".[67] Beyond the legislative and formal adjustment, the Soviets fully comprehend that American bipolar policy was largely shaped by the domestic debate and began considering measures to ease Carter's domestic dilemmas. They even considered inviting Senator Jackson – the champion of free emigration of Soviet Jews and the irreconcilable opponent of arms control – to Moscow.[68] Even more important, the Kremlin favoured some pragmatic concessions on human rights issues. Neutralization of the American critique and the strengthening of détente even touched on cooperative actions on human rights, at least in those areas in which the American public was particularly concerned: free emigration of Soviet Jews and the CSCE third basket. In early 1977, both the White House and the NCSJ registered a constant increase in the number of Soviet Jews allowed to leave the Soviet Union. Equally important, there were reasonable steps on some of the most controversial CSCE issues: some family-reunification cases found a solution, the jamming of Western radio was interrupted and the publication and circulation of Western books, newspapers, magazines and films was encouraged. The Soviets even approved the release of Mikhail Shtern from gaol and Vladimir Borisov from a psychiatric hospital, as well as the concession of an exit visa to many refuseniks, such as Ludmilla Alexeyeva and a member of the Georgian "Helsinki Group". Commenting on these concessions, Brzezinski pointed out that Carter's campaign "*is* having an impact on improvement of human rights abroad [emphasis in original]".[69] For this reason, Brzezinski could claim both that American pressures were producing an early success and that, despite early protests and criticism, Carter's firm stance on human rights did not destroy the possibility of relaunching détente and reaching a new SALT agreement.[70]

Western allies' reactions

While the White House tended to minimize its faux pas at the Moscow summit, the failure of the summit opened the Pandora's box of Western European doubts on Carter's human rights campaign. This was an unexpected result for a campaign that was meant to renew the American image abroad and to heal the rift between the United States and its Western allies that Carter had inherited from the Kissinger years. Moreover, Carter's foreign policy was based also on growing concern for human rights manifested by Western European governments and European supranational institutions. During the early 1970s, the European Community had taken centre stage in introducing human rights provisions in the Helsinki negotiations, as well as in addressing human rights abuses in North–South relations.[71]

In his first months in office, Carter had found mixed and contradictory responses coming from Western Europe. Public opinion and the press had generally been favourable to the human rights campaign. In early 1977, European media celebrated Carter as a new leader who succeeded in renewing America's image abroad through a human rights policy that was perceived as non-selective and universal. The London-based *Financial Times* celebrated Carter, who succeeded in giving America "a renewed confidence in itself", in which "the guilt of the Vietnam and Watergate periods has gone".[72] However hyperbolic, these opinions were shared by some prominent European politicians, such as President Giuseppe Saragat of Italy and the Christian Democrat

President of the German Bundestag, Karl Carstens. Polls conducted by the United States Information Agency confirmed that the European public perceived Carter's firm stance on human rights as a necessary reply to Soviet violations and abuses. Many Europeans, though not a majority, would support Carter's human rights policy even though this would weaken détente.[73] Conversely, many Western European governments, as well as EC institutions, cautioned Carter against making human rights a central issue in East–West relations, fearing that his open diplomacy could lead to a new crackdown on dissidents, as well as to new difficulties in East–West relations. Relations between the two Europes had been improving since the late 1960s and Carter's human rights diplomacy was now threatening this progress.[74] In March, for example, a Congressional mission in Strasbourg, which included Christopher Dodd, Donald Fraser, Tom Harkin and Douglas Walgren, noted that a "fair degree of concern" was emerging over American criticism of the Soviet record on human rights and the possibility of "a Soviet withdrawal" from the Helsinki Accords. In a separate note, Dodd pointed out "a definite desire on the part of the Europeans" to see the issue of human rights downplayed. Nevertheless, he also invited Carter not to accept such a pressure because "we should not be reluctant to state the facts as they are, and that, indeed, any conscious alteration of our stance on human rights … can only serve to weaken our overall position in the negotiations".[75]

Transatlantic disagreements on human rights multiplied over the following months. In part, they stemmed from different interpretations of what constitute human rights. Based on the tradition of national welfare systems and on a European social policy enshrined by the 1961 European Social Charter, most Western Europeans were comfortable with a broad definition of human rights that encompassed social and economic rights as well. Conversely, in his April speech Secretary of State Vance had been unequivocal: while the United States recognized social and economic rights as human rights, rights relating to the inviolability of the person would take precedence. Moreover, Europeans' scepticism towards Carter's human rights policy depended on its impact on détente. Since the early 1970s, Western Europeans had come to see détente as a dynamic process, whose aims were to promote and reinforce economic, cultural and social interconnections and exchanges between the two Europes, to make frontiers more permeable and, eventually, to overcome the Cold War in Europe.[76] Carter's firmness on Soviet human rights violations was a threat to all of this.

Not surprisingly, after the failure of the Moscow summit, Western European governments voiced their doubts on Carter's human rights stance more resolutely. President Giscard d'Estaing of France and Chancellor Schmidt of West Germany repeatedly thundered against the American overemphasis on human rights. Giscard d'Estaing did not hesitate to show his personal doubts. After avoiding an official meeting with Soviet émigré Andrei Amalrik, who had been expelled from the USSR in late 1976, he claimed that French foreign policy was based on "pragmatic actions", rather than public addresses in favour of dissidents in a foreign country. On another occasion, Giscard celebrated the success of quiet diplomacy and reciprocal accommodation, as opposed to the negative reactions open diplomacy and interference in domestic affairs could elicit.[77] The following month, in a *Newsweek* interview, the French president reiterated that Carter's open diplomacy on human rights put détente in jeopardy.[78]

Schmidt was even firmer. He dismissed Carter's human rights campaign as inconsistent with détente. For this reason, he also refused to meet Andrei Amalrik and threatened to withdraw the licences for Radio Free Europe and Radio Liberty that were broadcasting from West Germany. Based in Frankfurt, the radio stations were perceived as a major obstacle in détente on account of their growing coverage of dissidents' activities in Eastern Europe and in the Soviet Union.[79] Years later, Schmidt wrote in his memoirs: "from my European point of view of the situation, Carter's first response to Soviet policies in 1977 contained serious flaws. The accusation he publicly leveled over and over, that Soviet citizens were deprived of all human rights, could not, of course, alter their lives in any way, but it would inevitably embitter the Soviet leadership."[80] It is impossible to say how much of this condemnation stemmed from personal antipathy or divergent priorities for international relations. Nevertheless, the German Chancellor truly believed that Carter's campaign represented a major threat to the dialogue his country was developing with the Soviet Union and Eastern Europe. From an economic perspective, Germany was the European country that was benefiting the most from the dialogue with Eastern countries and the one that had most direct interest in stabilizing détente.[81] In addition, Carter's firm stance threatened another major success of German *Ostpolitik*, namely the constant increase in the number of ethnic Germans and GDR citizens emigrating to the Bundesrepublik (reaching over 60,000 each year between 1974 and 1977). During the two-year period between 1976 and 1977, nearly 8 million West Germans were allowed to cross the boundary and meet their relatives and friends living in the East. To Schmidt, these outcomes were made possible by quiet diplomacy, while the small drop in 1976 in the number of East Germans emigrating to the West was a direct effect of Carter's electoral slogans.[82] Finally, Schmidt's scepticism towards Carter's human rights policy was also a consequence of the German domestic debate where the CDU/CSU, the Christian Democrat opposition party, built on Carter's campaign and urged Schmidt to take a firm stance towards the GDR and its human rights violations. From Schmidt's perspective, convincing Carter to limit his public criticism of Soviet abuses could have assisted in the Chancellor's goal of containing domestic criticism.[83]

Even the British government took a nuanced stance and could not avoid underlining how Carter's campaign had increased international tensions. While officially supporting Carter's firm approach to human rights, Prime Minister James Callaghan and Foreign Minister David Owen expressed some concerns about how the American government was approaching human rights violations in the Soviet Union.[84] Between February and March, the British government tried to better understand the American stance with hopes of fostering a compromise within NATO on the role of human rights in East–West negotiations. After meeting Brzezinski, the British ambassador in Washington explained to his government the rationale for Carter's firmness. In a very detailed analysis, he underlined how Carter's approach to human rights in the USSR was meant to balance domestic pressures with his "personal commitment to human rights":

> [Carter] knows that he still faces hurdles ahead in securing Congressional approval for the international agreement which he hopes to reach, the Panama Canal, SALT II, a Middle East settlement, the control of conventional arms sales and negotiations with Latin America and in the far East, all contain elements which cannot fail to arouse the opposition of formidable domestic lobbies, strongly represented in Congress. ... Strong popular backing will be necessary to overcome his various opponents. This line of reasoning is at the centre of his thinking on human rights. By continuing to speak out, by reinforcing his remarks through concrete actions (such as asking Congress for more funds for Radio Liberty and Radio Free Europe) and by renouncing the concept of linkage, he is in effect asking the Soviet leadership to stand by their own definition of peaceful coexistence. He rejects the strand in Kissinger's thinking that it was right sometimes to sacrifice principle for expediency, which contributed to the distrust with which Kissinger came to be viewed by opponents of détente. He is thus establishing his credentials as a man of principle, fit to negotiate with the Soviet Union. In this way, he is seeking to outflank the conservative opposition, which he now faces in Congress and in the country to a SALT II treaty.

He also outlined two major risks in Carter's strategy. Internationally, Carter assumed that the Soviets were willing to accept the new rules of détente. Domestically, the president "may be asking more than the American public ... are able or willing to deliver. But his aims are imaginative and exciting."[85] Accordingly, the ambassador invited his government to fully support Carter's stance vis-à-vis the Soviet Union. To do that, he suggested, first, that British diplomats should explain to the Soviets that Carter attributed equal importance to the human rights campaign and negotiations for arms limitations and, second, to work for a common position among EC member states that should be close – or at least not hostile – to the American one.[86]

The British initiative seemed to produce a concrete outcome in April 1977, when EC foreign ministers agreed on a common declaration that recalled the importance of human rights in East–West relations and that EC members attributed great importance to respect for all CSCE principles.[87] A transatlantic split over human rights was avoided, but a cohesive Western attitude was still far off. On the eve of the Belgrade CSCE Review Conference, the United States had to face a further challenge: aligning European allies to speak with a single Western voice in Belgrade.

From early divisions to a human rights strategy for communist Europe

The failure of the Moscow summit in March 1977 and European criticism convinced the White House to revise its approach to bipolar affairs. For a very short period, from

April to July, bipolar cooperation took precedence over ideological competition and human rights were confined to quiet diplomacy and behind-the-scene channels.

Within the administration, Secretary of State Cyrus Vance, his principal adviser on Soviet matters, Marshall Shulman, and the American ambassador in Moscow, Malcom Toon, were firm proponents of a more cooperative attitude towards the Soviets. Toon was the first to point out explicitly that the human rights campaign was detrimental to détente. After Carter wrote to Sakharov in February, Toon invited the president to tone down his statements and to send Brezhnev two messages: a written note to clarify that his correspondence with Sakharov should not be considered an interference in Soviet affairs but a demonstration of the traditional American commitment to human rights, and a private message to reaffirm his personal commitment to détente and to respect Soviet sovereignty, as well as to explain that the "U.S. public and Congress feels much more deeply about human rights than apparently the Soviets think".[88] A few days later, he added that the situation was more serious than Washington perceived: "the Soviets see the human rights movement here as a direct challenge to their system and its image abroad. They also regard USG's public endorsement of the dissidents as blatant, impermissible interference in their internal affairs, as well as an effort to drive the wedge deeper between themselves and the non-ruling Western Communist Parties."[89]

Secretary of State Vance shared Toon's evaluations. He blamed American arrogance towards the Soviet Union and the polemics on human rights for the deadlock in SALT negotiations. He argued that the administration should relieve the pressure on the Soviets and avoid identification with the dissidents.[90] Indeed, when Vance met Soviet Minister Gromyko in May, arms control negotiations took centre stage, leaving human rights in the background. The meeting was a success, which allowed for an initial agreement on a basic scheme for a new SALT Treaty, and reinforced the position of those within the administration who were advocating reduced emphasis on human rights, and, eventually, a revision of the Jackson–Vanik amendment.[91]

Marshall Shulman shared Toon's assessment. Shulman had a long record of commitment to détente. Although he was aware that US–Soviet conflict had not come to an end, he believed that East–West tensions were based mostly on misperceptions and that relations could be improved. For this reason, he was among the first to propose a reversal on human rights in bipolar affairs. Already in January 1977, he had written in *Foreign Affairs* that:

> [I]t should be clear that the effort to compel changes in Soviet institutions and practices by frontal demands on the part of other governments is likely to be counterproductive. … It seems reasonable to believe that easing of repression is more likely to result from evolutionary forces within the society under prolonged conditions of reduced international tension than from external demands for change and the siege mentality they would reinforce.

To Shulman, the Moscow summit and its consequences confirmed his analysis. He blamed the United States for the sudden worsening in bipolar relations: the "deep cuts proposal" for the new SALT agreement, the human rights campaign, the lack of coordination in official declarations from White House representatives and the lack of any progress on trade relations had angered Moscow. Shulman argued that the White House needed to work for a radical improvement in bipolar relations through a new SALT proposal and a reduction of public criticism on human rights.[92]

Shulman's conclusions were confirmed by a new analysis made by Toon on the "prospects for ... a further deterioration". Toon listed a number of areas of growing misunderstanding between Washington and Moscow and blamed American open diplomacy on human rights as responsible for bipolar disagreements:

> In general, Soviets are still inclined to perceive our policies on human rights as directed specifically at them, and their reaction has been highly emotional. And there is always the chance that our relations may be further exacerbated by tougher Soviet measures against the dissidents – e.g. a Sharansky show trial.[93]

For this reason, Toon concluded that the administration should discuss human rights only through quiet diplomacy channels and strengthen trade relations with the Soviet Union, eventually modifying or repealing the Jackson–Vanik amendment.[94] To Vance, Toon and Shulman, normalization of trade relations and the repeal of the Jackson–Vanik amendment were key to stabilizing bipolar relations. A window of opportunity seemed to open when Soviet émigré Andrei Amalrik and Representative Paul Simon (D – Illinois) opposed the amendment. They were echoed by Senator Bob Dole (R – Kansas). In April, Dole submitted a proposal to authorize "certain credits or credit guarantees for the sale of agricultural products to non-market economy countries" that – not too implicitly – bypassed some of the restrictions of the Jackson–Vanik amendment. In June, Vance openly endorsed Senator Dole's proposal.[95]

In the same period, Secretary of Treasury Michael Blumenthal touched upon the repeal of the Jackson–Vanik amendment in a meeting of the Joint US–USSR Commercial Commission. However, he clarified that before any action to repeal the legislation could be taken, the Soviets should engage on three fronts: the Soviet press should avoid attacks on Carter, the conclusion of the Sharansky case should be acceptable to the American public and the Soviets should accept a more liberal policy concerning emigration and family reunification. Other representatives of the executive branch sent similar messages to their Soviet counterparts. During the plenary session, Blumenthal once again linked the prospect for détente and trade relations to the American political debate. A general improvement in bipolar relations – human rights included – would have a positive impact on a Congress that was extremely sensitive to human rights issues.[96]

The window to repeal the amendment immediately closed. Jackson and the NCSJ openly criticized the apparent new course on the Jackson–Vanik amendment and threatened to fight every single proposal the White House advanced on foreign policy issues.[97] Jackson's firmness forced the White House to back off. Vance retracted and assured Jackson that the administration opposed any attempt to repeal his amendment. Brzezinski invited the president to publicly reaffirm that the administration fully supported the Jackson–Vanik amendment and that it was opposed to the Dole proposal in order to avoid clashing with Jackson and his allies. With no hesitation, the president sent a handwritten note to Jackson in which he expressed his "doubts that the Jackson–Vanik amendment served the purpose of increasing Jewish outmigration from the Soviet Union", but he also clarified that he would enforce it and that the White House was determined not to support Dole's proposal.[98]

For the moment, the White House averted a clash with Jackson's forces. A cautious approach prevailed. With a view to upcoming difficult debates within Congress, the White House concluded that "we will need the full support of Jackson and other key Senators. Thus, it would be a major tactical mistake to launch an Administration initiative to repeal or modify the Jackson–Vanik and Stevenson amendment now."[99] However, this false move on the Jackson–Vanik amendment had two major consequences. First, many observers within the United States began to point out that Carter's human rights discourse was losing its strength. Jackson and Moynihan expressed their doubts on a foreign policy that they perceived as accepting Soviet claims on both human rights and arms control.[100] Second, disagreements within the administration grew. Hamilton Jordan and Zbigniew Brzezinski openly opposed Vance's suggestions. According to Jordan, Carter's broad programme for foreign affairs could face many problems in the US domestic debate. The administration had to develop "a comprehensive approach for winning public and Congressional support for specific foreign policy initiatives". To win over the opposition he argued that Carter should accept some conservative proposals:

To the extent that the issues we are dealing with have "liberal" or "conservative" connotation, our position on these particular issues is consistently "liberal." We must do what we can to present these issues to the public in a non-ideological way and not allow them to undermine your image as a moderate-conservative.[101]

Significantly, after reading the memorandum, Carter commented on it "to challenge Soviets for influence is conservative".[102]

Brzezinski, too, invited the president to publicly intervene on human rights in order to clarify the campaign's aims and contents because "some members in Congress are seizing on human rights as an excuse for blocking constructive initiatives in the area of development aid or at least as an opportunity for attaching all sorts of restrictive conditions on such aid".[103] He also invited Carter to continue with his firm stance on Soviet violations of human rights because:

Here I think we have done very well. Our commitment to human rights has put the Soviet leadership on the defensive in an area where it had free ride for at least the last eight years, and perhaps even for the last fifteen, if we count from the start of the Vietnamese War. The reason that Brezhnev et al are reacting so strongly to your insistence on human rights is not because they fear that we will make human rights a condition for our relations with them; they fear this insistence because they know that human rights is a compelling idea, and that associating America with this idea not only strengthens us, but it also generates pressures from within their own system. Ideologically, they are thus on the defensive.[104]

Brzezinski would repeat this idea several times over the following months. There was no reason to retreat from open diplomacy: not only did the Soviets continue to have high stakes in détente, but they were also on the defensive, thus proving the correctness of Carter's ideological weapon. Equally important, Brzezinski added, the American public was openly supporting firmness and open diplomacy.[105]

Over the summer of 1977, the administration definitely abandoned Vance's cautious approach. It openly addressed the case of Natan Sharansky, who had been accused of being a spy for the American government. The president himself denied publicly any connection between him and the administration, thus implying that the trial was a political one.[106] More importantly, the president signed three documents that defined the American approach to human rights violations in East–West relations: the Presidential Review Memorandum/NSC-28 on human rights, Presidential Directive 18 on bipolar relations and Presidential Directive 21 on Eastern Europe.

In July, Carter signed the Presidential Review Memorandum/NSC-28 on human rights. Prepared by the Christopher Group, the document defined a broad framework for Carter's human rights diplomacy. While it left many key questions on human rights unanswered, it offered a basic outline for a case-by-case approach to human rights. Accordingly, the study identified four groups of states –Western democracies, communist states, Third World nations and gross violators of human rights – recommending certain types of actions and expectations, ranging from public condemnation to economic sanctions.

Sharing Vance's cautious approach to human rights, the document called for a policy that would "keep in mind the limits" of American power, for the American "ability to change human rights practices in other society is limited", as well as the gravity of the violations and the existence of other American interests and national security considerations. As such, it envisaged a number of constraints on American actions, exceptions in the campaign and limited outcomes. The tone of the document, however, reflected Brzezinski's considerations on challenging the Soviet Union more than it echoed Vance's ideas. While it recognized that adopting human rights as a compass for foreign policy would substitute "in our dealings with non-communist countries a standard based on government behavior for an increasingly outmoded Marxist-non-Marxist standard", it conceived the human rights campaign as an assault on the Soviet Union. Ideologically, it would assist the United States "in the philosophical debate with the Soviet Union as to the type of society worth developing, thus helping us in those European states with competitive communist parties and in much of the Third World". Pragmatically, it would strengthen "the growth in the Soviet Union and Eastern Europe of democratic forces which may in time contribute to the development of more open societies".[107]

There was no contradiction between the proclaimed universal commitment to human rights and the anti-Soviet crusade it was proposing. First, a global approach to human rights would enhance the American commitment to "a world of nations whose systems of government and societies reflect individual and dignity and thus reject totalitarianism". A consistent approach to human rights in the world was a prerequisite for rebranding the image of the United States as a beacon of democracy and human rights, as well as for confronting the Soviet Union on ideological terms. Second, the Christopher Group was conscious that "Congress, the media, and the public" would judge the human rights campaign from its implementation in the Soviet case. Given such a prominence, it was fundamental to follow a consistent approach to Soviet violations.[108] The Christopher Group acknowledged that American efforts towards the promotion of human rights in the USSR and communist Europe "should remain firm and consistent but non-polemical", although "major changes … will not take place in the short-term". Nevertheless, it was possible to "positively influence trends in the long-term and encourage improvements in limited but important areas in the short-term".[109]

Reversing what Vance, Toon and Shulman had been advocating until that moment, PRM/NSC-28 specified that there was "no evidence that the U.S. human rights policy has yet impact on specific bargaining positions in important negotiations". Accordingly, human rights should become a fundamental part of bipolar détente. Making explicit what had become the distinguishing feature of Carter's human rights policy in the bipolar context, namely the connection between human rights and SALT as well as the interdependence between the American domestic debate and détente with the Soviets, the Christopher Group identified a clear strategy for the simultaneous promotion of human rights and the strengthening of détente. The White House had to use arms control and, eventually, the prospect for trade links as leverage for the advancement of human rights within the USSR and, at the same time, use human rights for the promotion of détente within the United States:

> Speaking out on human rights may be more tolerable to Moscow, and we may be therefore more effective, if we maintain approximately equal emphasis on our other major interests with respect to the Soviet Union. If we are making progress in other areas, e.g., SALT, the Soviets may be more responsive to our human rights approaches. We should tell the Soviets that while we do not link human rights to other issues, progress on that front will at least be conductive of progress on other fronts. Of course, while we deny a linkage, the Soviets have it within their power to create one.
>
> …
>
> Public and Congressional support for our policies toward the Soviet Union will be promoted by frank explanation and discussion of the realities of the human rights situation in the Soviet Union. Our cooperative relationship with the joint Legislative-Executive CSCE Commission can be useful in this regard.[110]

In August, Carter signed Presidential Directive 18 on "U.S. National Strategy" prepared by the Policy Review Committee. Despite the importance the White House attributed to North–South relations, the Soviet Union remained the central concern of the Carter administration. Bipolar affairs would continue to offer a mix of cooperation and confrontation, and, despite the limits on American power, the United States continued to enjoy many "critical advantages", such as allies "who genuinely share similar aspirations".[111] American diplomacy should have five major objectives: counterbalance

Soviet military power and "adverse influence in key areas, particularly Europe, the Middle East and East Asia"; "compete politically with the Soviet Union by pursuing the basic American commitment to human rights and national independence"; "seek Soviet cooperation" in resolving local conflicts that could multiply tensions between the United States and the Soviet Union; promote American security through negotiations with the Soviet Union for a new SALT Treaty; and "seek to involve" the Soviets in the management of global challenges.[112] Despite the emphasis on détente and arms control, Carter's Soviet policy would differ from that of the previous eight years. While Nixon and Kissinger had denied the importance of human rights and ideological competition with the Soviets, Carter and Brzezinski put human rights under the spotlight, considering them as a tool both to trigger a transformation of the Soviet system and to challenge it ideologically and for global influence.

Brzezinski's contribution to the Presidential Directive was clear: while détente was meant to stabilize bipolar relations, it should reinvigorate ideological competition, as he had been advocating since the late 1960s. His influence was even clearer in the third document adopted during the summer, Presidential Directive no. 21, "Eastern Europe". Since the mid-1960s Brzezinski had been advocating an American policy of "positive engagement of Eastern Europe" to stimulate differentiation within the Eastern bloc and to reduce Soviet influence over Eastern countries. Now it was time, NSC staff member Gregory Treverton wrote in April 1977, to "frame a coherent policy where one has not existed".[113] The Policy Review Committee debated four possible options:

1 bias towards Eastern European States that act with some independence of Moscow (presumably, Romania, Yugoslavia, Poland);
2 bias towards those that are somewhat liberal internally (e.g. Hungary, but not Romania);
3 bias towards those that are either relatively independent or liberal (all of the above);
4 efforts to expand US contacts across the board to the "minimum floor" now existing only with Poland, Romania and Yugoslavia.[114]

Presidential Directive 21 re-elaborated the four options, inviting the United States to "demonstrably show its preference for Eastern European countries that are either relatively liberal internally or relatively independent internationally" in order to "enhance their independence internationally and to increase their degree of internal liberalisation". This plan called for the United States to favour Poland and Romania through official visits to ensure the continuation of exchange programmes and the confirmation of MFN status; to improve relations with Hungary, in order to demonstrate that "its position is similar to Poland and Romania, including the possibility of a waiver of the Jackson–Vanik amendment"; and to limit relations with Bulgaria, Czechoslovakia and Eastern Germany until "there is demonstrated progress along one of the two dimensions".[115]

Information coming from activists across the Soviet bloc documented that it was possible to differentiate among countries of the Warsaw Pact based on human rights. The *Chronicle of Human Rights in the USSR* reported that "in Poland human rights activists are championing, with apparent success, the rights of the workers who protested against increased food prices".[116] American diplomats confirmed that both the Polish and the Yugoslav governments seemed to choose a more cooperative attitude to the American stance on human rights, showing some margins of tolerance for dissidents' activities. The Gierek government in Poland, in particular, showed a certain willingness to develop a dialogue with dissident intellectuals, in part because of its increasing dependence on Western capital and imports. For this reason, the Polish regime tried to improve its image abroad through some symbolic gestures and openings. For example, Gierek did not prevent the release and distribution of the film *Man of Marble*, which denounced the "cynicism and opportunism behind worker glorification". Even more important, he had promised amnesty for gaoled activists from the free trade union KOR.[117]

In December 1977, Carter paid an official visit to Poland, where he was welcomed warmly both by the Polish government and by opponents of Gierek's regime, who stood in the rain with signs reading "we count on you America. Don't let us down." Following the conclusions of Presidential Directive 21, and in part to alleviate the food shortage the country was facing at the time, Carter announced that the United States would grant Poland $500 million in loans and credit for agricultural products. As a result of Carter's visit to Poland, Gierek made some concessions with respect to emigration and his government made the unprecedented decision to broadcast the Carter–Gierek press conference in its entirety in Poland. Equally revealing, Polish authorities did not prevent the first lady, Rosalynn Carter, and Brzezinski from meeting the leader of the Catholic Church in Poland, Cardinal Wyszynski, who represented a powerful voice for many in the Polish opposition.[118] Indeed, Carter's December visit was the capstone of a constant trend aimed at presenting Poland as a communist country in which basic human rights were respected.[119]

The United States and the CSCE follow-up in Belgrade

The first general test for the human rights policy in bipolar affairs arrived in October, when the CSCE review conference opened in Belgrade. There, the United States could develop a strategy to differentiate among Soviet bloc countries, test Western cohesion on human rights and détente and prove to public opinion – both at home and abroad – the effective role human rights had in American policy towards the Soviet Union.[120]

In the weeks leading up to the conference, the Soviets cracked down on dissidents with a new wave of arrests that were supposed to curb contacts with Western activists. Andrei Amalrik commented in a letter to Carter that the Soviets were trying to erase the human rights movement in the Soviet Union before the opening of the conference.[121] Yet, they could not prevent information from circulating between East and West. A documented report prepared by the Moscow-based Commission to Investigate the Misuse of Psychiatry for Political Purposes, for example, was released in the West by the *Chronicle of Human Rights in the*

USSR and became the basis for a motion adopted by the British Royal College of Psychiatry condemning Soviet misuse of psychiatry that was then sent to all signatories of the CSCE.[122] Western networks for the promotion of the Helsinki Accords echoed dissidents' activities through petitions to their national governments, public demonstrations, conferences and some specific initiatives, such as the second "International Sakharov Hearings", a non-governmental tribunal that denounced Soviet repression, or the 1977 Venice Biennale, where Soviet and Czechoslovak dissidents' paintings were exhibited.[123] Similarly, the European Parliament passed a number of resolutions inviting EC institutions and member states to consider human rights and the fate of political dissidents in all their contacts with Eastern Europe and the Soviet Union, as well as to prioritize CSCE Basket III during the Belgrade conference.[124]

Washington's early attitude, however, was to downplay the importance of the meeting in order to safeguard the CSCE as a multilateral process and to prevent tensions within NATO. For this reason, the State Department proposed the creation of an ad hoc committee both to coordinate the departments and agencies involved in the CSCE process and to define some concrete proposals to be discussed with NATO allies.[125] While this blueprint preserved cohesion with the allies, it did not ensure a consistent approach to Carter's proclaimed "absolute commitment to human rights", nor was it able to match the high expectations Congress and NGOs had for the conference.

A first major change was the decision to involve the "Helsinki Commission" in this discussion. Vance even proposed enlarging the US diplomatic mission to include Dante Fascell and other commissioners and to grant them access to the State Department's classified materials relating to CSCE.[126] Brzezinski opposed Vance's proposal, because granting such a status to the commission could have limited Vance's "freedom of action" and led "other legislators to seek similar involvement on other subjects, such as SALT". Vance countered Brzezinski's point by outlining that the commission was established because of the non-cooperative attitude followed by the executive branch and ensured these consultations would have minimized the risk of Congressional action to impose a similar commission for SALT negotiations.[127] Moreover, Representative Dante Fascell and Senator Clifford Case, both members of the "Helsinki Commission", urged the White House to appoint all the members of their commission to the US delegation, while 127 Representatives and sixteen Senators invited American diplomats to name names in the case of victims of Soviet violations of human rights.[128]

These pressures did not modify the State Department's stance on the Belgrade conference until late August, when two changes occurred. First, Brzezinski convened a policy review meeting and a new consensus emerged on the opportunity to put the Soviets on the defensive on CSCE humanitarian provisions, assuming a tone in Belgrade that would be "neither shy nor demagogic".[129] Second, Undersecretary for Human Rights and Humanitarian Affairs Patricia Derian and her staff were disappointed at the dismissive attitude shown by the American delegation at the Belgrade preparatory meeting. American diplomats at Belgrade were in "a spiritual void" and seemed to have accepted the Soviet definition of "success" for the conference, which tended to downplay human rights. Derian and her staff blamed Ambassador Albert Sherer for the neglect of human rights:

> [He] is a principled gentleman, who defers to the Delegation's tactician on when to speak. Its tactician is genuinely insensitive to human needs, the deprivations governments can perpetrate on peoples. … He is Mr. CSCE, by his own definition exclusively qualified with a few other department officers to rate as member-diplomats in a political gathering (CSCE) they wish to make over into an exclusive debating club with the Soviets. The Club's dialogue is too precise, too politically explosive, and too important for common folk, Department principals, or most department officers to understand or influence. The hallmark of the Kissinger days was to subordinate the CSCE to our bilateral priorities with the USSR. The same U.S. message-bearers are there again, proving by their actions that the same priorities apply today. We won't precipitate World War III as a consequence. But we won't do much for people or our allies either.[130]

For this reason, Derian and Brzezinski suggested replacing this "relatively unknown State Department" official with Arthur Goldberg, a former Secretary of Labour, Supreme Court Justice, and president of the American Jewish Committee. Such a choice would have ensured "the visibility and the impact we desired", Brzezinski wrote in his memoirs.[131]

The administration then decided to ensure that all the members of the "Helsinki Commission" had the opportunity to take part in the diplomatic mission and, within days, Counselor Matthew Nimetz began consultation with prominent NGOs. The NCSJ, the Committee of Concerned Scientists and other organizations contributed to defining the American stance at the conference and provided Nimetz with their own proposals and information. Accepting their suggestions, Nimetz succeeded in co-opting NGOs, and he assured them that the American delegation at Belgrade would comprise diplomats, politicians and civil society representatives, in order to echo the "pluralism" of the American people and to receive firsthand information in respect of Basket III.[132]

In September, during an official visit to Washington, Gromyko reminded Carter that the Soviet Union would not tolerate any further American interference in its domestic affairs and hoped that Belgrade would be "an occasion for mutual accommodation, not accusation and counteraccusation, a constructive forum instead of a complaint box".[133] Things followed a different course. The State Department gave instruction to Goldberg to stick "with the interests and ideals of the American people, and with policy statements by the president, the Secretary of State and other high administration spokesmen". For this reason, Goldberg should "vigorously assert the obligations of all signatories of the Final Act to adhere to the accord in all aspects, including particularly human rights" and pursue "a full review of experience with implementation … special emphasis should be given to the poor implementation records of the Eastern countries, particularly in respect of Principle VII and Basket Three".[134]

The conference opened on 4 October 1977. In his opening speech, Goldberg briefly touched upon CSCE human rights provisions and the need to fully implement the Final Act. He avoided any direct polemics with Eastern European countries and with the Soviets. Rather, he clarified that the United States had no interest in criticizing the Soviets and claimed that his aim was to achieve a constructive and non-polemical dialogue with all nations.[135] EC member states welcomed Goldberg's attitude as it created enough room to pursue the EC's goals, namely, the strengthening of the process of détente and the promotion of the EC as an international player. Even the Soviets and their allies seemed satisfied with Goldberg's speech.[136]

Over the following days, however, Goldberg reversed his course and chose a firmer stance on human rights in order to respond to the American domestic debate. From Washington, Brzezinski informed Goldberg that the United States seemed to be "backpeddling on human rights". For this reason, he invited Goldberg to assume a firmer stance: "It looks like we have forgotten about the one issue that electrified the American people and the world."[137] One week later, Brzezinski was even more explicit and asked president Carter and all the administration to develop

> a coherent strategy – including priorities, timing and yes, linkages – for managing our dealings with the Soviet Union, including the barrage of arms control negotiations, and such major political issues as CSCE, human rights, and the Middle East. We need this strategy to guide our own planning and action, and to make sure we do not run into difficulty with Congress and the public on the Soviet front. For the American public, how the Soviet connection is managed is a central standard for evaluating the foreign policy performance and competence of any administration.[138]

Brzezinski's suggestion was to "speak out again publicly on the issue to disabuse the Soviets and to head off domestic charges that you are backing off human rights".[139]

Following Brzezinski's invitation, the American delegation in Belgrade started to name the names of countries in which violations occurred and to list the victims. In early November, Goldberg detailed to the State Department what American diplomats had discussed:

> October 26 – George Krimsky, thrown out of USSR because he had good contacts with Soviet dissidents; Robert Toth, picked up for spy charge but interrogated for 13 hours on Helsinki Watch Group members; Orlov, Ginzburg, Sharansky, who have been jailed for their Helsinki activities.

> October 28 – the 22 men (not named) who have been imprisoned for several years and whose only real "crime" was request for permission to emigrate.

> October 28 – Josef Begun, who was fired from job for requesting to emigrate, refused permission to rejoin his family, could not find other work and was arrested for parasitism.

> October 28 – an individual, Lev Gendin, … who since applying to emigrate to join his wife in 1970, has been prevented from working and is presently threatened with military conscription.

October 24 – Said that Czech people learned about Charter 77, and the harassment and deprivation of jobs through RFE.

October 18 – Charter 77 and Trials.

November 1 – Charter 77 and Soviet monitoring groups, first condemnation of psychiatric treatment of individuals confined for political views.[140]

Over the following months, Goldberg continued to name names. The Soviet Union and its allies vehemently protested, to the point that the Soviet ambassador threatened to withdraw from the conference if American attacks continued. Referring to Goldberg's accusations, the head of the Polish delegation stated that discussions over human rights were just a waste of time. He added that it seemed that some delegations were more concerned with the comments of their domestic press rather than the smooth running of the conference. For this reason, he invited Western delegations not to be "slaves" to their domestic political debates.[141]

Goldberg and the other American delegates often expressed their dissatisfaction with their European allies. From the American perspective, the relevance of human rights to the American people as well as Carter's willingness to show that a more reciprocal détente was possible pushed the United States towards a firmer stance. For their part, the EC Nine considered Belgrade as a test for their image as a unitary international player and as a tool to promote their conception of détente; thus, they were determined to avoid polemics between East and West.[142] Yet, Goldberg continued to oscillate between open criticism and more cooperative attitudes by recalling, for example, some progress made by the Soviets in relation to family reunification, free emigration and Western radio broadcasts. Even though such a strategy would not have made significant progress in respect of Basket III or introducing new proposals, it ensured the fulfilment of two major objectives: keeping cohesion with NATO allies and strengthening domestic support for a new SALT Treaty. As Goldberg wrote to the State Department in February 1978: "although I have never spoken publicly or privately of a linkage between what we do in Belgrade and SALT, I believe that failure to assert human rights vigorously here could strengthen opponents of a sensible SALT agreement".[143] Even Goldberg was unable to avoid linking the American stance on human rights to the prospect of a difficult Congressional debate for the new SALT II agreement.

By early December, Goldberg's continuing attacks imposed a deadlock on the conference. Consequently, the diplomatic delegations ended any discussion for new proposals and began to work on a final document that would focus only on preserving the Helsinki process. In mid-January 1978, Soviet ambassador Yuli M. Vorontsov circulated a draft document that was unacceptable to the United States since it omitted mention of human rights or humanitarian cooperation. According to Belgian diplomat and EC representative Louis Kawan, the Soviet proposal consisted of "vague wording which gives the impression that all is well; it says nothing about any shortcomings in implementation; and among the new proposals, it mentions only a few of Soviet origin".[144]

After months of fruitless negotiations, Ambassador Goldberg and all Western diplomats accepted the Soviets' proposal, which was finalized on 8 March 1978. It merely reaffirmed that all the signatory countries attributed great importance to the respect and promotion of the Helsinki principles and their willingness to summon a new review conference that was supposed to open in Madrid in 1980. In his concluding remarks, Goldberg did not hide his disappointment at the outcome of the conference as well as at the "profound disregard" for CSCE human rights provisions.[145]

As seen from Washington, however, the political outcome was different. To Brzezinski, many objectives had been achieved:

> A full and frank review of implementation, in which we have done quite well, and where Allied unity has been excellent, has now been completed. In the process: the Soviets have been pushed again to acknowledge the legitimacy of human rights as a topic of discussion between nations (the East both criticized our own record and made human rights proposals on its own); some States in the East, plus Yugoslavia, have done a little bit better at implementation; there will be another Belgrade-style [conference] in about two years; and over time the process can lead to improvements in the standards applied to government behavior and perhaps in the way governments actually behave.[146]

Even more important, within the United States, the administration succeeded in promoting its image as a staunch defender of human rights in the world. The cooperative relationship with the Fascell Commission and the many organizations of the "Helsinki lobby" allowed the American government to enhance and at the same time contain and direct their activities. In return, by approving the general stance the American diplomatic mission had assumed at Belgrade, NGOs contributed to shoring up Carter's credibility on human rights and had replied to those critics who, since late 1977, had argued that Carter's commitment to human rights was decreasing.[147] America's renewed firmness was commended, for example, by the NCSJ, which credited Goldberg and Carter for the increase in the number of Soviet Jews being allowed to leave the Soviet Union: "from some 1200/month last June to a present rate of about 1800/month, as the Belgrade meeting approached and got underway".[148] Even conservative Senators Jackson and Moynihan welcomed the American contribution to the Belgrade conference and sponsored a resolution commending Goldberg and the US diplomatic mission at the conference.[149]

There were, however, some problems. One was professional diplomats' critique of Goldberg's style. Ambassador Sherer's wife, Carroll Sherer, who was serving as a member of the US delegation at Belgrade, blamed Goldberg and Carter for the watered-down compromise at the end of the conference:

> Those who try to explain the Belgrade breakdown by blaming it on Soviet intransigence are off the mark. The fact is that Belgrade should have been approached more like a china shop than a bull pen; but it was not. The White House failed to understand the fragility of the new European dialogue which, like a newborn baby, it requires careful nursing or its very life would be easily jeopardized.[150]

This line of criticism was confined to diplomatic circles and staunch supporters of bipolar détente. The White House was more concerned with another critique, which was growing within Congress and among the general public. To many, Carter's campaign was assuming a purely anti-Soviet tone. It was time to reverse it, addressing allies' violations of human rights, easing criticism of the Soviet Union and, eventually, relaunching themes and proposals to strengthen bipolar cooperation and dialogue.

Conclusion

After fifteen months in office, the Carter administration assessed its human rights policy positively. It had achieved three positive outcomes. The first concerned the place of human rights in American foreign policy. Carter succeeded in giving human rights a central role in all major decisions on foreign policy and international affairs, while following a flexible and pragmatic approach. The administration seemed able to mediate between principles and realism. Second, Carter's campaign had found many supporters within the United States and Congress. Both liberals and conservatives commended Carter's firmness on human rights, although they had different reasons for doing so. The former enthusiastically supported the consistent approach that led Carter to criticize allies, as well as his commitment to preserve détente; the latter welcomed the open critique of the Soviets for their violations of human rights. This was the third major outcome. After a year of public criticism of the Soviet record on human rights, détente had not foundered on human rights polemics. Or at least, this was the dominant interpretation within the executive branch. Despite some protests coming from Moscow and the lack of any breakthrough in SALT negotiations, the Soviets continued to consider détente and a new arms control treaty high priorities. The White House was willing to partially recalibrate its approach to East–West relations in order to conclude SALT II, but human rights would continue to play a significant role, since the administration imagined it had enough room to advance both human rights and arms control.

Notes

1 J. Carter, "Inaugural Address", in *Public Papers of the Presidents of the United States: Jimmy Carter, 1977, Book I, January 1–June 22* (Washington, DC: US Government Printing Office, 1978), pp. 1–4; L. Bloomfield to Carter, "The Carter Human Rights Policy. A Provisional Appraisal", 16 January 1981, JCPL, ZBM, Box 34, Folder "NSA Accomplishment – Human Rights". See also, V.S. Kaufman, "The Bureau of Human Rights during the Carter Administration", *The Historian* 61:1 (1998), pp. 51–66; W.M. Schmidli, "Institutionalizing Human Rights in United States Foreign Policy: U.S.-Argentine Relations, 1976–1980", *Diplomatic History* 35:2 (April 2011), pp. 351–377.

2 J. Dumbrell, *The Carter Presidency: A Re-Evaluation* (Manchester and New York: Manchester University Press, 1993); D.F. Schmitz and V. Walker, "Jimmy Carter and the Foreign Policy of Human Rights: The Development of a Post-Cold War Foreign Policy", *Diplomatic History* 28:1 (January 2004), pp. 113–143; D.F. Schmitz, *The United States and Right-Wing Dictatorships* (Cambridge and New York: Cambridge University Press, 2006); I.N. Sneh, *The Future Almost Arrived: How Jimmy Carter Failed to Change U.S. Foreign Policy* (New York: Peter Lang, 2008).

3 Among the first to propose such interpretation G. Smith, *Morality, Reason and Power: American Diplomacy in the Carter Years* (New York: Hill and Wang, 1986).

4 Z. Brzezinski to Carter, "Weekly National Security Report", 19 February 1977, JCPL, ZBM, Box 41, Folder 3. See also, B. Keys, *Reclaiming American Virtue: The Human Rights Revolution of the 1970s* (Cambridge, MA: Harvard University Press, 2014), pp. 248–250; W.M. Schmidli, *The Fate of Freedom Elsewhere: Human Rights and U.S. Cold War Policy toward Argentina* (Ithaca, NY and London: Cornell University Press, 2013), pp. 92–106.

5 "Human Rights and Foreign Policy: Address by Secretary of State Cyrus R. Vance at the University of Georgia School of Law, Athens, Georgia", 30 April 1977, in E.P. Adam (ed.), *American Foreign Relations 1977: A Documentary Record* (New York: New York University Press, 1979), p. 165.

6 J. Carter, "Address at Commencement Exercises at University of Notre Dame", 22 May 1977, American Presidency Project, University of California-Santa Barbara: www. presidency.ucsb.edu/ws/idex.php?pid=7229 (accessed December 2018).

7 Ibid.

8 Schmidli, *The Fate of Freedom Elsewhere*; J.N. Green, *We Cannot Remain Silent: Opposition to the Military Dictatorship in the United States* (Durham. NC: Duke University Press, 2010). On the United States' support of authoritarian regimes in Latin America as a source of anti-Americanism during the 1970s; K. Coates, *Found Guilty: The Verdict of the Russell Tribunal Session in Brussels; the Verdict of the Second Russell Tribunal on Repression in Brazil, Chile and Latin America* (Nottingham: Bertrand Russell Peace Foundation, 1975).

9 Sneh, *The Future Almost Arrived*, p. 79.

10 C. Vance to American Embassy Moscow, 5 February 1977, JCPL, NSA – CF, Box 78, Folder 4.

11 *Department of State Bulletin*, 21 February 1977, p. 138.

12 Memorandum of Conversation between President Carter, Anatoly Dobrynin, Cyrus Vance, Z. Brzezinski, 1 February 1977, JCPL, NSA – SF, Box 34, Folder 1.

13 Memorandum for the President from the Vice President, "Meeting with Vladimir Bukovsky", 2 March 1977, JCPL, SS, Box 10, Folder 3/2/77.

14 D. Fascell, "Report on International Broadcasting", *Congressional Record*, 95th Congress, 1st Session, pp. 8732–8733; D. Binder, "Carter Requests Funds for Big Increase in Broadcasts", *New York Times*, 23 March 1977.

15 "Dissident Activity in Eastern Europe: An Overview", 1 April 1977; Memorandum, "The Soviet View of the Dissident Problem since Helsinki", May 1977; Memorandum, "The Spectrum of Soviet Dissent", May 1977, JCPL, NLC-7-17-5-4-7.

16 "Andropov to Central Committee, February 18, 1977 – U.S. Government Activities in Defense of Human Rights", in J. Rubenstein and A. Gribanov (eds), *The KGB File of Andrei Sakharov* (New Haven, CT and London: Yale University Press, 2005), pp. 223–224; P.B. Henze to Z. Brzezinski, "Effect of Foreign Broadcasts in the USSR", 2 May

1978, JCPL, NSA – CF, Box 79, Folder 6; P.B. Henze to Z. Brzezinski, "CIA Report on Results of Stepped-Up Publishing and Distribution Efforts to USSR & Eastern Europe", 18 December 1978, JCPL, NSA – CF, Box 3, Folder 12/78. See also, C.P. Peterson, *Globalizing Human Rights: Private Citizens, the Soviet Union, and the West* (Abingdon and New York: Routledge, 2012), pp. 49–50; R. Gates, *From the Shadows: The Ultimate Inside Story of Five Presidents and How They Won the Cold War* (New York: Penguin Books, 1998), pp. 91–94.

17 *Current Digest of the Soviet Press* 29:9 (1977).

18 *Chronicle of Human Rights in the Soviet Union* 25 (January–March 1977), p. 20.

19 KPPS Protocol 46/X, "About Directions to the Soviet Ambassador to Washington on the Question of Human Rights", 18 February 1977, JCPL, "Vertical Files", Box 114.

20 Z. Brzezinski to Carter, "Weekly National Security Report", 24 June 1977, JCPL, ZBM, Box 41, Folder 4.

21 Z. Brzezinski to Carter, "Weekly National Security Report", 19 February 1977, JCPL, ZBM, Box 41, Folder 3.

22 W.A. Harriman, "Memorandum of Conversation", 20 September 1976; W.A. Harriman, "Memorandum for Record of WAH's Talk with Governor Carter, Tuesday Morning, August 31, 1976", both in JCPL, Vertical Files, Box 114, Folder "USSR – Related Document".

23 J. Carter to L. Brezhnev, 26 January 1977, JCPL, ZBM, Box 18, Folder 2.

24 M. Del Pero, *The Eccentric Realist: Henry Kissinger and the Shaping of American Foreign Policy* (Ithaca, NY: Cornell University Press, 2010), pp. 110–142; J. Ehrman, *The Rise of Neoconservatism: Intellectuals and Foreign Affairs* (New Haven, CT and London: Yale University Press, 1995), pp. 97–136; J. Vaïsse, *Neoconservatism: The Biography of a Movement* (Cambridge, MA: The Belknap Press of Harvard University Press, 2010), esp. pp. 149–169.

25 D. Caldwell, "The Demise of Détente and US Domestic Politics", in O.A. Westad (ed.), *The Fall of Détente: Soviet–American Relations during the Carter Years* (Oslo and Boston: Scandinavian University Press, 1997), pp. 95–117; Tom W. Smith, "The Polls: American Attitudes toward the Soviet Union and Communism", *Public Opinion Quarterly* 47:2 (Summer 1983), pp. 277–292.

26 "The President's News Conference", 8 February 1977, in *American Foreign Policy. Basic Documents, 1977–1980* (Washington, DC: US Government Printing Office, 1983), pp. 558–559.

27 A. Lewis, "A Question of Humanity", *New York Times*, 28 February 1977; "Moral Policeman to the World?", *U.S. News and World Report*, 14 March 1977; Elizabeth Drew, "Reporter at Large: Human Rights", *New Yorker*, 18 July 1977.

28 J. Powell to J. Carter, "Soviet Dissidents", 21 February 1977, JCPL, SS, Box 9, Folder "2/21/77".

29 Ibid.

30 Memorandum of Conversation between President Carter, Anatoly Dobrynin, Cyrus Vance, Z. Brzezinski, 1 February 1977, JCPL, NSA – SF, Box 34, Folder 1.

31 Committee on the Present Danger, "Common Sense and the Common Danger", in C. Tyroler (ed.), *Alerting America: The Papers of the Committee on the Present Danger* (Washington, DC: Pergamon-Brassey's, 1984); J.W. Sanders, *Peddlers of Crisis: The Committee on the Present Danger and the Politics of Containment* (Boston: South End Press, 1983).

32 P. Nitze, "Assuring Strategic Stability in an Era of Détente", *Foreign Affairs* 54:2 (January 1976), pp. 207–232.
33 B. Weinraub, "Mondale Pledges U.S. Won't Cut Nato Funds", *New York Times*, 25 January 1977.
34 H.M. Jackson, "Memorandum for the President on Salt", 15 February 1977; J. Carter to H.M. Jackson, 17 February 1977, JCPL, SS, Box 9, Folder "2/18/77 (2)".
35 "Warnke to Head Arms Control Agency", *Washington Post*, 1 February 1977, P.C. Warnke, "Arms Control, Before Time Runs Out", *New York Times*, 9 February 1977. R.A. Strong, *Working in the World: Jimmy Carter and the Making of American Foreign Policy* (Baton Rouge: Louisiana State University Press, 2000), pp. 10–44.
36 R.L. Garthoff, *Détente and Confrontation: American–Soviet Relations from Nixon to Reagan* (Washington, DC: The Brookings Institution, 1994), p. 627; Senate, Committee on Foreign Relations, *On Nomination of Paul C. Warnke to be Director of the United States Arms Control and Disarmament Agency, with the Rank of Ambassador during his Tenure of Service: February 8 and 9 1977* (Washington, DC: US Government Printing Office, 1977).
37 American Council on Captive Nations to Carter, 7 March 1977, JCPL, WHCF, Box HU4, Folder "1/20/77–4/30/77"; "Support for President Carter's Rights Policy Is Theme of N.Y. Defense Rally", *Ukrainian Weekly*, 14 August 1977; A.M. Schindler to J. Carter, 18 February 1977; E. Gold to J. Carter, 22 June 1977, both in JCPL, "Office of Public Liaison", Box 54, Folder "Human Rights – Soviet Jewry"; Memorandum from G. McRae to the Executive Committee, 22 August 1977, CHRDR, AI USA Papers, Hawk Files, RG II, Series II.1, Box 5, Folder 8; J. Shestack to J. Carter, 5 March 1977, JCPL, WHCF, Box HU-1, Folder "3/1/77–3/31/77".
38 M. Rostropovich to J. Carter, 25 March 1977; J. Carter to M. Rostropovich, 5 April 1977, JCPL, WHCF, Box HU1, Folder "4/1/77–4/31/77".
39 Public Interest Opinion Research, "Polls Show Public Backs Carter on Human Rights – Even If Arms Talks Are Periled", 10 July 1977, NARA, RG 519, Box 14, Folder 6.
40 D.J. Pease to Jimmy Carter, 28 February 1977, JCPL, WHCF, Box HU-1, Folder "3/1/ 77–3/31/77"; H. Metzenbaum to J. Carter, 22 March 1977, JCPL, WHCF, Box HU-1, Folder "3/1/77–3/31/77".
41 F. Church in *Congressional Record*, 95th Congress, 1st Session, 2 March 1977, pp. 5838–5839; Benjamin Rosenthal in *Congressional Record*, 95th Congress, 1st Session, 3 March 1977, pp. 6133–6137.
42 "Senate Concurrent Resolution 7 – Submission of a Concurrent Resolution Relating to Freedom of Emigration", *Congressional Record*, 95th Congress, 1st Session, 26 January 1977, pp. 2218–2219. See also, the points raised by Jackson, Javits and Case in *Congressional Record*, 95th Congress, 1st Session, 2 March 1977, pp. 5826–5830.
43 H.M. Jackson, "Internationally Recognized Human Rights", *Congressional Record*, 95th Congress, 1st Session, 11 February 1977, pp. 4372–4373; D.P. Moynihan, "Remarks on Senate Concurrent Resolution 7", *Congressional Record*, 95th Congress, 1st Session, 2 March 1977, p. 5830; H.M. Jackson, "Human Rights and the Jackson–Vanik Amendment", JCPL, SS, Box 35, Folder "6.30.77".
44 J. Kemp to J. Carter, 25 March 1977, JCPL, WHCF, Box HU-1, Folder "3/1/77–3/31/77".
45 D. Fascell, "Opening Statement", in *Hearings Before the Commission on Security and Cooperation in Europe on Implementation of the Helsinki Accords – Human Rights*, 95th Congress, 1st Session, vol. 1 (Washington, DC: US Government Printing Office, 1976).
46 Sixty-three House Members to Carter, JCPL, WHCF, Box HU-1, Folder "2/1/77–2/28/77".

47 Fifty-seven Senate Members to J. Carter, 23 March 1977, JCPL, NSA–SF, Box 28, Folder 1.

48 J. Johnson to Carter, JCPL, WHCF, SF, Box HU-1, Folder 3.

49 "Response Favorable to Carter in Soviet", *New York Times*, 22 January 1977; N.V. Podgorny, "To His Excellency Jimmy Carter", *Pravda*, 21 January 1977, quoted in *Current Digest of Soviet Press*, 23 January 1977; P. Osnos, "Brezhnev: Ready to Work with Carter", *Washington Post*, 19 January 1977; "Initial Media Reaction to Presidential Inauguration", 22 January 1977 and "Foreign Media Reaction to Presidential Inauguration", 25 January 1977, both in JCPL, NSA, SF, Box 33, Folder 2; Memorandum from Z. Brzezinski to the President, "Soviet Reactions to Your Inauguration", 22 January 1977, JCPL, NSA – Coll. 1, Box 21, Folder 5.

50 A. Dobrynin, *In Confidence: Moscow's Ambassador to America's Six Cold War Presidents* (Seattle: University of Washington Press, 1995), pp. 380–383; M.P. Leffler, *For the Soul of Mankind: The United States, the Soviet Union and the Cold War* (New York: Hill and Wang, 2008), pp. 262–272; V. Zubok, *A Failed Empire: The Soviet Union in the Cold War from Stalin to Gorbachev* (Chapel Hill: University of North Carolina Press, 2007), pp. 254–255.

51 C. Bell, *The Costs of Virtue? President Carter and Foreign Policy* (Canberra: Australian National University, 1980); Mary DuBois Sexton, "The Wages of Principle and Power: Cyrus R. Vance and the Making of Foreign Policy in the Carter Administration" (PhD dissertation, Georgetown University, 2009).

52 Dobrynin, *In Confidence*, 390.

53 "The Soviet View of the Dissident Problem since Helsinki", May 1977.

54 Memorandum, Andropov and Rudenko to CC PCUS, "On Measures for Stopping Criminal Activities of Orlov, Ginzburg, Rudenko and Ventola", 5 January 1977: www.gwu.edu/~nsarchiv/NSAEBB/NSAEBB191/KGB%2001-20-1977.pdf (accessed July 2016); "Document 123: Andropov to Central Committee, February 18, 1977, U.S: Government Activities in Defense of Human Rights", in Rubenstein and Gribanov, *The KGB File of Andrei Sakharov*, pp. 223–224.

55 *Chronicle of Human Rights in the Soviet Union* 25 (January–March 1977), p. 23.

56 Ibid., p. 21; Y. Orlov, *Dangerous Thoughts: Memoirs of a Russian Life* (New York: Morrow, 1991), p. 194; P. Goldberg, *The Final Act: The Dramatic, Revealing Story of the Moscow Helsinki Watch Group* (New York: Morrow, 1988), p. 54; *Current Digest of the Soviet Press* 28:52 (26 January 1977).

57 *Chronicle of Human Rights in the Soviet Union* 25 (January–March 1977), p. 21.

58 *Current Digest of the Soviet Press* 29:9 (30 March 1977).

59 Dobrynin, *In Confidence*, pp. 390–391.

60 L. Brezhnev to J. Carter, 25 February 1977, JCPL, ZBM, Box 18, Folder 2.

61 Memorandum for the President, 18 March 1977, JCPL, ZBM, Box 1, Folder 3.

62 C. Vance, *Hard Choices: Critical Years in America's Foreign Policy* (New York: Simon & Schuster, 1983), p. 53.

63 Ibid., p. 54.

64 Ibid.

65 Ibid., p. 55. A similar point is in Dobrynin, *In Confidence*, p. 393.

66 Sanders, *Peddlers of Crisis*, pp. 241–244. A different interpretation, one that blames Carter's naiveté and diplomatic inexperience, is S. Talbott, *Endgame: The Inside Story of SALT II* (New York: Harper & Row, 1980), pp. 66–67.

67 Brezhnev quoted in Leffler, *For the Soul of Mankind*, p. 269.

68 Ibid.
69 NCSJ News Release, "Soviet Jews Emigrating from USSR this Year Surpass 1976 Figures", 5 December 1977, CJH, NCSJ Papers, Box 73, Folder 5; Memorandum from Z. Brzezinski for M. Costanza et al., "Human Rights Improvement", 16 May 1977, JCPL, NSA – SF, Box 28, Folder 2. See also, Zubok, *A Failed Empire*, pp. 233–236.
70 Z. Brzezinski to the President, "NSC Weekly Report #18", 24 June 1977, JCPL, ZBM, Box 41, Folder 4.
71 B. Keys, "Something to Boast About: Western Enthusiasm for Carter's Human Rights Diplomacy", in H. Notaker, G. Scott-Smith and D.J. Snyder (eds), *Reasserting America in the 1970s: U.S. Public Diplomacy and the Rebuilding of America's Image Abroad* (Manchester: Manchester University Press, 2016), pp. 229–244; M. Schultz and Thomas A. Schwartz (eds), *The Strained Alliance: US–European Relations from Nixon to Carter* (Cambridge: Cambridge University Press, 2010).
72 Z. Brzezinski to J. Carter, "Comments on President's Notre Dame Speech", JCPL, NSA – SF, Box 10, Folder "Human Rights 2/4/77".
73 Foreign Broadcast Information Service, "Special Memorandum: Initial Foreign Media Reactions to Presidential Inauguration", JCPL, NLC-7-33-2-2-4; Memorandum, USIA, "Foreign Media Reaction to President's Press Conference – February 9, 1977", JCPL, NSA – SF, Box 33, Folder 2; "West European Public Opinion on Key Human Rights Issues", Doc. S-25–77, NARA, RG 306 Records of the U.S. Information Agency, Box 17, Folder 25. See also Keys, "Something to Boast About", pp. 229–244.
74 S.A. Chapman, "The Economic Relations between the EEC and the CMEA: A Survey of Problems and Prospects", *La comunità internazionale* 40:3 (1985), pp. 421–449; Lincoln Gordon, with J.F. Brown, P. Hassner, J. Joffe and E. Moreton, *Eroding Empire: Western Relations with Eastern Europe* (Washington, DC: The Brookings Institution, 1987), pp. 435–436; A. Romano, "Untying Cold War Knots: The EEC and Eastern Europe in the Long 1970s", *Cold War History* 14:2 (2013), pp. 153–173.
75 J. Tuchman-Matthews to Z. Brzezinski, 4 May 1977, JCPL, NSA – SF, Box 28, Folder 2.
76 A. Romano, *From Détente in Europe to European Détente: How the West Shaped the Helsinki CSCE* (Brussels: Peter Lang, 2009), esp. pp. 219–228; G.H. Soutou, "The Linkage between European Integration and Détente", in N.P. Ludlow (ed.), *European Integration and the Cold War: Ostpolitik–Westpolitik, 1965–1973* (New York: Routledge, 2007), pp. 11–35, 24; F. Romero, S. Pons, "Europe between the Superpowers, 1968–1981", in A. Varsori and G. Migani (eds), *Europe in the International Arena during the 1970s* (Brussels and New York: Peter Lang, 2011), pp. 85–98. See also F. Romero, *Storia della Guerra fredda. L'ultimo conflitto per l'Europa* (Turin: Einaudi, 2009), p. 245.
77 Memorandum for the President, "Giscard Press Conference", 23 June 1977, JCPL, NLC-1-2-5-18-4.
78 Brzezinski to Costanza et al., "Human Rights Improvement". See also J. Hoagland, "France Bars Comments on East Bloc Dissidents", *Washington Post*, 23 February 1977; "Giscard, Schmidt on Détente", *Washington Post*, 19 July 1977; G.H. Soutou, "Three Rifts, Two Reconciliation: Franco-American Relations during the Fifth Republic", in D.M. Andrews (ed.), *The Atlantic Alliance under Stress: US–European Relations after Iraq* (Cambridge: Cambridge University Press, 2005), pp. 102–127.
79 Memorandum for Dr Brzezinski, "Concern Expressed by Chancellor Schmidt over RFE/RL", 29 June 1977, JCPL, NSA – CF, Box 22, Folder 2.

80 H. Schmidt, Men *and Power: A Political Retrospective* (New York: Random House, 1989), p. 182.

81 J. Aunesluoma, "Finlandisation in Reverse: The CSCE and the Rise and Fall of Economic Détente, 1968–1975", in O. Bange and G. Niedhart (eds), *Helsinki 1975 and the Transformation of Europe* (New York: Berghahn Books, 2008), pp. 98–113.

82 J. Renouard, "No Relief for a Troubled Alliance: Human Rights and Transatlantic Relations in the 1970s", in R. Haar and N. Wynn (eds), *Transatlantic Conflict and Consensus: Culture, History and Politics* (Cambridge: Cambridge Academic, 2009), pp. 145–162; O. Bange, "The Greatest Happiness of the Greatest Numbers … The FRG and the GDR and the Belgrade CSCE Conference (1977–1978)", in V. Bilandžić, D. Dahlmnn and M. Kosanović (eds), *From Helsinki to Belgrade: The First CSCE Follow-Up Meeting in Belgrade* (Bonn: Bonn University Press, 2012), pp. 225–253.

83 Memorandum from Cyrus Vance for the President, "Christopher Meeting with Biedenkopf", 16 March 1977, JCPL, NLC-128-12-6-15-4. See also CDU/CSU Group in the Bundestag, *White Paper on the Human Rights Situation in Germany and of the German in Eastern Europe* (Bonn, October 1977).

84 "President Carter and Human Rights in Europe" and "Telegram, Foreign Office to Washington", 20 February 1977, NA, FCO 28/3002; David Owen quoted in "Telegram 1005" from Washington to Foreign Office, 7 March 1977, NA, FCO 28/3237.

85 "Telegram no 1324 on President's Carter Foreign Policy", 25 March 1977, NA FCO 58/1160.

86 "Telegram 171: Détente and US/Soviet Relations", 23 March 1977, NA, FCO 58/1159; Memorandum, Michael Pike to Bryan Cartledge, "The US Approach to US/Soviet Relations", 2 July 1977, NA, FCO 58/1161; Memorandum, "Human Rights and Foreign Policy" for Certain Heads of Chancery, 14 December 1977, NA, FCO 28/3003.

87 European Political Cooperation: Ministerial Meeting, "Eastern Europe: Dissent and Human Rights", 18 April 1977, NA, FCO 58/1159.

88 American Embassy Moscow to State Department, 9 February 1977, JCPL, NSA – CF, Box 78, Folder 4.

89 American Embassy Moscow to State Department, 14 February 1977, JCPL, NSA – CF, Box 22, Folder 4.

90 M. Marder, "Soviets Criticized US on Salt, Human Rights", *Washington Post*, 28 March 1977; H. Smith, "Carter Warns He May Add Arms if Moscow Balks in Further Talks", *New York Times*, 31 March 1977; D. Oberdorfer, "Vance: Avoid Arrogance on Human Rights", *Washington Post*, 1 May 1977; Vance, *Hard Choices*, p. 46.

91 After the failure of the Moscow summit, a threefold proposal emerged in Washington. In the first part, the United States was willing to accept a Soviet request to follow the principles defined in the 1974 Vladivostok Agreement. The second part should address the most controversial issues, such as the Soviet "Backfire" bomber and the definition of "heavy missile". The third dealt with future commitments after the treaty came into force. Within this general scheme, the United States proposed to reduce the total ceilings from 2,400 to 2,200 launchers, with a sub-ceiling of 1,200 MIRVed missiles. In addition, it proposed a ban on mobile ICBMs. This provision would have forced the United States to abandon the MX programme. Z. Brzezinski to the President, "Salt", 23 April 1977, and Z. Brzezinski to the President, "Geneva Talks", 7 June 1977, both in JCPL, Vertical Files, Box 116. See also, S. Kaufman, *Plans Unraveled: The Foreign Policy of the Carter Administration* (DeKalb: Northern Illinois University Press, 2008), pp. 40–42.

92 M. Shulman, "On Learning to Live with Authoritarian Regimes", *Foreign Affairs* 55:2 (January 1977), pp. 326–338; Memorandum, from M. Shulman to C. Vance, "Some Observations on Current U.S.–Soviet Relations", 16 June 1977, JCPL, NLC-6-78-10-6-3.

93 Incoming Telegram 9160, from Ambassador to Secretary, "Prospect for U.S.–Soviet Relations", 25 June 1977, JCPL, NSA – CF, Box 78, Folder 7.

94 Ibid.

95 M. Wallach, "Report on Helsinki Commission Hearings", 14 January 1977, CJH, NCSJ Papers, Box 301, Folder 8; S. 1415, "A bill to amend the Trade Act of 1974 to authorize certain credits or credit guarantees for the sale of agricultural products to non market economy countries", 28 April 1977; and C. Vance to R. Long, 2 July 1977, LOC, DPMP, Box 1603, Folder 4.

96 B. Edgar to Mr Ross et al., "Draft Paper on Tradeoffs", 28 October 1977, JCPL, NLC-29-10-7-4-8.

97 H.M. Jackson to C. Vance, 13 July 1977, LOC, DPMP, Box 1603, Folder 4; H.M. Jackson to J. Carter, 17 June 1977, JCPL, CL, Box 51.

98 C. Vance to H.M. Jackson, 14 July 1977, LOC, DPMP, Box 1603, Folder 4; Z. Brzezinski to J. Carter, "Response to Senator Jackson Regarding the Dole Amendment", 22 July 1977, JCPL, CL, Box 51; J. Carter to H.M. Jackson, 26 July 1977, JCPL, CL, Box 51.

99 Z. Brzezinski to the Secretary of State and the Secretary of Treasury, "Follow Up to PRC Meeting on U.S.–Soviet Economic Relations: Tradeoffs", 13 September 1977, JCPL, NLC-29-10-7-1-1; Edgar to Ross et al., "Draft Paper on Tradeoffs".

100 H.M. Jackson, "Human Rights and the Jackson–Vanik Amendment", *Congressional Record*, 95th Congress, 1st Session, 14 June 1977, pp. 18895–18896; D.P. Moynihan, "Totalitarianism: The Central Challenge", in E.W. Lefever (ed.), *Morality and Foreign Policy: A Symposium on President Carter's Stance* (Washington, DC: Ethics and Public Policy Center, 1977), pp. 32–38. Even the British took note of the change in Carter's human rights campaign: Memorandum from K.B.A. Scott to Mr Crowe, "U.S. Foreign Policy: A European View", 26 August 1977, NA, FCO 28/3149.

101 H. Jordan to President Carter, June 1977, JCPL, CS, Box 34A, Folder 24: "Foreign Policy/Domestic Politics Memo Hamilton Jordan 6/77".

102 Ibid. In December, Jordan touched upon this problem once more. See Memorandum from H. Jordan to J. Carter, 3 December 1977, JCPL, CS, Box 34.

103 Z. Brzezinski to the President, "Weekly National Security Report #9", 16 April 1977, JCPL, ZBM, Box 41, Folder 3.

104 Z. Brzezinski to the President, "Weekly National Security Report #7", 1 April 1977, JCPL, ZBM, Box 41, Folder 3.

105 Z. Brzezinski to the President, "NSC Weekly Report #20", 8 July 1977, JCPL, ZBM, Box 41, Folder 4.

106 "Press Conference of the President of the United States", 13 June 1977, JCPL, Office of Public Liaison, Box 54, Folder "Human Rights – Soviet Jewry"; and "Statement by Department Spokesman – Shcharansky Trial", JCPL, NSA – CF, Box 79, Folder 5. See also B. Gwurtzman, "Carter Denies CIA Engaged Soviet Jew", *New York Times*, 14 June 1977.

107 Presidential Review Memorandum/National Security Council no. 28: Human Rights, JCPL, NLC-1002-A-246-1.

108 Ibid., p. 19.
109 Ibid., p. 17.
110 Ibid., p. 72.
111 Memorandum from the President for the Vice President et al., "Presidential Directive /NSC-18 – U.S. National Strategy", JCPL, WHCF, Box HU-1, Folder "8/1/77–8/31/77".
112 Ibid.
113 G. Treverton to Z. Brzezinski, "PRC Meeting on Europe, April 14, 1977", 13 April 1977, JCPL, ZBM, Box 24, Folder 28.
114 Ibid.
115 Memorandum from the President for the Vice President et al., "Presidential Directive /NSC-21 – Eastern Europe", 13 September 1977, JCPL, WHCF, Box HU-1, Folder "9/1/77–9/30/77".
116 "Three Months before Belgrade", *Chronicle of Human Rights in the Soviet Union*, January–March 1977.
117 "Poland Intellectuals Increase Their Challenge to the Government", 16 February 1977, JCPL, NSA – President's Daily Report Files, Box 1, Folder "2/15/77–2/28/77"; Flora Lewis, "Poland Softens Stand on Critics", *New York Times*, 20 January 1977; Peter Osnos, "Man of Marble: Getting at Poland's Core", *Washington Post*, 19 July 1977; "Poland Announces Amnesty that Might Free Dissidents", *Washington Post*, 20 July 1977.
118 B. Neikirik, "Warsaw Cool to Carter", *Chicago Tribune*, 30 December 1977; Z. Brzezinski, *Power and Principle: Memoirs of the National Security Adviser, 1977–1981* (New York: Farrar, Straus and Giroux, 1983), p. 298.
119 Z. Brzezinski to J. Carter, 15 March 1977, JCPL, NSA – President's Daily Report Files.
120 S.B. Snyder, *Human Rights Activism and the End of the Cold War* (New York and Cambridge: Cambridge University Press, 2012), pp. 81–114; Bilandžić, Dahlmnn and Kosanović, *From Helsinki to Belgrade*.
121 "From Helsinki to Belgrade", *Washington Post*, 9 August 1977; A. Amalrik to J. Carter, ADSA, AAP, Box 9, Folder 127.
122 *Chronicle of Human Rights in the Soviet Union*, March 1977.
123 Z. Brzezinski to the President, "Information Items: CSCE – Soviets and East Europeans Feel Pressure as Belgrade Conference Approaches", 15 March 1977, JCPL, NSA – President's Daily Report Files, Box 1, Folder "2/15/77–2/28/77". On the "Biennale del Dissenso" see F. Janouch and P. Zaccaria to A. Sakharov, 29 September 1977; P. Flores D'Arcais to E. and T. Yankelevich, 11 November 1977, both in ADSA, HRC, Box 4, Folder 48. On the International Sakharov Hearings, see L. Alexayeva's hearing, undated, ADSA, HRC, Box 13, Folder 1.
124 A.É. Gfeller, "Champion of Human Rights: The European Parliament and the Helsinki Process", *Journal of Contemporary History* 49:2 (2014), pp. 390–409.
125 A.A. Hartman to Z. Brzezinski, 17 March 1977, NARA, RG 59, WCP, Box 12, Folder 12; M. Nimetz to the Secretary, "Creation of a CSCE Policy Steering Group", 6 April 1977, NARA, RG 59, WCP, Box 12, Folder 12.
126 D. Fascell to C. Vance, 3 February 1977; C. Vance to D. Fascell, 28 February 1977, NARA, RG 519, Box 48, Folder "State Department Correspondence".
127 Z. Brzezinski to the Secretary of State, "Relations with the CSCE Commission", 14 March 1977, NARA, RG 59, WCP, Box 12, Folder 13; C. Vance to Z. Brzezinski, 22 March 1977, JCPL, ZBM, Box 13, Folder "3/10/77".

128 Ibid. See also, "Proposed Composition – Belgrade Conference", NARA, RG 519, Box 81, Folder 3.
129 Quoted in B. Walker, "Neither Shy nor Demagogic: The Carter Administration Goes to Belgrade", in Bilandžić, Dahlmnn and Kosanović, *From Helsinki to Belgrade*, p. 199.
130 Memorandum for P. Derian, "Summary Statement; Summary Conclusion; Recommendations – Trip to Belgrade", 11 August 1977, NARA, RG 59, WCP, Box 14, Folder 10.
131 Brzezinski, *Power and Principle*, p. 300.
132 Memorandum for M. Nimetz, "CSCE Meeting with NGOs, September 9, 1977", 8 September 1977, JCPL, OPL, Box 53, Folder "Human Rights – CSCE Helsinki Commission". See also E. Gold to Warren Christopher, 22 August 1977; Report of Presidium and Steering Committee of the World Conference on Soviet Jewry, "Soviet Jewry and the Implementation of the Helsinki Final Act", both in CJH, NCSJ Papers, Box 6, Folder "Jerry Goodman"; M. Mellman to the Executive Board of the Committee of Concerned Scientists, "The Helsinki Final Act/Belgrade Review Meeting", 15 June 1977, CJH, NCSJ Papers, Box 302, Folder 2; Memorandum prepared by the Helsinki Agreements Implementation Group, 15 September 1977, JCPL, OPL, Box 73, Folder 13. See, also, E. Vezzosi, "Gli scienziati statunitensi tra distensione e diritti umani: la Committee of Concerned Scientists negli anni Settanta", *Contemporanea* 19:3 (2016), pp. 419–435.
133 Memorandum of Conversation, "The President's Meeting with USSR Foreign Minister A.A. Gromyko", 23 September, JCPL, NSA – SF, Box 35, Folder 6.
134 Z. Brzezinski to the Secretary of State and others, "Instructions on CSCE", 7 October 1977, JCPL, NLC-15-82-2-2-1.
135 A. Goldberg, "Opening Speech", LOC, Arthur Goldberg Papers, Box 148, Folder 1.
136 A. Romano, "The European Community and the Belgrade CSCE", in Bilandžić, Dahlmnn and Kosanović, *From Helsinki to Belgrade*, pp. 205–224; U. Tulli, "The Limits of EPC? The EC Members at the Belgrade CSCE Review Conference", in G. Clemens (ed.), *The Quest for Europeanization: Interdisciplinary Perspectives on a Multiple Process* (Stuttgart: Franz Steiner Verlag, 2017), pp. 71–86.
137 Z. Brzezinski to the President, "NSC Weekly Report #32", JCPL, ZBM, Box 41, Folder 5.
138 Z. Brzezinski to the President, "NSC Weekly Report #33", JCPL, ZBM, Box 41, Folder 5.
139 Ibid.
140 "Incoming Telegram – Belgrade 7575: Soviet and Dutch Clash on Human Rights", from American Embassy Belgrade to Department of State, 2 November 1977; "Incoming Telegram – Belgrade 7616", from American Embassy Belgrade (Goldberg) to Department of State, 2 November 1977, both in NARA, RG 59, WCP, Box 14, Folder 16.
141 Quoted in M. Graf, T. Gülstorff, V. Lomellini, V. Gosheva Stoilova and B. Zaccaria, "The Shape of 'Détente' (1963–1979): European Détente and the Global Cold War?", *Zeitgeschichte* 6 (2011), pp. 409–435.
142 R. Lipshutz to J. Starr, "Belgrade, CSCE Trip", 3 March 1978: www.wilsoncenter.org/publication/global-politics-to-human-rights-the-csce-follow-meeting-belgrade-1977 (accessed March 2018). On the EC and the Belgrade conference see Romano, "The European Community".

143 "Incoming Telegram – Belgrade 0329", for the Deputy Secretary from Ambassador Goldberg, 3 February 1978, NARA, RG59, WCP, Box 8, Folder 4.

144 Ibid.

145 A. Goldberg, "Final Plenary Statement", 8 March 1978, LOC, Arthur Goldberg Papers, Box 148, Folder 2.

146 Z. Brzezinski to the President, "NSC Weekly Report no. 39", 9 December 1977, JCPL, ZBM, Box 41, Folder 5.

147 See, for example, R. Drinan, "Ambassador Arthur Goldberg Reviews the Belgrade Conference", 7 March 1978, *Congressional Record*, 95th Congress, 2nd Session, pp. 5957–58; W. Broomfield, "Tribute to Ambassador Arthur Goldberg", *Congressional Record*, 95th Congress, 2nd Session, pp. 8141–8142; M. Nimetz to the Deputy Secretary, "Support from NGOs for Our CSCE Efforts", 11 January 1978, NARA, RG59, WCP, Box 8, Folder 7.

148 A.S. Karlikov to M. Fine, "Belgrade Conference", CJH, NCSJ Papers Box 13, Folder "American Jewish Committee".

149 Senate Concurrent Resolution no. 75, "Praising the U.S. Delegation to the Belgrade Conference", 6 April 1978, *Congressional Record*, 95th Congress, 2nd Session, pp. 9012–9013.

150 C. Sherer, "Breakdown at Belgrade", *Washington Quarterly* 1:4 (1978), pp. 83–84. A similar point would be repeated by Ambassador A. Sherer in 1980. See A.W. Sherer, "Goldberg's Variation", *Foreign Policy* 39 (Summer 1980), pp. 154–159.

4

Coping with critics: the choice in favour of quiet diplomacy, 1978

After the CSCE review conference in Belgrade, the Carter administration modified its policy toward the Soviet Union. With the relevant exception of protests at the conclusion of the trials against activists of the Moscow-based Helsinki Group, the human rights initiative was confined to quiet diplomacy and private channels.[1] Historians tend to disagree on the rationale for such a change. Some have argued that Cuban and Soviet interventions in Africa dominated bipolar affairs. Accordingly, many have argued that there was no longer room for détente, nor for a human rights policy. The human rights campaign thus became a marginal aside during a hasty return to the militarization of American foreign policy.[2] To others, the decision to relegate human rights to quiet diplomacy was based on the negative reactions the campaign received abroad. Western European governments' pressures to revise the policy and Moscow's threats to interrupt détente and arms control negotiations forced the United States to rethink its human rights-based foreign policy.[3] This chapter will explain Carter's shift through a twofold rationale.

First, by late 1977 and early 1978, the Carter administration was satisfied with its accomplishments in bipolar relations. Despite Soviet protests and the many dissidents who were gaoled, Soviet authorities had yielded on some points the Americans had put pressure on. They followed a pragmatic cooperative approach, especially in those areas of particular concern to the United States, like the emigration of Soviet Jews, family reunification cases and a reduction in dissident convictions.[4] Many in the administration argued that moving human rights from open to quiet diplomacy would strengthen these trends, yield an acceptable solution to some specific cases and favour the conclusion of SALT II negotiations.

Second, the political debate within the United States favoured a major revision of the human rights campaign, especially in respect of US–Soviet relations. This point is clearly illustrated by the 1977 hearings summoned by the Fraser Committee on the early achievements of Carter's human rights policy, in which the White House was criticized by both liberals and conservatives. Edward Derwinski (R – Illinois), for example, attacked the administration for ignoring violations occurring within communist countries and tackling human rights abuses in allied countries. He provocatively asked, "Why is anti-Communism no longer part of our foreign policy? Why are we embracing Cuba and rejecting a longtime ally like Argentina?" At the other end of the political spectrum, liberal Leo Ryan (D – California) accused the administration of being "bold when it is safe and good politics – like criticizing the treatment of Soviet Jews – while expressing only mild disapproval" when criticizing traditional allies, such as South Korea and the Philippines.[5] Many began to point out the limits, shortcomings and contradictions of a campaign that the president himself had defined as absolute and universal. Far from ensuring a new consensual principle for American diplomacy and for the renewal of détente with the Soviets, as Carter had hoped, the human rights campaign had to cope with the duality that marked the rise of human rights in American political discourse.

In early 1978, the White House seemed willing to focus on criticism from liberals and those who called themselves "new internationalists". Building upon Western Europe's doubts and negative Soviet public reactions, they lashed out at the anti-communist theme they saw in Carter's campaign. To them, the White House should have rediscovered the global dimension of the human rights campaign and, at the same time, worked for the conclusion of the SALT II agreement. In coping with this criticism, however, the White House left its flank exposed to conservative critics. The Soviets' non-cooperative attitude further tested the limits of Carter's difficult equilibrium between firmness and dialogue.

An anti-Soviet campaign: liberals and realists against Carter's human rights

By late 1977, National Security Advisor Brzezinski's main concern for the continuation of the human rights campaign came from domestic politics, not international relations. As he explained to the president:

> Relations between Congress and the administration in the human rights area are at a very low ebb. It is hard to accept, given your own deep commitment to this issue, but most human rights advocates in Congress believe that, were it not for their continuing pressure and vigilance, the administration would renege on its commitment to human rights.[6]

To avoid any further worsening, Brzezinski made several proposals. The first was the creation of a human rights foundation. This new forum was meant to perform a variety of tasks, such as providing financial grants to human rights initiatives, working with human rights NGOs, publishing reports on the global respect for human rights and leading an international debate on the role of human rights in the world. Its creation would also strengthen White House connections with activists and Congress and, eventually, amplify activists' voices. Brzezinski went on to suggest other measures, such as a presidential speech for Human Rights Week, a campaign for the ratification of the Genocide Convention, the issuance of a presidential directive on human rights and a number of "working meetings – chaired by the vice president – with prominent congressional human rights advocates". Participants in these meetings "will not hear the Administration's position, but [they will] think through the problems involved in implementing legislation … and actively participate in working out mutually satisfactory resolutions".[7]

Brzezinski's conclusions were shared by Anthony Lake, director of the Policy Planning Staff, who gave his provisional assessment of the human rights campaign in January 1978. After listing several meaningful developments, Lake pointed out that the campaign had led to many improvements, without damaging other US interests "in any quantifiable way". Despite Soviet protests, Lake remarked that the human rights campaign did "not seem yet to have interfered with SALT and other arms control negotiations, or US–Soviet dealings in other areas".[8] According to Lake, problems could emerge from the domestic debate, where "Congressmen most interested in human rights … remain skeptical of our actions" because "our role in legislation has so far been largely reactive, and is seen by many as damage-limiting. It is generally believed that we would not be applying human rights criteria if Congress had not ordered us to do so." The paramount problem, Lake concluded, came from "congressional unhappiness with perceived softness in our application of the policy, combined with the desire of many Congressmen to seem tough".[9] Lake's conclusions were discussed within the administration. Many agreed with him. The only critical voice came from Southeast Asia expert Alan Romberg, who criticized Lake's paper for underestimating "the degree of skepticism and cynicism on the Hill about the administration's human rights policy".[10] Despite this difference, these early evaluations of the human rights campaign shared the idea that the political debate within the United States and Congressional scepticism, not Soviet reactions, were the major obstacle to the promotion of human rights in East–West relations.

Major American newspapers shared a similar understanding of the human rights campaign. Since late 1977, many op-eds had started to criticize Carter's human rights campaign for its shortcomings, mistakes and selectiveness. While many highlighted Carter's determination to tackle human rights abuses in specific targets, such as the Soviet Union or Argentina, others claimed that the president was "losing faith" in his human rights crusade, something that was now becoming a "nasty headache" for the entire administration and causing dissatisfaction among human rights advocates in Congress.[11]

To Stanley Hoffmann, a political scientist at Harvard University and sympathetic critic of Carter's foreign policy, two basic dilemmas afflicted Carter's human rights policy. The first emerged from bipolar relations and the precarious equilibrium between human rights and détente. Hoffmann felt that the Carter administration was unable to devise an appropriate approach to the Soviet Union, enshrined between cooperation and confrontation. "The issue of human rights, by definition, breeds confrontation. … Raising the issue touches on the very foundations of a regime, on its sources and exercise of power … it is a dangerous issue." The human rights campaign was in opposition to détente because it "almost inevitably increases tensions with our enemies. If it is pursued very avidly, it diminishes the chances of cooperation on a number of other world order issues." A second major problem was related to the lack of consistency in the implementation of a policy that had been presented as universal and, at the same time, pragmatic:

[I]f the United States is too selective about which countries to denounce, it risks becoming hypocritical (for instance, if it singles out only its foes and spares its friends). If it pursues the cause of human rights everywhere, in an almost crusading manner, that is likely to be a highly self-destructive ordeal. But if the policy becomes merely verbal, it will be a splendid demonstration of impotence.[12]

The short circuit between theory and practice of the human rights campaign had an impact both within the executive branch and in relations with Congress. Hoffmann claimed that the administration lacked a clear definition of priorities, problems and objectives for its international actions; the resulting confusion amplified problems with a resurgent Congress: "In order to get Congress back into some form of order, it is important to know what is desired." The lack of clear priorities prevented the administration from developing a good working relationship with Congress, which "interferes with practically everything" and left no room for the executive branch.[13]

Hoffmann's points were confirmed by both the debate within the administration and the debate between the White House and Congress. Since late 1977, the executive branch had experienced bureaucratic infighting on the extent, nature and objectives of the human rights campaign. On a general level, regional desks within the State Department considered human rights as a major threat to their natural aim, namely keeping good relations with states and national governments. A policy that was based on interferences in domestic affairs, public criticism and, eventually, economic sanctions did not favour friendly relations with other countries.

There were also specific problems. Diplomats and State Department officials became increasingly vexed at Patricia Derian's appointment as the head of the Bureau for Human Rights and Humanitarian Affairs. Derian came from the civil rights movement. During the 1960s she had contributed to the creation of Mississippians for Public Education, a white women's group in favour of public school desegregation. In 1968, she became president of the Loyalist Democrats Group, which opposed segregationists among the Democratic ranks in Mississippi. Within the Carter administration, Derian supported a firm stance on human rights. She came to see the promotion of human rights abroad through the lens of her direct experience with the civil rights movement. Accordingly, she assumed an uncompromising stance and advocated a policy that would distance the United States from authoritarian allies, starting with Chile, Argentina and the Philippines. In her understanding, her mission was not to introduce human rights into foreign policy decisions; it was preventing other concerns from eclipsing human rights considerations.[14]

Her background as an activist was not matched by an adequate understanding of State Department mechanisms and administrative culture, and Derian often fought against this machinery. For their part, diplomats soon identified Derian as an inexperienced outsider, with a radical position on human rights and unable to handle the delicate equilibria of international relations. As William Michael Schmidli has argued, the State Department's "unique culture" also had the practical consequence of excluding Derian's office from the flow of information circulating between US diplomatic posts and "the geographic and functional bureaus" of the department. Accordingly, Derian became aware of many decisions with "human rights implications only after a position had been drafted by the geographic bureaus and delivered to the secretary".[15]

Other departments also expressed strong opposition to prioritizing human rights. The Defense, Treasury and Agriculture departments, for example, did not spare criticism of Derian's attempts to cut off foreign assistance to regimes with a poor record on human rights. In early 1978, Undersecretary of State Lucy Benson threatened to resign should military aid not be exempt from scrutiny by both Derian's staff and the Christopher Group, the task force in charge of implementing the human rights campaign. Similarly, the Department of Agriculture succeeded in exempting the Food for Peace programme from the Christopher Group even when authoritarian regimes with a poor record on human rights were the beneficiaries of economic aid. Over the following months, even funding for the International Monetary Fund, the Ex-Im Bank, the International Development Association and the recently established International Fund for Agricultural Development were exempted from the scrutiny of both the Christopher Group and the Bureau for Human Rights.

The same Christopher Group contributed to confusion and friction within the administration. When it was established to coordinate the implementation of the human rights policy, it assumed a pragmatic and ad hoc approach, which by definition had no clear standards and formulas. Some within the group lamented an excessive centralization of decisions among Christopher's closest aides. Others complained that the mission itself was too strict, since many assistance programmes were excluded from its scrutiny. Just one year after pledging an absolute commitment to human rights, the Carter administration had to narrow the areas in which the human rights campaign would be implemented.[16]

The outcome was an even more confusing human rights policy. Since its inception, the administration had to balance between a universal and global commitment and the will to develop a pragmatic, case-by-case approach. The list of countries exempted from human rights considerations – or in which human rights were not the decisive factor in shaping American foreign policy – was getting longer. As Anthony Lake noted in early 1978, the administration had taken a strong position on Latin American abuses. Elsewhere, exceptions were becoming too numerous.[17] The administration wanted, for example, to normalize relations with China; therefore, it put human rights considerations aside in that country's case. By the end of 1978, the administration was fully aware of public surveillance and harassment of Chinese activists of the so-called Democracy Wall Movement. Nevertheless, it continued with its determination not to raise Chinese human rights violations.[18] Similarly, security concerns and Cold War priorities took precedence over human rights in Iran, South Korea, the Philippines,

Israel, Egypt, Saudi Arabia, North Yemen and Indonesia, despite reports on human rights abuses in these countries.

The trajectory of human rights in US–Brazilian relations is quite revealing. Tensions between Brazil and Washington had been growing since Carter's election, as a consequence of American criticism of human rights abuses and Carter's non-proliferation policy, which had become a major obstacle for the 1975 nuclear deal between Brazil and West Germany. By early 1978, the administration was determined to improve bilateral relations. Carter even paid an official visit to Brazil in March. Moreover, by spring 1978, the State Department began pointing out that recent improvements had been taking place in Brazil. The conclusion was that Brazil remained "a human rights problem country, but it is not a serious human rights problem country. ... Brazil [is] on an upward trend and [is] arguably better than a number of other important countries, Indonesia, the Philippines, Iran."[19]

The State Department's conclusion, however, elicited protest from human rights activists. As the *Los Angeles Times* commented in July 1978, the idea of human rights improvements

> appears nearsighted in light of what is actually happening in Brazil. As recently as April, 1977 Brazilian President Ernesto Geisel arbitrarily suspended Congress when that body pressed for judicial reform, especially the reestablishment of the habeas corpus in political cases. Nowadays, government decrees and broader "institutional acts" allow government authorities to override constitutional guarantees of due process and to hold, without trial, anyone considered a threat to "national security". ... Amnesty [International] also noted in its most recent annual report that, "although brutal and violent arrests of political prisoners have diminished, Amnesty International is concerned at increasing reports of the torture and ill-treatment of people ... suspected of ordinary crimes".[20]

Congressional supporters of a firmer stance on human rights were disappointed by what they perceived as a reversal in Carter's human rights policy. To those Representatives and Senators close to the new internationalists' ideas, not only was the president unable to meet their expectations, but he also appeared to have given an anti-Soviet boost to his human rights stance. The silence on Chinese violations of human rights, arms transfers to South Korea, the continuing good relations with Iran or the decision to withdraw from the International Labour Organization were denounced as some of the many contradictions in what the president called "a total commitment to human rights".[21] Joshua Eilberg (D – Pennsylvania), for example, criticized the administration's decision to lift the arms transfer embargo against Turkey given "the harsh treatment that religious minorities and political prisoners are subjected to in Turkey or the treatment that Greek Cypriots have received". Despite "the importance of Turkey in the NATO alliance", Eilberg admitted, "reports on continuing violations of human rights in Turkey and on the island of Cyprus" could not be tolerated any longer.[22] To address similar situations in which conflicting interests were at stake, Jonathan B. Bingham (D – Connecticut) invited the White House to define clear and strict criteria for foreign aid.[23] Similarly, Robert Lagomarsino (R – California) lashed out at "the apparent double standard which the Carter administration is applying toward the various Third World countries".[24] Even Ted Kennedy (D – Massachusetts) criticized Carter's selective pragmatism toward Nicaragua because, despite the reduction in aid, the White House had decided to maintain a $150 million military training programme, which clearly contradicted Carter's proclaimed total commitment to human rights. In April 1978, a State Department official cautioned that the general Congressional attitude was that "the administration has been inconsistent in applying its human rights policies, giving harsher treatment to small countries where we have little security or economic interest". In sum, to advocates of a human rights-based foreign policy, the pursuit of human rights was becoming the exception rather than the rule.[25]

Beyond criticism, Carter's liberal critics introduced legislation requiring the administration to define a new strategy to reaffirm the global aim of the human rights campaign. In February 1978, for example, Tom Harkin (D – Iowa) introduced an amendment to the law authorizing funding to international financial institutions. The amendment would prevent any loans to all countries that engaged in a consistent pattern of gross violations of human rights. The proposal, Frank Moore from the Congressional liaison office commented, could find many supporters in both Houses because "voting for human rights is popular and consistent with a perception of your goals". Nevertheless, the Treasury and State departments opposed such inflexible language on the grounds that it would be ultimately be detrimental to human rights.[26]

Other initiatives targeted the 1979 Security Assistance Act. In March 1978, two organizations close to the liberals within the Democratic Party, the Coalition for a New Foreign and Military Policy and Americans for Democratic Actions, coordinated a campaign to oppose the law that they felt did not take human rights into proper consideration. In their official communiqué they explained, "the first security assistance programme written entirely by the Carter administration continues in many cases to justify military aid and arms sales on overriding principles of national security that are so broad and diffuse that U.S. support for human rights can amount to little more than a series of statements of concern".[27] The report by the Coalition for a New Foreign and Military Policy argued that, far from promoting human rights in the world, the United States was committed "to supporting suppression of opposition to the recipient government – the very opposite of a human rights policy".[28] House Minority Leader Robert Michel (R – Illinois) shared this conclusion. In May, he introduced an amendment requiring human rights reports on all countries of the world. The administration "vigorously opposed" the proposal for several reasons: it was an unjustified interference in domestic affairs of countries that did not receive American military aid, it did not contribute to the real advancement of human rights and it was a "substantial additional burden" on Derian's Bureau of Human Rights and Humanitarian Affairs.[29] When Donald Fraser introduced three amendments to Sec. 502 of the Security Assistance Act, he posed a new challenge to the administration. His amendments urged, first, that the United States deny security assistance to any country "which engages in a consistent pattern of gross violations of internationally recognized human rights";

second, the State Department draw up monthly reports to Congress on commercial exports of munitions; and third, that "under no circumstances" should the United States furnish military education and training to governments that violate human rights.[30] The administration was opposed because, as Brzezinski and Lake explained, the amendments denied the necessary flexibility for the promotion of human rights and "would further complicate our dealings both with foreign governments and with Congress".[31]

The White House succeeded in preventing Congress from passing these proposals. However, it received several invitations to reconsider the role of human rights in bipolar relations. In February, for example, the American Committee on East–West Accords, an American lobby in favour of improving relations with the Soviet Union, proposed a conference on "Common Sense in US–Soviet Relations". The conference concluded with a bipartisan appeal in favour of détente and hoped that the administration would work for the conclusion of a SALT II Treaty, the repeal of the Jackson–Vanik amendment and a new general approach to human rights in East–West relations.[32] Sovietologist Stephen Cohen, one of the participants in the conference, noted that the White House ought to discuss human rights problems only through quiet diplomacy channels because there was "no alternative to détente". To face those global challenges that required a cooperative attitude by the Soviets, the administration had to develop a comprehensive dialogue, because:

> Détente is too important to be left to governments alone. A variety of nongovern-
> mental American organizations and citizens have been pursuing these kinds
> of relations, sometimes in the face of official American indifference and even
> obstructionism, for many years. They should be encouraged, and their ideas and
> expertise solicited, so that détente will become not merely fuller government-to-
> government relations, but institution-to-institution, profession-to-profession,
> citizen-to-citizen relations …. Meanwhile, the American government should make
> its own direct contribution by, among other things, promoting trade by granting
> to the Soviet Union favorable tariff and credit provisions, funding larger and more
> diverse exchanges of people, and pressing for liberalized entry-visa procedures
> and fewer travel restrictions in both countries.

Within this "reinforced détente", Cohen concluded, "what the United States can and should do is influence Soviet liberalization *indirectly* [emphasis in original] by developing a long-term American foreign policy, and thereby an international environment, that will strengthen reformist trends and undermine reactionary ones inside the Soviet Union".[33] Similarly, Harvard sociologist David Riesman pointed out "the danger of the human rights campaign": the ideological assault that was at the core of the campaign in favour of the Jackson–Vanik amendment in 1973/74 – and which was now the very foundation of Carter's human rights initiative – was weakening détente, the only possible policy to contain Soviet activism abroad.[34] George F. Kennan shared this conclusion. He considered Carter's open diplomacy both an obstacle to a new SALT Treaty and, paradoxically, a boost for an eventual new crackdown on dissidents.[35]

Congress immediately relaunched these conclusions. Many liberals were concerned by the deadlock in SALT II negotiations, which they believed was a consequence of Carter's open diplomacy on human rights.[36] For this reason, in early 1978, the White House was swamped by letters and appeals urging the administration to define new priorities in bipolar relations. Ted Kennedy, for example, urged Vance to resort to any means necessary to reach a conclusion in SALT II negotiations, and, in February, five Senators signed an appeal for the removal of the Jackson–Vanik amendment. Similarly, Senators Alan Cranston (D – California) and Jacob Javits (R – New York) and House Majority Whip John Brademas invited the White House to "meet and talk with the Soviet Delegation of Parliamentarians" that at the time was paying an official visit to Congress, as "a demonstration of presidential interest would make this exchange more substantive, bringing home to the Soviets and to the Congress that these visits have significant political value".[37]

Stabilizing détente to promote human rights

Not only did the administration follow the Congressional invitation to meet the delegation, it also made a number of conciliatory gestures toward the Soviets. All major executive officials refrained from criticizing the Soviets on human rights (with the exception of the trials against Orlov and Sharansky). They also reiterated the American commitment to the conclusion of a new SALT Treaty and to increased bilateral trade. This was not a reversal in Carter's stance on human rights in East–West relations nor an abandonment of dissidents in the USSR. Rather, the administration discussed their plight through quiet diplomacy channels. In April 1978, Brzezinski proposed a prisoner exchange to Ambassador Dobrynin, which would "remove an irritant, and would prevent the further emotionalism of the relationship. That would enable [Carter] to move more rapidly on SALT, probably by late summer or early fall."[38] Over the same period, Secretary of State Cyrus Vance searched for a new equilibrium between the diplomacy of human rights and the need to make progress on arms control.

By April 1978 the new equilibrium seemed to have achieved some concrete results. During a meeting in Moscow, Vance and Gromyko succeeded in discussing both human rights and arms control. Not only did Vance officially protest at the Soviet decision to continue the trials against members of the Moscow-based "Helsinki Group", but he also handed Gromyko a list of refuseniks, prepared by the NCSJ. Once back in Washington, Vance explained to the NCSJ president, Jerry Goodman, that Gromyko had assured him he would find a solution to those cases.[39]

The most significant progress was on negotiations for SALT II. Many contentious issues were addressed and a general structure for the treaty was defined. To the satisfaction of the American negotiators, Gromyko agreed to the 1,200 limit on MIRVed ballistic missiles within a larger ceiling of 2,250 ICBMs for both countries.[40] However, there were still many knots to untangle. The Soviets refused to suspend the production of the "Backfire" bomber or to discuss methods for verifying compliance with the ceilings stipulated by the treaty. Equally important, the White House had to define a clear strategy to sell the new treaty to the American public and Congress and, if necessary – Brzezinski suggested – the president had to start negotiations with Senators Jackson and Nunn.[41]

These problems were two sides of the same coin: domestic consensus around the new treaty could only increase through a more cooperative Soviet attitude on those issues that were under the spotlight of the American political debate, as the "Backfire" or verification criteria were. Consequently, despite the real progress in negotiations between the United States and the Soviet Union, the Moscow meeting was subject to a number of critiques from journalists, pundits and conservative politicians. Senator Jackson, for example, lashed out at the inept American negotiation strategy.[42] Furthermore, Gromyko's firm opposition to any discussion of the trials of Orlov and other dissidents, as well as his rejection of any discussion of the involvement of Soviet (and Cuban) troops in Central Africa and in the Horn of Africa, where a war erupted between Somalia and Ethiopia in 1977, further strengthened domestic critics of Carter's new course.[43]

Notwithstanding these problems, the administration was unanimous in considering the Moscow summit as important for progress on Soviet relations. Its results strengthened those who, like Vance or Shulman, were advocating a major initiative to improve bipolar relations and a minor emphasis on human rights. During a meeting of the Interagency Coordinating Committee for U.S.–Soviet Affairs, Marshall Shulman and Undersecretary of State Mark Schneider pointed out the progress made on human rights and SALT negotiations. The Soviet reaction to the Vance mission, Shulman emphasized, had been positive, and the Soviets were now exhibiting a more pragmatic and cooperative attitude on human rights. Schneider clarified that "a more liberal policy has been followed in terms of Jewish emigration. The first quarter of [the] year has seen a 48 percent increase over 1977." Despite Soviet authorities' actions against Sharansky, Shulman pointed out that frank discussions on human rights between Washington and Moscow were continuing.[44]

To strengthen these positive trends, Shulman and Schneider proposed repealing the Jackson–Vanik amendment, although they admitted supporters of the amendment were still numerous both in Congress and among the public. For this reason, they argued that the issue should be officially discussed only after the ratification of the SALT II Treaty in order to not undermine the White House. Until that moment senior State Department official William Leurs had proposed that the administration should not explain to the Soviets its project and, at the same time, it should also test the ground with moderate members of Congress and major organizations that had contributed to Jackson's campaign in favour of his amendment.[45]

Accordingly, while American diplomats invited the Politburo to allow more Soviet Jews to emigrate and to make some progress in respect of the Helsinki Final Act, Marshall Shulman and Al Moses, Special Advisor on Jewish Affairs, tried to develop a dialogue with some of the organizations that constituted the NCSJ. Domestic negotiations were doomed to fail from the start, since among the thirty-nine organizations that were part of the NCSJ, only the American Jewish Congress and the Union of

Councils for Soviet Jews gave a lukewarm welcome to the idea of a possible repeal of the Jackson–Vanik amendment.[46]

Beyond the domestic debate, two further events convinced the White House to abandon any initiative to repeal the Jackson–Vanik amendment: the crisis in the Horn of Africa and the "season of trials" against activists of the Moscow-based Helsinki Watch group. Not only did these events demonstrate the limits of American diplomacy in influencing Soviet behaviour, but they also fuelled suspicions and new critiques towards Soviet intentions, eventually bolstering those who accused Moscow of exploiting détente to threaten the United States.

Quiet diplomacy in trouble: Africa, the neutron bomb and the season of trials

Between 1975 and 1976, the Angolan civil war was pivotal in discrediting Henry Kissinger's realpolitik. Even during the Carter years, Africa remained a Cold War hotspot where global rivalries continued to grow. A new crisis erupted in 1977. In March, the Front for the National Liberation of the Congo (FNLC), a group of about 2,000 Katangan Congolese soldiers, entered the Zairian province of Shaba from Angola to affirm the independence of the area. Zairian president Mobutu seized on the Cuban involvement in Angola and the ties between Cuban troops and Katangan volunteers to denounce the invasion as a Cuban–Soviet aggression. Appeals to the Organization of African Unity on this basis made little progress. While the OAU condemned the invasion, there was no concern regarding the alleged communist involvement. Similarly, American reactions were lukewarm. Realism and idealism intertwined in rejecting Mobutu's appeal. First, Carter's strategy for Central Africa relied on Nigeria, Zaire's rival, as the key player in the region. Second, for an administration that had come to power promising to make human rights a fundamental tenet of its foreign policy, Mobutu's appeal could not easily be accepted on account of his regime's shameful human rights record. Moreover, following Vance's regionalist approach to international affairs, the administration tended to regard Africa's problems as regional, not global. Carter himself claimed, at first, that there was no evidence of Cuban involvement.[47] Furthermore, with the long shadows cast by the Vietnam War and the Angola fiasco over the political debate, it was unlikely that Congress would have supported military involvement in Central Africa. For all these reasons, the Carter administration denied military aid to Zaire, authorizing only the shipment of non-military supplies. International military support, however, arrived to Mobutu in April from France, Morocco and Egypt and was fundamental to repel the invasion.[48]

In a repetition of this crisis, Katangan rebels regrouped and invaded the Shaba region in May 1978. Once more, Mobutu alleged direct Cuban responsibility. This time, however, the United States took a firmer position. In part, this was a consequence of domestic politics. Within the United States, Carter's popularity was decreasing significantly – his approval among Americans dropped from 56 per cent in November 1977 to 39 per cent in April 1978 as a result of a perception of him being soft on communism and for failing to check "Cuban–Soviet adventurism in Africa".[49] In part, the administration recognized the failure of its non-involvement policy in 1977. Accordingly, the United States openly supported France and Belgium in their military interventions, transporting around 2,500 troops in Zaire. Much to Secretary of State Cyrus Vance's chagrin, the White House could not handle the crisis as a regional conflict. It was evolving into a Cold War confrontation. Meeting Gromyko in late May, Carter voiced American concern and outrage over Soviet and Cuban involvement and "adventurism" in Africa. He also claimed that he "had no doubt that the Soviet Union could have prevented" the invasion.[50]

Bipolar relations and the domestic debate over détente were further poisoned by events in the Horn of Africa. The Horn of Africa was not immune to global rivalry between the United States and the Soviet Union. Its strategic position en route to the Suez Canal and close to the Arabian peninsula fostered the superpowers' interest in the region. In 1953, the United States signed a military alliance with Ethiopia, while, after decades of military assistance, the Soviets concluded a Treaty of Friendship with Somalia in 1974. The situation started to change – apparently to the benefit of the Soviet Union – in early 1977 when the pro-American Selassie government in Ethiopia was overthrown in a military coup. After some confusion, this led to the creation of Menghistu's pro-Soviet regime. Although both Somalia and Ethiopia were now part of the Soviet camp, this did not prevent Somali from claiming sovereignty over the Ogaden region, which was part of the Ethiopian state. As tensions grew, the Soviets sided with the larger and strategically more important Ethiopia.[51] Moreover, abandoning revolutionary Ethiopia would have created both new tensions between the Soviet Union and China and enough room for an autonomous Cuban intervention in the region.[52]

The Carter administration followed with apprehension the latest developments in the region. In March 1977, Brzezinski urged his staff to define some guidelines for approaching the area.[53] Within days, the administration halted its military assistance to Ethiopia because of the blatant violations of human rights occurring there. Later, in April, the State Department ordered the American ambassador in Somalia to test President Siad Barre's willingness to drop out of the Soviet orbit and enter the American area of influence.[54]

Benefiting from Eritrean rebellions against Ethiopia and presuming American support, the Somali government invaded the Ogaden region in July. Moscow ensured consistent military aid to Ethiopia. By the end of 1977, more than 1,500 Soviet military advisers and 3,000 Cuban troops were operating there. At first, the Carter administration seemed quite willing to stay out of the crisis. The war did not represent a major threat to American security or interests, and the memory of the Vietnam War was strong enough to prevent any military operation. Also, Secretary of State Cyrus Vance was determined to follow his regionalist approach to Third World crises, thus avoiding any direct intervention that would have turned the crisis into a Cold War confrontation. Moreover, both Somalia and Ethiopia had been condemned by the Carter administration for their constant violations of human rights, and, finally,

Somalia, now moving closer to the United States, was the aggressor.[55] With these arguments, Vance and Defense Secretary Harold Brown opposed any thought of military intervention.

Brzezinski took the opposite stance. He disagreed with Vance on their evaluation of the crisis and its relationship to détente. To Vance, Soviet and Cuban involvement demonstrated Soviet opportunism. Yet, it did not modify the local nature of the conflict. Accordingly, the United States should favour a diplomatic solution to the crisis, one that would not hamper SALT negotiations. In other words, for Vance détente was a strictly compartmentalized process in which there was no room for linkage between SALT negotiations and all other bipolar issues. To Brzezinski, Soviet action was part of a broader plan to expand Moscow's influence in the Middle East and on global oil supply. Brzezinski's points were echoed by Robert Gates, who pointed out growing Soviet interest in Angola, Guinea, Nigeria, Tanzania and, in particular, Rhodesia. To avoid the expansion of Soviet influence over the Persian Gulf and of its involvement in Africa, Gates argued that the United States should vigorously react to Soviet actions. American action was even more urgent because of the political debate within the United States, where the White House was facing mounting criticism of being weak on the Soviet Union.[56]

As the Soviet–Cuban presence increased, Carter started to agree with Brzezinski's analyses. While he refused any arms transfer to Siad Barre's regime, he nevertheless authorized programmes for the modernization of the American strategic arsenal. He also obtained the commitment of NATO allies to increase their defence spending, and, despite the human rights campaign, favoured the rearmament of Somalia's neighbouring countries, encouraging regional allies to provide the Barre regime with military equipment and considering also the delivery of military planes (F-5 and C-130) to Sudan. Washington also tried to develop a dialogue with the Non-Allied Movement, urging the Yugoslav and Indian governments to mediate with Cuba in order to encourage Havana's disengagement from the area.[57] Finally, Carter publicly pointed out that Soviet actions in the Horn of Africa were contrary to détente and that Soviet and Cuban withdrawal was a precondition for a positive conclusion of the SALT II agreement.[58]

While the Kremlin's intervention in the Horn did not cause a major rupture in bipolar relations, as Nancy Mitchell has recently argued, it nevertheless forced Carter to assume a firmer stance and to modify his administration's linkage strategy. The linkage, which Carter had first disowned and then used to strengthen the domestic consensus for détente, was now at the top of his agenda. It was not Kissinger's rigid linkage in which every single progress in arms limitation was strictly linked to other negotiations, but it was what historian Robert Strong defined as "commonsense linkage". Under this approach, the Soviets would be made to understand that SALT II ratification would be possible only if they followed a more cooperative strategy, both in domestic and in international affairs.[59] Yet, the Soviets did not share Carter's reasoning. On the contrary, over the following months not only did they continue their military action in Africa, but they also began trials against prominent human rights activists, which triggered an anti-Soviet surge within the United States. In this climate, many voiced their concerns about Carter's approach to détente. Ronald Reagan, for example, claimed that:

> The Soviet goal is obvious: to secure a permanent foothold for itself on the Red Sea. If the Soviets are successful – and it looks more and more as if they will be – then the entire Horn of Africa will be under their influence, if not their control. From there, they can threaten the sea-lanes carrying oil to Western Europe and the United States, if and when they choose. More immediately, control of the Horn of Africa would give Moscow the ability to destabilize those governments on the Arabian Peninsula which have proven themselves strongly anti-communist. ... Unless the White House can bring itself to understand these realities, it is not too much to say that in a few years we may be faced with the prospect of a Soviet empire of protégés and dependencies stretching from Addis Ababa to Cape Town.[60]

Similarly, in a caustic comment, Representative John Ashbrook (R – Ohio) denounced that the war in the Horn of Africa marked the definitive end of détente:

> I have always been fascinated at how people throw around the word détente like it really means something. As we all know, this magical word supposedly describes current relations between the United States and the Soviet Union. But is there any substance behind this word? ... There is no détente at all. The Soviets have not restrained their activities. They have not changed their behavior. Instead, the Soviets have continued their policies of aggression throughout the world. Probably their most impressive military venture at this time is on the continent of Africa ... it is apparent that détente is a word without substance. The Soviets continue to do what they want to do, without regard to the policy of détente. Détente is dead. Or perhaps it was never really alive.[61]

Over the following weeks, the critiques of conservatives and cold warriors were fuelled by another controversial development, Carter's decision to postpone the development of the neutron bomb. The dispute over the new warhead emerged in the summer of 1977 when an unclassified Congressional document made vague references to the classified programme to develop the bomb. While at the time this programme was not controversial, it "sparked a passionate debate", forcing Carter to return "to a kind of policy limbo ten months later".[62] The entire episode would amplify Carter's reputation for indecisiveness. Yet, for the moment, many agreed with *Washington Post* columnists Rowland Evans and Robert Novak, who argued that with this decision Carter was ensuring another major victory to the Soviets.[63] In the same newspaper, Walter Pincus highlighted that the burden from Carter's decision fell on American allies. For this reason, the House Committee on Armed Services was preparing a letter to protest against Carter's action that, Pincus commented, reduced Western security. Senator Robert C. Byrd (D – West Virginia) believed that Carter had to reverse the decision in order to contain conservatives' critique of his foreign policy and SALT II negotiations.[64] In early May 1978, the Coalition for a Democratic Majority, an organization close to Jackson's Democrats and to the Committee on the Present Danger, issued a press release denouncing the administration:

> The Carter administration is continuing a pattern of international accommoda-
> tion and retreat, which is weakening our nation's standing in the world, just as
> it is weakening the administration's standing at home, breeding division among
> Democrats and giving round to Republicans. ... We have yielded to Soviet pressure
> on human rights, the neutron bomb and, it appears, in the SALT negotiations. We
> have avoided any meaningful response to the Soviet–Cuban rampage in Africa.[65]

With Carter on the defensive in relation to his bipolar policy, the Soviets announced the beginning of trials against the members of the Moscow-based Helsinki Group and, specifically, against Yuri Orlov, Natan Sharansky and Aleksandr Ginzburg. The White House was aware that these trials represented a litmus test for its entire bipolar policy. A strong reaction could precipitate a disruptive chain of events, anger the Soviets and sanction the end of détente. A weak reaction would dis-avow Carter's commitment to human rights and undermine the domestic basis of détente and SALT II. For this reason, the administration had begun discussing its possible reaction to the trials as early as February 1978, when Ambassador Melvyn Levitsky presented a detailed strategy to cope with the ongoing Sharansky case. Before the beginning of the trial, Levitsky invited the administration to issue some general declarations to "state our concerns and record our position, but also to pre-serve the possibility of working for Sharansky's release after the trial". Among pos-sible measures, Levitsky invited Marshall Shulman to clarify American diplomatic protests to journalists and Congressional leaders and to persuade every "influ-ential American who has good relations with the Soviets (e.g. Averell Harriman, Armand Hammer, Donald Kendall) to take up the Sharansky case". During the trial, Levitsky wrote, the administration should avoid any direct polemics with the Soviets and "take into consideration other elements of U.S.–Soviet relations, such as other human rights cases, on-going negotiations". However, it was also oppor-tune to postpone all official visits and meetings with Soviet officials.[66] Inevitably, Levitsky's suggestions for the post-trial period were even vaguer. The presi-dent and the secretary of state should release an appeal to Soviet authorities for Sharansky's release, while Brzezinski should develop a behind-the-scenes initiative with Dobrynin to explain the importance the Sharansky case had for the American public, for Congress and for the continuation of détente. If necessary, Brzezinski could propose some "exchanges between the Soviets and countries holding leftist prisoners". He continued that should these initiatives have failed or sentencing be more severe than expected, the White House would need to adopt some specific measures:

1 postpone or cancel high-level visits, such as those by Kreps, Bergiand and Califano;
2 postpone or cancel bilateral meetings;

3 we could also look for practical steps to take in the trade area. The only feasible action would be in the export of licensing field, however, since wheat sales are heavily influenced by domestic considerations;

4 slow down cooperative exchange activities under the scientific and cultural agreements;

5 take the offensive at multilateral meetings. We could instruct our delegations to various UN organizations to raise the Shcharanskiy case publicly in strong terms.[67]

However, the memorandum concluded that if these initiatives failed "it will be difficult to justify going back to business as usual and any attempt to get this moving again will be viewed with suspicion in the United States". In the following months, the White House followed Levitsky's suggestions, avoiding any direct presidential involvement in the controversy. Prominent officials explained to the Soviets that the conviction of Orlov, Ginzburg and Sharansky would cause sharply deterioration in bipolar relations. Yet, American pressures did not produce any positive outcome. In mid-May 1978, the Soviets concluded the first trial and sentenced Yuri Orlov to seven years' imprisonment and five years' internal exile. The State Department immediately denounced this "gross distortion of internationally accepted standards of human rights".[68]

The sentences fuelled transnational protests. The European Parliament approved a resolution that condemned the Soviet Union, while EC foreign ministers issued an official release to protest at the sentences.[69] Public demonstrations, rallies and protest marches took place in Rome, Paris and Bonn. From Western European and American cities, petitions were addressed to NATO countries and many international organizations calling for measures to boycott and punish the Soviets. A major initiative targeted the 1980 Olympic Games, which were slated to be hosted by the Soviets in Moscow. In Great Britain, for example, Liberals, Conservatives and many Labour supporters joined human rights activists in an official "Campaign to Remove the Olympics from Moscow". In France, a new organization was established to promote a human-rights based boycott of the Olympic Games, the "COBOM – Comité de boycott des Jeux olympiques de Moscou".[70] In April 1979, it published a long manifesto demanding "no sports in the Gulag" because of the Soviets' brutal repression of dissidents and constant human rights violations.[71]

Protests gained momentum in the United States as well, intertwining a genuine indignation regarding human rights violations with the growing criticism of Carter's weak approach to the Soviets. The Committee of Concerned Scientists and the recently established Scientists for Sakharov Orlov Shcharansky coordinated a campaign to decry the sentence as a violation of the Helsinki Agreements. A nineteen-scientist delegation announced it would not participate in a scientific meeting in the Soviet Union, while fifteen Nobel laureates signed an appeal expressing their concern for the plight of Soviet Helsinki monitors.[72] Congress immediately joined the protests. When the sentence was announced, both House and Senate unanimously passed a resolution urging the president to "continue to express U.S. opposition to the imprisonment of members of the Soviet Helsinki Groups". Speaking on the Senate floor, Daniel Patrick Moynihan clarified the meaning of the sentence and its implications for bipolar dialogue:

> One thinks of this in terms of the recent statements by Secretary Vance, who … in an interview in *Time* magazine said that when President Carter and Mr. Brezhnev meet he was sure they will find they share the same hopes and aspirations. What are the hopes and aspirations of the head of the Soviet State that could behave this way – send a man to prison for seven years, because he sought to exercise the most elemental human rights of following the conduct of his own government?[73]

Pressed by domestic critics, President Carter publicly condemned the sentence. He announced the cancellation of Secretary Califano's mission to Moscow and the possibility of cancelling a presidential meeting with Gromyko.[74] This last point was quite controversial within the administration. According to NSC staffer Jessica Tuchman-Matthews, the president should have met Gromyko to "hit (him) hard on human rights [and to] go beyond the regular litany – Orlov, Sharansky, Ginzburg – to mention some other cases: apolitical ones that demonstrate the truly needless cruelty of Soviet policy".[75] Carter revised his decision and accepted Tuchman-Matthews' suggestion. The day before the meeting with Gromyko, he also publicly affirmed the existence of an indirect linkage between Soviet violations of human rights, Soviet military activism in the Horn and arms control:

> We ought not necessarily to let Soviet action in other areas interfere with the progress of SALT. But … unless the Soviets do honor the constraints on basic human rights, unless they also honor constraints on their involvement in places like Africa, that it will have a strong adverse effect on our country and make it much more difficult to sell to the American people and to have ratification in Congress of a SALT agreement if it should be negotiated between me and Brezhnev and those who work under us. So, I never have favored the establishment by me or Brezhnev of a linkage between the two, saying that if the Soviets and the Cubans stay in Ethiopia, for instance, we would cancel the SALT talks. I think that the SALT agreement is so important for our country, for the safety of the entire world, that we ought not to let any impediment come between us and the reaching of a successful agreement. But there is no doubt that if the Soviets continue to abuse human rights, to punish people who are monitoring the Soviets' compliance with the Helsinki agreement, which they signed on their own free will, and unless they show some constraints on their own involvement in Africa and on their sending Cuban troops to be involved in Africa, it will make it much more difficult to conclude a SALT agreement and to have it ratified once it is written.[76]

During his meeting with Gromyko, Carter protested at Soviet violations of human rights, presented the Orlov case as a threat to détente and required the Soviets to respect the Helsinki Final Act.[77]

White House official protests peaked with Carter's speech at the Annapolis Naval Academy in early June 1978. In a long-meditated speech on the state of bipolar relations, Carter addressed both Soviet actions and those domestic critics who were advocating a tougher stance on the Soviets.[78] While he acknowledged the serious worsening in bipolar relations, he nevertheless blamed the Soviet Union for it and warned its leaders that their actions in Africa and their repression at home were undermining détente and arms control:

> To be stable, to be supported by the American people, and to be a basis for widening the scope of cooperation, then détente must be broadly defined and truly reciprocal. Both nations must exercise restraint in troubled areas and in troubled times. Both must honor meticulously those agreements which have already been reached to widen cooperation, naturally and mutually limit nuclear arms production, permit the free movement of people and the expression of ideas, and to protect human rights.[79]

Carter was launching a double challenge to the Soviets. Domestically, the president noted that "by their actions, they've demonstrated that the Soviet system cannot tolerate freely expressed ideas or notions of loyal opposition and the free movement of peoples". Internationally, he emphasized that the United States was seeking cooperation with all countries, even with the nations of Eastern Europe and with the People's Republic of China to forge a world "which is more responsive to the desire of people everywhere for economic well-being, social justice, political self-determination, and basic human rights". Finally, in the best-known part of his speech, Carter highlighted that the Soviet Union had to "choose either confrontation or cooperation" because "the United States is adequately prepared to meet either choice".[80]

Carter's speech did not produce the expected results. At home, many agreed with journalists Rowland Evans and Robert Novak's analysis that Carter had mixed Vance's more conciliatory vocabulary with Brzezinski's hawkish one: "like ordering from a Chinese Menu, the president was taking one from column A and one from column B".[81] In Moscow, Brezhnev underestimated the impact of his decisions on bipolar relations. During a Politburo meeting, he dismissed Carter's firmness: with Congressional elections approaching – he claimed – the American president was falling under the "usual influence of the most shameless anti-Soviet types and ringleaders of the military-industrial complex of the United States". For this reason – Brezhnev insisted – the Soviet Union should reject American pressures. Rather, it should respond with firmness:

1 We should come forward in our press (simultaneously in all of the main newspapers) with a large and serious declaration, calling it, let's say, "Concerning the policy of the Carter government". We should ... say directly that in the policy of the United States changes are taking place, which are dangerous for the affairs of peace. Under the curtain of lies and slander on the USSR and other socialist countries concrete matters are being perpetrated, directed against peace and

détente. ... Attempts at clumsy interference in our internal affairs are being perpetrated. ...

2 We should come forward with a collective declaration of governments – participating in the Warsaw Pact regarding the results of the session of the Council of NATO.

3 We should come forward with a special declaration of the Soviet government on African affairs. In this document we should categorically refute and expose the imperialist intentions with regard to the policy of the Soviet Union and other socialist countries in Africa.[82]

Ambassador Dobrynin confirmed Brezhnev's analyses. From Washington, he explained that Carter had to juggle different and often conflicting pressures. According to Dobrynin, the White House had no interest in interrupting détente with the Soviets. Not only were "influential political and business circles" in favour of détente, but also the vulnerability of Carter's position in the 1980 presidential elections, "if he goes into these elections as the president who caused a strategic arms agreement with the Soviet Union to fail", was forcing the White House to continue détente.[83] For these reasons, Dobrynin invited Soviet leaders to continue their operations in Africa and the trials against those "renegades like Shcharansky". The administration "was forced to retreat and to announce its intention to continue the Soviet–American negotiations on SALT ... and to declare that that agreement meets the interests not only of the Soviet Union, but also the national interest of the United States. *The Russians won this mini-confrontation* – such is the conclusion of the local political observers."[84]

The Soviet inability to fully understand Carter's precarious equilibrium and the evolution of the American political debate was clear. By blaming the United States for the worsening in bipolar relations, the Politburo underestimated how its own actions fuelled opposition to détente and Carter's opponents. But even Carter's strategy proved to be flawed. He had imagined human rights and détente as two extremities of a political blanket. By hitting the Soviets on human rights, he hoped to shelter détente from domestic critics. Through the strengthening of détente, he was trying to both ideologically challenge the Soviets and to promote human rights in the Soviet bloc. By the time of the trials, it was clear that neither Brezhnev nor domestic critics of détente were willing to retreat from their positions and to negotiate. Carter's political blanket proved too narrow to cover both extremes, as a major emphasis on human rights angered the Soviets and the shift to quiet diplomacy definitely alienated the domestic public.

Over the following days, the Soviets took a harder stance and denounced American interference. *Pravda* launched a postcard campaign to protest against Carter's statements. In early July, Brzezinski reported to the president that hundreds of postcards with this message overwhelmed the White House:

Mister President!
Human rights that you speak so much about begin at home. We address you, Mr. President, an appeal to take concrete actions in your country, to denounce and stop the political trials of the American civil rights fighters.

Adding our voice to the broad international campaign of solidarity with political prisoners in the US jails we are expecting from You mister President, decisive actions in defense of justice.

We urge: freedom to the freedom fighters!!![85]

Protests were followed by new sentences against dissidents. On 21 June 1978 refuseniks and human rights activists Ida Nudel and Vladimir Slepak were sentenced to four and five years of exile, respectively. On 9 July, Soviet authorities announced that the trials of Ginzburg, Sharansky and Filatov would take place in three different cities far from Western journalists and diplomats. To Brzezinski, the choice of the date just before the opening of the Geneva negotiations between Vance and Gromyko revealed the Soviets' understanding of Carter's positions:

> The Soviets have concluded that they can safely ignore our earlier protestations. I think the time is ripe for a strong statement of condemnation of the Soviets – and let the Soviets link this to SALT if they choose. ... [Y]our credibility on human rights is now at stake, and Cy should tell Gromyko in no uncertain terms that your administration intends to speak up. Moreover, it would be good if State was instructed to do so, because if you alone do so the newspapers will be full of stories, attributed to State Department officials, critical of your position on human rights.[86]

Similarly, Jessica Tuchman-Matthews argued that the decision to start the trials on the eve of the Geneva summit between Vance and Gromyko was "a test asking us in the full view of the international community: how much do you care about human rights?". Should the United States fail to respond, she claimed, nothing would prevent the Soviets from launching a major wave of repression. To make matters worse, she concluded, this would have had negative consequences within the United States: "it will not be difficult for US press and public opinion to draw the obvious connection". For this reason, she suggested cancelling the scheduled Vance–Gromyko meeting or issuing a presidential statement to explain to both the Soviets and the American public that "we are proceeding with the meeting only because SALT is in the US interest and in the interest of global peace".[87]

Congress took a firmer stance. After a meeting at the White House, Senators Jackson and Moynihan lashed out at Carter's decision to continue with SALT negotiations. To Jackson, Vance's mission was "the wrong signal at the wrong time", while Moynihan denounced the administration for "acquiescence in what is happening, acquiescence that verges on complicity".[88] Others joined the camp of those urging to stop SALT negotiations. Donald W. Riegle (R – Michigan), for example, argued that the trials jeopardized both the reliability of the Soviet Union and the credibility of détente:

> What value is one to place on the pledges and guarantees of a government of this sort? What is the meaning and value of the word of the Soviet government when it comes to international arrangements? What can one expect from Soviet pledges

concerning the Helsinki Accords, or a possible SALT agreement? How can they mean any more than the guarantees the Soviet Union makes to its own people, its own national flesh and blood? I cannot imagine a SALT treaty I could support with a nation that terrorizes its own people. I cannot see the value of an expanded trading relationship with a government that brutalizes dissenters who act within the bounds of the Soviet constitution. I am ashamed of the conduct of the Soviet government and I must urge my own government to do nothing that would give aid and comfort to a Soviet regime that would devour its own people.[89]

The White House was not indifferent to these appeals. Nevertheless, it opted for a strategy that could convey its outrage to the Soviets without any repercussions for the SALT negotiations. For this reason, in July 1978 Vance flew to Geneva to help finalize the new treaty and, at the same time, to protest against the Soviet trials. Once in Switzerland, he met Avital Sharansky, the dissident's wife, and openly condemned the violation of the Helsinki Agreements. He warned the Soviets that their actions had "exacerbated relations" and "led to a gap between [the United States and the Soviet Union] on a number of issues".[90] Vance's protests fell on deaf ears. On 14 July, Soviet authorities sentenced Aleksandr Ginzburg to eight years of forced labour, while Ivan Filatov was sentenced to death.

For the administration, domestic protests and Soviet disregard of Vance's objection made a firm reaction more pressing. Many organizations of the "Helsinki lobby", which until that moment had been generally supportive of Carter's human rights policy, began to criticize the White House's approach and discussed retaliatory measures. The NCSJ proposed freezing all cultural, scientific and technological programmes, suspending all bilateral negotiations and abandoning the SALT II talks. A few dozen activists from the Student Struggle for Soviet Jewry demonstrated in front of Aeroflot headquarters in New York, rhetorically asking to be transferred to Moscow and gaoled as political prisoners.[91] The American chapter of Amnesty International and Khronika Press announced the publication of a special volume collecting all the Soviet editions of the *samizdat Chronicle of Current Events*.[92]

Politicians also wasted no time in criticizing Carter's weak reactions to the sentences. Senator Dole and Congressmen Zeferetti, Jeffords, Kildee and Young wrote to the White House asking for the adoption of stronger measures.[93] Jessica Tuchman-Matthews reported that Jackson was drafting a proposal for a ninety-day suspension in issuing trade licences to the Soviet Union. More importantly, "a long parade of Senators and Congressmen testified before the CSCE Commission" suggesting some firmer measures, such as a complete economic boycott, the suspension of SALT negotiations and even withdrawal "from the Helsinki Final Act". According to Tuchman-Matthews, the president should prevent Congress from further action and consider measures "suspending all trade, government-sponsored exchanges, and technology transfer with the Soviet Union", because:

While it may appear ... that growing pressure will make it easier for the president to take strong steps, in reality the opposite is true. If the president acts in response to Congressional pressure he will get no positive credit for doing that whatever he does, and will be perceived as weak by many. I think that political realities demand a rethinking of your desire to calibrate the US response so as to save stronger actions for the sentencing and subsequent acts. If we wait it will be too late – Congress will have pre-empted all but the most extreme steps, and the president will reap nothing but a political loss.[94]

Carter agreed and condemned the sentences. From Bonn, where he was paying an official visit, and on the same day that the dissidents' sentences were announced, he underscored that the Soviet action was a "reminder that, so late in the 20th century, a person can be sent to jail simply for asserting his basic human rights. ... The struggle for human liberties is long and difficult, but it will be won. There is no power on Earth that can long delay its progress."[95] After his return to the United States, he cancelled two official missions in the Soviet Union, those of the director of the Environmental Protection Agency and the Secretary of Housing and Urban Development, and postponed a meeting of scientists from both countries. He then suspended all high-level meetings.[96] Carter also cancelled the contract for the sale of computers to TASS and introduced a specific procedure for the export of oil and gas technology to the Soviet Union. Finally, he urged Brzezinski to define a strategy on how to exploit American economic and technological advantages within the bipolar confrontation.[97]

Yet again, renewed American firmness did not produce the expected results within Soviet relations or domestically. The genie was out of the bottle and the administration did not know how to reverse it. The White House measures paled in comparison with the radical tone of the anti-Soviet campaign that was developing in American society and in Congress. While commenting on the decision to stop high-technology transfers, Jackson and Moynihan repeated on 19 July 1978 that the only concrete measure the White House had to implement was an interruption in SALT negotiations.[98] Jack Kemp and Patricia Schroeder urged the White House to demand that the International Olympic Committee deny Moscow the right to host the 1980 Olympic Games. On 26 July, the Senate voted on a resolution to reinstate visa restrictions on foreign members of communist parties, which the Carter administration had removed just one year before in order to comply with CSCE provisions. It was a retaliatory decision, but, as Raymond Garthoff has argued, it also signalled "that if the Soviets could violate the Helsinki Accord, then the United States could too". In a similar manner, Republican Robert Dole introduced a resolution calling on the Federal government to cancel all scientific and cultural programmes, to rethink American participation in the CSCE process and to suspend SALT negotiations. Senator Robert C. Byrd (D – West Virginia) felt there was no chance for ratification of the SALT II Treaty in Senate.[99] Over the following days, demands to stop SALT negotiations multiplied. Jackson and Moynihan were joined by Republicans Bob Dole, Nick Vento and candidate Newt Gingrich.[100] In a similar manner, Senator Packwood (R – Oregon) urged the Federal government "to begin a process" to renounce the CSCE that the Soviets had turned into "a fraudulent document", while Senator Percy urged the State Department to summon a meeting of all CSCE foreign ministers to condemn Soviet violations of the Final Act.[101]

Conclusions

Events from May to July 1978 undermined Carter's initiatives in bipolar relations. American protests did not bring about any decisive change in the Soviets' actions, either in terms of human rights violations or their growing involvement in the Horn of Africa. On the contrary, the Soviets' commitment to the continuation of the trials against members of the Moscow Helsinki Group demonstrated the limits of American diplomacy. The meaning of the trials, as *New York Times* journalist David Shipler commented, was indisputable. On the one side, Soviet authorities had sent a clear message to dissidents, to their Western supporters and to the Carter administration that neither public nor private pressure would intimidate them. On the other side, the Soviets were pointing out the limits of détente and were acting to "dramatize what détente does and does not mean here: that its centerpiece is arms control, and that it does not imply acquiescence to American demands for internal social change".[102]

Despite the growing frustration in international affairs, it was within the United States that Carter's strategy vacillated the most. Within the administration, tensions over the human rights diplomacy multiplied. The clash between Carter's dovish Secretary of State, Cyrus Vance, and his more hawkish National Security Advisor, Zbigniew Brzezinski, became uncontainable. Once again, everything revolved around détente and linkage. Vance felt that any American action to reduce Soviet influence in Africa or to support dissidents and human rights activists in the Soviet Union should be designed to prevent any consequences for arms control. The conclusion of the new SALT Treaty was too important to be jeopardized by any other initiative. Conversely, Brzezinski believed that Soviet actions and the evolution of the American political debate imposed a reappraisal of Carter's approach to bipolar affairs. To the National Security Advisor, the White House ought to clarify that Soviet actions in the Horn and against dissidents increased the obstacles to the conclusion of SALT II. Carter wavered and oscillated between the two. He alternately drew from their different vocabularies, but, by early July, he declared publicly that Soviet repression and actions in the Horn were damaging the prospects for SALT ratification.

Finally, in a political climate where anti-communism and doubts on détente were strengthening, the Carter administration discovered that it was unable to control the relationship between human rights and arms control. Congressional initiatives, such as the demand to interrupt SALT negotiations or to exit the CSCE, were a direct critique against Carter's actions. Before signing the SALT II Treaty, the administration needed to find a new legitimation for both the bipolar dialogue and its quiet diplomacy on human rights.

Notes

1 J.A. Rosati, "The Rise and Fall of America's First Post-Cold War Foreign Policy",
   in H.D. Rosenbaum and A. Ugrinsky (eds), *Jimmy Carter: Foreign Policy and Post-
   Presidential Years* (Westport, CT: Greenwood Press, 1994), pp. 35–52; G. Smith,
   Morality, Reason and Power: American Diplomacy in the Carter Years (New York: Hill
   and Wang, 1986); D. Skidmore, "Carter and the Failure of Foreign Policy Reform",
   Political Science Quarterly 108:4 (Winter 1993–1994), pp. 699–729; S. Kaufman, *Plans
   Unraveled: The Foreign Policy of the Carter Administration* (DeKalb: Northern Illinois
   University Press, 2008).

2 W. Lafeber, "From Confusion to Cold War: The Memoirs of the Carter Administration",
   Diplomatic History 8:1 (January 1984), pp. 1–12; T.M. Nichols, "Carter and the Soviets.
   The Origins of U.S. Return to a Strategy of Confrontation", *Diplomacy and Statecraft*
   13:2 (June 2002), pp. 21–42; O.A. Westad (ed.), *The Fall of Détente: Soviet American
   Relations during the Carter Years* (Oslo and Boston: Scandinavian University Press,
   1996); D.J. Sargent, *A Superpower Transformed: The Remaking of American Foreign
   Relations in the 1970s* (Oxford and New York: Oxford University Press, 2015),
   pp. 261–295.

3 R.L. Garthoff, *Détente and Confrontation: American–Soviet Relations from Nixon
   to Reagan* (Washington, DC: The Brookings Institution, 1994); O. Njølstad, "Keys
   of Keys? SALT II and the Breakdown of Détente", in Westad, *The Fall of Détente*,
   pp. 34–71.

4 Z. Brzezinski to M. Costanza et al., "Human Rights Improvement", 16 May 1977, JCPL,
   NSA – SF, Box 28, Folder 2; CIA, National Foreign Assessment Center, "Significant
   Developments Related to the U.S. Stand on Human Rights – USSR & Eastern Europe",
   14 April 1978, JCPL, NLC-31-39-1-15-8. Even the Helsinki Commission reported
   some limited progress in Soviet compliance with CSCE human rights provisions: see
   Commission on Security and Cooperation in Europe, *Hearings: Information Flow,
   Cultural and Educational Exchanges*, 95th Congress, 1st Session (Washington, DC:
   US. Government Printing Office, 1978).

5 R.B. Boettcher, "The Role of Congress in Deciding United States Human Rights
   Policy", in N. Kaufman Hevener (ed.), *The Dynamics of Human Rights in U.S. Foreign
   Policy* (New Brunswick, NJ: Transaction, 1981), pp. 279–290.

6 Z. Brzezinski to the President, "Human Rights", 3 December 1977, JCPL,
   NLC-126-10-7-1-2.

7 Ibid. As Brzezinski suggested, the White House began a series of meetings with human
   rights leaders from both Houses. The first to participate in such meetings were House
   Democrats Diggs, Fraser, Harkin, Obey, Pease, Wilson, Wright, and Republicans
   Buchanan, Conte, Young. The first Senators to be received at the White House to
   discuss human rights were Democrats Cranston, Humphrey, Inouye, Kennedy and
   Republicans Case, Javits, Mathias, Pearson. J. Tuchman-Matthews to F. Moore,
   "Meeting with Congressional Human Rights Advocates", 5 January 1978, JCPL, WHCF,
   Box HU-2, Folder "1/11/78–31/1/78".

8 A. Lake to the Secretary, "The Human Rights Policy: An Interim Assessment", 20
   January 1978, NARA, RG 59, WCP, Box 19, Folder 1.

9 Ibid.

10 A.D. Romberg, through Mr Kreisberg, to A. Lake, "Human Rights", 6 February 1978, NARA II, RG 59, WCP, Box 19, Folder 1.

11 T. Szulc, "Is Jimmy Carter Losing Faith? The Plot Against Human Rights", NARA, RG 59, WCP, Box 15, Folder 8; "Tears and Sympathy for the Shah", *New York Times*, 17 November 1977; L. Oelsner, "Civil Liberties Group Says the President Has 'Erratic' Record", *New York Times*, 29 January 1978; J. Amuzegar, "Rights, and Wrongs", *New York Times*, 29 January 1978; R. Burt, "Carter Asks for No Cut in Arms Aid to Marcos Despite Negative Human-Rights Report", *New York Times*, 6 February 1978; K. Elliott House, "U.S. Officials Worry Over Inconsistencies in Human Rights Plan", *Wall Street Journal*, 11 May 1978. The quotation is from a memorandum written by S. Oxman for P. Derian, 10 March 1978, NARA, RG 59, WCP, Box 19, Folder 13.

12 S. Hoffmann, "The Hell of Good Intentions", *Foreign Policy* 29 (Winter 1977–1978), pp. 3–26.

13 Ibid.

14 W.M. Schmidli, *The Fate of Freedom Elsewhere: Human Rights and U.S. Cold War Policy toward Argentina* (Ithaca, NY and London: Cornell University Press, 2013), pp. 85–88.

15 E.S. Maynard, "The Bureaucracy and Implementation of U.S. Human Rights Policy", *Human Rights Quarterly* 11:2 (May 1989), pp. 175–248; A. Glenn Mower, Jr, *Human Rights and American Foreign Policy: The Carter and Reagan Experiences* (Westport, CT: Greenwood, 1998, pp. 61–67; V.S. Kaufman, "The Bureau of Human Rights during the Carter Administration", *The Historian* 61:1 (1998), pp. 51–66; Schmidli, *The Fate of Freedom Elsewhere*, pp. 95–106.

16 Schmidli, *The Fate of Freedom Elsewhere*, p. 95; Kaufman, *Plans Unraveled*, pp. 30–32; Sargent, *A Superpower Transformed*, p. 255–260.

17 A. Lake to the Secretary, "The Human Rights Policy: An Interim Assessment", 20 January 1978, NARA, RG 59, WCP, Box 19, Folder 1.

18 Cable from Peking to Secretary of State, December 1978, JCPL, ZBM, Staff Evening Report File, Box 17, Folder1.

19 McNeil to Oxman, "Brazil Fingerprint Computers", 17 April 1978, NARA, RG 59, WCP, Box 16, Folder 4.

20 C. Arnson and M.T. Klare, "Human Rights: Here Is the Noble Theory … But Is This the Practice, At Least in Brazil?", *Los Angeles Times*, 2 July, 1978.

21 See, for examples, D. Fraser, "Freedom and Foreign Policy", *Congressional Record*, 95th Congress, 1st Session, 20 May 1977, pp. 15845–15848; D. Fraser, "US Participation in ILO", *Congressional Record*, 95th Congress, 1st Session, 20 September 1977, pp. 30005–30006.

22 J. Eilberg, "Whitewash on Human Rights in Turkey?", *Congressional Record*, 95th Congress, 2nd Session, 4 April 1978, p. 8963.

23 J. Bingham, "Foreign Aid and Human Rights", *Congressional Record*, 95th Congress, 2nd Session, 22 March 1978, p. 3152.

24 R. Lagomarsino, "Double Standard on Human Rights", *Congressional Record*, 95th Congress, 2nd Session, 13 April 1978, pp. 10183–10184.

25 E. Kennedy, "Human Rights and Nicaragua", *Congressional Record*, 95th Congress, 2nd Session, 10 February 1978, pp. 3281–3283.

26 F. Moore to the President, "Weekly Legislative Report", 18 February 1978, JCPL, Plains Files, Box 20, Folder 3; Cyrus Vance to H. Reuss and T.P. O'Neill, 11 May 1978, NARA, RG 59, WCP, Box 16, Folder 3.

27 P. Derian to the Deputy Secretary, "Critique of Human Rights Reports by Coalition for a New Foreign and Military Policy", 27 March 1978, NARA, RG 59, WCP, Box 15, Folder 18.

28 Ibid.

29 R. Michel, "Human Rights" *Congressional Record*, 95th Congress, 2nd Session, 1 May 1978, p. 12019; and Draft of a Memorandum, NARA, RG 59, WCP, Box 15, Folder 17.

30 D.T. Kenney to All Assistant Secretaries, "Fraser Human Rights Amendments", 4 May 1978, NARA, RG 59, WCP, Box 16, Folder 1.

31 Anthony Lake to the Deputy Secretary, "The Fraser Amendments", 29 April 1978, NARA, RG 59, WCP, Box 16, Folder 1; Kenney to All Assistant Secretaries, "Fraser Human Rights Amendments".

32 C. Marcy (ed.), *Common Sense in U.S.–Soviet Relations* (Washington, DC: American Committee on East–West Relations; New York: Norton, 1978).

33 Stephen F. Cohen, "Soviet Domestic Politics and Foreign Policy", in Macy, *Common Sense in U.S.–Soviet Relations*, pp. 11–28.

34 D. Riesman, "The Danger of the Human Rights Campaign", in Marcy, *Common Sense in U.S.–Soviet Relations*, pp. 49–55.

35 G.F. Kennan, "Needed: A New American View of the USSR", in Marcy, *Common Sense in U.S.–Soviet Relations*, pp. 27–35.

36 R.W. Kasten-Meier, *Congressional Record*, 95th Congress, 2nd Session, 16 May 1978, pp. 13991–13993.

37 E. Kennedy to Cyrus Vance, 15 January 1978, JCPL, CL, Box 49, Folder "Correspondence 01/78–02/78"; Cranston, Brademas Javits and others to Z. Brzezinski, 10 January 1978, JCPL, NSA – CF, Box 79, Folder 4.

38 Z. Brzezinski to the President, "NSC Weekly Report no. 64", 23 June 1978, JCPL, ZBM, Box 41, Folder 6.

39 Memorandum of Conversation between Gromyko and Vance, JCPL, Vertical Files, Box 114; J. Goodman, in Memorandum from J. Goodman to the File, March 1978, CJH, Jerry Goodman Papers, Box 8, Folder 3.

40 C. Vance to the Department of State, 20 April 1978, JCPL, NSA, ZBM, SF, Box 56, Folder 3.

41 Z. Brzezinski to the President, "NSC Weekly Report #56", JCPL, ZBM, Box 41, Folder 6, and Memorandum from Z. Brzezinski for the President, "NSC Weekly Report #79", JCPL, ZBM, Box 41, Folder 8.

42 D.K. Shipler, "Vance and Gromyko Confer 6 Hours on Arms Issues", *New York Times*, 21 April 1978; B. Gwertzman, "Arms Pact Progress Indicated in Moscow", *New York Times*, 22 April 1978; "Jackson Calls U.S. Inept in Arms Talks with the Soviet", *New York Times*, 23 April 1978; M. Marder, "Vance Informs Carter of Limited Advances on Salt in Moscow", *Washington Post*, 25 April 1978.

43 Memorandum of Conversation between Gromyko and Carter, "Salt, CTB, Africa, Human Rights", 27 May 1978, JCPL, Vertical Files, Box 114; Westad, *The Fall of Détente*, pp. 187–206.

44 Memorandum, "Meeting of the Interagency Coordinating Committee for U.S.–Soviet Affairs", 2 May 1978, JCPL, NLC-12-27-1-2-6.

45 Ibid.

46 Memorandum to E. Sanders et al., "The Union of Council for Soviet Jews", 20 November 1978, JCPL, Special Advisor on Jewish Affairs – Moses, Box 13, Folder "Sakharov Article"; See also Memorandum from J. Goodman, "Jackson Amendment", 5 January 1979, CJH, Jerry Goodman Files, Box 8, Folder 3.

47 *Department of State Bulletin*, 18 April 1977, p. 361.

48 T.P. Odom, *Shaba II: The French and Belgian Intervention in Zaire in 1978* (Fort
    Leavenworth, KS: Combat Studies Institute, 1993), pp. 17–30; P. Gleijeses, "Truth or
    Credibility: Castro, Carter, and the Invasions of Shaba", *International History Review*
    18:1 (1996), pp. 70–103.

49 Gleijeses, "Truth or Credibility", pp. 70–103; George H. Gallup, *The Gallup Poll: Public
    Opinion, 1972–1977*, vol. 2 (Wilmington, NC: Scholarly Resources Inc., 1978), p. 1239.

50 Memorandum of Conversation between Gromyko and Carter, "Salt, CTB, Africa,
    Human Rights".

51 O.A. Westad, *The Global Cold War: Third World Interventions and the Making of Our
    Times* (New York: Cambridge University Press, 2005), pp. 250–286. Fidel Castro
    could have played a major role in influencing Soviet decision to support Ethiopia.
    Back from the Horn of Africa, Castro explained to Honecker that "Ethiopia has a
    great revolutionary potential. So there is a great counterweight to Sadat's betrayal in
    Egypt." See "The Cold War in Southern Africa and in the Horn of Africa", *Cold War
    International History Project Bulletin* 8/9 (Winter 1996), p. 20.

52 M.P. Leffler, *For the Soul of Mankind: The United States, the Soviet Union and the Cold
    War* (New York: Hill and Wang, 2008), pp. 278–279.

53 PRM/NSC-21, "The Horn of Africa", 17 March 1977: http://nsarchive.gwu.edu/
    carterbrezhnev/docs_global_competition/Tab%202/19770401%20–%20The%20
    Horn%20of%20Africa,%20Presidential%20Review%20Memorandum.pdf (accessed
    August 2019).

54 Memorandum, Policy Review Committee Meeting, 11 April 1977, JCPL, ZBM, Box 24,
    Folder "Meetings PRC 10".

55 Z. Brzezinski, *Power and Principle: Memoirs of the National Security Adviser,
    1977–1981* (New York: Farrar, Straus and Giroux, 1983), p. 316. The most detailed
    analyses are N. Mitchell, *Jimmy Carter in Africa: Race and the Cold War* (Palo Alto,
    CA: Stanford University Press and Woodrow Wilson Center Press, 2016) and D.R.
    Jackson, *Jimmy Carter and the Horn of Africa: Cold War Policy in Ethiopia and
    Somalia* (Jefferson, NC: McFarland & Co., 2007). See also, R. Thornton, *The Carter
    Years: Toward a New Global Order* (New York: Paragon House, 1991), pp. 180–185.

56 Z. Brzezinski to the President, "NSC Weekly Report #36", 11 November 1978,
    JCPL, ZBM, Box 41, Folder 5. On differences between Vance and Brzezinski, see
    Memorandum, Special Coordinating Committee, 2 March 1978, in J.M. Hanhimäki
    and O.A. Westad (eds), *The Cold War: A History in Documents and Eyewitness
    Accounts* (Oxford and New York: Oxford University Press, 2003), pp. 542–546;
    Mitchell, *Jimmy Carter in Africa*, pp. 401–446.

57 Thornton, *The Carter Years*, pp. 134–179. Carter to Tito and Carter to Morarji Desai,
    10 February 1978, both in JCPL, ZBM, Box 28, Folder SCC 56.

58 J. Carter, "The President's News Conference", 12 January 1978, and "Address at Wake
    Forest University", 17 March 1978, *Weekly Compilation of Presidential Documents*,
    vol. 14, pp. 56–58 and pp. 529–535; Memorandum of Conversation between Gromyko
    and Carter, "Salt, CTB, Africa, Human Rights". See also Garthoff, *Détente and
    Confrontation*, pp. 653–657; C. Vance, *Hard Choices: Critical Years in America's Foreign
    Policy* (New York: Simon & Schuster, 1983), p. 73; Kaufman, *Plans Unraveled*, p. 122;
    F. Romero, *Storia della Guerra fredda. L'ultimo conflitto per l'Europa* (Turin: Einaudi,
    2009), pp. 266–270.

59 Mitchell, *Jimmy Carter in Africa*, pp. 401–446; Strong, *Working in the World*, p. 103.

60 R. Reagan, "America's Purpose", 25 July 1978: www.reaganlegacy.org/speeches (accessed August 2015).

61 J. Ashbrook, "Détente is Dead – or Was It Ever Really Alive?", *Congressional Record*, 95th Congress, 2nd Session, 2 May 1978, pp. 12265–12266.

62 Strong, *Working in the World*, pp. 123–152.

63 R. Evans and R. Novak, "Behind the Neutron Decision", *Washington Post*, 10 April 1978; R. Evans and R. Novak, "How Our Nuclear Policy Benefits the Kremlin", *Washington Post*, 13 April 1978; G.F. Will, "Back to the Backfire Argument", *Washington Post*, 13 April 1978.

64 W. Pincus, "Carter Given Alternatives to Barring Neutron Bomb", *Washington Post*, 6 April 1978.

65 "Coalition for a Democratic Majority Joins Criticism of Foreign Policy", *Washington Post*, 6 May 1978.

66 Memorandum, from M. Levitsky for the Secretary et al., "The Shcharansky Case", 18 February 1978, JCPL, NLC-15-94-6-1-5.

67 Ibid.

68 C. Vance for the President, "Orlov Given Maximum Sentence", 18 May 1978, JCPL, NLC-128-13-8-12-4.

69 "Rapport fait au nom de la commission politique sur les résultats de la rencontre de Belgrade prescrite par l'Acte Final de la Conférence de Helsinki sur la sécurité et la coopération en Europe, 3 mai 1978", HAEU, PE0 2829; "Rapport fait au nom de la commission politique sur la situation de la Communauté Juive en Union Soviétique, 7 novembre 1978", HAEU, PE0 2837; Confidential Meeting of Foreign Ministers and President of the Commission, 20 May 1978, HAEU, EN-1145.

70 Telegram, 10 July 1978, IOC Archives, PT-KILLA-MEMO-M001-4105 (June–July 1978); Alliance Anticollectiviste Universelle's Appeal to Killanin, 29 August 1979, IOC Archives, JO-1980-BOYCO- 205639; "Moscou80: Boycott des jeux Olimpiques", IOC Archives, JO-1980-BOYOCO-205444; Association of Ukrainians in Great Britain, "Appeal to the International Olympic Committee", July 1979, IOC Archives, JO-BOYCO-20433.

71 Appeal from the COBOM, April 1979, IOC Archives, JO-BOYCO-205444.

72 P. Simon, "Scientists Protest Arrests of Orlov, Shcharansky", *Congressional Record*, 95th Congress, 2nd Session, 12 May 1978, p. 13535; "Nobel Winners Protest Soviet Dissident Trials", *New York Times*, 20 May 1978; B. Gwertzman, "U.S. Scientists Cancel Trip in Protest Over the Trial of Orlov", *New York Times*, 21 May 1978; T. O'Toole, "Orlov's Sentence Causes Third U.S. Physicist Group to Cancel Russian Trip", *Washington Post*, 3 June 1978; "A Small World in Support of Orlov", *New Scientist*, 11 November 1978.

73 D.P. Moynihan, "Human Rights in the USSR", *Congressional Record*, 95th Congress, 2nd Session, 18 May 1978, pp. 14265–14267.

74 Vance to President, "Orlov Given Maximum Sentence".

75 Jessica Tuchman to Z. Brzezinski, "Gromyko Visit – Human Rights", 26 May 1978, JCPL, NLC-6-79-6-17-5.

76 Jimmy Carter, "The President's News Conference: Q&A", 25 May 1978: www. presidency.ucsb.edu/ws/index.php?pid=30852&st=&st1#axzz1q1Wpv7Yy (accessed October 2016).

77 Memorandum for Dr Brzezinski, "Carter–Gromyko Meeting", 27 May 1978, JCPL, Vertical Files, Box 114.

78 Memorandum from J. Fallows for the President, "Naval Academy Speech", 23 May 1978, JCPL, SS, Box 90, Folder "Annapolis Speech 5/23/78"; Memorandum from R. Hertzberg, J. Doolittle and G. Smith for the President, 26 May 1978, JCPL, SS, Box 89, Folder "Annapolis Speech 6/7/78 (2)".

79 "Annapolis Speech", 6 June 1978, JCPL, SS, Box 89, Folder "Annapolis Speech 6/6/78 (1)".

80 Ibid.

81 R. Evans and R. Novak, "The Divided President", *Washington Post*, 14 June 1978. See also "Carter on Soviet: An Ambiguous Message", *New York Times*, 9 June 1978; R. Craston, "United States–Soviet Relations. The Administration View", *Congressional Record*, 95th Congress, 2nd Session, 22 June 1978, p. 18389.

82 "Brezhnev's Speech in Politburo on Foreign Affairs Issues, 8 June 1978", in Westad, *The Fall of Détente*, pp. 207–210.

83 "Dobrynin's Political Report to Gromyko on Soviet–American Relations, 11 July 1978", in Westad, *The Fall of Détente*, pp. 213–220.

84 Ibid.

85 "Soviet Postcards Campaign", 7 July 1978, JCPL, ZBM, Box 41, Folder 6.

86 Memorandum from Z. Brzezinski for the President, "NSC Weekly Report #66", 7 July 1978, JCPL, ZBM, Box 41, Folder 6.

87 Memorandum from J. Tuchman-Matthews for Z. Brzezinski, "Human Rights", 7 July 1978, JCPL, WHCF, Box HU-2, Folder "8.1.77–8.31.77".

88 J. Hoagland, "U.S. Soviet Talks Must Continue, Vance Declares", *Washington Post*, 11 July 1978; "Salt and the Soviet Trials", *Washington Post*, 12 July 1978; W. Pincus, "Trials Provoke Anger on Hill", *Washington Post*, 12 July 1978.

89 D.W. Riegle, "Shcharansky and Ginzburg", *Congressional Record*, 95th Congress, 2nd Session, 11 July 1978, p. 20152.

90 Memorandum of Conversation, "Vance–Gromyko Meeting", 13 July 1978, JCPL Vertical Files, Box 115.

91 J. Goodman to the File, 30 October 1978, CJH, NCSJ Papers, Box 7, Folder "Jerry Goodman"; L. Maitland, "Leaders Across the U.S. Denounce Sentencing of Dissidents", *New York Times*, 15 July 1978.

92 Paul B. Henze to Z. Brzezinski, "Peter Reddaway on Chronicle of Current Events", 26 July 1978, JCPL, NSA File, Country Files, Box 80, Folder 1.

93 L.G. Denend and M. Albright to Z. Brzezinski, "Congressional Mail", 28 July 1978, JCPL, WHCF, Box CO59, Folder 165.

94 J. Tuchman to Z. Brzezinski, "Human Rights – USSR", 12 July 1978, JCPL, NSA File, Subject Files, Box 28, Folder 2.

95 Jimmy Carter, Press Release, 14 July 1978: www.presidency.ucsb.edu/ws/index.php?pid=31080&st (accessed August 2015).

96 Garthoff, *Détente and Confrontation*, p. 674.

97 A list of the measures adopted by the White House is in J. Watson to T. Bradley, 21 September 1978, JCPL, WHCF, Box CO-59, Folder CO-165. See also, PRM/NSC-42: "Framework of US Strategy for US Non Military Competition with the Soviet Union" and PRM/NSC-44: "Export of Oil and Gas Production Technology to USSR".

98   "Daniel Patrick Moynihan Commends the Denial of Technological Export", 19 July
     1978, LOC, DPMP, Box 2795, Folder 9.
99   Senate Resolution 506, "A resolution expressing the sense of the Senate with respect
     to the compliance of the Soviet Union with the provisions on human rights of the
     Final Act of the Conference on Security and Cooperation in Europe, also known as
     the Helsinki Accords", 95th Congress, 2nd Session, July 1978; R.L. Garthoff, *Détente
     and Confrontation: American–Soviet Relations from Nixon to Reagan* (Washington,
     DC: The Brookings Institution, 1994), p. 675.
100 N. Gingrich to J. Carter, 28 August 1978, JCPL, WHCF, Box FO-43, Folder 61,
     "1/20/77–12/31/78"; Nick Vento, in *Implementation of the Helsinki Accords*, vol.
     7: *Hearings on Repercussions of the Trials of the Helsinki Monitors in the USSR before
     the Commission on Security and Cooperation in Europe*, 95th Congress, 2nd Session,
     1978 (Washington, DC: US Government Printing Office, 1978), pp. 33–35, 106;
     Memorandum from M. Wallach for J. Goodman, "Soviet Helsinki Violations Hint at
     Likely Salt Actions, Dole Says", 11 August 1978, CJH, NCSJ Papers, Box 302, Folder 2.
101 H.M. Jackson, "The 1978 Nobel Peace Prize for the Helsinki Monitors in USSR",
     Congressional Record, 95th Congress, 2nd Session, 14 July 1978, p. 20789; Robert
     Packwood, "The Helsinki Accord", *Congressional Record*, 95th Congress, 2nd Session,
     14 July 1978, p. 20908; J. Kemp, "Trials and Olympic Games", *Congressional Record*,
     95th Congress, 2nd Session, 17 July 1978; D.J. Bennet to Senator Percy, 14 August
     1978, JCPL, WHCF, Box CO-59, Folder CO-165, "9/1/79–12/31/79".
102 D.K. Shipler, "Shcharansky Treason Case – Which Begins Today – May Be Indicator
     of Foreign and Domestic Policy", *New York Times*, 10 July 1978.

5

Critics' triumph: quiet diplomacy, SALT II and the invasion of Afghanistan, 1979–1980

From late 1978 and throughout 1979, SALT II dominated bipolar relations and the political debate within the United States. Its realization, however, had to overcome two obstacles.

The first emerged from bipolar relations. The events of early 1978 had poisoned American–Soviet relations and weakened détente. American pressures had not prevented the USSR and Cuba from intervening in the war between Ethiopia and Somalia, nor had they succeeded in stopping the trials of Natan Sharansky and other prominent dissidents. Negotiations on arms control, which had made significant initial progress in April, had also stalled. If Washington and Moscow wanted to sign a new SALT Treaty, they had to move swiftly to mend the diplomatic break and improve relations between the two countries. The second problem arose from the debate within the United States. Since 1977, Carter had tried to appease conservative critics, but after 1978, both Congress and the American public had grown sceptical of Soviet intentions, détente and Carter's foreign policy.

Against this background, Carter's human rights initiative became a marginal aside in bipolar policy; it was not completely abandoned, yet it had only secondary importance compared to the conclusion of SALT II. Beyond the attempt to strengthen détente, the administration concluded that the Soviets were making some significant although pragmatic and selective progress, especially in those areas to which the American public was paying particular attention. The White House believed that discussing human rights through quiet diplomacy channels and avoiding public references to the plight of dissidents could strengthen these trends.

However, the White House was hardly alone in focusing on Soviet violations of human rights, nor was it in full control of the issue. CSCE norms and human rights in East–West relations were under global scrutiny. The European Parliament, for example, had emerged as a champion of human rights and was continuously debating resolutions on human rights violations in the Soviet bloc.[1] The election of Poland's Cardinal Karol Wojtyla as Pope John Paul II in October 1978 gave a fresh boost to human rights activists across the bloc. In March 1979, his first encyclical letter, *Redemptor hominis*, directly discussed human rights:

The rights of power can only be understood on the basis of respect for the objective and inviolable rights of man. The common good that authority in the State serves is brought to full realization only when all the citizens are sure of their rights. The lack of this leads to the dissolution of society, opposition by citizens to authority, or a situation of oppression, intimidation, violence, and terrorism, of which many examples have been provided by the totalitarianism of this century. Thus the principle of human rights is of profound concern to the area of social justice and is the measure by which it can be tested in the life of political bodies.[2]

Nor was American attention toward human rights in East–West relations decreasing. Congress in particular continued to consider human rights both a high priority in East–West relations and a yardstick to evaluate any foreign initiative put forth by the Carter administration. During the Congressional debate on the ratification of the SALT II Treaty, for example, both opponents and supporters of the treaty often invoked the state of human rights in the Soviet Union to justify their stance on arms control.

With Moscow's invasion of Afghanistan in December 1979, Carter's difficult balance between cooperation and confrontation, arms control and human rights ended. Détente was dead, and with it the United States had lost all major tools to promote human rights in the Soviet Union. Similarly, the White House no longer needed to legitimize détente within the United States through a firm human rights stance. Nevertheless, the issue of human rights remained on Carter's bipolar agenda, although it assumed an almost exclusively propagandistic role in denouncing Soviet repression.

A new quiet diplomacy to improve bipolar relations

After the "season of trials" in mid-1978, when the Soviets sentenced prominent dissidents, the United States and the Soviet Union moved swiftly to heal the rift of the previous months. As Soviet Ambassador Anatoly Dobrynin wrote in his memoirs, by late 1978, communication between the administration, the Soviet embassy in Washington and the Kremlin intensified, favouring significant progress on arms control.[3] This progress involved a number of technical issues. The US government agreed to postpone the deadline for compliance with the treaty at the end of 1981 and not, as requested previously, in May of the same year. For their part, the Soviets renounced to a ban on all air-to-surface missiles (ALCM) with a range of more than 2,500 km. Even more importantly, Moscow accepted that the treaty could include some verifiability tools (still to be defined) and renounced encryption systems that could have nullified the controls. Moreover, the Americans recognized the Soviet right to build thirty "Backfire" bombers per year as long as they had no intercontinental capacity. By late February 1979, the SALT II Treaty was ready.[4]

Convergence on arms control was matched by a general improvement in bipolar relations, including human rights. According to a CIA analysis, after the trials of

Orlov, Sharansky and Ginzburg, Soviet authorities were "seeking to improve Moscow's image and to stem the wave of protests abroad. ... Moscow's latest moves seem[ed] calculated to reduce frictions with the US." Indeed, the analysis continued, the Soviets had postponed or suspended many trials, while some convictions had been commuted to less severe measures, as in the case of Maria Slepak, Aleksandr Zinoviev and Eduard Kuznetsov.[5] In August, the NSC confirmed this trend and predicted that the Soviets were ready for "a few more cautious conciliatory gestures". Figures were encouraging; by the end of July, no more dissidents had been arrested, and the number of Jews who were allowed to leave the Soviet Union was constantly growing. To the NSC, "the Soviets may now feel they are in a better position to make a few more public gestures to underline their compliance with the CSCE Final Act without risking a resurgence of activism". It was then possible to expect "more concessions, such as the revelation that Sakharov's step-daughter and her family will be allowed to emigrate, or raising the level of Jewish emigration".[6]

The Carter administration decided to respond positively to the Soviets' actions. A constructive response to the Soviet "new course" on human rights was supposed to strengthen these trends and, at the same time, to foster a major improvement in international relations. In late September, Marshall Shulman explained to the House Foreign Affairs Committee that "a number of steps on the Soviet side in recent weeks suggests that the Soviet Union wishes to reverse the tide of events":

- The court action against two American correspondents, who had been charged with slander as part of an effort to limit Western news reporting on Soviet dissidents, was termed.
- An American businessman who had been charged with currency violations apparently in retaliation for the arrest of two Soviet citizens for espionage was allowed to leave the country after a transparently contrived trial.
- The inhumane severity of sentences in human rights cases has been relatively reduced in the most recent series of trials, following the conviction of Shcharanskiy, and the Soviet leadership has agreed to allow a number of families to leave the country who had previously been denied permission to do so. The level of Jewish emigration from the Soviet Union has continued to rise and is now higher than at any time since 1973.[7]

There was a concrete "opportunity for us to put the U.S.–Soviet relationship on a more realistic and steady course". As a corollary, Shulman implied that human rights issues should be relegated to quiet diplomacy.[8] Within days, Secretary of State Vance echoed Shulman's points. During a meeting with a group of Senators who would pay an official visit to Moscow in November, he admitted that "the dissident trials have left [a] bad aftertaste", but that "the problems of the summer have largely abated".[9]

Accordingly, over the following months, White House officials avoided polemics on the human rights situation in the USSR. In November, for example, Carter decided not to meet writer "half dissident, Andrei Voznesensky", although it would have "served as a stimulus to keep intellectual life open in the Soviet Union". Similarly,

National Security Advisor Brzezinski decided not to participate in a solidarity event with Soviet Jews because of his "sensitive role in US–Sov[iet] relations".[10] Around the same time, State Department spokesperson Hodding Carter announced that those scientific meetings that had been suspended as a retaliation for the trials would resume in February. He specified that "the human rights picture in the Soviet Union had improved considerably", as the increase in the number of Soviet Jews who were allowed to emigrate and information about "judicial repression against dissidents" demonstrated.[11] Nevertheless, human rights abuses in the Soviet Union remained on the American agenda. Diplomats and White House officials discussed privately with their Soviet counterparts some specific cases, such as the situation of a group of Soviet Pentecostals who were denied the right to emigrate and had taken shelter in the American embassy.[12] On other occasions, American officials and diplomats urged the Soviets to find acceptable solutions to ongoing human rights cases before they became public. Soviet authorities seemed to cooperate with American demands: they granted a visa to Elena Bonner, Andrei Sakharov's wife, to travel to Italy for treatment of her wartime eye injury; they authorized four Volga German families to emigrate; and they postponed until late 1979 the trials of the members of the Lithuanian Helsinki Group.[13]

The most significant development concerning human rights in bipolar relations was the conclusion of a delicate year-long negotiation Brzezinski personally conducted with Dobrynin to arrange an exchange of prisoners.[14] Talks were interrupted in mid-1978 because of the Soviet trials of prominent dissidents. To make matters even more difficult, the Soviets feared that the exchange could create a new Bukovsky affair: when Vladimir Bukovsky had been released in 1976 in a prisoner exchange with Chilean communist leader Louis Corvalan, he became a staunch critic of both détente and Soviet leaders. In September, Brzezinski suggested to the Soviet ambassador that it might be best to "quietly arrange for the resolution of the more glaring cases". This "would in itself contribute to a better atmosphere [and] make SALT ratification easier". Dobrynin replied that the Soviet leadership was inclined to discuss some specific cases, and that it was in favour of commuting Ivan Filatov's death sentence. Yet, he also clearly explained that "Sharansky could not be involved in any discussion because his case has become symbolic and the Soviet leaders feel very strongly about it". He then proposed the release of the Vins family, but Brzezinski refused. "Since the exchange [was] designed to have a positive political effect – Brzezinski pointed out – focusing on essentially obscure cases would not serve the political purposes of such accommodation."[15] Negotiations continued until April 1979, when they agreed on exchanging Valdik Enger and Rudolf Chernyayev, two Soviet UN officials charged with espionage, for five dissidents: Aleksandr Ginzburg, Valentyn Morotz, Georgy Vins and the two Soviet Jews who in 1970 had hijacked a plane in order to escape from the Soviet Union, Mark Dymshits and Eduard Kuznetsov.[16]

Around the same time, the Carter administration began reconsidering the political and economic sanctions introduced after the 1978 trials. In December 1979, official meetings resumed. A delegation led by Michael Blumenthal and Juanita Kreps, Secretaries of Treasure and Commerce respectively, participated in a conference in Moscow to discuss the possibility of increasing trade relations between East and West.[17]

A concrete step was the idea to lift the embargo on technology sales that the president had announced just a few months earlier. In his memoirs, Brzezinski underlined that the State Department and the Department of Commerce had autonomously approved the request by Dresser Industries, of Texas, for export licences for oil and gas technologies to the Soviet Union. This *fait accompli* angered Carter and Brzezinski.[18] Yet, some recently declassified documents cast doubt on Brzezinski's account. By mid-August, the entire administration was discussing the possibility of lifting the ban on these licences. Beyond the economic relevance of the sale, as Vance, Blumenthal and Kreps argued, the sale of licences would significantly improve bipolar relations. Brzezinski and his staff had a different view. General William Odom, who at the time was a military aide at the NSC, urged Brzezinski and Carter not to lift economic sanctions against the Soviet Union to avoid a major confrontation with Senator Jackson and his supporters.[19] Another opponent was Samuel Huntington, at the time a member of Brzezinski's staff. Huntington opposed the export licences for both national security reasons and the opportunity to keep an economic and technological advantage over the Soviets.[20] Odom and Huntington's points were resumed by Brzezinski in late August:

> Proceeding [with the technology transfer] as if nothing has happened would be to play into Senator Jackson's hands, in addition to perhaps generally hurting our national security. However, to revoke the licenses would be preemptive and would now send an excessively negative signal to the Soviet Union. Therefore, on balance I recommend a suspension on both national security and foreign policy grounds. National security grounds are most specific in the Dresser case, but there are also broader foreign policy considerations in the transfer of oil technology to the Soviet Union. In essence, as the DSB assessment suggests, "it would allow the Soviets to enter the natural oil and gas fields throughout the world with advanced drilling technical competence, presenting increased opportunities for them to exert their policy influence".[21]

Nevertheless, Vance's line prevailed. It was a natural choice, since it was consistent with the political will to improve bipolar relations. At the same time, it represented a response to growing protests coming from the American business community. Between July and September, many entrepreneurs reacted negatively to the decision to impose economic sanctions on the Soviet Union. To James V. Jones, president of Dresser Industries, Carter's economic sanctions were "sheer idiocy" because "placing oil technology under government control will virtually hand American export business to foreign competitors on a silver platter".[22]

The removal of the embargo was also consistent with other options the White House had been discussing since August. One concerned the sale of computers to TASS that the White House had prevented in retaliation for the dissidents' convictions. In April 1979, Carter reversed his previous decision. In announcing it, he ambiguously claimed that the "total communication capability" of the computer was decreased by "about 77%", thus implying that national security considerations, not human rights, had suspended the sale.[23] The other option was the possibility of a major initiative to repeal the Jackson–Vanik amendment. The administration had already discussed and abandoned the idea of repealing the Jackson–Vanik amendment in 1977, for the White House feared that such a decision could damage the possibility of ratifying the SALT II Treaty, given the intractable opposition from Senator Henry Jackson, his supporters and many NGOs, as well as the AFL-CIO. However, since then a number of changes had occurred, both at home and abroad, and the administration began reconsidering a major initiative in this area.

First, the Soviets seemed to have adopted a more cooperative attitude. On the eve of the Vienna summit for the signing of SALT II, Moscow wanted to improve bipolar relations. In November 1978, the Soviet journal *Novyj Mir* published a roundtable on human rights pointing out the many measures the Soviets had adopted to comply with international standards. Even more importantly, by early 1979, not only did the Soviets conclude the prisoner exchange on Brzezinski's terms, but they also allowed a growing number of Soviet Jews to emigrate. In sum, Moscow was enhancing its credibility as a human rights champion, and also offering a hand to the White House for the difficult Senate ratification of the SALT II Treaty.[24]

Second, economic data reinforced the idea that the Jackson–Vanik amendment was detrimental to American trade and production. Already at the end of June 1977, the Politburo had informed Secretary of Commerce Kreps that American imports had fallen by 50 per cent compared to the previous year. These figures were aggravated by the expansion of commercial relations between the Soviet Union and other Western countries. The 1978 figures confirmed that Soviet exchanges with the United States were lower than those with France, Japan and, above all, West Germany. Both the administration and the business community blamed the Jackson–Vanik amendment as a legislative measure that obstructed American penetration into the Soviet market.[25]

Third, the definitive establishment of diplomatic relations with China, which was announced in December 1978 and completed on 1 January 1979, created two opportunities for the normalization of trade relations with the Soviets. Granting MFN status to the Soviet Union would have contributed to containing Moscow's irritation with Carter's normalization of relations with China. At the same time, many in the administration had concluded that a vast majority of members of Congress were in favour of granting MFN status to China.[26] For this reason, the administration could have asked Congress to make the Jackson–Vanik amendment more flexible and to link the granting of MFN status to China with a similar action for the Soviet Union.

Finally, albeit briefly, the administration believed that many in Congress would favour a repeal of the Jackson–Vanik amendment. In early January, Dante Fascell, Adlai Stevenson III and Charles Vanik publicly announced that the Soviets had met the requirements of the Jackson–Vanik amendment and, consequently, that they were in favour of granting MFN status to the Soviets.[27] Their positions were quite significant, since they were prominent Democrats with a major commitment to the promotion of human rights in the Soviet Union: Vanik had co-authored the language of the Jackson–Vanik amendment, Fascell was the chairman of the Congressional Helsinki Commission and Adlai Stevenson had authored an amendment to the 1974 Ex-Im Bank Act that put a ceiling on credits to the Soviet Union.

Relying on these considerations, Vance and Blumenthal defined a strategy for trade normalization with the Soviet Union in late January 1979. According to them, figures relating to emigration from the Soviet Union could allow the president to grant MFN status without modifying existing legislation. To win Congressional support, they proposed linking the granting of MFN status to the Soviet Union to a similar action with regard to China and specified that the White House – not the Kremlin – should guarantee that yearly figures were met.[28]

Nevertheless, the proposal encountered determined opposition within the administration. On 20 March, Stu Eizenstat, Carter's chief domestic adviser, took a firm position against the proposal on the grounds that it lacked "adequate consultations with Jewish groups and right before what will be a difficult SALT ratification process", and any eventual action on the Jackson–Vanik front could "complicate passage of SALT and may hurt politically in the Jewish community".[29] The following day, Frank Moore (assistant to the president for Congressional liaison) and Hamilton Jordan came out against any "premature" action to repeal the Jackson–Vanik amendment because:

1. Although congressman Vanik may be receptive to this approach, Senator Jackson certainly will not, and can be expected to oppose us. This will surely lead to a debate not only on Soviet human rights, but other unpleasant Soviet activity around the world. Such a debate before SALT is submitted to the Senate will further aggravate an already dangerous anti-Soviet climate, making the reception for SALT that much more difficult.
2. An issue as controversial as this requires extensive Congressional consultation with numerous committees and individual members. ...
3. We do not believe that the Jewish community is united on MFN for the Soviets. Some Jewish leaders may see MFN for Russia as inevitable ... but in our brief discussions with AIPAC, we have found no support for the idea. They may be brought around, but this will require additional discussions with them. We do not need another battle with this group if it can be avoided.

For these reasons, they concluded, "we recommend that you postpone your decision on MFN for China and the Soviet Union until consultations are completed and SALT II is submitted".[30] Accordingly, in April, Vance and Blumenthal explained to Dobrynin that the administration would consider granting MFN to the Soviet Union only after SALT ratification.[31] Once again, everything revolved around SALT II, which was supposed to be signed at the Vienna summit in June 1979. Yet, before the Vienna summit, the administration had to explain to the American public the rationale for moving the human rights campaign to quiet diplomacy.

Domestic problems I: NGOs and quiet diplomacy

With the 1977/1978 CSCE review conference in Belgrade, it had become clear that the Carter administration attributed great importance to activists and networks for the promotion of human rights. In those months, diplomat Matthew Nimetz had established a cooperative relationship with major organizations of the so-called "Helsinki lobby". Over the following months, the White House and the State Department maintained strict contact with many NGOs, calling them periodically for briefings on the results of, and obstacles to, the human rights campaign or on measures taken by the American government. Contact intensified between late 1978 and early 1979. The rationale was threefold. Firstly, these meetings were a recognition of NGOs' contribution to Carter's campaign. As the president clarified during a ceremony at the White House for the thirtieth anniversary of the Universal Declaration of Human Rights, global awareness of human rights was made possible by "Amnesty International, the International Commission of Jurists, the International League for Human Rights, and many other nongovernmental human rights organizations" that "document[ed] widely those practices that destroy the lives and minds of many human beings".[32] Secondly, White House attention to NGOs and activists could contribute to Carter's campaign for the ratification of the human rights treaties that were stalling on the Senate floor. Both the White House and many NGOs believed that broad grassroots action would favour their ratification.[33] Finally, the White House needed to explain to activists the reasons that had led the administration to privilege quiet over open diplomacy in addressing Soviet violations of human rights.

In early 1979, many leading NGOs seemed to be in favour of Carter's new quiet diplomacy on Soviet violations of human rights. Many shared the administration's analysis of progress made by the Soviets in their compliance with the Helsinki Final Act and its human rights provisions. Amnesty International and the International League for Human Rights, for example, underlined that many sentences were commuted to less severe measures.[34] Similarly, by late 1978, the NCSJ confirmed the White House's figures on the number of Soviet Jews allowed to emigrate; although the Soviets' "bizarre" legal procedures did not change, nearly 29,000 Soviet Jews succeeded in leaving the country (the highest numbers since 1973). To the NCSJ, another positive aspect was that for the first time since the end of the Second World War, Soviet authorities were assuming a more conciliatory attitude towards Jewish culture. After decades of assimilation and denial of Soviet Jews' identity, the Kremlin had now authorized the reopening of a few Jewish theatres and was not obstructing the circulation of religious books. The Jewish minority remained one of the most discriminated against, the NCSJ concluded, but the Soviet authorities' attitude now seemed more tolerant.[35] Other NGOs favoured Carter's shift to quiet diplomacy because they had traditionally assumed a conciliatory attitude towards détente. Bipolar dialogue, they had consistently argued, was a prerequisite for any action in defence of dissidents and quiet diplomacy could serve both the strengthening of détente and the promotion of human rights. In addition, many influential organizations such as the NCSJ and the Committee of Concerned Scientists favoured the ratification of the SALT II Treaty as a way to promote peace and security. Even the Polish-American Congress, for example, expressed its "conditional support of the SALT II Treaty". Nevertheless, activists and NGOs were urging the White House to place human rights alongside the SALT II Treaty in its discussions with the Soviets.[36]

Problems with NGOs emerged when the administration began discussing the repeal of the Jackson–Vanik amendment. The NCSJ threatened to coordinate an international campaign against such an action.[37] This problem opened a Pandora's box of NGOs' fears and doubts at Carter's reversal. Following the example of the NCSJ, many activists began to question Carter's shift in favour of quiet diplomacy and to urge a firmer stance on human rights in East–West relations. In February 1979, the Committee of Concerned Scientists made public that it had given the White House's science and technology adviser a list of scientists and dissidents whose plight was particularly significant to American scientists.[38] Similarly, between April and May 1979, the American section of Amnesty International coordinated a number of demonstrations and initiatives to protest at violations of human rights in the USSR. The organization demanded the immediate release of activists of the Helsinki groups, protested at the harassment of Vladimir Shelkov, an eighty-three-year-old Protestant pastor, and threatened to exploit the upcoming Olympic Games in Moscow to inform the world about political repression in the Soviet Union.[39]

The gap between the White House's silence and the growing number of NGO initiatives fuelled a new debate on Carter's human rights and bipolar policies. The American press criticized Carter's weakness; he was now perceived as a leader who was not able to keep his promises.[40] Conservative *Washington Post* columnists Evans and Novak accused the administration of having abandoned dissidents: "Human rights, the shining emblem of Jimmy Carter's foreign policy, vanished almost without a trace in Vienna" because "Brezhnev said nyet and meant it."[41] When, in September, the Senate Dirksen Office Building hosted the third edition of the International Sakharov Hearings, the press denounced the administration's abandonment of its human rights commitments. During this initiative, intentionally modelled as a public trial against Soviet authorities, Soviet émigrés, academicians, journalists and activists charged that, contrary to what the Carter administration was claiming, repression in the Soviet Union had never decreased and accused the White House of neglecting its commitment to human rights. To the *Wall Street Journal*, the aim of the International Sakharov Hearings was to "provide a disturbing reminder to the Carter administration that the only world leader who currently pursues a coherent policy on human rights is Leonid Brezhnev".[42]

Even the creation of Helsinki Watch, a new NGO whose name assumed a major emphasis on CSCE human rights provisions, was perceived by many as an implicit criticism of Carter's weak stance on Soviet violations of human rights because, as the *Washington Post* commented, "individual rights are too important to leave to governments alone. Governments have other concerns which sometimes take precedence."[43] In reality, after some initial hesitation,[44] the White House supported the creation of the organization. The original idea for Helsinki Watch had emerged in the White House entourage on the initiative of Ambassador Arthur Goldberg, who had led the American delegation to the Belgrade CSCE review conference.[45] Goldberg's initiative was not rooted in disappointment with Carter's human rights strategy; rather, it was based on the recognition that the State Department and the Congressional

"Helsinki Commission" needed "a private counterpart" to keep the Helsinki process "honest and active".[46] During a Congressional hearing, he expressed his hope that a citizens' monitoring group could be established in the United States, as had happened in the Soviet bloc:

> Private individuals have a lot to do, outside of government. It's a great anomaly to me that while in the Soviet Union, in Czechoslovakia, in Poland, under conditions of repression, private individuals have had the courage to organize private groups but that in our country individuals have not organized a monitoring group. I would hope they would, as an indication that individuals in our country, in addition to government, have a great interest in the implementation of the Final Act.[47]

The crucial boost to Goldberg's project came from the Ford Foundation and its president, McGeorge Bundy. Bundy persuaded Goldberg to involve Robert Bernstein, CEO of Random House and chairman of the Fund for Free Expression, in the monitoring group. Bernstein's interest in intellectual freedom in Eastern Europe dated back to a 1973 book fair in Moscow where he made contact with Soviet dissidents. Bernstein agreed to form the new monitoring committee and identified some collaborators, including Jeri Laber, an expert on the Soviet Union, Edward Kline, founder of Khronika Press, which had published much *samizdat* literature in the United States, and Aryeh Neier, former executive director of the American Civil Liberties Union.[48] In January 1979, the Ford Foundation awarded the US Helsinki Watch Committee a two-year $400,000 grant. The State Department and the Congressional "Helsinki Commission" provided the new NGO with a list of "several dozen people from a broad ideological and political spectrum whose names and credentials would be such as to attract instant attention when they announce a position [and] representatives of many aspects of American life" to be involved in the project.[49] Goldberg, Bernstein, Laber and Kline inaugurated the US Helsinki Watch Committee in February 1979 and succeeded in co-opting several experts in human rights and communist affairs.[50] After that, its activities constantly increased, ranging from the publication of detailed reports to appearances at Congressional hearings. In September, Executive Director Jeri Laber even succeeded in meeting with Helsinki monitors in Russia, Ukraine and other Eastern European countries. As scholar Daniel C. Thomas points out, the US-based watch group "immediately became a major fixture in the transnational network and gained a prominent voice in U.S. policy making on the CSCE, Eastern Europe and the Soviet Union".[51]

For the moment, however, Helsinki Watch contributed to cast doubt on Carter's policy towards Soviet violations of human rights. Although Helsinki Watch never criticized the White House, one of its first communiqués warned of the peril that the CSCE Final Act would "drift into history as a remnant of an idealistic but futile experiment" without an independent monitoring body, thus reinforcing the idea that the Carter administration was retreating from its stance on human rights.[52]

Domestic problems II: Congressional reactions

The White House's problems with activists paled in comparison to those with Congress. The decision to prioritize bipolar cooperation and SALT II over confrontation and human rights was difficult to reconcile with the growing anti-détente attitudes of American society and Congress. As early as May 1978, pollster Patrick Caddell explained to the president that the American public was moving toward more conservative opinions, and that SALT II "seem[ed] destined to be caught in the vertex [sic] of these larger concerns over our defense and foreign policy posture. I fear that a SALT agreement will not be judged on its own merits but rather become a vehicle for these concerns. Given the attitudes we see emerging, SALT could become a firestorm."[53] Over the following months, two major developments within the United States confirmed this analysis.

The first development came from a number of polls that showed the American public's growing dissatisfaction with détente and anxiety with bipolar relations. By late 1978, 40 per cent of American citizens believed that the Soviet Union was enjoying a condition of strategic superiority, while only 14 per cent believed that the United States still had some military advantage.[54] If compared with data from previous years, this projection was even worse; in 1977, 31 per cent of Americans believed that the strategic equilibrium was in favour of the Soviets; in 1976, only 26 per cent had a similar perception.[55] Other polls confirmed the growing scepticism toward SALT II. In April 1978, for example, 53 per cent of American citizens urged the administration to take a firmer stance vis-à-vis the Soviet Union, while only 32 per cent believed that the administration should reduce bipolar tensions. By the end of the year, 52 per cent urged an increase in the military budget. Similarly, approval ratings dropped from 70 per cent in early 1978 to 42 per cent in November; on the eve of the June 1979 Vienna summit they would decline even more, dropping to 32 per cent.[56]

The second development was the results of the midterm elections, which confirmed a conservative turn in American politics. This shift had begun earlier and had multiple roots. Economic difficulties played a major role in shaping US citizens' negative perception of the Carter administration. Yet, Carter's perceived soft stance on Communism was a major target in the Republicans' campaign. The vote confirmed a general strengthening of the Republican Party and, within both parties, of their more conservative wings. "The big losers", as *Washington Post* columnist Robert G. Kaiser commented, "were liberals, whose rank and morale were both depleted."[57] Democrats kept the majority in the House, but lost fifteen seats. Many "new internationalists" failed to secure re-election, particularly Joshua Eilberg and human rights champion Donald Fraser. In the Senate, Democrats lost a net of three seats, although they succeeded in keeping a 58:41 majority. Liberal Republicans Clifford Case (New Jersey) and Edward Brooke (Massachusetts), and Democrats Richard Clark (Iowa), James Abourezk (South Dakota), Thomas J. McIntyre (New Hampshire), Wendell Anderson (Minnesota) and William Hathaway (Maine) were among the most prominent losers.

The electoral result was at the centre of a meeting between Secretary of State Vance and Senator Moynihan. They agreed that the new Senate would be more hostile to the White House's foreign policy, "with a rigid Republican right growing in confidence and votes" and the president "having to put together any number of coalitions to win different issues". To Moynihan, things were complicated by the growing friction within the Democratic Party:

> In foreign affairs there are in fact two Democratic parties. ... I described in brief the ideological conflict which then formed between the McGovernites and those of us who, without having necessarily supported the old positions, very much opposed the new ones. I explained that this was a battle about real things. That each side felt the other to be hateful and wrong and dangerous and divisive. A certain coming together occurred in 1976. I put it to him that as a member of the drafting committee for Democratic platform I had written most of the foreign policy planks of the platform. ... Then the election, and our great shock .... Almost without exception he and the President had appointed to the Department of State persons of the opposite camp from us, persons who were not only different in their views but who regarded us as the enemy. As the Secretary's enemy.[58]

Moynihan felt it was time to relaunch cooperation between the White House and Jackson's wing of the Democratic party. However, the Secretary of State replied that it would be difficult to develop a dialogue with Jackson, since its "attacks on him and the president were personal".[59] By the time this conversation took place, Jackson, who had never concealed his opposition to détente and arms control, had launched a major assault on Carter's policy with respect to the Soviet Union. After the 1978 Soviet trials, he accused the president of conducting a selective human rights policy, showing more firmness and determination against allied authoritarian regimes than against the Soviets. To Jackson, this policy was detrimental and paradoxical for the promotion of human rights:

> Many share my continuing dismay at the American policy on human rights that finds it convenient to criticize the petty dictatorships, with which the world unhappily abounds, but inconvenient to speak out about the Soviet system that inspires repression around the world. Thus it is that the Administration speaks more about the abuses of human rights in Chile, the Philippines, Argentina, and Guatemala, while speaking less about violations of human rights in the Soviet Union. ... Only with sensible priorities can we hope to forge an effective policy out of the impulse to support the cause of international human rights. Only by reasserting our concern at the denial of basic rights in the Soviet Union can we make credible our concern about basic rights elsewhere.[60]

In addition, Jackson believed that the administration was damaging national security through the continuation of détente and arms control negotiations with the Soviets. The evolution of the human rights campaign was emblematic of such a tendency, for he believed that Carter's foreign policy had become "an unsettling mixture of moralism, malaise, and retrenchment".[61]

Jackson's critique was not new. He had been an outspoken opponent of détente since the early 1970s and a staunch supporter of a firm stance on Soviet violations of human rights. What most worried the White House was that, first, by late 1978 Jackson had shown his unwillingness to negotiate with the executive branch regarding foreign policy issues and, second, that his ideas seemed to be now shared by a majority of members of Congress. In February 1979, for example, Democrat Mario Biaggi (New York) invited Carter to recalibrate his foreign policy and his approach to SALT II in order "to force additional concessions from the Soviets", such as "releasing their strangle-hold on its captive nations". Just a few weeks later, Republican Robert Michel noted that the "the essential qualities" of Carter's human rights-based foreign policy were its "inconsistency and lack of fairness".[62]

Neoconservative political scientist Jeane Kirkpatrick summarized this set of critiques and objections in November 1979. A member of the Committee on the Present Danger, Kirkpatrick announced that the failure of Carter's human rights campaign was "now clear to everyone except for its architects". Her analysis was based on a re-evaluation of the totalitarian model, as opposed to authoritarian regimes, and on what she denounced as Carter's double standards on human rights. To Kirkpatrick, two major differences existed between right-wing authoritarian regimes and Soviet communism. Firstly, in a major realist undertaking, Kirkpatrick focused on their international alignment. Whereas Soviet communism was unequivocally identified as the enemy, traditional authoritarian regimes were "not only anti-communist, they were positively friendly to the United States". The second difference was the possibility that authoritarian regimes could evolve into democracies: "Although there is no instance of a revolutionary socialist or communist society being democratized, right-wing autocracies do sometimes evolve into democracies – given time, propitious economic, social and political circumstances, talented leaders, and a strong indigenous demand for representative government." Blaming Carter for the revolution in Nicaragua, where leftist guerrillas had overthrown dictator Anastasio Somoza in 1979, Kirkpatrick claimed that external interference in authoritarian regimes would not favour their democratic transition. Not only was Carter's liberal agenda, she continued, responsible for the overthrowing of an allied regime, but it had also abandoned the commitment to fight totalitarianism. This was a deceptive and dangerous foreign policy, Kirkpatrick concluded, that had allowed "a dramatic Soviet military build-up … and a dramatic extension of Soviet influence in the Horn of Africa, Afghanistan, southern Africa, and the Caribbean" and that "not only failed to prevent the undesired outcome, but actively collaborated in the replacement of moderate autocrats friendly to American interests with less friendly autocrats of extremist persuasion".[63]

Kirkpatrick succeeded in offering a coherent analysis of neoconservatives' critique of Carter's human rights policy, which was accused of displaying an uncertain, flawed and unacceptable morality that failed to cope with the reality of Soviet power.[64] This would become the political manifesto of Carter's neoconservative opponents, who characterized his administration as the culmination of a decade-long appeasement toward the Soviet Union.[65] For the moment, Kirkpatrick's analysis was increasingly echoed by the American public and by Congress. Even the Helsinki Commission, which had generally assumed a supportive stance toward Carter's human rights policy, was now more sceptical and manifested its discontent with the Carter administration. In early 1979, for example, Dante Fascell, the Chairman of the Helsinki Commission, explained to Secretary Vance that the new official American attitude toward Soviet violations of human rights weakened any possible action to defend Soviet dissidents and raised doubts about the approach the United States would follow at the CSCE Madrid conference, which was supposed to take place in 1980.[66] Even more importantly, some members of the Helsinki Commission openly questioned the data that the administration was using to represent some progress and therefore legitimatizing the shift in favour of quiet diplomacy. Robert Drinan, for example, pointed out that "the Soviet Union has twisted and distorted the provisions of the Helsinki Final Act for their own political ends" and that the "Soviet record [was] still dismally poor".[67]

In this political climate, Carter's decision to remove the sanctions that had been introduced after the 1978 trials offered a new opportunity to attack the White House. The very same day that the embargo on the sale of computers to TASS was lifted, Jackson and Moynihan released a harsh communiqué against an action that "mock[ed] the Administration's policy of promoting human rights".[68] Even the April 1979 exchange of prisoners found many critics. John Ashbrook (R – Ohio), for example, compared Carter's dual standards on human rights to George Orwell's "doublethink", namely "the ability to believe completely in two contradictory ideas". In this case, he claimed:

> We swapped two Soviet spies convicted in this country for buying some of our defense secrets in return for Soviet citizens who have been oppressed and brutalized in the Soviet Union for exercising freedoms we take for granted. ... [W]hat I do object to is the doublethink attitude of the White House and the press in hailing this release as an example of the improvement in Soviet internal policies and in Soviet–United States relations. What improvement? Quite the opposite. The dissidents left because there is no improvement internally in that repressive society in Russia.[69]

With the Vienna summit for the signing of the SALT II Treaty getting closer, many raised their voices in favour of a firmer stance on Soviet violations of human rights. Senators Abraham Ribicoff (D – Connecticut), Jacob Javits (R – New York) and Howard Baker (R – Tennessee), whom the administration considered crucial for the ratification of the SALT II Treaty, invited the president to intervene in defence of "all the Prisoners of Conscience who still languish in Soviet prisons, labor camps and remote sections of that country".[70] Commenting on this letter and "numerous calls, visits and letters from persons representing Jews who are either in Soviet jails or in exile or who have been prevented from leaving the Soviet Union", presidential adviser Edward Sanders proposed that members of the American delegation at the Vienna meeting could raise the cases of prominent dissenters with Soviet officials.[71]

The White House listened carefully to these messages and assumed a firmer stance vis-à-vis the Soviets. In June, just days before the Vienna summit, Carter announced that the United States would develop the MX missile. Back from Europe, he accepted Jackson's, Sam Nunn's (D – Georgia) and John Tower's (R – Texas) proposal to expand the military budget, announcing a 5.6 per cent increase in defence spending. Furthermore, the administration publicly addressed Soviet violations of human rights. On 10 June, the day before flying to Vienna, Brzezinski received the five dissidents who had been exchanged for Soviet spies at the White House. Finally, in Vienna, American diplomats and officials discussed all bipolar problems encompassing human rights, arms control, the Ogaden War and bilateral trade relations. However, the only concrete achievement was the signing of the SALT II Treaty, since discussions on CSCE and human rights were ineffectual.[72]

On 1 August 1979, on the fourth anniversary of the signing of the Helsinki Final Act, Carter welcomed representatives from NGOs and the "Helsinki Commission" at the White House for an official ceremony. During the meeting, the president explicitly stigmatized Eastern countries' inability to comply with the CSCE human rights provisions:

[I]n the German Democratic Republic, harsh new laws designed to restrict contact with foreigners will take effect today, on the anniversary of Helsinki. In Czechoslovakia, members of the Charter 77 movement remain in prison, facing trial for their dedication to basic human freedoms. In the Soviet Union, organizations established to monitor compliance with the Helsinki agreement have been harassed and their members jailed. Acts like these are totally inconsistent with pledges made at Helsinki.[73]

Now that the treaty was signed, the president could abandon his diplomatic caution on human rights and resume a firmer stance. This was intended to deflect domestic criticism. The administration was aware that it was now impossible to develop a dialogue with Jackson and other "irreconcilable" critics of détente, as it had hoped for in early 1977. Rather, through a firmer stance on Soviet violations on human rights, it hoped to contain their opposition and eventually to dialogue with moderate critics of détente: "I can envision winning SALT without Jackson and possibly even without Baker", an anonymous staff member confessed to the *Wall Street Journal*, "but without Nunn, we are dead."[74]

In June, Carter addressed Congress on the Vienna summit and the SALT II Treaty. The president did not abandon his confidence that the treaty, and, indeed, bipolar dialogue, was in America's best interest. With realism, he admitted that détente did not end competition between two "fundamentally different visions of human society and human destiny". He defended the content of the new arms control agreement and expounded on the many advantages the US democratic system enjoyed. Even the human rights campaign was a further demonstration of American strength: "The support for human rights – balanced by the concrete example of the American society – has aligned us with peoples all over the world who yearn for freedom."[75] Like many of

Carter's major initiatives on bipolar policy, this speech pointed out that détente was not a new form of appeasement and it did not hinder America's will to defend its values.

Less than a month later, on 9 July, the Senate Committee on Foreign Relations began its hearings on SALT II. Even the timing of early hearings favoured the overlap between arms control and human rights. The following day, in a special session, both the House and the Senate paid official tribute to the trials of Sharansky and Ginzburg. The following week, Congress remembered "captive nations". For this reason, Representative William Broomfield (R – Michigan) reminded his colleagues:

> Captive Nations week 1979 assumes a special significance, not only because it is the 20th anniversary of congressional action … but also because of recent American efforts to more fully assess our political, economic and military relationships with the Soviet Union and the People's Republic of China, the two largest captive empires. … Heartless and deceitful communist activities in empires like the Soviet Union not only undermine the spirit of détente but also the spirit of individually. The recent harassments, arrests, and exiles of Soviet dissidents, the persistent Soviet repression of stubborn opposition to Russification, are indicative of the mind-set of the communist leadership. Moreover, these activities tend to undermine the spirit of such international agreements as Helsinki and SALT to which the Soviets are signatories.[76]

However, the fight for ratification took place in the Senate, and its first round took place in the Committee on Foreign Relations. Between July and November, a number of politicians, diplomats, academics, experts and pundits of bipolar affairs participated in its hearings. Both supporters and opponents of the SALT II Treaty explained how they perceived the link between the new treaty and human rights in the Soviet Union. In an extensive exchange with diplomat George Vest, for example, Senator Stone (D – Florida) recalled the plight of dissidents and, specifically, the prisoner exchange to underline that the Soviet Union was not a reliable partner in international negotiations and, accordingly, the United States should renounce the SALT II Treaty:

> Stone: Am I correct that the family of Alexander Ginsburg, his mother, his wife, his two small sons and his ward, a 19-year-old boy who has been a member of his family since 1974, is still in the Soviet Union?
>
> Vest: I do not know the exact details on that, sir. I would have to get that and report it to you.
>
> Stone: Is it correct that the Soviet authorities have refused to let the boy leave, that they have inducted him into the army despite one medical commission's findings that he is too ill to serve, that they have assigned him to a construction battalion in Northern Russia [and] that they interfere with his correspondence with Mrs. Ginsburg? …?
>
> Vest: This is an area, which we have been discussing with the Soviets and pressing them on. …

Stone: Finally, am I correct in saying that in the matter of Sergei Shibalyev, the Soviet authorities are, in effect, circumventing their agreement with us by invoking a technicality, which goes clearly against the spirit and intent of the understanding that we have reached?

Vest: Regarding that case, sir, I would have to look into the matter and report back to you. I just do not have the information automatically on hand. I am not trying to evade the answer.

Stone: These are important issues. The Helsinki Commission, which the Congress has set up to monitor the Final Act, today is hearing Mr. Moroz and Mr. Ginsburg as witnesses. It is very important because Americans want to be assured that if we negotiate a bargain with the Soviets, a specific bargain as this one was, they will keep to it and we will see to it that they keep it. If they do not keep it and we do not see to it that they keep it, what good would an agreement be? If they do not keep a small, clearly monitored agreement, like the prisoner exchange, then how can we really rely on a large, difficult-to-monitor issue such as SALT?[77]

On the opposite side, Albert Vorspan, a member of the Union of American Hebrew Congregations, explained that his organization supported the new treaty because:

We believe that SALT II must be examined and measured and judged on its own merits. Our support for SALT II in no way signifies our approval of Soviet domestic or international policies. The SALT II Treaty is of momentous intrinsic moral and strategic interest. It is deserving of ratification on its own merits. If the world disappears into a nuclear holocaust, our concerns for human rights and peace become irrelevant. Human life is the ultimate civil and human right.[78]

In September, a new problem emerged. Frank Church, Chairman of the Senate Committee on Foreign Relations, denounced the presence of Soviet troops in Cuba, harking back to the 1962 missile crisis. Harshly criticized by Republicans and fearing not being re-elected, Church accused the Carter administration of having allowed a Soviet military presence in Cuba. Accordingly, together with John Tower (R – Texas), he proposed postponing the discussion of the new SALT Treaty until the resolution of the crisis. In early October, Carter was forced to intervene; although the combat unit was not "capable of attacking the United States", it represented a "very serious matter and that this status quo [was] not acceptable". However, in his concluding remarks, he explained that "the brigade issue [was] not the occasion for a return to the Cold War. … The greatest danger to American security tonight is not a brigade of Soviet troops in Cuba. It is not Cuban divisions in Africa. The greatest danger to all the nations of the world including the United States and the Soviet Union is the threat of nuclear holocaust."[79] Carter's remarks ended the dispute over the Soviet brigade in Cuba, although it did not stop his opponents' critiques.[80] On 9 November, the Senate Committee on Foreign Relations invited the Senate to ratify the SALT II Treaty. However, the Commission's vote (nine in favour of ratification; six against it) was below the two-thirds majority required to ratify international treaties. The following month, when the

Senate Committee on Armed Services endorsed ratification with ten votes in favour and seven abstentions, it was clear that the treaty had no concrete chance of being ratified.[81] Nevertheless, these problems would disappear soon after the Soviets invaded Afghanistan in December 1979.

The Soviet invasion of Afghanistan and the end of détente

Over the summer, Congressional debate on SALT II was a cause of concern for the White House but international changes were equally troubling.

In Central America, political instability was on the rise. Following his human rights commitment, Carter had cut off financial and military aid to many right-wing regimes in the area. Somoza's regime in Nicaragua was among these. Yet, since late 1977 instability and riots had been growing in the country, culminating in Somoza's fall and the Marxist *Frente Sandinista de Liberación Nacional* taking power. With a major departure from traditional containment, the Carter administration did not cut either diplomatic relations with the new regime or financial aid. Rather, fearing that a firm stance would turn Nicaragua into a new Cuba, the Carter administration tried to improve relations with Nicaragua through food and medical aid, official diplomatic recognition and a $75 million emergency economic package. Carter's response to the Sandinista revolution angered his conservative opponents. They blamed Carter's human rights policy for destabilizing Somoza. Moreover, they were outraged at Carter's lack of firmness vis-à-vis a new Marxist government in Central America. To them, the issue was not avoiding a new Cuba, but confronting it, for Nicaragua was already a Marxist government.[82]

The Middle East was another major source of crisis. In Iran, the Carter administration was late in understanding the growing opposition to the Shah's regime. The United States had long supported the Shah. Iran was a vital ally to Washington – for oil supplies and for containment in the Middle East. The country was also supposed to represent a successful experiment in modernization: Carter called it "an island of stability in one of the most troubled areas of the world" during a New Year toast in Tehran. The Shah, however, had grown increasingly unpopular in Iran, with Islamic clergy fiercely opposed the his reforms. In January 1979 protesters forced the Shah to flee. An Islamic republic, headed by religious leader Ayatollah Ruhollah Khomeini, was then declared. The US could do nothing but helplessly observe what Brzezinski promptly described as "the most massive defeat since the beginning of the Cold War, overshadowing in its real consequences the setback in Vietnam".[83] In the following weeks, the Carter administration minimized its attention to radical Islamism, keeping its focus on the minority communist component in the Iranian revolution. Yet, with the Vietnam shadow still over Washington, the administration decided not to intervene.

In November 1979, revolutionaries stormed the American embassy in Tehran and held fifty-two Americans hostage. The militants threatened to kill the hostages or try them as spies. The Carter administration tried unsuccessfully to negotiate for the hostages' release. In April 1980, as pressure mounted, Carter approved a daring rescue attempt. To the nation's dismay, the rescue mission failed. Ted Koppel – at the time a little-known journalist who had predicted that the crisis would last only a couple of days – launched a nightly programme titled "America Held Hostage" which picked up an average of 12 million viewers.[84]

The Iranian revolution produced another, less dramatic but equally shocking, effect. It struck international markets, with a radical reduction in oil production from 5.8 million barrels a day in July 1978 to 445,000 barrels a day in January 1979. A little more than a year after the beginning of the Iranian revolution, oil prices had almost tripled. For American consumers, the summer of 1979 was the summer of gasoline shortages and endless queue at fuel stations. A Gallup poll from late May 1979 reported that approval of Carter's policy had faded to 37 per cent. While this was primarily an outcome of the state of the economy, foreign policy issues were relevant. A couple of months before, only 45 per cent of respondents to a *New York Times*–CBS survey had approved his foreign policy. By June, this was down to 36 per cent.[85] To Carter's critics, these were further demonstrations of his flawed and misguided foreign policy. As scholars Daniel Yankelovich and Larry Kagan wrote, the American public tied together SALT II, the oil shock and the crisis in Central America: "it felt bullied by OPEC, humiliated by the Ayatollah Khomeini, tricked by Castro, out-traded by Japan and out-gunned by the Russians".[86] The impact of these multiple crises became clear in December, when Senator Byrd admitted that the Senate would reschedule the discussion of the SALT Treaty because "the environment in the Senate would not be conducive to concentrating on the treaty".[87]

A new crisis in the Middle East flared up on Christmas Eve, when Soviet tanks invaded Afghanistan. When news of the invasion reached the international community, condemnation was almost unanimous. The most outraged reaction came, unsurprisingly, from the United States. Carter himself had to admit: "The action of the Soviets has made a more dramatic change in my opinion of what the Soviets' ultimate goals are than anything they've done in the previous time that I've been in office."[88]

The administration followed events in Afghanistan with growing concern. The foreign policy elite speculated on the reasons for Moscow's intervention. George Kennan thought that Soviet actions should not be perceived as a threat to Western security. On the contrary, Moscow's action reflected "defensive rather than offensive [Soviet] impulses". Moscow's fears resulted from a number of overlapping problems, including the prospect of losing control over the friendly Afghan regime, the prospect of the growth of radical Islamists' influence on Muslim areas within the Soviet Union and the risk of growing Chinese influence in the region. In a similar manner, Vance's chief adviser for Soviet affairs Marshall Shulman argued that the Soviet decision was based on an overestimation of the possible risks of Afghan instability and on the fear that the United States could militarily intervene in Iran. Accordingly, Shulman urged the administration to avoid any excessive punitive measures and to continue with the efforts to ratify the SALT II Treaty. A second explanation underlined the Soviet leaders' opportunism. In a clear attack on Carter's conduct of bipolar affairs, Henry Kissinger suggested that the Soviets believed that the United States would not challenge their actions because it had failed to do so in the Horn of Africa. Additionally, Kissinger stated that Moscow had concluded that détente had deteriorated to the point that it had nothing to lose.[89]

Brzezinski proposed another interpretation. Recalling his 1978 analysis of the "arc of crisis" that spread over the Middle East and that could be exploited by the Soviets to gain global influence, Carter's NSA argued that Moscow saw Afghanistan as a step toward the oil-rich Arabian peninsula and the Indian Ocean.[90] These analyses were flawed by a substantial misunderstanding of the problems and transformations in the area, above all the emergence of a radical Islamism that was equally opposed to both Western modernization and to the Soviet Union. They also revealed Brzezinski's inability to escape his Cold War perspective. Nevertheless, they defined Carter's response to the Afghan crisis. To some extent, it was a natural outcome since the administration was caught by surprise by the invasion and Brzezinski had been offering for years an apparently coherent analysis of Soviet motivations. In part, it was also a consequence of growing difficulties and problems in bipolar relations. Finally, it was a policy shaped by ongoing domestic debate, where criticisms of American weakness vis-à-vis Soviet assertiveness were constantly strengthened.[91]

While Brzezinski would later claim that the United States prompted the Soviet Union to invade Afghanistan so that Moscow could get its "Vietnam", he nevertheless admitted that "the initial effects of the intervention [were] likely to be adverse for us". Domestically, the administration now had to face some negative transformations triggered by the invasion:

> A. The Soviet intervention is likely to stimulate calls for more immediate U.S. military action in Iran. Soviet "decisiveness" will be contrasted with our restraint, which will no longer be labelled as prudent but increasingly as timid; B. At the same time, regional instability may make a resolution of the Iranian problem more difficult for us, and it could bring us into a head-to-head confrontation with the Soviets; C. SALT is likely to be damaged, perhaps irreparably, because Soviet military aggressiveness will have been so naked; D. More generally, our handling of Soviet affairs will be attacked by both the right and the left.[92]

Abroad, new problems would emerge with Arab allies and with Pakistan, as well as with China, that "will certainly note that Soviet assertiveness in Afghanistan and in Cambodia is not effectively restrained by the United States".[93] To make things worse, the timing of the invasion in "the first week of the new decade" was "symbolic and significant".[94] For these reasons, Brzezinski clarified, a firm strategy had to be developed because "Afghanistan is the seventh state since 1975 in which communist parties have come to power with Soviet guns and tanks, with Soviet military power and assistance (Vietnam, Angola, Laos, South Yemen, Cambodia, Ethiopia, and now probably Afghanistan)".[95] The conclusion was clear. The administration had to develop "a genuinely punitive reaction" to the Soviet Union.[96] In less than two days, Brzezinski's staff prepared a long list of retaliatory measures.[97] On 2 January 1980, Carter approved twenty-six decisions, encompassing the suspension of SALT II, the withdrawal of the American ambassador from Moscow and a reduction in diplomatic personnel, a grain embargo against the Soviet Union and another on advanced technology, a break in trade negotiations, new Radio Free Europe/Radio Liberty and Voice of America broadcasts to Muslims in the Soviet Union and Central Asia, the idea of promoting a boycott of the 1980 Moscow Olympic Games, assistance to Pakistan and to Afghan rebels and the strengthening of military ties with China.[98]

Brzezinski invited Carter to become a new Truman. Before doing that, however, the president had first to align Congress and public opinion on his new stance. Accordingly, he repeatedly intervened to denounce Soviet aggression and emphasized the need for a firm response. On 8 January 1980, the president declared that the Soviet invasion was a "sharp escalation" in the already "aggressive history" of the Soviet Union. Comparing the Afghan crisis to the 1956 invasion of Hungary and the 1968 repression of the Prague Spring, Carter recalled that those countries "were basically subservient to the Soviet Union; they were not independent nations in control of their own affairs", while Afghanistan was "a sovereign nation, a non-aligned nation, a deeply religious nation".[99] Days later, he pointed out that Moscow's aggression was a threat to regional stability and to global oil supplies. For a nation that had spent the previous summer waiting in line to pump gasoline, the fear of Soviet control over oil was an invitation to support the president's new course. On 23 January, Carter delivered his State of the Union Address. The new "Carter doctrine", as the speech came to be known, presented the invasion as "the most serious threat to the peace since the Second World War" and concluded that it was impossible "to conduct business as usual with the Soviet Union":

> The region which is now threatened by Soviet troops in Afghanistan is of great strategic importance: It contains more than two-thirds of the world's exportable oil. The Soviet effort to dominate Afghanistan has brought Soviet military forces to within 300 miles of the Indian Ocean and close to the Straits of Hormuz, a waterway through which most of the world's oil must flow. The Soviet Union is now attempting to consolidate a strategic position, therefore, that poses a grave threat to the free movement of Middle East oil. ... Meeting this challenge will take national will, diplomatic and political wisdom, economic sacrifice, and, of course, military capability. We must call on the best that is in us to preserve the security of this crucial region. Let our position be absolutely clear: An attempt by any outside force to gain control of the Persian Gulf region will be regarded as an assault on the vital interests of the United States of America, and such an assault will be repelled by any means necessary, including military force.[100]

The new American doctrine, defined by Brzezinski's analyses and developed with the language of conservative and neoconservative critics of Carter's foreign policy, definitely abandoned détente and negotiations with the Soviets to fully embrace traditional containment.[101]

This shift was met with domestic approval. Political scientist Stanley Hoffmann welcomed this "useful restatement of containment". For the first time since 1978, approval ratings surged.[102] The American public welcomed Carter's step back from his ideologically competitive and reciprocal détente to traditional containment. Lee Hamilton (D – Indiana) commented on the "change in his thinking on defense" and the decision to "deploy armed forces abroad, a stronger Atlantic alliance, a more visible naval presence in the Indian Ocean", while Republican Jacob Javits lauded Carter's prudence in managing the crisis.[103] Senator Jackson welcomed Carter's turn to containment, although he noted some unclear points.[104] Still, the level of support was below what the White House expected, and many critics denounced Carter's tardiness in assessing and recognizing the Soviet threat.[105] Eldon Rudd (R – Arizona), for example, pointed out that:

> The President's State of the Union speech marked a reversal of his attitude toward the danger of the Soviet Union and international communism. This was the same president who only three years ago stated that he was proud to lead the effort to rid our Nation of an inordinate fear of communism. ... The Soviets have been encouraged in their objectives by the President's action over the past three years – his cancellation of the B1 bomber and the neutron antitank weapon, his veto of the nuclear aircraft carrier, and his slowing of the cruise and MX missile programs in order to win Soviet agreement on the new SALT II Treaty.[106]

Despite scant bipartisan support, Carter's speech represented the definitive acceptance of a renewed strategy to globally contain the Soviet Union. Although reactive and defensive, from Moscow the new "Carter doctrine" was the formal and definitive enunciation of what Carter had been trying to do since 1977: delegitimizing and eventually overthrowing the Soviet government. The human rights campaign, the ambivalent attitude towards arms negotiations, the lack of any progress in international trade, the increase in NATO's budget and the development of new weapons were just early steps in an anti-Soviet crusade that – after the "Afghan pretext" – could be completed.[107]

Human rights initiatives after Afghanistan

A major change in the human rights campaign was spurred by Brzezinski's proposal to respond to the Soviet invasion of Afghanistan. From his perspective, Soviet military aggression legitimized an explicit anti-Soviet redefinition of Carter's campaign. Denouncing Soviet violations of human rights "would fan an old irritant; would place [the] Soviets on defensive in international dialogue; it could really inject some long-term wedges in Soviet internal politics". It was the only proposal Carter rejected: he wrote a laconic "no" on the memorandum next to this specific point. To the president, the promotion of human rights abroad was too important to become a mere propaganda tool.[108] Yet, over the following months, American diplomatic action on human rights seemed to follow Brzezinski's suggestion. This was in part a consequence of sudden developments in the Soviet Union, where authorities cracked down on

Soviet dissidents. Even before the invasion began, the *Chronicle of Human Rights in the Soviet Union* reported an increase in "arrests, trials and searches" that have "affected all sectors of dissident activities". Only prominent leaders of the free emigration movement were not arrested, although, as the *Chronicle* explained, "Jewish emigration has declined approximately 50 percent (from 4,000 to 2,000 per month)".[109] The CIA confirmed these data. In a January report, it pointed out that "Moscow has intensified its campaign against the Soviet dissident movement" and that, for the first time since Carter's election, "new restrictions on Jewish emigration reportedly were introduced ... lowering the total for the first quarter of 1980 by more than 25 percent as compared with the same period last year".[110]

The Kremlin's decision to launch a major effort to curb dissent intertwined domestic and international considerations. At home, dissent was no longer limited to urban intellectuals and elites. Dissidents' ability to forge contacts with Western activists was a major threat to the Politburo. In addition, Andropov had concluded that "some anti-social elements in the USSR" were aiming to exploit the 1980 Moscow Olympic Games to conduct "their hostile activities". Arresting dissidents would prevent such actions.[111] Bipolar tensions and the downturn in East–West relations played a major role in shaping the new wave of repression. Now that détente was over, there was no reason to take into account Western pressures on a Soviet internal problem.

The action that most outraged Western observers was Moscow's decision to exile Andrei Sakharov to Gorkyi. Apparently, the decision was adopted soon after Sakharov's public demonstration against the invasion of Afghanistan.[112] Yet, the Politburo had already begun discussing such an action in 1973; it only avoided exiling him at that time in order to preserve détente and contain international criticism. A new proposal emerged on 26 December.[113] Brezhnev, Andropov, Gromyko and Ustinov agreed that "Sakharov was the initiator of all the anti-Soviet undertakings", that he "had a bad influence on other scientists" and, even more importantly, "the question of Sakharov has ceased to be a purely domestic question. He finds an enormous number of responses abroad. All the anti-Soviet scum, all this rabble revolves around Sakharov." For this reason, Soviet leaders agreed to silence him.[114] Now that détente was over, the Soviets had no reason to tolerate his activities any longer. However, as Jay Bergman recently suggested, the Politburo carefully pondered the most opportune solution. Based on the precedent of Solzhenitsyn's expulsion, Soviet authorities opted for domestic exile to a city virtually closed to Western journalists, where Soviet authorities could constantly monitor Sakharov's activities.[115]

As soon as news of Sakharov's exile reached the West, protests exploded. The White House officially denounced the "act of repression against a man who has struggled valiantly for human rights in the Soviet Union".[116] The American Academy of Sciences decided to suspend all its bilateral programmes with the Soviet Union and, over the following months, the French Académie des Sciences, the British Royal Society and a number of German, Italian and Belgian scientists announced that they would not participate in exchange programmes with the Soviet Union until Sakharov's release.[117] A variety of American Senators expressed their solidarity with Sakharov. Resolution 340 condemned the Soviet Union for its violations of the Helsinki Accords and for showing "by its actions towards Andrei Sakharov [that it was] an enemy of freedom".[118] In late January, George Brown (D – California) introduced a proposal that invited the United States government to end all its scientific programmes with the Soviet Union.[119] In early February, both Houses unanimously approved (402:0, 91:0, respectively) a resolution by Don Bonker (D – Washington) that urged President Carter to formally protest to the Soviets against Sakharov's exile and to use all necessary means to put an end to this blatant violation of human rights.[120] The action against Sakharov strengthened the White House's proposal to boycott the Moscow Olympic Games; although Carter resisted presenting the boycott as a human rights initiative, many Western European organizations and National Olympic Committees joined the pro-boycott camp because of Soviet violations of human rights and Sakharov's exile.[121]

Protests over human rights abuses did not diminish over the following weeks and encompassed other issues as well. Senator Dennis DeConcini (D – Arizona), for example, condemned the many "atrocities carried out by Soviet officials". From the House, Herbert Harris (D – Virginia) denounced the new crackdown on refuseniks.[122] Figures released over the following months confirmed Harris' point. In August, NCSJ Chairman Jerry Goodman wrote to Carter to point out that the decrease in the number of Soviet Jews who were allowed to leave the country was now stabilizing at around 800 per month and to urge him to formally protest. The following month, sixty-one Representatives signed a similar appeal addressed to the White House.[123]

Embracing demands from Congress, the White House vigorously protested at the new Soviet crackdown against dissidents and Soviets' poor record of compliance with the Helsinki Final Act. However, human rights issues would not receive the attention, resources and the political reflection they had until that moment. In the renewed Cold War, human rights became a propaganda tool to mark the difference between the United States and the Soviet Union. Undersecretary Patricia Derian, for example, pointed out "the suppression of dissent, the large numbers and harsh treatment of political prisoners, censorship of information, restrictions on freedom of emigration and travel, and denial of full religious freedom". To strengthen her point, Derian specified who the victims of this "intensified campaign to suppress dissent" were. She denounced the gaoling of Vladimir Klebanov, Aleksandr Podrabinek and many other activists from Helsinki Watch groups; she criticized the punishment of Tatiana Velkanova, who had been "sentenced to 4 years in a labor camp and 5 years in exile for compiling and printing reports on conditions in Soviet prisons", and the actions against Sakharov, who was "the veritable international symbol of human rights and scientific freedom". She claimed that Jewish emigration from the Soviet Union had "climbed to a record total of just over 50,000 in 1979 but stands at only 17,000 so far this year".[124] Months later, the new Secretary of State Edmund Muskie wielded the human rights weapon: the "Soviets dislike and fear our emphasis on human rights … because they know that what a powerful attraction freedom has for millions of people everywhere on Earth … the contrast between our system and closed societies of our adversaries is dramatically visible".[125]

The administration soon launched a major initiative to denounce abuses and violations of human rights in the USSR and in Afghanistan. In April 1980, Paul Henze prepared a memorandum on American actions to support Soviet dissidents. From his perspective, the White House had undertaken some important initiatives, but many others should be developed as well. The first action was to allocate "resources – both manpower and money to programs encouraging dissidence ... [have] not been proportionate to the high level of attention given this field in statements and demonstrative actions". He also invited the White House to do more to strengthen its international broadcasting capabilities because "Radio Liberty's current level of performance is only a fraction of its potential." He pointed out that the administration needed to allocate more resources to "book and publication programs for Eastern Europe and the USSR". Increased funding, Henze argued, would enable the United States to "exploit the new opportunities for penetrating the communist world with ideas and information which are constantly developing". In addition, Henze called on officials to exploit the national and religious "self-assertion" of Soviet Muslims, Ukrainians, Georgians and residents of the Baltic republics through the creation of a "tape-cassette distribution program". Brzezinski welcomed these suggestions and invited Henze "to organize a Soviet working group meeting to discuss possible ways of implementing these proposals".[126]

The United States developed a propaganda offensive targeting international organizations and fora as well. American diplomats denounced the new crackdown against dissidents, new restrictions on Jewish emigration, new actions to contain the "Helsinki monitoring groups" and the problem of Afghan refugees.[127] On this last point, Brzezinski explicitly urged the CIA to prepare an assessment of the worldwide refugee problem as "generated by Soviet initiatives". The final study was presented in May 1980. Although it did not find any "evidence that the Soviets deliberately attempt to create international refugees flows as a foreign policy weapon", it concluded that Soviet actions in Afghanistan, Cuba, the Horn of Africa and Indochina contributed to refugee flows:

> The influx of Afghan refugees into Pakistan began with the communist takeover of Afghanistan in April 1978, but the great majority fled the Soviet invasion of December 1979. ... From January 1979 to September 1979 the refugee flow into Pakistan averaged 15,000 per month, but increased to an average of 59,000 per month from September 1979 to January 1980. Since January ... the refugee population in Pakistan increased at a monthly rate of about 80,000.

In its conclusions, the document explained that "Marxist or communist-sponsored countries" had produced almost 5 million refugees.[128] Based on these figures, the American government urged its diplomatic personnel in international fora to denounce human rights abuses occurring in Cuba, Eastern Europe, Cambodia and Afghanistan.[129] In July 1980, several executive branch representatives participated in a conference in Warsaw on "Peace and Human Rights". The American delegation was led by Jerome Shestack, US ambassador to the UN Commission on Human Rights, who attacked the Kremlin for the plight of numerous dissidents. Carter even sent a personal message to the participants explaining how "world peace is indissolubly linked with human rights".[130] Not too subtly, the president was blaming the Soviets for their double aggression against Afghanistan and human rights.

The new American stance on human rights emerged clearly from the Helsinki process. On the one side, the executive branch did not hesitate in violating the principle of the Helsinki Accords by denying visas to several Eastern bloc scientists who had been invited to participate in a conference in California. Singularly enough, such an action did not outrage Helsinki Watch. It recognized that "at times the benefits which these exchanges provide may be outweighed by other considerations".[131] Conversely, a new discussion developed regarding the opportunity to participate in the Madrid CSCE review conference that was supposed to begin in late 1980. Many critics and opponents of Carter's Soviet policy urged American withdrawal from a process that was supposed to favour the Soviet Union. According to Ronald Reagan, "going to Madrid is negating what we thought we could accomplish by boycotting the Olympics. If the athletes can't go, why should the diplomats go?"[132] The Carter administration never considered such a hypothesis. Even more importantly, two new developments offered opportunities to chasten the Soviets and prove Western cohesion.

From August 1980, Poland was at the centre of international attention. With a mix of sympathy and anxiety, Western observers and governments followed strikes on the Baltic Sea, the creation of Solidarność (Solidarity), the shadow of the Soviet invasion and, later, Jaruzelski's decision to impose martial law in 1981.[133] In July 1980, the Polish government authorized a general increase in the prices of certain basic goods. In order to avoid a general protest, the government introduced this measure close to summer. However, this did not prevent a series of strikes in large industrial areas. The following month, protests grew and reached the Gdansk shipyards. The crisis was worsening. In addition to economic demands, workers urged the recognition of the right to strike, the possibility of forming independent trade unions, religious freedom and the release of gaoled dissidents. They were "totally political", as the American administration commented.[134] On the American side, a cautious attitude prevailed. The main concern was that the Red Army could intervene in the crisis. For this reason, Washington began to study possible economic sanctions to be imposed on the USSR and Poland should the invasion take place.[135] Considering the Polish crisis as a human rights catalyst or an effect of the "Helsinki process" would be wrong and naïve. Yet, it would be equally misleading not to acknowledge the demand for religious freedom or the frequent references to the Helsinki Agreements coming from Polish workers. However, for the moment, the main effect of the Polish crisis was to focus the spotlight on the USSR's ability to comply with CSCE provisions and to urge a firmer stance vis-à-vis the Soviet bloc at the Madrid review conference.

The second development took place within the United States, where the White House involved NGOs in the definition of its stance vis-à-vis the Madrid conference.[136] In late 1979, for example, the Aspen Institute published a collection of essays entitled *United States Human Rights Policy: From Belgrade en Route to Madrid*. They urged the White House to openly address Soviet violations of CSCE human rights provisions. Over the following months, all major NGOs defined their own priorities and suggestions for the White House. They all agreed on the necessity of openly denouncing Soviet actions.

The International League for Human Rights, for example, urged the White House to exploit the CSCE forum to address the poor conditions of Soviet prisoners, while the Committee of Concerned Scientists and the NCSJ repeatedly met Counselor Matthew Nimetz to explain their own priorities for the conference. For its part, Helsinki Watch published two booklets documenting the new crackdown against dissidents.[137]

The White House juggled these different pressures. The president replied to Reagan and listened to NGOs' demands. To prove his commitment to human rights in East–West relations, he summoned to the White House more than 300 representatives from NGOs and Congress to celebrate the fifth anniversary of the signing of the CSCE Final Act. During the ceremony, Carter stood up for the Final Act and for the decision to participate in the Madrid conference. He promised a firm stance and opened the American delegation at the conference to thirty representatives from NGOs. Given recent developments, participation in the Madrid review conference was even more important:

> The Soviet invasion of Afghanistan and the increasingly brutal occupation of that once free nation can no more be reconciled with the Helsinki pledges than it can be reconciled with the Charter of the United Nations. For invading a neighbor, the Soviet Union already stands condemned before the world. A hundred and four members of the United Nations condemned the Soviet Union and demanded the immediate withdrawal of its occupying troops. If they are still there at the time of the Madrid conference, we will continue the pressure for the withdrawal of those Soviet troops.[138]

Finally, during the ceremony, the president announced that Griffin Bell and Max Kampelman would lead the American delegation to the conference. This harbingered a firmer stance on Soviet human rights violations. Kampelman, in particular, was close to Jackson's Democrats and to neoconservatives, and was a prominent leader of the American-Jewish community with a strong record of activism on behalf of Soviet Jews.[139]

Kampelman would not disappoint Carter, or the new American president, Ronald Reagan, who took office just weeks after the opening of the Madrid conference. During the preparatory meeting, Kampelman set the tone of the American approach to the conference: "The Soviets and their allies have made it clear that they want to cut down drastically the review of implementation phase of the main meeting. This is unacceptable."[140] In addition, since the preparatory meetings, Kampelman succeeded in maintaining a strong cohesion with NATO allies. Of course, the growing sense of crisis in East–West relations played a major role in such an outcome: although some differences between the shores of the Atlantic remained, all Western delegates agreed that considering a firm review of Soviet violations of CSCE human rights provisions was paramount. However, as Sarah Snyder has argued, contrary to what Ambassador Goldberg had done in Belgrade in 1977, Kampelman paid specific attention to NATO allies and visited many Western capitals to define a common CSCE position.[141] A final explanation for renewed NATO unity on the CSCE process was based on the growing influence of NGOs and activists; Western European delegates had to meet NGOs expectations just as much as American diplomats. The fact that Madrid became "a city of dissidence", as *Le Monde* wrote, and to which the White House contributed through supporting the opening of a Helsinki Watch office in Madrid, multiplied pressures on Western delegates to take a cohesive stance on human rights.[142]

When the Madrid conference officially opened, Kampelman reiterated the official American position vis-à-vis the CSCE process:

> No one should doubt American constancy to the powerful ideals of the CSCE process, to the preservation and enhancement of human freedom, to respect for the sovereignty and independence of all states, and to the effort to establish greater military security and cooperation among us.[143]

Similarly, co-chairman Griffin Bell openly referred to the Russian monitors Yuri Orlov and Natan Sharansky, as well as the Ukrainian Mykola Rudenko and Lithuanian Viktoras Petkus. "When Andrei Sakharov was banished", he lamented, "some of our best hopes for a spirit of security and cooperation in Europe were banished." Another delegate invited Soviet leaders to engage in peaceful ideological competition with the United States. He warned communist signatories that arresting Helsinki monitors only "created a situation in which those of us all over the world join our voices with theirs and become with them Helsinki monitors".[144]

The Soviet Union was on the defensive, and the United States was leading the human rights offensive. Although Moscow had perceived Carter's entire campaign as an ideological assault and as intolerable interference in its domestic affairs, Carter's human rights policy had now lost much of its significance and had become a mere propaganda effort. It was no longer necessary to balance competition and cooperation, open and quiet diplomacy. It was necessary to expose the Soviets to international criticism and work for their isolation via the issue of human rights.

Conclusions

In late 1978, the Carter administration had to choose whether to relaunch the bipolar dialogue or continue on the path of firmness. Behind this decision lurked the paradox and contradiction of Carter's bipolar policy since 1977. On the one side, any action aimed at strengthening détente at the international level entailed its internal weakening. On the other side, everything that the American government could do to legitimize the dialogue with the Soviet Union and arms control within the United States drew a firm rejection from the Soviet side, and thus a decline in the possibility of finalizing the SALT II Treaty. The Carter administration chose détente with the Soviet Union. This would have made it possible to consolidate the limited progress that the USSR had made in the field of human rights and to conclude negotiations on arms control. The corollary of this approach was the return to quiet diplomacy on human rights, the removal of sanctions introduced after the trials of Orlov, Sharansky,

Filatov and Ginzburg and potentially the revision of the Jackson–Vanik amendment that had imposed trade restrictions on the Soviets. These initiatives, however, were not supported by the American public, now increasingly opposed to détente.

The search for a balance between firmness and dialogue ceased in December 1979, when the Soviet invasion of Afghanistan precipitated the end of détente. With it, the Carter administration's attempt to give stability to bipolar relations, strengthening détente, arms control, the Helsinki agreements and respect for human rights, also sank. However, human rights did not disappear from American politics, becoming a permanent feature of bipolar relations and also an issue in the presidential campaign. As Senators Jackson and Moynihan had already done in Congress and Jeane Kirkpatrick in *Commentary*'s pages, now Ronald Reagan, the Republican candidate, repeatedly accused Carter of not giving enough support to the human rights campaign. He did so, for example, from a stage before the Statue of Liberty, with Stanislaw Walesa, father of the famous Polish trade union leader at his side, denouncing the "sad result" of the Carter administration.[145] He reiterated this point in a number of direct attacks and official communiqués. One of these, issued just days before the opening of the Madrid CSCE review conference, restated the entire panoply of charges and critiques conservatives had levelled at Carter's foreign policy:

In 1977, Mr. Carter proclaimed that he would make human rights a fundamental tenet of his foreign policy. Yet, here again, the Carter Administration has not lived up to its promises: this is not a human rights policy.

1. The Carter Administration has failed to condemn systematic Soviet violations of the Helsinki Accords;
2. The Carter Administration sought to dissuade the AFL-CIO from giving even modest financial assistance to the workers in Poland, who had so bravely struggled to win the basic human right of free association;
3. The Carter Administration supported the Pol Pot communist Cambodian regime, which had slaughtered millions of its own people, in the United Nations. ...

To effectively fulfil the Helsinki Accords, we need a vigorous and consistent human rights policy. Yet, at the last review conference in 1977, the Carter Administration, though speaking boldly to the public, spoke timidly to the Soviets. The signal must have been clear to the Soviet leaders: Carter's human rights policy toward the Soviet empire and its captive nations was meant only for domestic political consumption. ... Its support for our cultural and informational programs has declined over the last four years, while the misinformation and propaganda programs of our adversaries have grown. Nor has it focused world attention on the flagrant violations of the Helsinki accords by the Soviet Union, such as when the Soviet Union resumed jamming Voice of America radio broadcasts to prevent the people under its control from hearing of the courageous Polish workers and their struggle. America in effect ratified this blatant act of hypocrisy.[146]

Reagan's words recalled how Carter's attempted balance between human rights and détente – a dangerous chimera that the outgoing administration had chased unsuccessfully – had failed. What did not fail was the prominent role human rights would assume in American foreign policy and East–West relations.

Notes

1 A.É. Gfeller, "Champion of Human Rights: The European Parliament and the Helsinki Process", *Journal of Contemporary History* 49:2 (2014), 390–409.
2 John Paul II, *Redemptor hominis* (Rome: Edizioni Paoline, 1979).
3 A. Dobrynin, *In Confidence: Moscow's Ambassador to America's Six Cold War Presidents* (Seattle: University of Washington Press, 1995), pp. 415–418.
4 S. Kaufman, *Plans Unraveled: The Foreign Policy of the Carter Administration* (DeKalb: Northern Illinois University Press, 2008), pp. 179–180; R.L. Garthoff, *Détente and Confrontation: American–Soviet Relations from Nixon to Reagan* (Washington, DC: The Brookings Institution, 1994), pp. 880–810.
5 CIA, Bureau of Intelligence and Research, "The Dissident Trials: An End in Sight?", 28 July 1978, JCPL, NLC-SAFE-17B-12-64-9-2.
6 W. Hyland to the President, "Information Items: Dissident Update for the USSR and Eastern Europe", August 1978, JCPL, NLC-1-3-4-1-2.
7 M. Shulman, "An Overview of U.S.–Soviet Relations", *Department of State Bulletin* 78:33 (September 1978), pp. 28–33.
8 Ibid.
9 "Soviet Union; For Ribicoff Committee", 8 November 1978, in "Global Competition and the Deterioration of U.S.–Soviet Relations, 1977–1980", International Conference at Fort Lauderdale, 1995 (unpublished manuscript), vol. 4, pp. 426–429.
10 Z. Brzezinski to J. Carter, "Meeting with Andrei Voznesensky", 6 November 1978, JCPL, ZBM, Box 80, Folder 11/78; E. Sander to Z. Brzezinski, "Solidarity Day", 20 March 1979, JCPL, Special Advisor on Jewish Affairs – Moses, Box 3, Folder "Brzezinski".
11 Commission on Security and Cooperation in Europe, 99th Congress, 2nd Session, *Documents of the Helsinki Monitoring Group in the USSR and Lithuania (1976–1986)* (Washington, DC: US Government Printing Office, 1986), pp. 293–294.
12 P. Tarnoff to Z. Brzezinski, 17 April 1980, "US Government Initiatives on Behalf of Human Rights in the USSR and Eastern Europe", JCPL, ZBM, Box 29, Folder 6 "4/79–4/80".
13 Ibid.
14 Z. Brzezinski to the President, "US-USSR Prisoner Exchange", 10 August 1978, JCPL, NLC-SAFE-39C-19-63-6-4.
15 Memorandum of Conversation between Z. Brzezinski and Anatoly Dobrynin, 20 September 1978, JCPL, ZBM, Box 19, Folder 5.
16 Office of the White House Secretary, Press Release, 27 April 1979, JCPL, ZBM, Box 19, Folder 2.
17 Garthoff, *Détente and Confrontation*, p. 679.
18 Z. Brzezinski, *Power and Principle: Memoirs of the National Security Adviser, 1977–1981* (New York: Farrar, Straus and Giroux, 1983), pp. 323–324.

19 W. Odom to Z. Brzezinski, 15 August 1978, JCPL, NLC-10-14-3-17-4.
20 S. Huntington to Z. Brzezinski, "The Dresser Case", 12 August 1978, JCPL, NLC-10-14-3-17-4. See also S. Huntington, "Trade, Technology and Leverage: Economic Diplomacy", *Foreign Policy* 32 (Autumn 1978), pp. 63–106.
21 Z. Brzezinski to the President, "Dresser Case" 29 August 1978, JCPL, NLC-12-24-1-4-7.
22 "Using Trade to Influence Russia", *Business Week*, 24 July 1978; "The Rising Sentiments Against Sales to Russia", *Business Week*, 11 September 1978; "Exports of Oil Technology Is Reexamined", *Wall Street Journal*, 30 August 1978; G. Conderarci, "Sole of Oil-Pipe Gear to Soviets is Cleared by Administration", *Wall Street Journal*, 28 September 1978.
23 "Carter Reverses on Tass Computer Sale", *Washington Post*, 6 April 1979; S.T. Sherman to Rauer H. Meyer, 26 January 1979, JCPL, BM, Box 80, Folder 2/79. See also D.C. Thomas, *The Helsinki Effect: International Norms, Human Rights, and the Demise of Communism* (Princeton, NJ: Princeton University Press, 2001), p. 217.
24 C.P. Peterson, *Globalizing Human Rights: Private Citizens, the Soviet Union, and the West* (Abingdon and New York: Routledge, 2012), p. 101.
25 "The Wrong Strategy", *Business Week*, 31 July 1978; L. Silk, "Toward More Soviet Trade", *New York Times*, 10 December 1978. See also, Bruce Parrott (ed.), *Trade, Technology and Soviet American Relations* (Bloomington: Indiana University Press, 1985), pp. 334–336; Garthoff, *Détente and Confrontation*, p. 679; A.P. Dobson, *U.S. Economic Statecraft for Survival, 1933–1991: Of Sanctions, Embargoes and Economic Warfare* (London: Routledge, 2002), pp. 238–248.
26 Henry M. Jackson to J. Carter, 13 October 1978, HMJP, 3560/6/1/41.
27 C. Vance to the President, "Charlie Vanik", 13 January 1979, JCPL, Plains File, Box 39, Folder 3; M. Nimetz to the Deputy Secretary, "Jackson–Vanik", 23 May 1979, NARA, RG 59, WCP, Box 9, Folder 10. See also P. Buwalda, *They Did Not Dwell Alone: Jewish Emigration from the Soviet Union, 1967–1990* (Washington, DC: Woodrow Wilson Center Press; Baltimore, MD: Johns Hopkins University Press, 1997), pp. 132–134.
28 C. Vance and M. Blumenthal to the President, 21 January 1979, Cyrus R. Vance and Grace Sloane Vance Papers, Yale University, Libraries and Manuscripts, Box 12, Folder 91.
29 S. Eizenstat to the President, "Waiver Authority", 20 March 1979, JCPL, WHCF, Box CO-60, Folder CO-165, "1/1/79–4/30/79".
30 F. Moore and H. Jordan to the President, "Vance/Blumenthal Proposals", 21 March 1979, JCPL, CL – Moore, Box 37, Folder "Memorandum from Frank Moore".
31 Garthoff, *Détente and Confrontation*, pp. 800–801.
32 "The White House Commemoration on the 30th Anniversary of the Declaration of Human Rights", JCPL, Bureau of Ethnic Affairs, Box 30, Folder "Human Rights – 12/78".
33 Z. Brzezinski to the President, "Human Rights", 3 December 1977, JCPL, NLC-126-10-7-1-2,; Joint Declaration by Amnesty International USA, International Commission of Jurists, International League for Human Rights, "To Ratify the Covenants", 10 December 1978; and David Hinkley (Amnesty International USA) to Marina Wallach (NCSJ), 5 April 1979; both in NCSJ, Accession I-181A; Box 201, Folder 6.
34 C. Vance to the President, 28 December 1978, JCPL, NLC-7-19-4-2-8.

35 I. Levkov, "The Establishment of a Jewish Theater in Birobidzhan", 19 December 1978, CJH, NCSJ Papers, Box 4, Folder "Mailings 1978"; E. Kline, "The Helsinki Process. A Balance Sheet", ADSA, HRC, Box 21, Folder 8.

36 M. Kac and M. Gottesman (Committee of Concerned Scientists) to President Carter, 7 June 1979, CJH, NCSJ Papers, Box 221, Folder "Committee of Concerned Scientists"; R. Evans and R. Novak, "The Kremlin's Good Will", *Washington Post*, 25 May 1979; Polish-American Congress to the President, 5 December 1979, JCPL, Staff Offices – Ethnic Affairs: Aiello Files, Box 7, Folder "Madrid Conference".

37 M. Wallach to J. Goodman, "NCSJ Meeting with Secretary Blumenthal – 11/28/1978", 1 December 1978, CJH, NCSJ Papers, Box 71, Folder 2; "Jackson Amendment: What is to Be Done?", 5 February 1979, CJH, Jerry Goodman Papers; Box 8, Folder 3; J. Goodman to Board of Governors and Interested Parties, "Legislative Update; Other Actions Recommendations", 27 July 1979, CJH, NCSJ Papers, Box 332, Folder 4; E. Gold, "Why Alter the Jackson–Vanik Amendment?", *New York Times*, 26 April 1979.

38 Memorandum, from M. Mellman to members of the board of the CCS, "Meeting with Frank Press", 9 February 1979, CJH, NCSJ Papers, Box 221, Folder "Committee of Concerned Scientists".

39 Amnesty International News Release, "Amnesty Condemns Treatment of Helsinki Monitors", 24 June 1979, CJH, NCSJ Papers, Box 201, Folder 6; *Chronicle of Human Rights in the Soviet Union* 34 (April–June 1979).

40 "Whetting the Soviet Appetite", *New York Times*, 4 May 1979; A. Abrams, "Ginzburg: Exile Worse Than Prison", *Washington Post*, 5 May 1979; B. Gwertzman, "Russians Did Little More than Sign Helsinki Accords", *New York Times*, 6 May 1979; "A Freed Soviet Dissident Sees No Easing on Rights", *New York Times*, 11 May 1979; R.G. Kaiser, "Released Dissident Tells of Activists' Suffering in Soviet Prison Camps", *Washington Post*, 12 May 1979; B. Gwetzman, "Kissinger's Revival of Linkage", *New York Times*, 2 August 1979; "Soviet Forced Labor Making Olympic Charms, Panel Told", *Los Angeles Times*, 29 September 1979; A. Shanker, "Where We Stand", *New York Times*, 21 October 1979.

41 R. Evans and R. Novak, "Human Rights: Carter Blinked First", *Washington Post*, 29 June 1979.

42 "Brezhnev's Human Rights Policy", *Wall Street Journal*, 28 September 1979.

43 D. Doder, "Helsinki Watch Unit Set To Monitor U.S. on Rights", *Washington Post*, 18 March 1979; "Superfluous Panel on Helsinki Accords", *New York Times*, 5 March 1979; "U.S. Helsinki Watch with a Purpose", *New York Times*, 13 March 1979.

44 J. Greenwald to Bernstein 29 May 1978, CHRDR, HRW, Box 68, Folder 8.

45 A. Goldberg to the Files, "U.S. Monitoring Groups", 18 November 1977, LOC, Arthur Goldberg Papers, Box 151, Folder 5. See also W. Korey, *NGOs and the Universal Declaration of Human Rights: A Curious Grapevine* (New York: St. Martin's Press, 2001), p. 237; J. Laber, *The Courage of Strangers: Coming of Age with the Human Rights Movement* (Cambridge, MA: Public Affairs, 2002), pp. 96–98.

46 Quoted in Peterson, *Globalizing Human Rights*, p. 87.

47 Thomas, *The Helsinki Effect*, p. 150.

48 P. Slezkine, "From Helsinki to Human Rights Watch: How an American Cold War Monitoring Group Became an International Human Rights Institution", *Humanity. An International Journal of Human Rights, Humanitarianism and Development* 5:3 (Winter 2014), pp. 345–370.

49 J. Greenwald to R. Bernstein, 29 May 1978; A. Friendly to D. Fraser et al., "Proposed Agenda for the Committee on Human Rights and Fundamental Freedoms", 14 March 1979, both in CHRDR, HRW, Record Group 7: Helsinki Watch, Box 68, Folder "U.S. Department of State – Correspondence".

50 See, for example, R.L. Bernstein to L. Alexeyeva, 9 May 1979, CHRDR, HRW, Box 42, Folder 6 "Files of Jeri Laber: USSR – Academic Freedom Project".

51 Thomas, *The Helsinki Effect*, p. 151.

52 Helsinki Watch News Release, "US Citizens' Group Forms Helsinki Watch Committee: Will Monitor Compliance with Human Rights Provisions of Helsinki Accords and Cooperate with Groups in Other Countries", February 1979, CHRDR, HRW, Record Group 7: Helsinki Watch, Box 53, Folder 7. See also S.B. Snyder, *Human Rights Activism and the End of the Cold War* (New York and Cambridge: Cambridge University Press, 2012), pp. 115–134; Peterson, *Globalizing Human Rights*, pp. 87–88.

53 P. Caddell to the President and H. Jordan, 10 May 1978, JCPL, Staff Office Files – Rafshoon, Box 60, Folder "Salt (5)".

54 Kaufman, *Plans Unraveled*, p. 117.

55 Ibid.

56 Ibid.; S. Huntington, "Renewed Hostility", in J. Nye (ed.), *The Making of America's Soviet Policy* (New Haven, CT: Yale University Press, 1984), pp. 277–278; D. Caldwell, "U.S. Domestic Politics and the Demise of Détente", in O.A. Westad (ed.), *The Fall of Détente: Soviet American Relations during the Carter Years* (Oslo and Boston: Scandinavian University Press, 1996), p. 101. See also T. Stevens, "Poll Shows Few Support SALT Treaty", *Congressional Record*, 96th Congress, 1st Session, 21 March 1979, pp. 5648–5649.

57 R.G. Kaiser, "In the Upper Chamber, Things Seem to Be Going – Right", *Washington Post*, 9 November 1978. See also R.D. Johnson, *Congress and the Cold War* (New York and Cambridge: Cambridge University Press, 2006), pp. 240–241.

58 Memorandum of Conversation between D.P. Moynihan and C. Vance, 28 December 1978, LOC, DPMP, Box 39, Folder 1.

59 Ibid.

60 H.M. Jackson, "The Balance of Power and the Future of Freedom", 24 April 1979, HMJP, Accession no. 3560-06/13/78.

61 Ibid.

62 M. Biaggi in *Congressional Record*, 96th Congress, 1st Session, 15 February 1979, p. 2620; R.H. Michel, "The Administration's Foreign Policy Failure", *Congressional Record*, 96th Congress,1st Session, 25 April 1979, p. 8718.

63 J. Kirkpatrick, "Dictatorships and Dual Standards", *Commentary* 68:5 (November 1979), pp. 34–45.

64 A. Gleason, *Totalitarianism: The Inner History of Cold War* (Oxford and London: Oxford University Press, 1995), pp. 198–200.

65 H.M. Jackson to ABC News, HMJP, Accession no. 3560-06/13/22.

66 D. Fascell to C. Vance, 17 January 1979, NARA I, RG 519, Box 48, Folder "Department of State Correspondence".

67 R. Drinan, "Soviet Record on Helsinki – Still Dismally Poor", *Congressional Record*, 96th Congress, 1st Session, 28 February 1979, pp. 3553–3554.

68 "Statement by Senators Henry M. Jackson and Daniel Patrick Moynihan", 9 April 1979, LOC, DPMP, Box 2797, Folder 5.

69 J. Ashbrook, "Carter Administration Doublethink", *Congressional Record*, 96th Congress, 1st Session, 30 April 1979, pp. 9065–9066.

70 Ribicoff, Javits and Baker to President Carter, 14 June 1979, JCPL, WHCF, Box CO-60, Folder "165 5/1/79–5.31.7/9".

71 E. Sanders to the President, "Soviet Prisoners, Refusenicks, and Dissidents", 6 June 1979, JCPL, WHCF, Box CO-60, Folder "5/1/79–5/31/79"; Z. Brzezinski to the President, "Decisions on Summit Objectives", 24 May 1979, JCPL, ZBM, Box 20, Folder "Alpha Channel 5/79–8/79".

72 Kaufman, *Plans Unraveled*, pp. 181–182; Garthoff, *Détente and Confrontation*, pp. 798–813.

73 "Statement on the Fourth Anniversary of the Signing of the Final Act in Helsinki", 1 August 1979, in *Public Papers of the Presidents of the United States: Jimmy Carter, 1979, Book I, June 23–December 31* (Washington, DC: US Government Printing Office, 1981), p. 1352.

74 A.R. Hunt, "Little Giant: In the Salt Debate, Sen. Sam Nunn's Role Could Prove Decisive", *Wall Street Journal*, 22 March 1979; "Carter May Yield to Hawks to Gain Votes for Salt", *Christian Science Monitor*, 7 May 1979; G. Sperling, "Ratification: 70 Senators Undecided", *Christian Science Monitor*, 19 June 1979.

75 J. Carter, "Address Delivered Before a Joint Session of the Congress", 18 June, 1979, in *Public Papers of the Presidents of the United States: Jimmy Carter, 1979, Book I*, pp. 1087–1092.

76 J. Kemp, *Congressional Record*, 96th Congress, 1st Session, 18 July 1979, pp. 19343–19344; and W. Broomfield, *Congressional Record*, 96th Congress, 1st Session, 18 July 1979, p. 19345.

77 Committee on Foreign Relations, Senate, *The Treaty between the U.S. of America and the USSR on the Limitation of Strategic Offensive Arms and the Protocol Thereto, Together Referred as the Salt II Treaty, Both Signed at Vienna, Austria, on June 18, 1979, and Related Documents, Part II, Hearings Before the Committee on Foreign Relations, United States Senate, 96th Congress, 1st Session* (Washington, DC: US Government Printing Office, 1979), pp. 360–361.

78 Ibid., Part IV, p. 140.

79 "President's Address to the Nation, RE: Soviet Brigade in Cuba", 10 January 1979, JCPL, SS, Presidential Files, Box 133, Folder "President's Address to the Nation".

80 Kaufman, *Plans Unraveled*, pp. 185–187.

81 Abstentions came from five Republicans, Independent H. Byrd and Democrat H. Cannon.

82 W.M. LeoGrande, *Our Own Backyard: The United states in Central America, 1977–1992* (Chapel Hill: University of North Carolina Press, 1998), pp. 54–56.

83 Z. Brzezinski to the President, "NSC Weekly Report #83", 28 December 1978, JCPL, ZBM, Box 42, Folder 2.

84 O.A. Westad, *The Global Cold War: Third World Interventions and the Making of Our Times* (New York: Cambridge University Press, 2005), pp. 290–300; Kaufman, *Plans Unraveled*, pp. 196–199; D. Yergin, *The Prize: The Epic Quest for Oil, Money and Power* (New York: Simon & Schuster, 1991), pp. 674–698.

85 "Approval of Carter Falls to 37% Low, Polls Find", *New York Times*, 31 May 1979; "New Poll Gives Kennedy Big Lead over the President", *New York Times*, 24 June 1979; A. Clymer, "Carter Is Edged in Poll by Reagan and Ford; Kennedy Leads Both", *New York Times*, 1 July 1979

86 D. Yankelovich and L. Kagan, "Assertive America", *Foreign Affairs* 59:3 (1980), pp. 696–713.

87 C. Mohr, "Iran Issue Detracts from Arms Treaty", *New York Times*, 4 December 1979.

88 "Transcript of President's Interview with Frank Reynolds on Soviet Reply", *New York Times*, 1 January 1980.

89 House Subcommittee on Europe and the Middle East of the Committee on Foreign Affairs, *An Assessment of the Afghanistan Sanctions: Implications for Trade and Diplomacy in the 1980s* (Washington, DC: US Government Printing Office, 1981), pp. 14–19; "George F. Kennan, on Washington's Reaction to the Afghan Crisis: Was This Really Mature Statesmanship?", *New York Times*, 1 February 1980; "M. Shulman to Cyrus Vance on US–Soviet Relations after Afghanistan, February 15, 1980", in Westad, *The Fall of Détente*, pp. 351–357

90 Z. Brzezinski to the President, "NSC Weekly Report #81", 28 December 1978, JCPL, ZBM, Box 42; Z. Brzezinski to the President, "NSC Weekly Report #87", 2 February 1979, JCPL, ZBM, Box 42; Z. Brzezinski to the President, "Reflections on Soviet Intervention in Afghanistan", 26 December 1979, JCPL, NSA – SF, Box 1, Folder "Afghanistan 4-12/79".

91 Yankelovich and Kagan, "Assertive America".

92 Brzezinski to the President, "Reflections on Soviet Intervention in Afghanistan".

93 Ibid. See also Z. Brzezinski's interview in *Le Nouvel Observateur*, 15–21 January 1998.

94 Z. Brzezinski to the President, 9 January 1980, JCPL, NSA – CF, Box CO-1 "Afghanistan", Folder 1.

95 Z. Brzezinski to the President, 3 January 1979, JCPL, ZBM, Box 17, Folder "Southwest Asia – Persian Gulf – Afghanistan".

96 Ibid.

97 Z. Brzezinski to the President, 29 December 1979, JCPL, ZBM, Box 17, Folder "Southwest Asia – Persian Gulf – Afghanistan".

98 Memorandum for the Vice President et al., "Results of the NSC Meeting", 2 January 1980, JCPL, ZBM, Box 17, Folder "Southwest Asia – Persian Gulf – Afghanistan, 12.26.79–1.4.80".

99 Jimmy Carter, "Situation in Iran and Soviet Invasion of Afghanistan Remarks at a White House Briefing for Members of Congress", 8 January 1980: www.presidency.ucsb.edu/documents/situation-iran-and-soviet-invasion-afghanistan-remarks-white-house-briefing-for-members (accessed December 2018).

100 Draft, "The Carter Doctrine or Carter's Arc of Defense", 9 January 1980, JCPL, NSA – CF, Box CO-1 "Afghanistan", Folder 2.

101 J.W. Sanders, *Peddlers of Crisis: The Committee on the Present Danger and the Politics of Containment* (Boston: South End Press, 1983), pp. 236–238.

102 Stanley Hoffmann, quoted in D.J. Sargent, *A Superpower Transformed: The Remaking of American Foreign Relations in the 1970s* (Oxford and New York: Oxford University Press, 2015), pp. 260–261.

103 L. Hamilton, "The Presidential Messages: The State of the Union", 6 February 1980, *Congressional Record*, 96th Congress, 2nd Session, p. 2227.

104 "Reaction to the Speech is Sharply Partisan", *New York Times*, 24 January 1980.

105 L. Gelb, "Beyond the Carter Doctrine", *New York Times Magazine*, 10 February 1980.

106 E. Rudd, "Assessing the President Actions Against Soviet Aggression", *Congressional Record*, 96th Congress, 2nd Session, 24 January 1980, p. 758.

107 "CPSU CC Politburo Decision with Report by Gromyko, Andropov, Ustinov, Ponomarev": www.gwu.edu/~nsarchiv/NSAEBB/NSAEBB57/r13.pdf (accessed October 2014).

108 Memorandum for the Vice President et al., "Results of the NSC Meeting".

109 "Arrests and Trials: The Campaign against Dissent", *Chronicle of Human Rights in the Soviet Union* 36 (October–December 1979), pp. 5–8.

110 CIA, "USSR: Suppression of Dissidents", JCPL, NLC-23-59-4-1-7.

111 Quoted in Peterson, *Globalizing Human Rights*, pp. 102–103

112 A. Austin, "Sakharov Proposed Soviet Withdrawal", *New York Times*, 3 January 1980. See also "The Exile of Sakharov", *Chronicle of Current Events* 56 (30 April 1980), pp. 74–77; V. Zubok, *Zhivago's Children: The Last Russian Intelligentsia* (Cambridge, MA and London: The Belknap Press of Harvard University Press, 2009), pp. 331–334.

113 Andropov and Rudenko to Central Committee, "The Case against Andrei Sakharov", 26 December 1979, in J. Rubenstein and A. Gribanov (eds), *The KGB File of Andrei Sakharov* (New Haven, CT and London: Yale University Press, 2005), pp. 243–246.

114 Ibid., p. 247.

115 J. Bergman, *Meeting the Demands of Reason: The Life and Thoughts of Andrei Sakharov* (Ithaca, NY: Cornell University Press, 2009), p. 281.

116 "U.S. Assails Moscow on Sakharov; 'Very Serious View'", *New York Times*, 23 January 1980.

117 M. Kenward, "Western Science Supremos Criticize the Soviets", *New Scientist*, 21 February 1980; "7,900 Scientists Boycott Soviet to Protest Jailing of Dissidents", *Chronicle of Higher Education*, 27 October, 1980; Andropov to Central Committee, "Responses in the West to Sakharov's Banishment", 24 January 1980, in Rubenstein and Gribanov, *The KGB File of Andrei Sakharov*, pp. 250–251. See also, C. Rhéaume, "Western Scientists' Reaction to Sakharov's Human Rights Struggle in the Soviet Union, 1968–1989", *Human Rights Quarterly* 30:1 (February 2008), pp. 1–20.

118 Sen. Res. 340, "Submission of a Resolution Regarding Andrei Sakharov", *Congressional Record*, 96th Congress, 2nd Session, 28 January 1980, pp. 833–844.

119 G. Brown, "Legislation Introduced to Limit United States–Soviet Scientific Exchanges in Response to Actions Against Andrei Sakharov", *Congressional Record*, 96th Congress, 2nd Session, 29 January 1980, p. 1043.

120 H. Con. Res. 272, "A Concurrent Resolution Expressing the Sense of the Congress that Andrei Sakharov Should Be Released from Internal Exile, Urging the President to Protest the Continued Suppression of Human Rights in the Soviet Union, and for Other Purposes", *Congressional Record*, 96th Congress, 2nd Session, 5 February 1980, pp. 1900–1905.

121 A.D. Sakharov, "Statement on the Moscow Olympics", in *Chronicle of Current Events* 56 (April 1980), pp. 86–88; D.B. Kanin, *A Political History of the Olympic Games* (Boulder, CO: Westview Press, 1981); U. Tulli, "Bringing Human Rights In: The Campaign against the 1980 Moscow Olympic Games and the Origins of the Nexus between Human Rights and the Olympic Games", *International Journal of the History of Sport* 33:16 (2016), pp. 2026–2045.

122 D. De Concini, "Civil Rights in the Soviet Union", *Congressional Record*, 96th Congress, 2nd Session, 6 February 1980, p. 2120; H. Harris, "The State of Soviet Jewry", *Congressional Record*, 96th Congress, 2nd Session, 22 January 1980, p. 263.

123 J. Goodman to the President, 21 August 1980, and A. Cranston, C. Pell et al. to the President, 4 September 1980, both in JCPL, Special Advisor on Jewish Affairs – Moses, Box 13, Folder "Sakharov Article".

124 "Statement by Assistant Secretary of State for Human Rights and Humanitarian
    Affairs (Patricia Derian) before the Subcommittee on International organizations
    of the House Foreign Affairs Committee", 16 September 1980, in *American Foreign
    Policy Basic Documents, 1977–1980* (Washington, DC: US Government printing
    Office, 1983), pp. 575–576.
125 *Department of State Bulletin*, December 1980, p. 8.
126 P. Henze to Z. Brzezinski, "Dissidence in Eastern Europe and the USSR – Are We
    Doing Enough?", 17 April 1980, JCPL, ZBM, Box Horn/Special, Folder 4/80.
127 E. Muskie to the President, "UN Meeting with Gromyko", 13 September 1980, JCPL,
    ZBM, Box 20, Folder "Alpha Channel 9.80–10.80".
128 L. Bloomfield to Z. Brzezinski, "Soviet Responsibility for Refugees", 28 May 1980,
    JCPL, NSA – CF, Box 83, Folder 4.
129 C. Vance to the President, "U.N. Human Rights Commission", 13 March 1980, JCPL,
    NLC-128-15-3-4-6.
130 Armand Hammer to E. Muskie, 25 July 1980, CHRDR, AI USA Papers, Box 1, Folder
    "Documents Released on Appeal (1)".
131 Orville H. Schell (Helsinki Watch) to F. Press, 14 March 1980, CHRDR, HRW, Box
    63, Folder 11; Andy Sommer to the Executive Committee, "US Government's Visa
    Denial to Eastern Bloc Scientists", CHRDR, HRW, Box 53, Folder 7
132 R. Reagan in *CSCE Digest*, 27 June 1980. Even European allies seemed to criticize
    the Carter administration: see Vance to the President, 8 February 1980, JCPL,
    NLC-128-15-2-6-5.
133 General Jaruzelski justified the introduction of martial law as the lesser evil and as an
    unpopular, yet necessary measure to prevent Soviet invasion. Recently declassified
    sources from Russia and Poland tend to shed new light: on the one side, the Soviets
    had never made plans for a military intervention, on the other, Jaruzelski urged the
    Soviets to give military support to his actions. See M. Signifredi, *Giovanni Paolo II
    e la fine del comunismo. La transizione in Polonia* (Milan: Guerini e associati, 2013),
    pp. 141–161; M. Kramer, *Soviet Deliberation during the Polish Crisis, 1980–1981*,
    Special Working Paper No. 1, Cold War International History Project, Woodrow
    Wilson International Center for Scholars, 1999; V. Zubok, *A Failed Empire: The
    Soviet Union in the Cold War from Stalin to Gorbachev* (Chapel Hill: University of
    North Carolina Press, 2007), pp. 265–272; M. Byrne and A. Paczkowski (eds), *From
    Solidarity to Martial Law: The Polish Crisis of 1980–1981: A Documentary History*
    (Budapest and New York: Central European University Press, 2007).
134 Memorandum for Z. Brzezinski, "Evening Notes", 25 November 1980, JCPL,
    NLC-1-17-7-9-6.
135 E. Muskie to the President, 15 December 1980, JCPL, NLC-128-16-1-6-5;
    E. Muskie to Carter, 6 January 1981, JCPL, NLC-128-16-3-2-7; Memorandum for
    Z. Brzezinski, "Paper on Sanctions in the Polish Context", 1 January 1981, JCPL,
    NLC-123-124-7-7-3.
136 Cyrus Vance to the President, "Dante Fascell on CSCE. The Madrid Conference",
    29 October 1979, JCPL, NLC-128-15-2-6-5.
137 *United States Human Rights Policy: From Belgrade en Route to Madrid* (Washington,
    DC: Aspen Institute for Humanistic Studies, 1979). See also Memorandum from
    D. Hirsch (Committee of Concerned Scientists) for Members of the Board,
    "Madrid CSCE Review Conference", 29 August 1980; "Briefing Material for the U.S.

Delegation to the Madrid CSCE Review Conference", CJH, NCSJ Papers, Box 221, Folder "Committee of Concerned Scientists"; NCSJ, "Aide Memoire Submitted to President Jimmy Carter", 4 September 1980, CJH, NCSJ Papers, Box 288, Folder "US Government 1976–1980, 1982". Finally, see also Memorandum from C. Vance for the President, 7 February 1980, JCPL, NLC-128-15-2-5-6; The International League for Human Rights, "Press Conference on Andrei Sakharov", 30 January 1980, CHRDR, HRW, Record Group 7 "Helsinki Watch", Box 63, Folder 4.

138 "Remarks of the President at a Ceremony Commemorating the 5th Anniversary of the Helsinki Accords", 29 July 1980, CHRDR, HWR, Record Group 7 "Helsinki Watch", Box 68, Folder 8.

139 Ibid.

140 Remarks by M.M. Kampelman, 10 September 1980, JCPL, Staff Offices, Ethnic Affairs, Aiello Files, Box 7, Folder "Madrid Conference".

141 S.B. Snyder, "The CSCE and the Atlantic alliance: Forging a New Consensus in Madrid", *Journal of Transatlantic Studies* 8:1 (2010), pp. 56–68.

142 *Le Monde*, 12 November 1980. See also W. Korey, *The Promises We Keep: Human Rights, the Helsinki Process and American Foreign Policy* (New York: Institute for East–West Studies, 1993), p. 101; Laber, *The Courage of Stranger*, pp. 120–124.

143 Quoted in S.B. Snyder, *Human Rights Activism and the End of the Cold War* (New York and Cambridge: Cambridge University Press, 2012), p. 137.

144 *American Foreign Policy Basic Documents, 1977–1980*, pp. 454–456.

145 L. Cannon, "Castigating the Betrayal of Workers' Aspirations", *Washington Post*, 2 September 1980; A.L. Goldman, "In Jersey City, Polish Father Savors Son's Victory", *New York Times*, 1 September 1980. See also S. Wilentz, *The Age of Reagan: A History, 1974–2008* (New York: HarperCollins, 2008), pp. 99–126.

146 Reagan Bush Committee, "News Release: Statement by Governor Ronald Reagan on Human Rights and the Helsinki Accords", 17 October 1980, ADSA, HRC, Box 27 Ad., Folder 18.

Conclusion

In November 1981, the editors of *Commentary* posed three questions regarding President Carter's human rights policy to a group of eighteen American intellectuals:

1 What role, if any, should a concern for human rights play in American foreign policy? Is there a conflict between this concern and the American national interest?
2 Does the distinction between authoritarianism and totalitarianism seem important to you? If so, what follows from it in practice? If not, what distinctions would you make in judging and dealing with non-democratic regimes?
3 Does the approach of the Reagan administration, to the extent that it can be inferred from statements of the president and other high officials, compare favorably or unfavorably with the Carter administration's human rights policy?[1]

Their replies drew a negative assessment of Carter's years. Unsurprisingly, only former National Security Advisor Zbigniew Brzezinski defended the actions of the Carter administration, arguing that Carter's experience had favoured a "massive political awakening around the world. The idea of human rights, once so narrowly confined to a small portion of mankind, is becoming today the central and most compelling force for political change throughout the world." Brzezinski also claimed two other major successes: through its human rights campaign, the United States had succeeded in ideologically challenging the Soviet Union and in reaffirming its basic political values, "values that were somewhat in eclipse during the preceding years".[2]

All other commentators censured Carter's campaign. While recognizing that his emphasis on the promotion of human rights had been innovative and represented an important boost to their special place in American foreign policy, his agenda was perceived as flawed, contradictory and naïve.

Participating in the forum, international jurist Richard Falk was among those who made a negative assessment of Carter's experience:

A non-selective emphasis on human rights of the sort associated with the initial two years of the Carter Presidency seems ill-advised and unsustainable. In fact, it was quietly abandoned as impractical. As directed against allies and friends, it seemed simultaneously ineffective, interventionary, and self-defeating, while as against adversaries it complicated negotiations and relations without enhancing human rights. The Carter approach to human rights could not finally be reconciled with a world of states or with the practical pursuit of U.S. interests in the world.[3]

Falk's observations were an exemplar of a strand of criticism that many liberals and new internationalists addressed to Carter's human rights-based foreign policy. For them, after a promising start, President Carter's campaign turned out to be selective and contradictory, and was abandoned after 1978. They also argued that the human rights campaign took on a mainly anti-Soviet character, undermining its initial universalism, creating new frictions with the Soviet Union and, in the end, damaging bipolar détente. But this was a minority position. A more common critique underlined Carter's inability to respond to the Soviet threat, as the White House had directed its human rights campaign against some allied regimes while ignoring Soviet totalitarianism. Jeane Kirkpatrick, Nathan Glazer, Oscar Handlin and Seymour Martin Lipset were among the intellectuals interviewed by *Commentary* who detailed how Carter's foreign policy did not pay enough attention to the Soviet Union and its human rights abuses. What was lacking in Carter's human rights policy, Lipset concluded, was "a practical moralism, a commitment to democracy and human rights which is tied to national interest".[4]

Beyond the partisan nature of many of these opinions, the symposium provides insight into the significance of Carter's human rights campaign to American foreign policy and to the American political debate, as well as for its impact on East–West relations.

Human rights moved to the centre of international relations and especially of American foreign policy in the early 1970s. As part of a global surge and drawing on different sources, American interest in human rights emerged as a legislative challenge to Richard Nixon and Henry Kissinger's perceived realist and amoral foreign policy: Democrats and Republicans, liberals and conservatives, and new internationalists and neoconservatives agreed on defining human rights as a new priority in American foreign policy.[5] This consensus was undermined by a different political understanding of human rights. To liberals and new internationalists, the issue of human rights was linked to freeing American foreign policy from the constraints of the Cold War and renewing American action in international relations. To them, the new universalism of human rights offered a viable foreign policy agenda for an era of growing interdependence. To conservatives and neoconservatives, the issue of human rights was an ideological weapon to renew the Cold War and to suspend détente, which was perceived as a flawed and deceptive form of appeasement with Soviet totalitarianism.

Carter tried to craft a synthesis between these two understandings. In the electoral campaign, he advocated a human rights-based foreign policy to renew the American image abroad and to respond to the moral bankruptcy of previous years. Trying to reconcile the different approaches to human rights, he identified them as a new political compass for America's actions abroad that could infuse new moralism into America's international actions and define a new consensual principle to replace discredited containment. Once elected, Carter gave priority to human rights in the bureaucratic machinery of the State Department, appointing former civil rights activist Patricia Derian to the new post of Undersecretary for Human Rights and asking each regional office of the department to appoint a human rights specialist. In his early decisions, human rights considerations led to cutting off financial aid to many traditional American allies. Above all, with the adoption of Presidential Review Memorandum 28, the Carter administration defined the guidelines for a human rights policy that aspired to be universal and pragmatic: universal because it would influence all foreign policy decisions, pragmatic because it would take into account the available tools and leverages as well as potential costs and limits.[6] Realism and idealism intertwined in the implementation of the policy, as well as in the definition of its objectives.[7] However, the outcome was a human rights policy that encompassed different and sometimes opposing meanings and objectives. Human rights were about moral necessities and national interests, about bolstering US power and restraining military interventionism, about regaining ideological primacy vis-à-vis the Soviet Union, as well as defining new principles to deal with non-communist countries. The Carter administration's policy encompassed all of these elements at times. It adopted a flexible and pragmatic approach to human rights, adapting its proclaimed total commitment to the local specificities of each case.

Carter's human rights policy gave rise to a number of differences and conflicts. The administration struggled to identify which rights mattered the most, the objectives and tools of its policy, as well as its implementation and limits. The lower-level executive bureaucracy resisted fully embracing human rights. Within the State Department, for example, mid-level officials and career diplomats were more concerned with keeping friendly relations with authoritarian foreign governments rather than castigating them on human rights abuses. Political differences often turned into personal animosity. Patricia Derian and her staff were often considered outsiders, with their maximalist approach to human rights. At higher levels, Secretary of State Cyrus Vance and National Security Advisor Zbigniew Brzezinski offered two different and opposing understandings of the role and the scope of human rights in American foreign policy. On the one hand, Vance advocated a pragmatic approach to human rights, one that should take into consideration the limits on American "power and wisdom", avoiding "doctrinaire plans". To him, human rights should be a leading principle moving American foreign relations beyond the Cold War mentality, but it should not become a "mechanistic formula".[8] On the other hand, Brzezinski tended to appreciate human rights policy for its impact on bipolar relations. He did not contend that the human rights policy should consider the limits of American power, nor that it demanded a consistent approach in order to be effective. However, to the National Security Advisor, the human rights policy should have aimed at competing "politically with the Soviet Union by pursuing the basic American commitment to human rights and national independence".[9]

Outside the executive branch, the Carter administration struggled to impose its human rights agenda on Congress. It did not develop its human rights policy from a *tabula rasa*. It had to engage residual distrust of executive from the Nixon and Ford eras and it had to participate in dynamics created by the earlier Congressional actions on the human rights community. Those members of Congress who paid specific attention to human rights often expressed their views to the White House on the directions, achievements and shortcomings of the human rights campaign. For their part, the president and White House officials regularly consulted both conservative and liberal members of Congress, but month after month, Congress began questioning the soundness of Carter's policy. Not only did the division between Carter and Congress over how to pursue foreign policy demonstrate the limits on executive power in the late Cold War, especially on human rights issues, but it also became a bitter defeat for the Carter administration's attempt to build a lasting consensus on foreign policy through human rights.

Carter's determination to develop a quasi-universal human rights policy did not mean that the US president ignored Cold War imperatives, promoting moralism in US foreign affairs at the expense of power. As Carter himself later wrote, "the demonstration of American idealism was a practical and realistic approach to foreign affairs, and moral principles were the best foundation for the exertion of American power and influence".[10] Indeed, the Carter administration designed its human rights policy in order to keep idealism and realism together. Far from being "a morality without power" or a policy that ignored the Soviet threat, as many neoconservatives claimed, Carter's human rights policy paid specific attention to bipolar relations.

Benefiting from Brzezinski's reflections on détente, which he though should become more reciprocal and ideologically aggressive, and on the "Helsinki process" that gave the United States the chance to loosen Soviet control over Eastern Europe, Carter embraced human rights as a weapon against the Soviet Union. He did so indirectly, through a coherent commitment to their universal promotion abroad, thus distancing the United States from numerous authoritarian right-wing regimes. He did so in relation to Eastern Europe, using human rights and the CSCE as a wedge to distance some Eastern European states from the Soviets. Finally, he directly used human rights to challenge the Soviet regime to protect its citizens' fundamental freedoms. Carter's foreign policy never rejected the Cold War. Rather, through the human rights campaign, it renewed it. What Carter rejected was a static vision of bipolar confrontation. As the president himself clarified in one of his major foreign policy speeches, for more than twenty years the United States had fought the USSR through "the flawed and erroneous principles and tactics of our adversaries, sometimes abandoning our own values for theirs. We've fought fire with fire, never thinking that fire is better quenched with water."[11] Carter not only distanced himself from the Vietnam War experience and the militarization of Cold War policies; he also renewed American strategy in order to ideologically challenge the Soviet Union. Human rights could provide the "water" to extinguish the Soviet fire.

If ideological competition through human rights provided the administration with a competitive element in bipolar relations, the Carter administration was also determined to revive bipolar détente and reach a new SALT Treaty to limit the arms race. From the time of his election, Carter pledged to renew bipolar dialogue, avoiding Kissinger's mistake and making it more reciprocal. He never doubted that détente should continue and that arms control negotiations were a priority for the United States. Once in the White House, he immediately worked towards a new SALT II Treaty and the strengthening of détente, eventually considering new trade and economic ties between Moscow and Washington.

Like the human rights campaign, however, détente entailed major divisions between Carter's top foreign policy advisers. Secretary of State Vance entered office determined to broaden the foreign policy agenda of the United States and to address new challenges emerging during the 1970s. He took a firm stance in defence of détente and arms negotiations with the Soviets, believing that a new SALT Treaty was in the best interests of both superpowers. For this reason, he constantly thundered against linking arms control negotiations to human rights and other contentious issues in bipolar relations.[12] On the other hand, National Security Advisor Zbigniew Brzezinski's vision of détente combined containment, ideology and the rationalization of bipolar competition. From the start of the administration, Brzezinski argued that détente meant stabilizing the international system and avoiding a major crisis between superpowers, not renouncing ideological competition.

While the division between Vance and Brzezinski was real, it should not be exaggerated. In the first place, Carter was aware of these differences and, as White House Chief of Staff Hamilton Jordan recalled, the president had a clear plan for the division of labour within his administration: "Cy would be the doer, Zbig the thinker, and Jimmy Carter would be the decider."[13] Second, since the election, Carter had agreed more with Brzezinski's analyses than with Vance's. While agreeing with Vance on the importance of arms control and on the fact that this was the most likely area to produce a concrete outcome, President Carter never abandoned confrontation with the Soviets, nor the will to challenge them ideologically through a consistent approach to global human rights violations.

Following Brzezinski's recommendations, the Carter administration developed a concept of détente that was both minimal and ambitious. Détente was not "the panacea" to "end competition between two radically different systems, each with its own interests", the president claimed in 1978. Rather, it was "an antidote to the uncontrolled competition between the United States and the Soviet Union".[14] Where Kissinger and Nixon had envisioned bipolar dialogue as a new form of geopolitical containment of Soviet power with no place for ideological confrontation, to Carter and Brzezinski it was the basis for avoiding a military showdown between superpowers and to launch a new ideological competition. Human rights offered the perfect ideological weapon. The White House conceived its human rights campaign and détente as being complementary and interdependent. By preserving and strengthening détente with the Soviets, Carter hoped to ease Soviet internal repression and to make the Soviets more responsible for upholding CSCE human rights provisions. By introducing a competitive ideological strand and challenging the USSR on human rights issues, Carter hoped to provide domestic legitimacy for détente in the face of a growing opposition to bipolar dialogue.

Had this strategy worked, Carter's bipolar policy would have formed a "virtuous circle": the more the Soviets respected human rights, the more détente would have been approved in the United States; the more détente continued, the more respect for human rights would have become a reality in the Soviet system. Therefore, the Carter administration envisioned a foreign policy that could balance cooperation and confrontation, developing a continuous negotiation between domestic opponents of détente and the Soviets. While the president himself publicly denied the existence of a linkage between arms control and human rights, this sort of linkage was the very essence of his bipolar policy. Human rights and arms control were the two extremes of a single political action.

With benefit of hindsight, such a policy was based on three ultimately flawed assumptions. First, the White House underestimated Soviet resistance to the human rights campaign and overestimated Soviet interest in the continuation of a form of détente that entailed ideological confrontation through human rights. Carter and Brzezinski's views on détente were hardly compatible with the Soviet conception, which was based on the recognition of an equal status between the superpowers and non-interference in domestic affairs. Despite continuous Soviet protests at American interference in Soviet politics, Brzezinski and many other White House officials concluded that the human rights campaign had no negative impact on SALT or other negotiations. They also continuously expressed satisfaction with the accomplishments of the human rights campaign in bipolar affairs. The Soviets' pragmatic concessions in those areas to which the American public was paying specific attention such as free emigration of Soviet Jews or CSCE humanitarian provisions led them to conclude too optimistically that Carter's campaign was having a positive impact on human rights in the Soviet Union. In reality, Soviet response to Carter's human rights campaign was more complicated. Beyond protests and pragmatic concessions, it also included a new crackdown on dissidents and new trials. The Sharansky case, for example, was a demonstration that to the Soviets, there were insurmountable limits that Carter's campaign should not trespass. Neglecting Soviet protests and outrage at the human rights campaign, the Carter administration failed to understand how its human rights initiative contributed to eroding mutual trust and, in the end, détente.

Second, the domestic consensus for a human rights-based foreign policy was illusory, precarious and short-lived. Far from reconciling liberal with conservative visions of human rights, Carter's campaign exacerbated their differences. To liberals, Carter's human rights emphasis should have signalled a new course for American foreign policy, one that was free of anti-communism and more suitable to a more complex, pluralistic and interdependent international system. To conservatives, human rights should renew the ideological challenge to the Soviet system and suspend any notion of bipolar détente. Frustrated by the selective standards of the human rights campaign, liberal members of Congress were the first to try to expand the scope of human rights provisions. Conservatives did the same, but they tried to give Carter's campaign an overly explicit anti-Soviet tone.

Finally, Carter's strategy was based on a negotiation process with partners – the Soviet Union and American opponents of détente – who had no interest in negotiating on their counterparts' terms. Between 1977 and 1979, the Politburo attempted to address US pressure by allowing more Soviet Jews to leave the country, postponing or in some cases cancelling trials of dissidents, facilitating the reunification of families separated by the Cold War, interrupting the jamming of Western radio and reducing censorship of *samizdat* publications, Western literature and even films. The Soviets were not willing to make other concessions to American pressures, but their actions were insufficient for domestic conservative and neoconservative opponents of détente, who believed that neither the Soviets nor the Carter administration went far enough.

Between 1977 and the Soviet invasion of Afghanistan, Carter oscillated between open and quiet diplomacy, more cooperative initiatives and firmer confrontation. Dissenting voices within the administration soon increased. By mid-1978, Soviet protests and European allies' criticism of Carter's open diplomacy on human rights fuelled new critiques within the United States. To many liberals and new internationalists, Carter had given an anti-Soviet twist to his proclaimed universal human rights campaign and was jeopardizing détente and the conclusion of a new SALT II Treaty. To cope with this critique and to strengthen Soviet pragmatic concessions on human rights, the White House moved the human rights campaign to quiet diplomacy. This shift, however, occurred at a time when the Soviets were concluding the trials of prominent dissidents, and American attention was focused on Soviet and Cuban involvement in the Horn of Africa. Accordingly, the White House discovered it was not in full control of the issue of human rights in East–West relations. Domestic critics and transnational NGOs did not tone down their denunciations of Soviet abuses. Furthermore, to domestic critics of détente, such a change represented a betrayal of Carter's commitment to the promotion of human rights and a further demonstration of the dangers of détente. Many began asserting that the Carter administration had abandoned Soviet dissidents, directing its human rights policy against American allies and consequently weakening the US position in international relations. Combining realism and idealism, power and morality, the neoconservatives denounced Carter's flawed morality that had ignored the Cold War and national security.

Carter's strategy ultimately failed, trapped as it was in a crucial contradiction: the more the administration openly discussed Soviet abuses of human rights, the more the Soviets grew sceptical of bipolar dialogue; the more the administration relegated the issue to quiet diplomacy and private meetings, the more critics and opponents within the United States accused the president of retreating from his total commitment to human rights. Caught in this contradiction, Carter lost the domestic support he had managed to garner in 1976, and the critics of détente, helped by the Iran hostage crisis, the subsequent oil shock and the invasion of Afghanistan, won the 1980 election with Ronald Reagan.

Despite Carter's defeat, human rights remained a central concern of American foreign policy. With an early reversal from the attempt to marginalize human rights, the Reagan administration incorporated them into a conservative strategy of democracy promotion to roll back communism.[15] After the end of the Cold War, human rights took on a central role in American attempts to redefine the international system. Human rights were part of President Bush's attempt to inaugurate a "new world order", as they were at the core of Democratic President Bill Clinton's enlargement doctrine. However, actions did not meet these aspirations. Despite significant attention to human rights, abuses and violations continued with limited objections from the international community or the United States. The attacks on 11 September 2001 marked a low point in the trajectory of human rights in American foreign policy. In the War on Terror, not only did the United States collaborate with some of the most repressive regimes in the world, it also became a human rights violator. In sum, over the last three decades, human rights have proved to be a fundamental concern or American foreign policy, but their place remains contested. This is hardly surprising looking at the emergence of human rights in American foreign policy and their role in Carter's foreign policy. Although the end of the Cold War has freed human rights from their conceptual and practical links to bipolar antagonism, human rights continue to generate sharp conflict, assume different meanings and define different political ends – as happened during the Carter years.

Notes

1 "Human Rights and American Foreign Policy. A Symposium", *Commentary* 79 (November 1981), pp. 25–63. The eighteen American intellectuals were: W. Barret, P.L. Berger, Z. Brzezinski, N. Chomsky, M. Decter, R. Falk, N. Glazer, O. Handlin, S. Hook, J. Kirkpatrick, M. Lerner, S.M. Lipset, C.W. Maynes, E.J. McCarthy, R. Nisbet, M. Novak, M. Peretz, B. Rustin.
2 Z. Brzezinski, ibid.
3 R. Falk, ibid., p. 35.
4 S.M. Lipset, ibid., p. 49.
5 D.P. Forsythe, *Human Rights and U.S. Foreign Policy: Congress Reconsidered* (Gainesville: University of Florida Press, 1988); K. Cmiel, "The Emergence of Human Rights Politics in the United States", *Journal of American History* 86 (December 1999), pp. 1231–1250; B. Keys, "Congress, Kissinger, and the Origins of Human Rights Diplomacy", *Diplomatic History* 34:5 (2010), pp. 823–852.
6 D.F. Schmitz and V. Walker, "Jimmy Carter and the Foreign Policy of Human Rights: The Development of a Post-Cold War Foreign Policy", *Diplomatic History* 28:1 (January 2004), pp. 113–143.
7 PRM-NSC-28: Human Rights, JCPL, NLC-1002-A-246-1.
8 C. Vance, "Human Rights and Foreign Policy", *Department of State Bulletin* 76 (23 May 1977), p. 506.
9 PRM-NSC-28: Human Rights.

10 J. Carter, *Keeping Faith: Memoirs of a President* (New York: Bantam Books, 1982), p. 143.
11 J. Carter, "Address at Commencement Exercises at University of Notre Dame", 22 May 1977, American Presidency Project, University of California-Santa Barbara: www.presidency.ucsb.edu/ws/idex.php?pid=7229 (accessed December 2018).
12 C. Vance, *Hard Choices: Critical Years in America's Foreign Policy* (New York: Simon & Schuster, 1983), p. 136.
13 J.M. Hanhimäki, *The Rise and Fall of Détente: American Foreign Policy and the Transformation of the Cold War* (Washington, DC: Potomac Books, 2013), p. 105.
14 Interview with the President, 11 July 1978, in *Public Papers of the Presidents of the United States: Jimmy Carter, 1978, Book II, June 30–December 31* (Washington, DC: US Government Printing Office, 1979), pp. 1272–1277.
15 R. Sinding Søndergaard, "'A Positive Track of Human Rights Policy': Elliott Abrams, the Human Rights Bureau, and the Conceptualization of Democracy Promotion, 1981–1984", in R. Pee and W.M. Schmidli (eds), *The Reagan Administration, the Cold War, and the Transition to Democracy Promotion* (Basingstoke: Palgrave Macmillan, 2018), pp. 31–53.

Select bibliography

Archival collections and manuscripts

Andrei D. Sakharov Archives, Houghton Library, Harvard University, Cambridge, MA.
Center for Human Rights Documentation and Research, Columbia University, New York.
Center for Jewish History, New York.
Cyrus R. and Grace Sloane Vance Papers, Manuscript and Archives Repository, Yale University, New Haven, CT.
Gerald R. Ford Presidential Library, Ann Arbor, MI.
Henry M. Jackson Papers, University of Washington, Seattle, WA.
Historical Archives of the European Union, Florence.
IOC Archives at the Olympic Studies Center, Lausanne, Switzerland.
Jimmy Carter Presidential Library, Atlanta, GA.
Manuscript Division, Library of Congress, Washington, DC.
National Archives, Kew, London.
National Archives and Record Administration, College Park, MD and Washington, DC.

Published documents

Commission on Security and Cooperation in Europe. *Documents of the Helsinki Monitoring Group in the USSR and Lithuania (1976–1986)*, 99th Congress, 2nd Session. Washington, DC: US Government Printing Office, 1986.
Commission on Security and Cooperation in Europe. *Hearings Before the Commission on Security and Cooperation in Europe on Implementation of the Helsinki Accords – Human Rights*, 95th Congress, 1st Session, vol. 1. Washington, DC: US Government Printing Office, 1976.
Commission on Security and Cooperation in Europe. *Hearings: Information Flow, Cultural and Educational Exchanges*, 95th Congress, 1st Session. Washington, DC: US Government Printing Office, 1978.
Committee on Foreign Relations, Senate. *The Treaty between the U.S. of America and the USSR on the Limitation of Strategic Offensive Arms and the Protocol Thereto, Together*

Referred as the Salt II Treaty, Both Signed at Vienna, Austria, on June 18, 1979, and Related Documents, Part II, Hearings Before the Committee on Foreign Relations, United States Senate, 96th Congress, 1st Session. Washington, DC: US Government Printing Office, 1979.

Committee on International Relations. Congress and Foreign Policy, 1975. Washington, DC: Government Printing Office, 1976.

Congressional Record (various editions and volumes).

CSCE Digest (various editions and volumes).

Department of State. Report to Congress on the Human Rights Situation in Countries Receiving U.S. Security Assistance. Washington, DC: US Government Printing Office, 15 November 1975.

Department of State Bulletin (various editions and volumes).

Foreign Relations of the United States (various editions and volumes).

House Committee on Foreign Affairs. Human Rights and U.S. Foreign Policy, Hearings Before the Subcommittee on International Organizations, 96th Congress, 1st Session. Washington, DC: US Government Printing Office, 1979.

House Committee on Foreign Affairs, Subcommittee on International Organizations and Movements. Human Rights in the World Community: A Call for US Leadership. Washington, DC: Government Printing Office, 1974.

House Committee on Foreign Affairs, Subcommittee on International Organizations and Movements. International Protection of Human Rights: The Work of International Organizations and the role of U.S. Foreign Policy. Hearings, 93rd Congress, 1st Session. Washington, DC: US Government Printing Office, 1974.

House of Representatives, Subcommittee on International Political and Military Affairs of the Committee on International Relations. Hearings on H.R.9466 (S.2679) and Related Bills to Establish a Commission on Security and Cooperation in Europe. Washington, DC: US Government Printing Office, 1976.

House Subcommittee on Europe and the Middle East of the Committee on Foreign Affairs. An Assessment of the Afghanistan Sanctions: Implications for Trade and Diplomacy in the 1980s. Washington, DC: US Government Printing Office, 1981.

Legislative Reference Service of the Library of Congress. Aspects of Intellectual Ferment and Dissent in the Soviet Union. Washington, DC: US Government Printing Office, 1968.

Legislative Reference Service of the Library of Congress. Aspects of Intellectual Ferment in the Soviet Union. Washington, DC: US Government Printing Office, 1966.

Public Papers of the Presidents of the United States (various editions and volumes).

Senate Committee on Foreign Relations. Establishing a Commission on Security and Cooperation in Europe, Report No. 94-756. Washington, DC: US Government Printing Office, 23 April 1976.

Senate Committee on Foreign Relations. On Nomination of Paul C. Warnke to be Director of the United States Arms Control and Disarmament Agency, with the Rank of Ambassador during his Tenure of Service: February 8 and 9 1977. Washington, DC: Government Printing Office, 1977.

Essential secondary sources

The following are more or less important sources for the ideas expressed in this book. Complete bibliographical references may be found in the chapter endnotes.

Apodaca, Claire. *Understanding US Human Rights Policy: A Paradoxical Legacy*. New York: Routledge, 2006.

Auten, Brian J. *Carter's Conversion: The Hardening of American Defense Policy*. Columbia: University of Missouri Press, 2008.

Bell, Coral. *The Costs of Virtue? President Carter and Foreign Policy*. Canberra: Australian National University, 1980.

Betts, Paul. "Socialism, Social Rights, and Human Rights: The Case of East Germany." *Humanity: An International Journal of Human Rights, Humanitarianism, and Development* 3:3 (Winter 2012): 407–442.

Bilandžić, Vladimir, Dittmar Dahlmnn and Milan Kosanović (eds). *From Helsinki to Belgrade: The First CSCE Follow-Up Meeting in Belgrade*. Bonn: Bonn University Press, 2012.

Bradley, Mark P. *The World Reimagined: Americans and Human Rights in the Twentieth Century*. New York: Cambridge University Press, 2016.

Brinkley, Douglas. "The Rising Stock of Jimmy Carter: The Hands-On Legacy of Our Thirty-Ninth President." *Diplomatic History* 20:4 (Fall 1996): 505–530.

Brzezinski, Zbigniew. *America in the Technetronic Age*. New York: School of International Affairs, Columbia University, 1967.

Brzezinski, Zbigniew. *Power and Principles: Memoirs of the National Security Adviser, 1977–1981*. New York: Farrar, Straus and Giroux, 1983.

Brzezinski, Zbigniew. *The Soviet Bloc: Unity and Conflict*. Cambridge, MA: Harvard University Press, 1960.

Brzezinski, Zbigniew. "The Soviet Political System: Transformation or Degeneration?" *Problems of Communism* 15:1 (January 1966): 1–15.

Brzezinski, Zbigniew, and William E. Griffith. "Peaceful Engagement in Eastern Europe." *Foreign Affairs* 39 (July 1961): 642–653.

Buchanan, Tom. "The Truth Will Set You Free: The Making of Amnesty International." *Journal of Contemporary History* 37:4 (October 2002): 575–597.

Cahn, Anne H. *Killing Détente: The Right Attacks the CIA*. University Park: Pennsylvania University Press, 1998.

Caldwell, Dan. "The Legitimization of the Nixon–Kissinger Grand Design and Grand Strategy." *Diplomatic History* 33:4 (September 2009): 633–652.

Carter, James E. *Keeping Faith: Memoirs of a President*. New York: Bantam Books, 1982.

Cmiel, Kenneth. "The Emergence of Human Rights Policy in the United States." *Journal of American History* 86:3 (1999): 1231–1250.

Cmiel, Kenneth. "The Recent History of Human Rights." *American Historical Review* 109:1 (February 2004): 117–135.

Craig, Campbell, and Frederik Logevall. *America's Cold War: The Politics of Insecurity*. Cambridge, MA: Harvard University Press, 2010.

Del Pero, Mario. *The Eccentric Realist: Henry Kissinger and the Shaping of American Foreign Policy*. Ithaca, NY: Cornell University Press, 2010.

Del Pero, Mario. "'Which Chile, Allende?' Henry Kissinger and the Portuguese Revolution." *Cold War History* 11:4 (2011): 625–657.

Dumbrell, John. *The Carter Presidency: A Re-Evaluation*. Manchester and New York: Manchester University Press, 1993.

Ehrman, John. *The Rise of Neoconservatism: Intellectuals and Foreign Affairs*. New Haven, CT and London: Yale University Press, 1995.

Feingold, Henry L. *"Silent No More": Saving the Jews of Russia. The American Jewish Effort, 1967–1989*. Syracuse, NY: Syracuse University Press, 2006.

Ferguson, Niall, Charles Maier, Manela Erez and Daniel J. Sargent (eds). *The Shock of the Global: The 1970s in Perspective*. Cambridge, MA: Harvard University Press, 2010.

Forsythe, David P. *Human Rights and U.S. Foreign Policy: Congress Reconsidered*. Gainesville: University of Florida Press, 1988.

Friedrich, Carl J., and Zbigniew Brzezinski. *Totalitarian Dictatorship and Autocracy*. Cambridge, MA: Harvard University Press, 1956.

Garthoff, Raymond L. *Détente and Confrontation: American–Soviet Relations from Nixon to Reagan*. Washington, DC: The Brookings Institution, 1994.

Gati, Charles (ed.). *Zbig: The Strategy and Statecraft of Zbigniew Brzezinski*. Baltimore, MD: Johns Hopkins University Press, 2013.

Gleason, Abbott. *Totalitarianism: The Inner History of Cold War*. Oxford and London: Oxford University Press, 1995.

Gleijeses, Piero. *Conflicting Missions: Havana, Washington, and Africa, 1959–1976*. Chapel Hill and London: University of North Carolina Press, 2002.

Gleijeses, Piero. "Truth or Credibility: Castro, Carter, and the Invasions of Shaba." *International History Review* 18:1 (1996): 70–103.

Goldberg, Paul. *The Final Act: The Dramatic, Revealing Story of the Moscow Helsinki Watch Group*. New York: Morrow, 1988.

Hanhimäki, Jussi M. *The Flawed Architect: Henry Kissinger and American Foreign Policy*. Oxford and New York: Oxford University Press, 2004.

Hanhimäki, Jussi M. *The Rise and Fall of Détente: American Foreign Policy and the Transformation of the Cold War*. Washington, DC: Potomac Books, 2013.

Hanhimäki, Jussi M. "They Can Write It in Swahili: Kissinger, the Soviets and the Helsinki Accords." *Journal of Transatlantic Studies* 1:1 (Spring 2003): 37–58.

Hoffmann, Stanley. "The Hell of Good Intentions." *Foreign Policy* 29 (Winter 1977–1978): 3–26.

Johnson, Robert D. *Congress and the Cold War*. New York and Cambridge: Cambridge University Press, 2006.

Kaufman, Robert G. *Henry M. Jackson: A Life in Politics*. Seattle and London: University of Washington Press, 2000.

Kaufman, Scott. *Plans Unraveled: The Foreign Policy of the Carter Administration*. DeKalb: Northern Illinois University Press, 2008.

Keys, Barbara. *Reclaiming American Virtue: The Human Rights Revolution of the 1970s*. Cambridge, MA: Harvard University Press, 2014.

Keys, Barbara. "Something to Boast About: Western Enthusiasm for Carter's Human Rights Diplomacy." In *Reasserting America in the 1970s: U.S. Public Diplomacy and the Rebuilding of America's Image Abroad*, ed. Hallvard Notaker, Giles Scott-Smith and David J Snyder, 229–244. Manchester: Manchester University Press, 2016.

Kissinger, Henry A. *Diplomacy*. New York: Simon & Schuster, 1994.

Korey, William. *The Promises We Keep: Human Rights, the Helsinki Process and American Foreign Policy*. New York: Institute for East–West Studies.

Leffler, Melvyn P. *For the Soul of the Mankind: The United States, the Soviet Union and the Cold War*. New York: Hill and Wang, 2008.

Marcy, Carl (ed.). *Common Sense in U.S.–Soviet Relations*. Washington, DC: American Committee on East–West Relations; New York: Norton, 1978.

Mieczkowski, Yanek. *Gerald Ford and the Challenges of the 1970s*. Lexington: University Press of Kentucky, 2005.

Mitchell, Nancy. *Jimmy Carter in Africa: Race and the Cold War*. Palo Alto, CA: Stanford University Press and Woodrow Wilson Center Press, 2016. ◆

Moyn, Samuel. *The Last Utopia: Human Rights in History*. Cambridge, MA: Harvard University Press, 2010.

Muravchik, Joshua. *The Uncertain Crusade: Jimmy Carter and the Dilemmas of Human Rights Policy*. Washington, DC: American Enterprise Institute for Public Policy Research, 1988.

Nathans, Benjamin. "The Disenchantment of Socialism: Soviet Dissidents, Human Rights and the New Global Morality." In *The Breakthrough: Human Rights in the 1970s*, ed. Jan Eckel and Samuel Moyn, 33–47. Philadelphia: University of Pennsylvania Press, 2013.

Nichols, Thomas M. "Carter and the Soviets. The Origins of U.S. Return to a Strategy of Confrontation." *Diplomacy and Statecraft* 13:2 (June 2002): 21–42.

Nitze, Paul. "Assuring Strategic Stability in an Era of Détente." *Foreign Affairs* 54:2 (January 1976): 207–232.

Orbach, William. *The American Movement to Aid Soviet Jews*. Amherst: University of Massachusetts Press, 1979.

Peretz, Pauline. *Let My People Go: The Transnational Politics of Soviet Jewish Emigration during the Cold War*. Piscataway, NJ: Transaction Publishers, 2015.

Peterson, Christian P. *Globalizing Human Rights: Private Citizens, the Soviet Union, and the West*. Abingdon and New York: Routledge, 2012.

Renouard, Joe. *Human Rights in American Foreign Policy: From the 1960s to the Soviet Collapse*. Philadelphia: University of Pennsylvania Press, 2016.

Rhéaume, Charles. "Western Scientists' Reaction to Sakharov's Human Rights Struggle in the Soviet Union, 1968–1989." *Human Rights Quarterly* 30:1 (February 2008): 1–20.

Ribuffo, Leo P. "Is Poland a Soviet Satellite? Gerald Ford, the Sonnenfeldt Doctrine and the Election of 1976." *Diplomatic History* 14:3 (Summer 1990): 385–403.

Romano, Angela. *From Détente in Europe to European Détente: How the West Shaped the Helsinki CSCE*. Brussels: Peter Lang, 2009.

Rosati, Jerel A. "Continuity and Change in the Foreign Policy Beliefs of Political Leaders: Addressing the Controversy over the Carter Administration." *Political Psychology* 9:3 (September 1988): 471–505.

Rubenstein, Joshua, and Alexander Gribanov (eds). *The KGB File of Andrei Sakharov*. New Haven, CT and London: Yale University Press, 2005.

Sanders, Jerry W. *Peddlers of Crisis: The Committee on the Present Danger and the Politics of Containment*. Boston: South End Press, 1983. ✦

Sargent, Daniel J. *A Superpower Transformed: The Remaking of American Foreign Relations in the 1970s*. Oxford and New York: Oxford University Press, 2015. ◆

Schapiro, Amy. *Millicent Fenwick: Her Way*. New Brunswick, NJ: Rutgers University Press, 2003.

Schmidli, William M. *The Fate of Freedom Elsewhere: Human Rights and U.S. Cold War Policy toward Argentina*. Ithaca, NY and London: Cornell University Press, 2013.

Schmitz, David F. *The United States and Right-Wing Dictatorships*. Cambridge and New York: Cambridge University Press, 2006.

Schmitz, David F., and Vanessa Walker. "Jimmy Carter and the Foreign Policy of Human Rights: The Development of a Post-Cold War Foreign Policy." *Diplomatic History* 28:1 (January 2004): 113–143.

Schultz, Matthias, and Thomas A. Schwartz (eds). *The Strained Alliance: US–European Relations from Nixon to Carter*. Cambridge: Cambridge University Press, 2010.

Skidmore, David. *Reversing Course: Carter's Foreign Policy Domestic Politics, and the Failure of Reform*. Nashville, TN: Vanderbilt University Press, 1996.

Slezkine, Peter. "From Helsinki to Human Rights Watch: How an American Cold War Monitoring Group Became an International Human Rights Institution." *Humanity. An International Journal of Human Rights, Humanitarianism and Development* 5:3 (Winter 2014): 345–370.

Sneh, Itai N. *The Future Almost Arrived: How Jimmy Carter Failed to Change U.S. Foreign Policy*. New York: Peter Lang, 2008. •

Snyder, Sarah B. *From Selma to Moscow: How American Activists Transformed U.S. Foreign Policy*. New York: Columbia University Press, 2018. •

Snyder, Sarah B. *Human Rights Activism and the End of the Cold War*. New York and Cambridge: Cambridge University Press, 2012.

Søndergaard, Rasmus Sinding. "'A Positive Track of Human Rights Policy': Elliott Abrams, the Human Rights Bureau, and the Conceptualization of Democracy Promotion, 1981–1984." In *The Reagan Administration, the Cold War, and the Transition to Democracy Promotion*, ed. R. Pee and W.M. Schmidli, 31–53. Basingstoke: Palgrave Macmillan, 2018.

Strong, Robert A. *Working in the World: Jimmy Carter and the Making of American Foreign Policy*. Baton Rouge: Louisiana State University Press, 2000.

Stuckey, Mary E. *Jimmy Carter, Human Rights, and the National Agenda*. College Station: Texas A&M University Press, 2008.

Suri, Jeremi. "Détente and Human Rights: American and West European Perspectives on International Change." *Cold War History* 8:4 (November 2008): 527–545.

Suri, Jeremi. *Henry Kissinger and the American Century*. Cambridge, MA: Harvard University Press, 2007. •

Suri, Jeremi. *Power and Protest: Global Revolution and the Rise of Détente*. Cambridge, MA and London: Harvard University Press, 2003.

Thomas, Daniel C. *The Helsinki Effect: International Norms, Human Rights, and the Demise of Communism*. Princeton, NJ: Princeton University Press, 2001.

Thornton, Richard. *The Carter Years: Toward a New Global Order*. New York: Paragon House, 1991.

Tulli, Umberto. "Bringing Human Rights In: The Campaign against the 1980 Moscow Olympic Games and the Origins of the Nexus between Human Rights and the Olympic Games." *International Journal of the History of Sport* 33:16 (2016): 2026–2045.

Vaïsse, Justine. *Neoconservatism: The Biography of a Movement*. Cambridge, MA: The Belknap Press of Harvard University Press, 2010.

Vance, Cyrus. *Hard Choices: Critical Years in America's Foreign Policy*. New York: Simon & Schuster, 1983.

Vaughan, Patrick. "Beyond Benign Neglect: Zbigniew Brzezinski and the Polish Crisis of 1980." *Polish Review* 64:1 (1999): 3–28.

Westad, Odd Arne (ed.). *The Fall of Détente: Soviet–American Relations during the Carter Years*. Oslo and Boston: Scandinavian University Press, 1997. •

Westad, Odd Arne, and Jussi M. Hanhimäki (eds). *The Cold War: A History in Documents and Eyewitness Accounts*. Oxford and New York: Oxford University Press, 2003.

Westad, Odd Arne, and Melvyn P. Leffler (eds). *The Cambridge History of the Cold War*, vols 1–3. Cambridge and New York: Cambridge University Press, 2010.

Wilentz, Sean. *The Age of Reagan: A History, 1974–2008*. New York: HarperCollins, 2008.

Williams, Phil. "Détente and US Domestic Politics." *International Affairs* 61:3 (July 1985): 431–447.

Zelizer, Julian E. "Détente and Domestic Politics." *Diplomatic History* 33:4 (September 2009): 633–652.

Zubok, Vladislav. *Zhivago's Children: The Last Russian Intelligentsia*. Cambridge, MA and London: The Belknap Press of Harvard University Press, 2009.

Index

Abourezk, James 23, 162
Abrams, Elliott 2
Abzug, Bella 60
Afghanistan 3–4, 7, 164
    American reaction to the invasion
        171–173
    human rights after the invasion 174–179
    Soviet invasion of 169–171
Albert, Carl 51, 76n17
Alexeyeva, Ludmilla 95
Amalrik, Andrei 85, 96, 100–105
American Conference on Soviet Jewry 28
    see also National Conference on Soviet
        Jewry
Amnesty International 1, 22, 33, 45n123,
        52, 62, 84, 90, 127, 142, 159–160
Anderson, Wendell 162
Andropov, Yury W. 29, 93, 174
Angola 48–52, 67, 132
Arbatov, Georgy 86, 94
arc of crisis 171
Ashbrook, John 135, 165

"Backfire" bomber 89, 117n91, 130–131, 157
Barre, Siad 133–134
Belgrade conference 7, 74, 98, 105–111,
        122, 158, 160, 177–178
    see also Conference on Security and
        Cooperation in Europe
Bell, Griffin 178–199
Benson, Lucy 126
Bergman, Jay 174
Bergold, Henry E. 55
Bernstein, Robert 161

Biaggi, Mario 164
Bingham, Jonathan B. 127
Blaustein, Jacob 12
Block, Herbert "Herb" 34
Bloomfield, Lincoln 1
Blumenthal, Michael 100, 155–158
Bonker, Don 175
Bonner, Elena 50, 155
Borisov, Vladimir 95
Borstelmann, Thomas 36
Brademas, John 51, 76n17, 130
Bradley, Mark Philip 12
Brandt, Willy 35
Brazil 21, 23, 84, 90, 127
Brezhnev, Leonid 17, 34, 50, 56, 87, 93–94,
        99, 138–140, 160, 174
Bricker, John W. 14–15
Brock, William 31
Brooke, Edward 91, 162
Broomfield, William 167
Brown, George 175
Brown, Harold 134
Brown, Sam 60
Brzezinski, Zbigniew 5–6, 16, 48, 82, 85,
        90, 92, 94–97, 100–108, 110, 123–
        124, 129–131, 133–136, 139–144,
        145n7, 155–157, 166, 169, 173–176,
        190, 193–194
    arc of crisis 171–172
    electoral campaign 63–70
    rivalry with Vance 71–73, 106, 139, 192
    see also Kissinger, Henry A.; Vance,
        Cyrus R.
Buckley, James 53, 57

Bukovsky, Vladimir 62, 85, 93, 155
Bundy, McGeorge 161
Byrd, Robert C. 135, 143, 170, 185n81

Caddell, Patrick 60, 162
Califano, Joseph A. 136, 138
Callaghan, James 97
Canis, Bill 55
Cannon, Jim 54
Carstens, Karl 96
Carter, Hodding 155
Carter, Rosalynn 105
Case, Clifford 52–55, 91, 106, 145n7
Castro, Fidel 148n51, 170
Chalidze, Valery 29
Chernyayev, Rudolf 155
China 12, 64–65, 139, 157–158
    human rights in China 52, 126–127, 167
    normalization of relations 16–18, 170–172
Christopher Group 82, 102–103, 126
Christopher, Warren *see* Christopher Group
Church, Frank 58, 91, 168
Clark, Richard 162
Coalition for a Democratic Majority 135
Cohen, Stephen 129
Commission on Security and Cooperation
    in Europe *see* Helsinki Commission
Committee of Concerned Scientists 107,
    137, 159–160, 178
Committee on the Present Danger 4, 89,
    136, 164
Conference on Security and Cooperation
    in Europe 7, 27–36, 50–56, 85,
    95, 105–111, 143–144, 158–161,
    165–166, 177–179
    see also Helsinki conference; Belgrade
        conference; Madrid conference
Congress 1, 2, 5, 6, 11, 14, 18–19, 67–70
    after Afghanistan 172
    and the emergence of human rights
        19–56
    opposition to Carter's foreign policy
        123–144, 153, 157–169
    support for Carter's foreign policy 85,
        89–92, 96, 98–103
Conquest, Robert 30
Corvalan, Louis 155
Cranston, Alan 26, 130, 145n7

CSCE *see* Conference on Security and
    Cooperation in Europe
Cuba 4, 93, 168–169, 176
    Cuban military involvement in Africa
        49–50, 132–138
    see also Soviet brigade in Cuba; Horn of
        Africa

Daniel, Yuli 27
decolonization 49
    and human rights 10, 15, 20
DeConcini, Dennis 175
Democratic Party 128
    divisions over foreign policy 6, 48,
        163–164
    during the presidential elections of 1976
        58–63
Derian, Patricia 106–107, 125–128, 175,
    192
Derwinski, Edward 122
détente 16–19
    Afghanistan 169–173
    Brzezinski, Zbigniew 64–68, 70–72
    domestic criticism 30–32, 37, 56–63,
        134–136, 143–144, 154–158,
        193–195
    human rights 4–7, 30–36, 51–56, 88–111,
        130–132, 154–158, 193–195
    Soviet military interventions 48–50,
        132–136
    Vance, Cyrus R. 71–72
    Western Europe 95–98, 105–111
    see also Kissinger, Henry A.; Nixon,
        Richard
Dobrovolsky, Alexey 27
Dobrynin, Anatoly 45n122, 50, 56, 85, 86,
    88, 92, 130, 136, 140, 153, 155, 158
Dodd, Christopher 29, 96
Dole, Bob 55, 100, 143
Domenici, Pete 91
Donald, Fraser 23–26, 37, 96, 122, 128,
    145n7, 162
    see also Fraser Committee
Douglas, William 28
Dresser Industries 156
Drew, Elizabeth 60, 69
Drinan, Robert 26, 165
Dymshits, Mark 155

Eilberg, Joshua 53, 127, 162
Eizenstat, Stu 62, 158
emigration from the Soviet Union 7,
  27, 31–33, 52, 54, 61–63, 93, 95,
  100, 105, 109, 122, 131, 154, 158,
  174–176, 195
  see also Jackson–Vanik amendment;
  Nativ
Enger, Valdik 155
Ethiopia 82, 131–134, 171
Etzold, Thomas H. 21
European Community *see* European
  Economic Community
European Economic Community 10, 21,
  34–35, 96, 137, 152
Evans, Rowland 56, 57, 135, 139, 160

Falk, Richard 22, 190–191, 197
Fascell, Dante 21–22, 54–56, 73, 91, 106,
  110, 157, 165
  see also Helsinki Commission
Fenwick, Millicent 52–55
Filatov, Ivan 141–142, 155, 180
Ford, Gerald 35–37, 48–50, 55–60, 63,
  68–69, 73, 193
Foreign Assistance Act of 1973 23
Foreign Assistance Act of 1974 26
Frankel, Max 68
Fraser Committee 23–24
  see also Donald, Fraser
Friendly, Alfred 36
Fulbright, William 15

Galanskov, Yuri 27
Gardner, Richard 64, 69
Garthoff, Raymond 143, 185
Gates, Robert 134
Geneva summit 141–142
Gierek, Edward 105
Gingrich, Newt 143
Ginzburg, Aleksandr 27, 85, 108, 136,
  137–142, 154–155, 167, 180
Giscard d'Estaing, Valéry 96
Goldberg, Arthur J. 28, 107–110, 160–161,
  178
Goodman, Jerry 53, 130, 175
Gromyko, Andrej 35, 87, 93–94, 99, 107,
  130–133, 138, 141, 174

Hamilton, Lee 173
Harkin, Tom 26, 96, 128, 145n7
Harriman, W. Averell 87, 136
Harrington, Michael 33
Hatfield, Mark 91
Hathaway, William 162
Helms, Jesse 33, 91
Helsinki Commission 6, 48–56, 73, 85, 91,
  106–107, 157, 161, 165–166
  see also Fascell, Dante; Fenwick, Millicent
Helsinki conference 34–36
  see also Conference on Security and
  Cooperation in Europe
Helsinki groups 85, 95, 108, 122, 130–132,
  136, 144, 155, 160–161, 175
Helsinki Watch 160–161, 175, 177–179
Henze, Paul 175–176
Hertzberg, Hendrik 48
Hoffmann, Stanley 124–125, 172
Holbrooke, Richard 62
Holman, Frank 14
Horn of Africa 4, 132–135, 144, 164, 166,
  176
  Cuban military intervention 133–134
  Soviet military intervention 133–134
  see also Ethiopia; Somalia
Horner, Charles 31
Hughes, Harold 22
human rights
  Carter's policy 1–2, 4–7, 82–88, 98–111,
    122–126, 130–132, 136–137,
    152–158, 192–197
    domestic criticism 124–130, 137–139,
      141–144, 158–159
    domestic support 89–92, 110
    historians' evaluation 3–4, 86
  during the 1976 electoral campaign 56–74
  emergence in American foreign policy
    10–11, 18–38
  Soviet violations 27–36, 50–54, 100,
    108–109, 130–137
  see also détente; open diplomacy; quiet
    diplomacy
*Human Rights in the World Community:
  A Call for U.S. Leadership* 24
  see also Donald, Fraser; Fraser
    Committee
Huntington, Samuel 156

International Sakharov Hearings 51, 106, 160
Iran
    exception to the human rights campaign
        126–127
    revolution 169–172, 196
Isaacson, Walter 64

Jackson, Henry M. 2, 4, 28–35, 58–63,
        89, 91, 94–95, 100–101, 110, 131,
        141–143, 156–158, 163–166, 173,
        178
Jackson–Vanik amendment 27–32, 52,
        62, 99, 100–101, 129, 130–132,
        157–158, 160
Jaruzelski, Wojciech 177, 188n133
Javits, Jacob 28, 91, 145n7, 165, 173
Jeffords, Jim 142
Johnson, Lyndon B. 10, 28, 61–62, 66, 71
Jones, James V. 156
Jordan, Hamilton 101, 158, 173

Kagan, Larry 170
Kaiser, Robert G. 162
Kampelman, Max 178
Kawan, Louis 109
Kemp, Jack 91, 143
Kennan, George F. 14, 129, 170
Kennedy, Edward 23, 128, 130
Kennedy, Ted *see* Kennedy, Edward
Keys, Barbara 10, 36, 69
Khomeini, Ruhollah 170
Khrushchev, Nikita S. 27
Kildee, Dale 142
Kirkpatrick, Jeane 3, 7, 60, 164–165, 180,
    191
Kissinger, Henry A. 4, 6, 30, 57, 87–88, 91,
    95, 98, 104, 107, 132, 134, 170–171,
    191, 194
    détente 16–18, 49–50
    electoral campaign of 1976 59–63,
        67–68, 73
    Helsinki Commission 55–56
    human rights 19–20, 23, 25–27, 32–35,
        37–38
    see also Brzezinski, Zbigniew; détente;
        Nixon, Richard
Klebanov, Vladimir 175
Kline, Edward 161

Korey, William 22, 28, 55
Kreps, Juanita 136, 155–157
Krimsky, George 85, 108
Kristol, Irving 33
Kuznetsov, Eduard 154–155

Laber, Jeri 161
Lagomarsino, Robert 128
Lahkova, Vera 27
Lake, Anthony 124, 126, 129
Lance, Bert 59
Laxalt, Paul D. 91
Lech, Stanislaw 180
Lefever, Ernest 1–2
Leigh, Monroe 55
Leurs, William 131
Levitsky, Melvyn 136–137
Lewis, Anthony 88
linkage 87–89, 109, 134, 138
Lord, Winston 25

Maddox, Lester 59
Madrid conference 165, 177–179
    see also Conference on Security and
        Cooperation in Europe
Man of Marble 105
Manekovsky, Irene 62
Mansfield, Mike 15, 55
Mariam, Menghistu Haile 133
M'Baye, Keba 54
McCarthy, Joseph 22
McCloskey, Robert J. 52
McCrisken, Trevor 16, 38, 40
McGregor, Burns James 33
McIntyre, Thomas J. 162
Meany, George 33
Metzembaum, Howard 90
Michel, Robert 76n17, 128, 164
Mills, Wilbur 31
Mitchell, Nancy 3, 134
Mobutu, Sese Seko 140
Mondale, Walter 55, 62, 85
Moore, Frank 136, 158, 182
Morotz, Valentyn 155
Moscow Helsinki Group 136, 152
    see also Conference on Security and
        Cooperation in Europe; Helsinki
        groups

Moscow summit of 1977 92–95, 98–99,
    117n91, 131
Moscow summit of 1978 130–132
Moses, Al 131
most favoured nation 31, 104, 157–158
    see also Jackson–Vanik amendment
Moyn, Samuel 6, 36
Moynihan, Daniel P. 2, 62, 91, 101, 110,
    138, 141, 163, 165, 180
Muravchik, Joshua 3
Muskie, Edmund 175
MX missile 117n91, 166, 173

National Conference on Soviet Jewry (NCSJ)
    31, 53–54, 62, 90, 95, 100, 107, 110,
    130, 131, 142, 159, 160, 175, 178
Nativ 27–28
NCSJ *see* National Conference on Soviet
    Jewry
neoconservatives 2, 3, 6, 7, 37–38, 59, 87,
    91, 164, 172, 178, 191, 193, 196
    see also Jackson, Henry M.; Kirkpatrick,
    Jeane; Moynihan, Daniel P.
neutron bomb 89, 135–136
new internationalists 6, 22–24, 37, 61, 84,
    92, 123, 127, 162, 191
"New Left" 16
Nicaragua 82, 128, 164, 169
Niebuhr, Reinhold 59, 84
Nimetz, Matthew 107, 159, 178
Nitze, Paul 89
Nixon, Richard 4, 16–21, 24, 31–35, 37, 60,
    66, 88, 104, 191, 193–194
Novak, Robert 56–57, 135, 139, 160
Nudel, Ida 141
Nunn, Sam 131, 166

Odom, William 156
Ogaden War *see* Horn of Africa
Olympic Games 91, 137, 143, 160, 172–177
open diplomacy 6, 63, 83–89, 105–111
    criticism of 99–101, 123–130
    European reactions 95–98
    Soviet protests 92–95
Orlov, Yuri 7, 33, 50, 52, 54, 108, 115,
    130–131, 136–138, 154, 179
Owen, David 97
Owen, Henry 64, 70

Packwood, Bob 143
Palach, Jan 29
Pease, Don J. 90
Petkus, Viktoras 179
Pincus, Walter 135
Pinochet, Augusto 21, 82
Podrabinek, Aleksandr 175
Poland 51, 93, 104–105, 152, 161, 177, 180,
    188n133
Pompidou, George 35
Ponce De Leon, Clara 20
Pope John Paul II *see* Wojtyla, Karol
Powell, Jody 88
Presidential Directive (18) 102–103
Presidential Directive (21) 102, 104–105
presidential elections of 1976 55–63
Presidential Review Memorandum/
    NSC-28 102–103, 192
prisoner exchange 130, 155, 157, 167
Proskauer, Joseph 12

quiet diplomacy 6–7, 32, 99, 100, 122–123,
    129–132, 152–161, 165, 196
    during the Nixon administration 18, 25
    and Western Europe 96–97

Reagan administration *see* Reagan, Ronald
Reagan, Ronald 1–2, 178
    opposition to Carter 135, 177–178,
    180–181
    opposition to Ford and Kissinger 34–35,
    57
Republican Party 33, 35, 55–58, 143,
    162–163
Ribicoff, Abraham 28, 165
Riegle, Donald W. 141
Riesman, David 129
Rockwell, Norman 12
Romberg, Alan 124
Roosevelt, Franklin D. 11–13, 31, 61
Rosenthal, Benjamin 91
Rostow, Eugene 89
Rostropovich, Mstislav 90
Rubenstein, Joshua 1
Rudd, Eldon 173
Rudenko, Mykola 179
Russell Tribunal 21
Ryan, Leo 123

Sakharov, Andrei D. 29, 31, 35, 50–51, 62, 85, 88, 99, 137, 154–155, 174–175, 179
SALT *see* Strategic Arms Limitation Talks
SALT II *see* Strategic Arms Limitation Talks
Sanders, Edward 165
Sargent, Daniel J. 8
Schmidli, William Michael 126
Schmidt, Helmut 96–97
Schmitz, David 3
Schneider, Mark 131
Schroeder, Patricia 143
Security Assistance Act of 1979 128
Selassie, Haile 133
Shaba 132
Sharansky, Avital 142
Sharansky, Natan 7, 50, 85, 93, 100, 102, 108, 130–131, 136–138, 140–142, 152, 154–155, 179, 195
Shelkov, Vladimir 160
Sherer, Albert 107, 121n150
Sherer, Carroll 110
Shestak, Jerome 90
Shipler, David 144
Shtern, Mikhail 95
Shulman, Marshall 99–100, 103, 131, 136, 154, 170
Simon, Paul 100
Sinyavsky, Andrei 27
Sirotin, Alexander 28
Slepak, Maria 154
Slepak, Vladimir 62, 85, 93, 141
Sneh, Itai Nartzizenfield 3
Snyder, Sarah B. 30, 40n30, 68, 178
Solidarność 177
Solzhenitsyn affair 33–34, 49
Solzhenitsyn, Aleksandr 33–36, 49, 57–58, 174
Somalia 131–134, 152
    see also Ethiopia; Horn of Africa
Somoza, Anastasio 164, 169
Sonnenfeldt doctrine 56, 67
Sonnenfeldt, Helmut 56, 67
South Korea 25, 58, 86, 90, 123, 127
Soviet anti-semitism 27–29, 31
Soviet brigade in Cuba 4, 168
Soviet Jews 7, 27–33, 62–63, 95, 110, 122–123, 132, 155, 157, 175, 178, 196

    see also emigration from the Soviet Union; Jackson–Vanik amendment
Soviet Trials 7, 27, 100, 102, 109, 122, 130–132, 136–138, 140–144, 154–155, 160, 163, 165–167, 179, 195–196
    see also Sharansky, Natan; Orlov, Yuri; Ginzburg, Aleksandr
Sparkman, John 52
Sprague, Mansfield 55
SS-20 missiles 4
Stettinius, Edward 12
Stevenson, Adlai III 101, 157
Stone, Richard 167–168
Strategic Arms Limitation Talks (SALT) 2–6, 17–18, 30, 34, 55, 57, 70, 72–74, 87–91, 94, 98–100, 103–104, 106, 109–111, 122–124, 129–131, 134–136, 138, 141–144, 152–159, 162, 165–171, 179, 194–196
Strong, Robert 134
Student Struggle for Soviet Jewry 142

Thomas, Daniel C. 161
Tillich, Paul 59
Toon, Malcom 94, 99–100, 103
Tower, John 166, 168
Trilateral Commission 3, 63–64, 71
Truman, Harry S. 13, 61, 132
Tuchman-Matthews, Jessica 138, 141–142
Tverdokhlebov, Andrei 29

Udall, Morris 58
Ustinov, Dmitry 93, 174

Vance, Cyrus R. 48, 70–73, 82–83, 85, 90, 92, 94, 96, 99–103, 106, 130–134, 136–144, 154, 156, 158, 163, 165, 170, 192, 194
    see also Brzezinski, Zbigniew
Vanik, Charles 31, 158
Velkanova, Tatiana 175
Vento, Nick 143
Vest, George 167–168
Vienna summit 157–160, 162, 165–166
    see also Strategic Arms Limitation Talks

Vietnam War 15–18, 59, 62, 67, 71, 73, 95, 132–133, 171
  and human rights 5, 11, 21, 36, 84, 193
Vins, Georgy 155
Vorontsov, Yuli M. 109
Vorspan, Albert 168

Walgren, Douglas 96
Walker, Vanessa 3
Warnke, Paul 4, 89–90
Wattemberg, Ben 60
Wiesel, Elie 27–28

Will, George F. 34
Wojtyla, Karol 152
Wren, Christopher 52
Wurtman, Stuart A. 62
Wyszynski, Stefan 105

Yankelovich, Daniel 170
Yates, Sidney 52, 76n17
Young, Andrew 82

Zeferetti, Leo C. 142
Zinoviev, Aleksandr 154